Global Perspectives on Sports and Christianity

While the relationship between sport and religion is deeply rooted in history, it continues to play a profound role in shaping modern-day societies. This edited collection provides an interdisciplinary exploration of this relationship from a global perspective, making a major contribution to the religious, social scientific and theological study of sport.

It discusses the dialectical interplay between sport and Christianity across diverse cultures, extending beyond a Western perspective to include studies from Africa, South America and Asia, as well as Europe, the UK and the US. Containing contributions from leading experts within the field, it reflects on key topics including race, gender, spirituality, morality, interfaith sport clubs, and the significance of sport in public rituals of celebration and mourning. Its chapters also examine violent sports such as boxing and mixed martial arts, as well as reflecting on the cult of sporting celebrity and the theology of disability sport.

Truly international in scope, *Global Perspectives on Sports and Christianity* is fascinating reading for all those interested in the study of sport, sociology and religion.

Afe Adogame is the Maxwell M. Upson Professor of Christianity and Society at Princeton Theological Seminary, USA.

Nick J. Watson is Associate Professor of Sport and Social Justice in the School of Sport at York St John University, UK.

Andrew Parker is Professor of Sport and Christian Outreach in the School of Sport and Exercise at the University of Gloucestershire, UK.

Routledge Research in Sport, Culture and Society

Global Perspectives on Sports and Christianity

Edited by Afe Adogame,
Nick J. Watson and
Andrew Parker

Routledge
Taylor & Francis Group

LONDON AND NEW YORK

First published 2018
by Routledge
2 Park Square, Milton Park, Abingdon, Oxon OX14 4RN

and by Routledge
711 Third Avenue, New York, NY 10017

Routledge is an imprint of the Taylor & Francis Group, an informa business

British Library Cataloguing in Publication Data
A catalogue record for this book is available from the British
Library

Library of Congress Cataloging in Publication Data
A catalog record for this book has been requested

ISBN: 978-1-138-82852-0 (hbk)
ISBN: 978-1-315-73835-2 (ebk)

Typeset in Sabon
by Wearset Ltd, Boldon, Tyne and Wear

MIX
Paper from
responsible sources
FSC® C013604

Printed and bound by CPI Group (UK) Ltd, Croydon, CR0 4YY

To Major General Ishola Williams for opening my eyes to research on the nexus of religion and sport; to my Dad, Rufus Adogame for his sportsmanship over five decades prior to retirement; and in loving memory of my Mum, Caroline Adogame

(Afe Adogame)

For my extended family, for which I am most thankful: Dave (69), Jenny, Kerry, Simon (Bill and Buddy) and Rob, Kelly (Orla and Neve) – and in remembrance of 'Aunty She'

(Nick Watson)

For Susie

(Andrew Parker)

Contents

Contributors

Olutayo Charles Adesina is Professor of History and Director, Centre for General Studies, University of Ibadan, Nigeria. He has served with distinction as the Head of the Department of History, (2001–2003) and (2006–2008), where he has been a full professor since 2007. He has been a Visiting Professor, Kennesaw State University, Georgia, USA. The focus of his works on sub-Saharan Africa has either singly or generally summoned intersections of local, national, regional and global history. His major publications include: *Globalization and Transnational Migrations: Africa and Africans in the Contemporary Global System* (with Akanmu Adebayo, Cambridge Scholars Publishing, 2009), *Marginality and Crisis: Globalization and Identity in Contemporary Africa* (with Akanmu Adebayo and Rasheed Olaniyi, Lexington Books, 2010), *Critical Perspectives on Peace, Conflict and Warfare in Africa* (with Olukoya Ogen and Noah Echa Attah, Obafemi Awolowo University Press, 2012). His most recent publication is *Nigeria in the Twentieth Century: History, Governance and Society* (Connel Publications, 2017).

Afe Adogame is the Maxwell M. Upson Professor of Christianity and Society at Princeton Theological Seminary, and a leading scholar of the African religious diaspora. He holds a PhD in History of Religions from the University of Bayreuth in Germany and has served as Associate Professor of World Christianity and Religious Studies, and Director International at the School of Divinity, New College, The University of Edinburgh, UK. He is the author of *The African Christian Diaspora: New Currents and Emerging Trends in World Christianity* (Bloomsbury Academic, 2013), and the editor/co-editor of several books including *The Public Face of African New Religious Movements in Diaspora: Imagining the Religious 'Other'* (Ashgate, 2014), *Africa in Scotland, Scotland in Africa: Historical Legacies and Contemporary Hybridities* (Brill, 2014), and *Engaging the World: Christian Communities in Contemporary Global Societies* (Regnum Edinburgh Centenary Series.

Regnum, 2014). He is the Secretary General of the International Association for the History of Religions (IAHR).

Rose Mary Amenga-Etego is a Senior Lecturer in Religious Studies at the Department for the Study of Religions, University of Ghana, Legon and a Research Fellow at the Research Institute for Theology and Religion (RITR), University of South Africa, South Africa. Her research interests include African Indigenous Religions, Gender Issues in Religion and African Culture, African Sexuality, and African Indigenous Religions and Sustainable Development. Her publications include 'Engaging the Religio-Cultural Quest in Development: An African Perspective' (*Theological Studies*, October 2016), 'Akokɔ bere so nim Adekyee: Women's Interpretation of Indigenous Oral Text' (in *Unravelling and Reweaving Sacred Canon in Africana Womanhood*, Lexington Books, 2015) and *Mending the Broken Pieces: Indigenous Religion and Sustainable Rural Development in Northern Ghana* (Africa World Press, 2011). She is also a co-editor of *Unraveling and Reweaving Sacred Canon in Africana Womanhood* (Lexington Books, 2015) and *Religion and Gender-based Violence: West African Experience* (with Mercy Amba Oduyoye, Asempa, 2013).

Brian Brock is a Reader in Moral and Practical Theology at the University of Aberdeen. He is the Managing Editor of the *Journal of Religion and Disability*. He has also written monographs on the use of the Bible in Christian ethics (*Singing the Ethos of God*, William B. Eerdmans Publishing, 2007; *The Malady of the Christian Body*, Cascade Books, 2016) as well as the ethics of technological development (*Christian Ethics in a Technological Age*, William B. Eerdmans Publishing, 2010). He has published two books that approach theological questions through interviews; most recently one that extensively cross-examines the theology of the internationally renowned American theologian and ethicist, Stanley Hauerwas (*Beginnings*, Continuum International Publishing, 2016; *Captive to Christ, Open to the World*, Cascade Books, 2014). He is also editor (with Professor John Swinton) of *Theology, Disability and the New Genetics: Why Science needs the Church* (Continuum International Publishing, 2007) and *Disability in the Christian Tradition: A Reader* (William B. Eerdmans Publishing, 2012).

David Chidester is Professor of Religious Studies and Director of the Institute for Comparative Religion in Southern Africa (ICRSA) at the University of Cape Town in South Africa. He is the author or editor of over 20 books in North American studies, South African studies, and comparative religion. His major publications include *Salvation and Suicide: Jim Jones, the Peoples Temple, and Jonestown* (Indiana University Press, 1988; revised edition 2003); *Authentic Fakes: Religion and American*

Popular Culture (University of California Press, 2005); *Christianity: A Global History* (Penguin; Harper Collins, 2000); *Savage Systems: Colonialism and Comparative Religion in Southern Africa* (University of Virginia Press, 1996); *Wild Religion: Tracking the Sacred in South Africa* (University of California Press, 2012); and *Empire of Religion: Imperialism and Comparative Religion* (University of Chicago Press, 2014). He has twice received the American Academy of Religion's Award for Excellence in Religious Studies.

Seán Crosson is the Acting Director of the Huston School of Film & Digital Media, NUI Galway and the PI of the Sport & Exercise Research Group in the Moore Institute, NUI Galway. His current research project examines the representation of sport in film and popular culture, the subject of a range of publications including his monograph *Sport and Film* (Routledge, 2013) and the co-edited collection *Sport, Representation and Evolving Identities in Europe* (Peter Lang, 2010). He is currently completing a monograph examining the depiction of Gaelic games in film. He is President of the European Federation of Associations and Centres of Irish Studies (EFACIS).

James C. Deming is Associate Professor of the History of Christianity in Modern Europe. His interests are in the social and cultural history of Christianity. Among other topics, he teaches courses in the history of European Christianity and poverty, Christianity and nature, the 'dechristianisation' of Europe, and the history of Church, Sports and Leisure. Previously he published primarily on French Protestantism. At present his research focus has shifted to the history of football and European Christianity. His publications include *Religion and Identity in Modern France: The Modernization of the Protestant Community in Languedoc, 1815–1848* (University Press of America, 1999), 'Martyrs for Modernity: The Three-Hundredth Anniversary Jubilee of the French Reformation and the Catholic/Protestant Debate on the Huguenot Martyrs' (in *From Persecution to Pluralism: Religious Minorities and the Enforcement of Conformity in Western Europe since the Reformation*, Peter Lang, 2007) and 'Philip Schaff, Europe, and American Exceptionalism' (*The Journal of Presbyterian History*, spring/summer 2006).

Tom Gibbons is Senior Lecturer in Sports Studies at Teesside University, UK and one of the Elders at Amazing GRACE Church in Teesside. He has an MA in the Sociology of Sport from the former 'Centre for Research into Sport & Society' (CRSS) at the University of Leicester and became a Christian in 2008 while studying part-time for his PhD (later awarded at Teesside in 2013). He has published research in a range of academic journals and has a number of chapters in edited books. His first monograph was titled *English National Identity and Football Fan Culture: Who are ya?* (Ashgate, 2014) and he has since co-edited two further texts titled *The Impact of the 2012 Olympic and Paralympic Games: Diminishing Contrasts, Increasing Varieties* (Palgrave, 2015) and *Sport and English National Identity in a 'Disunited Kingdom'* (Routledge, 2017). He is keen to develop a Christian approach to the sociology of sport and is currently co-editing a special edition of the journal *Sport in Society* on the topic of Christian social scientific approaches to sport.

Grant Jarvie is Professor (Chair of Sport) with the University of Edinburgh and Honorary Professor with the University of Toronto. He has held three established chairs at three different Universities and is a former University Vice-Principal and Acting Principal. He is an advisor to both the Scottish and UK Governments and the Scottish Football Association. Recently described by a Member of the House of Lords as one of the most authoritative voices on sport and its wider role in international development and social cohesion, he has most recently published *Sport, Culture and Society* (Routledge, 2017).

James Jones, The Right Reverend KBE served as Bishop of Hull 1994–1998 and as Bishop of Liverpool 1998–2013. In 2010 he was appointed by the British Government to chair the Hillsborough Independent Panel, which reported in 2012. It led to the quashing of the original inquests and to the setting up of a new inquest which became the longest running in British legal history and returned a determination of 'unlawful killing' of the 96 Liverpool football fans at the Hillsborough Stadium in Sheffield in 1989. In the 2017 New Year's Honours List he was nominated by the Prime Minister to the Queen to be made a Knight Commander of the Order of the British Empire (KBE) for 'services to the bereaved and to justice'. His speeches, articles, sermons and broadcasts on the BBC are available on his website Bishop James Jones.Com.

Nils Martinius Justvik is Associate Professor in History at the Institute for Religion, Philosophy and History at the University of Agder, Norway. He holds a PhD in History (2007) on the topic Sport and Christianity in the 'Bible Belt' of Norway 1945–2000. His two Masters theses, in Christianity and History, also focus on the regional history of the 'Bible belt' in Norway; Protestants' relations to the Labour Movement and the relationship between the liberal theologian and his theologically conservative congregation in a rural community. In 2014 he produced a historiographical article in the *Journal of Religion & Society* comparing his doctoral thesis to three milestones of the US literature of Muscular Christianity. In spring 2017 he published the hundred years history of Vest-Agder regional organisation of Norwegian Sports Association. In

2016 he started writing the history of Aust-Agder regional organisation of Norwegian Sports Association. A book will be published late 2018.

Eloísa Martín is a tenured Professor of Sociology at the University of Rio de Janeiro, in Brazil, and the co-chair of SEPHIS-the South-South Exchange Programme for the Research on the History of Development. She has been working in the Sociology of Religion since she was an undergrad student – especially theory, Catholicism, and popular religion. She has been elected Executive Secretary for two terms (2003–2007) and Vice-President (2007–2009) of the Association of Social Scientists of Religion in Mercosur (ACSRM), and is currently Secretary/Treasurer of the International Sociological Association Research Committee on Sociology of Religion (2014–2018). Since 2010 she has been the Editor of *Current Sociology*. She was Editor (and co-founder) of *Ciencias Sociales y Religión/Ciências Sociais e Religião* (Social Sciences and Religion) from 1999 to 2010; Associate Editor of *Sociedade & Estado* (State & Society) from 2008 to 2011; and collaborates as a board member and consultant for journals and book collections in the USA, Australia and Europe.

Andrew Parker is Professor of Sport and Christian Outreach and Co-director (with Nick Watson) of the Centre for Sport, Spirituality and Religion (CSSR) in the School of Sport and Exercise at the University of Gloucestershire, UK. His research interests include: sport and spirituality, sport and social identity, and sport and marginalised youth. He has served on the editorial boards of the *Sociology of Sport Journal* (2005–2008) (Human Kinetics), *Qualitative Research* (2001–present) and is a former co-Editor of the *International Journal of Religion and Sport* (2010–2012).

Jeremy Treat (PhD, Wheaton College) is Pastor for Preaching and Vision at Reality LA and Adjunct Professor of Theology at Biola University. He is the author of *The Crucified King: Atonement and Kingdom in Biblical and Systematic Theology* (Zondervan, 2014).

Jonathan Tuckett earned his PhD at the University of Stirling and has worked variously between there and the University of Edinburgh as a teaching fellow. He primarily works in Religious Studies where he specialises in Method and Theory with a particular emphasis on Philosophy of Social Science. His current research focuses on how to understand the concept of 'religion' in the framework of intersubjectivity using philosophical phenomenology.

Abel Ugba is Senior Lecturer in the School of Arts and Digital Industries, University of East London, London. His professional and academic background is in journalism and sociology, having obtained an MA in

Journalism (Dublin City University, Ireland) and a PhD in Sociology (Trinity College, Dublin, Ireland). His research, teaching and academic writing have focused on media, religion, international development and Europe's new African diasporas. He has published books, articles, book chapters and commissioned reports on African diasporic religion, as well as on migrant media. He is the author of *Shades of Belonging: African Pentecostals in Twenty-First Century Ireland* (Africa World Press, 2009).

Nick J. Watson is Associate Professor Sport and Social Justice in the School of Sport, York St John University, UK. His research and practice is interdisciplinary and is accessible to a wide audience and broadly focuses on issues surrounding 'social justice' in sport, in particular, the relationship between sport and Christianity. His most recent research projects examine fatherlessness, faith and mentoring in and through sports, theological understandings of well-being in elite sport, the practice of sport chaplaincy/psychology and the effectiveness of sport-Dementia initiatives. He has co-authored/edited a number of books and journal special editions and has been the Co-Director of two University centres of excellence and convener of two international conferences. He has worked with the Sport and Church Office of the Vatican, the Church of England, Sport Chaplaincy UK and the public theology think-tank, Theos. He is an Associate Editor of the *Journal of Disability and Religion*, and reviews work for various sport social science and theology journals. He is also a Director and Trustee of The Island, York, UK (2013–), a charity that provides mentoring services for vulnerable children.

Corey L. Williams (PhD, Edinburgh) is Assistant Professor of Anthropology and Global Christianity at Leiden University, The Netherlands. As an anthropologist of religion, his current research interests include interreligious encounter in Nigeria and African immigrant religious networks in California, USA. He serves as the General Secretary for the African Association for the Study of Religions and as Co-Chair of the World Christianity Unit for the American Academy of Religion. He is also the Sub-Saharan Africa Coordinator and Moderator for the 'Islam in the Modern World' project (2017–2020), sponsored by the Leiden Islam Academy and the Ministry of Foreign Affairs, The Hague, The Netherlands.

Foreword

Sport is a global phenomenon. Whether we are thinking of elite sport with mass spectator interest and considerable commercial backing, or participative sport enjoyed at grass roots level though tinged with consumerism and disclosing a huge range of motivations, sport is everywhere. If 'the unexamined life is not worth living', it is also true that unexamined sport is not worth playing, and this timely volume brings multiple perspectives to bear on this pervasive cultural practice.

Many contemporary sports players and spectators may be more or less oblivious to the religious origins of sport (one need only think of the ancient Olympics, of the Etruscan funeral rites that became the Roman games, and of the likely pagan origins of primitive forms of 'football'), and to the ways in which sport and religion have often enjoyed a symbiotic relationship through the centuries. But increasingly scholars of religion have turned their attention to sport, both investigating that history and analysing contemporary sport for its quasi-religious aspects. Theologians have asked about sports theological *raison d'etre*, and its place in God's purposes. Social scientists and historians discovered sport earlier, and both approach the subject from different angles and with different interests, as do psychologists, and those interested in migration, gender politics and ethnicity. There is a rich diversity of academic perspectives now offered on sport and this collection of essays illustrates many of these various approaches and how their perspectives interlock and mutually illuminate one another. Some scholars deliberately adopted *inter*disciplinary and *trans*disciplinary methods, enriching the whole project and opening up further possibilities for research into the multi-faceted phenomenon of sport, and for collaborative effort to that end.

But the volume also has another major strength. Much academic writing on sport to date has been male, white and Western. In this, it might be argued, it mirrors so much of the reality of contemporary sport itself. Western readers will be increasingly aware of very important contributions in the field from female scholars, and this volume indicates a further welcome broadening of diversity. Against the Western-centric trend, essays here shed light on sport as experienced in multiple continents, and through research whose writers do not share many of the assumptions about sport, identity, religion and society, that many researchers have hitherto taken for granted. This volume takes us to Argentina, Nigeria, Ghana, South Africa, Norway and Scotland, as well as the United States and England.

Global Perspectives on Sports and Christianity is a timely and significant volume in this broadening field of study. It will indicate to its readers some of what is possible given the range of current approaches, stretch horizons of interest through the diversity of its content, and should stimulate further research across the gamut of disciplines.

Dr Robert Ellis
Faculty of Theology and Religion
University of Oxford

Introduction

Afe Adogame, Nick J. Watson and
Andrew Parker

The 1970s marks a significant watershed in the historiography of 'Religion and Sport(s)' as a field of study but also increasingly so in its evolvement and development as an interdisciplinary and transdisciplinary endeavour. While sports have been studied primarily from the perspectives of social science, law, ethics and the various dimensions of human difference, most notably 'race' and gender, Rebecca Alpert (2015) aptly indicates that adding religion to the conversation underscores the importance of sports as one of the most popular and significant dimensions of human experience in the twenty-first century. Her recent book is illuminating not simply because it explores the complex relationship between religion and sports, providing some definitional clarity, but more importantly because it provides a useful pedagogical twist to the field, 'taking case studies based on actual events to test ... theoretical knowledge in real-life situations.' (p. 4). Alpert remarks, 'examining actual cases will connect classroom learning to real life, develop new perspectives on religion and sports, and provide a chance to respond to the challenges and conflicts in this arena' (p. 4).

Previous work in the area has identified that while there is an ever-increasing literature base, there is a serious lack of empirical research in the field of sport and religion (see Jarvie and Thornton, 2012; Parker, Watson and White, 2016; Watson and Parker, 2014). Research endeavours, scholarly gatherings, journal contributions and practical initiatives that focus on sport and religion have exponentially increased during the last decade. However, these discourses are limited to contexts of countries and of disciplines. For example, the vast majority of research on the sport-religion interface has come from the US, and has typically focused on a narrow evangelical manifestation of Christianity. There is little, except for Catholic reflection on sport from the Vatican, from mainland Europe and on non-western understandings of religion and sports. Most of the contributions published in the USA or the UK for instance, do not take into account developments on the European continent or in Canada, not to mention Africa, Latin America and Asia. And yet important sporting events are characterised by their international dimension.

This edited collection provides an interdisciplinary exploration of the relationship between sports and Christianity from a 'global' perspective. This clearly differentiates the book from previous social science-based scholarship in the area, and thus, demonstrates its originality. Indeed, previous monographs and anthologies in this area have tended to focus on 'western' understandings of the sport and Christianity relationship (e.g. Parry, Watson and Nesti, 2011; Watson and Parker, 2013) especially from a North-American evangelical standpoint (e.g. Baker, 2007; Higgs and Braswell, 2004; Hoffman, 2010; Overman, 2011; Price, 2001; Scholes and Sassower, 2013). Conversely, this book includes chapters on the dialectical relationship between sports and Christianity across diverse global cultures, non-western (Africa, Asia) and western perspectives (Europe and North America), something that makes this volume attractive and readable across a broad range of disciplines and geographical settings.

There is a considerable amount of existing social science literature that examines sport in non-western contexts, something that is reflected in the Routledge Research in Sport, Culture and Society series (e.g. Majumdar, 2009), alongside related academic outputs. For example, social science literature on sport in Africa (e.g. Alegi and Bolsmann, 2010; Booth, 1998), Asia (e.g. Bromber, Krawietz and Maguire, 2012; Chakraborty, Chakrabarti and Kingshuk, 2009; Hong, 2009), Russia (Orttung, 2013), South America (Wood and Johnson, 2009) and reflections on spirituality in Australian sporting locales (Crotty and Hess, 2016). In addition, there is a burgeoning literature that examines the spread of the 'muscular Christian' ethos through the vehicle of British colonialism in the mid-late nineteenth century (e.g. Majumdar, 2008; Mangan, 2001). However, to our knowledge there is no detailed reflection on this topic from the perspective of religion, theology (Christianity), and sociology beyond these western-centric analyses. It is from these perspectives that this book contributes to work in this area.

There is, however, a wealth of literature in the disciplines of theology and religious studies that address understandings of Christianity across the globe and issues concerning different world religions (Cooper, 2013; Kalu, 2008; Tennent, 2007; Walls, 2002), and thus provide appropriate starting points for our discussion. The need and rationale for further research, that explores sport and non-western understandings of Christianity (and other religions), is therefore considerable. Within the context of a relatively new and rapidly expanding field of practical theology, this book provides a unique and important addition to the current literature for both undergraduate and postgraduate students, and serves as a point of reference for academics from a wide-range of related fields including: theology and religious studies, cultural studies, psychology, health studies, ethics and sports studies (i.e. sociology, psychology, history, and philosophy/ethics, World Christianity, world religions, African studies, migration and diaspora studies etc.). The book may also be of interest to physical educators, sports coaches, sports chaplains and sport psychologists, who wish to adopt a more 'holistic' approach to their work.

Two events that helped to galvanise our reflection on sports from the perspectives of religion, theology and sociology were the interdisciplinary workshop/seminar 'Religion and Sport: Past, Present and Future' held at the University of Edinburgh, UK (27 March 2013) and the Inaugural Global Congress on Sports and Christianity, held at York St John University, UK (24–28 August 2016) respectively. Conversations before, during and beyond these pivotal meetings have underscored the urgency in further interrogating the intersecting and interlocking relationship between sport and religion, in this case Christianity and indigenous religions.

The Special Issue, 'Religion and Sports', *Studies in World Christianity* (2015, 21.3) took the discourse on religion and sport one step further by exploring correlations between football and culture and religion, interaction processes that are also of interest to religious studies and mission theology; how sporting celebrities are rarely discussed within the broader realms of theological debate, and ways in which academic discourse that centres on the lives and lifestyles of celebrity sports stars can provide fruitful ground for critiquing the role of sport in modern-day society. This collection of chapters also addresses ways in which traditional world-views of supernatural causality have influenced the nature and practice of Christianity, the innovative ways in which contemporary Pentecostal/charismatic churches have reinvented alternative religious spaces; and unpacks the legitimacy of claims that athletes in extreme sports may encounter the mystical and sublime, when examined through a Christian theological lens.

The timing of the book is concurrent with the shift towards debates surrounding spirituality and wellbeing both within other academic disciplines (i.e. the medical sciences and psychology) and within wider culture (Theos, 2013, 2016). Alpert (2015: 3) points to sports and religion as two core strands of everyday life that are deeply rooted in global cultures, maintaining that 'both spheres can be enriching and ennobling influences, and both can be the locus for social evils – greed, corruption, commercialism, racism, sexism, homophobia, xenophobia'. Studying the interconnections between sports and religion gives us an opportunity to understand how these key aspects of society influence our political and cultural lives and provide ways to understand human experience and its meaning and purpose. Since modern sport is often intertwined with commercial and political agendas, the book attempts to provide an important corrective to the 'win at all costs' philosophy of modern sport that cannot always be fully understood through secular ethical inquiry.

New multidisciplinary research initiatives should interrogate and explore wide-ranging questions, such as, how sporting pursuits from physical activity to organised and competitive/elite sport can be a potentially powerful and cost-effective way of supporting a range of development, health, wellbeing, and peace objectives, and how awareness might be raised surrounding the crucial need to integrate sport and physical activity into policies and programmes across a range of sectors, including health, education, economic and social development (Adogame, 2015: 195). Such a focus highlights the potential of sport as a viable and practical tool for the realisation of sustainable development, health, wellbeing, peace and transformation; and also how sport programmes and interventions implemented in an equity-driven and culturally relevant way might give opportunity to women, persons with disabilities and young people to exhibit their core skills and values. Moreover, research interest should focus on the relationship between sport, religion and spirituality as an aspect of wellbeing but in a much more complex and varied way than that of the ideology and practice of muscular Christianity. It is against this backdrop that this edited book therefore draws crucial attention to the ambivalence of sport(s) and religion (Christianity) from a global perspective.

The book is structured around three main sections. Part I centres on transdisciplinary considerations; Part II on non-western perspectives on the sport-Christianity relationship; and Part III on western perspectives on sport and Christianity.

Part I comprises two chapters. Tom Gibbons' opening chapter revisits the marginalisation of religion in the sociological analysis of sport over the last two decades, and addresses this void through identifying Christian approaches to sociology that are yet to be drawn upon by sociologists. In this exploratory chapter, Gibbons calls attention to what appears to be a significant lacuna in the expanding research on the multidisciplinary topic area of sports and Christianity and presents a challenge to the secular bias that has saturated the sociology of sport. In Chapter 2, Jeremy Treat aptly remarks how sports that currently capture the public imagination across the globe have largely evaded the attention of Christian theologians. There seem to be two polar responses: some dismiss sports as merely games, while others worship sports as nearly a god. Treat argues that when viewed through the lens of Scripture, sports are more than a game, less than a god.

Part II features seven chapters, addressing non-western perspectives on sport and Christianity. David Chidester explores the enduring relationship between football and Christianity and indigenous religious traditions in South Africa. Introduced by the British military in the nineteenth century, football was adopted by African Christian converts at mission schools and churches, becoming a part of African Christian life like literacy, wage labour and European clothing. As football developed to become the most popular African sport during the twentieth century, it was attended by indigenous rituals of strengthening and healing, drawing upon an African traditional religious heritage. During the World Cup in 2010, three religions were on display – Christianity, African Traditional Religion, and the religion of football. By analysing the Christian prayers, the ancestral rituals, and the contests over ownership of sacred symbols, such as the vuvuzela, in the religion of football in South Africa, the chapter identifies three important features of World Christianity – mediations with indigeneity, negotiations with local sovereignty and transactions with a global economy.

Eloísa Martín provides a novel, non-classical approach at understanding the intersection between religion and popular culture or a sport-religion interface, and understanding religion as a template for fan practices. She proposes to look at this approach from a new perspective: not understanding sport as a civil religion, but rather understanding soccer fandom as a practice of the sacred and, ultimately, as a form of 'religious' socialisation. Drawing from her rich ethnographic notes on practices of the sacred among young men in Argentina, Martín underscores how the presence of the sacred in everyday life is broadly viewed as a trend that unifies working class cultures in Latin America; it is visible in rituals, feasts, devotions and miracles, as well as in daily activities. A person's relations with the sacred are part of daily life, developed in and through 'secular' practices.

In Chapter 5, Olutayo Adesina adopts the historical and empiricist traditions to exemplify the complex relationship between culture, memory, reality and the senses. He establishes a dialogue that demonstrates the significance of place, space and time in the game of soccer. Following a useful discussion of the ways in which generations of Yoruba Nigerians engage the game of soccer, he analyses how traditional religious credo, values and ideas have also come to incorporate a multitude of perspectives that question and at the same time reinforce old ideas of winning football matches. Taking its cue from the antics and enthusiasm of Ganiyu Elekuru (a.k.a. Baba Eleran), head of the supporters' club of the Ibadan-based Industrial Investment and Credit Corporation (IICC) football club and his rumoured love for the occult, the narrative juxtaposes the past image of football enthusiasm with the glory of modern football.

Soccer (football) has not only taken centre stage in Ghana's sporting activities, it continues to engender greater public display of emotions and nationalism. The Ghanaian Church is not exempt from this show of patriotism. Yet, the disparity in support by Ghanaian Christians and the Church as a whole is creating concern for gender activists, feminist theologians and scholars of religions in Ghana. Rose Mary Amenga-Etego (Chapter 6) examines the role of Ghanaian Christians and the Church in the promotion of soccer in Ghana on the one hand and the creation of gender inequalities in the sport on the other. In turn, she demonstrates how historical allegations of occult practices within male soccer are being challenged by the modern-day Christian Church. Continuing this theme of spiritual juxtaposition in and through sport, Chapter 7 is based on Corey Williams's interaction with a group of male footballers in Kaduna, Nigeria in early 2010. Known as the 'Interfaith FC', this diverse group – consisting of Hausa Muslims, Gbagyi Muslims, Gbagyi Christians, and Igbo Christians – was initiated as a grassroots Christian response to violence surrounding the implementation of *Shari'a* in 2000. Despite ongoing tension in the region, including targeted threats at the group, they continued to meet and play together. Drawing upon participant observation and qualitative interviews conducted with select members, Williams explores how the group understands sport and utilises it to facilitate and promote ethnoreligious cooperation. Particular attention is given to how sport relates to and is constructed within a Nigerian Christian identity.

In Chapter 8, Jonathan Tuckett explores the religious heritage of martial arts; perceiving Kendo and Taekwondo as forms of naturalisation; and suggesting that 'religion' and 'nationalism' are ways of categorising non-dominant and dominant modes of naturalisation. He considers how Kendo can be conceived as a 'nationalistic' mode of naturalisation and Taekwondo as a 'religious' mode of naturalisation, thus coming to some conclusion on how these modes of naturalisation interact with more traditionally conceived 'religious' modes like Christianity. In another vein, the dalliance between religion and sports has been politicised and given wider recognition in recent times. Public display of religious belonging by sports people has traditionally been more common in the US than in Britain. Yet this notion has been challenged in recent years both by the ever-increasing public display of religious symbolisms by UK-based elite sports performers, and by the thickly religious tone of related media coverage. Such trends were aptly demonstrated in March 2012 when Premier League footballer Fabrice Muamba collapsed and suffered a cardiac arrest while playing for Bolton Wanderers in a high-profile televised game against Tottenham Hotspur. In Chapter 9, Abel Ugba utilises data obtained from selected national and local newspapers in Britain (2012–2013) and websites in the aftermath of this event to examine the trajectories and implications of the public display of faith by the footballing fraternity. He also interrogates how and to what extent the rising phenomenon of faith in English football signals a new attitude to public displays of faith in British society.

Part III comprises seven chapters that address western perspectives on sport and Christianity. To this end, Chapter 10 is informed by findings from a Church of Scotland research report led by the author, Grant Jarvie, and undertaken between 2013–2014. The chapter focuses upon the relationship between sport and competition and how a Christian response might articulate both the negative and positive effects of competitiveness in sport. The author draws on further international examples in order to contribute to a more global perspective on sport, competition and Christianity. The chapter attempts to analyse bible references about sport, the etymology of competition and how the relationship between sport, competition and Christianity can impact on the freedoms that athletes have. Nils Martinius Justvik's focus is on Protestantism and sport in the 'Bible Belt' of Norway in the first half of the twentieth century and in Chapter 11 he explains why sport – 'any display of human joy of life' – was so harshly rejected in many of the communities in this part of Norway. To better understand what kind of religiosity developed in the area in the decades around 1900, and what challenges the communities and the various popular movements face with respect to religion, Justvik explores the history of the regional branch of the YMCA, focusing on the changing attitudes to sport in this geographical locality in the first half of the twentieth century.

In recent years, academic discussion surrounding the lives and lifestyles of celebrity sports stars has provided fruitful ground for critiquing the role of sport in modern-day society. Rarely, however, has celebrity been discussed in relation to the sport-media-spirituality nexus. Drawing upon literature concerning the historical development of celebrity and sociological analyses of celebrity as a concept, in Chapter 12 Andrew Parker and Nick Watson argue that celebrity status is situated at the heart of an individualised and ideologically grounded late capitalist culture in which visual media is central to the production of social identities. In turn, Parker and Watson seek to uncover ways in which celebrity status and 'stardom' might be viewed as powerful signifiers in terms of popular cultural perceptions of sports performers. In so doing they consider some of the sporting icons of more recent years and analyse how their images have been managed and manipulated in order to depict specific messages relating to notions of faith, religion and spirituality.

Two major disasters have occurred at Ibrox Park, home of Glasgow Rangers Football Club, in 1902 and 1971 respectively. In both cases, public efforts were made to unite the city in memorial to the victims and consolation for their families. These rituals can reinforce social bonds as well as expose underlying conflicts that otherwise were suppressed. James C. Deming (Chapter 13) critically examines the place and priorities of religious figures and institutions in these rites of grief. In particular, the author concentrates on church leaders' use of the tragedies to evaluate football's status in the late-Victorian era and the 1960s. Even though the hostility and violence resumed soon after the time of mourning had faded, the influence of rituals of public mourning was great enough that moments of commemoration marking anniversaries of the tragedy were observed with proper decorum.

Christianity has been an enduring feature of the mainstream sports film from its emergence in the early twentieth century, such that religious icons, references and rituals have now become naturalised as a familiar and recurring aspect of the genre. Religious figures have also taken lead roles in sports films, occasionally as athletes or employing sport as a means of instilling discipline and character in young people. In more recent years, Christianity has continued to feature prominently within the genre. Seán Crosson (Chapter 14) provides an overview of the historical development and ideological importance of Christianity in the sports film, drawing mostly on films from the US, but also sports films from other countries including Britain.

Nick Watson and Brian Brock (Chapter 15) provide a theological analysis of two violent combat sports, boxing and Mixed Martial Arts (MMA, also known as cage fighting). The titles of the biographies of a number of well-known professional Christian boxers and the fact that 'roughly 700 churches in the United States have begun incorporating MMA [Mixed Martial Arts] into their ministry in some capacity' raises a host of ethical quandaries and seeming paradoxes for the theologian. The authors contribute to academic theological reflection on boxing and MMA, providing a brief cultural history of both to contextualise their theological analysis, while at the same time discussing theories of violence, and applying theological ethics to examine the ethical problems and paradoxes that exist for Christians who participate in, or watch, boxing or MMA.

Part III ends with a chapter (Chapter 16) by James Jones on the Hillsborough Football Disaster, highlighting the role of the Church of England in the Hillsborough Independent Panel. Jones provides a chronological, descriptive and reflective narrative about his own roles as Bishop of Liverpool (1998–2013) and as Chair of the Hillsborough Independent Panel (2010–2012), as a kind of raw material for those who wish to explore and research the role of the Church of England and one of its pastors in contemporary society. Even when the dynamics of a culture push an individual to the forefront that narrative is always woven out of the many stories of others who have played their own part. Thus, the work of the Hillsborough Independent Panel was the summation of the efforts of expert colleagues and of a dedicated secretariat who worked together to deliver the Terms of Reference, that had been shaped through consultation with the families. This led to the quashing of the verdicts of the original inquests and to the appointment of a new Coroner, Lord Justice Goldring, to oversee new inquests in 2013. After the longest inquest in British Legal history on 26 April 2016 the Jury overturned a verdict of accidental death and unanimously exonerated the fans of any responsibility and by a majority of 7:2 returned a determination of 'unlawful killing'.

In sum, *Global Perspectives on Sports and Christianity* aims not only to reflect on the ways in which the sport–Christianity relationship has developed over time, but also how it is variously played out by different individuals and groups in different geographical and cultural contexts. Moreover it aims to offer insights into the ways in which faith might be used as a means to negotiate and challenge the values and practices of modern-day sport, thereby creating more equitable and inclusive sporting experiences for those concerned. One example of how this might be achieved is through addressing issues of 'social justice' in the sports realm, such as, gender, race, religion, ethnicity, disability, sexuality and the many different forms of corruption, etc. Some of the chapters within this volume begin this discussion, not least the chapters addressing public justice issues surrounding the Hillsborough and Ibrox football disasters. Social justice is a foundational concept within the disciplines of theology and religious studies (e.g. Palmer and Burgess, 2012), and more recently, has become a 'hot topic' in the social scientific study of sport (e.g. Gottfried, 2014; Long, Fletcher and Watson, 2017; Schinke and Hanrahan, 2012). We believe that it is by way of such reflection that our understandings of the relationship between sport and Christianity can continue to thrive and that the desire for ongoing empirical scholarship will be stimulated and encouraged.

References

Adogame, A. (2015) Editorial 'Religion and Sport, Past, Present and Future', Special Issue on Religion and Sport, *Studies in World Christianity*, 21: 3, 193–200.

Alegi, P. and Bolsmann, C. (2010) *South Africa and the Global Game: Football, Apartheid and Beyond*, London: Routledge.

Alpert, R. (2015). *A Case Study Textbook on Religion and Sport*. West Sussex, UK: Columbia University Press.

Baker, W. (2007) *Playing with God: Religion and Modern Sport*, London: Harvard University Press.

Bromber, K., Krawietz, B. and Maguire, J. (eds) (2012) *Sport Across Asia: Politics, Cultures and Identities*, London: Routledge.

Booth, D. (1998) *The Race Game: Sport and Politics in South Africa*, London: Routledge.

Chakraborty, S.J., Chakrabarti, S. and Kingshuk, C. (eds) (2009) *The Politics of Sport in South Asia*, London: Routledge.

Cooper, D. (2013) *Christianity and World Religions: An Introduction to the Worlds of the Major Faiths*, Phillisburg, NY: P and P Publishing.

Crotty, M. and Hess, M. (eds) (2016). *Sport, War and Society in Australia and New Zealand*. London: Routledge.

Gottfried, S. (2014) Social Justice and Professional Sport, *International Journal of Applied Philosophy*, 28: 2, 373–389.

Higgs, R.J. and Braswell, M.C. (2004) *An Unholy Alliance: The Sacred and Modern Sports*, Macon, GA: Mercer University Press.

Hoffman, S.J. (2010) *Good Game: Christianity and the Culture of Sports*, Waco, TX: Baylor University Press.

Hong, F. (ed.) (2009) *Sport, Nationalism and Orientalism: The Asian Games*, London: Routledge.

Jarvie, G. and Thornton, J. (2012) Sport, Religion and Spirituality, in *Sport, Culture and Society: An Introduction (2nd edn)*, London: Routledge: 324–340.

Kalu, O. (ed.) (2008) *Interpreting Contemporary Christianity: Global Processes and Local Identities* (Studies in the History of Christian Missions), Grand Rapids, MI: Wm B. Eerdmans.

Long, J., Fletcher, T. and Watson, B. (eds) (2017) *Sport, Leisure and Social Justice*, London: Routledge.

Majumdar, B. (ed.) (2009) *Modern Sport – The Global Obsession*, London: Routledge.

Majumdar, B. (2008) *Cricket in Colonial India 1780–1947*, London: Routledge.

Mangan, J.A. (ed.) (2011) *The Cultural Bond: Sport, Empire and Society*, London: Routledge.

Orttung, R. (2013) *The 2014 Winter Olympics and the Evolution of Putin's Russia*, London: Routledge.

Overman, S. (2011) *The Protestant Ethic and the Spirit of Sport: How Calvinism and Capitalism Shaped America's* Games, Macon, GA: Mercer University Press.

Palmer, M.D. and Burgess, M. (eds) (2012) *The Wiley-Blackwell Companion to Religion and Social Justice*. Chichester, UK: Blackwell Publishing.

Parker, A., Watson, N.J. and White, J. (eds) (2016) *Sports Chaplaincy: Trends, Issues and Debates*, Farnham, UK: Ashgate.

Parry, J., Watson, N.J. and Nesti, M.N. (2011), *Theology, Ethics and Transcendence in Sports*, London: Routledge.

Price, J.L. (2001) *From Season to Season: Sports as American Religion*, Mercer Macon, GA: Baylor University Press.

Schinke, R.J. and Hanrahan, S.J. (2012) *Sport for Development, Peace, and Social Justice*, Morgantown, WV: Fitness Information Technology.

Scholes, J. and Sassower, R. (2013) *Religion and Sports in American Culture*, New York: Routledge.

Tennent, C.T. (2007) *Theology in the Context of World Christianity*, Grand Rapids, MI: Zondervan.

Theos (2013) *The Spirit of Things Unseen: Belief in Post-Religious Britain*, London: Theos.

Walls, A.F. (2002) *The Cross-Cultural Process in Christian History*, Maryknoll, NY: Orbis.

Watson, N.J. and Parker, A. (eds) (2013) *Sports and Christianity: Historical and Contemporary Perspectives* (foreword by Michael Novak), New York: Routledge.

Watson, N.J. and Parker, A. (2014) *Sport and the Christian Religion: A Systematic Review of Literature* (Foreword, Scott Kretchmar; Preface, Brian Brock), Newcastle upon Tyne, UK: Cambridge Scholars Publishing.

Wood, D. and Johnson, L. (eds) (2009) *Sporting Cultures: Hispanic Perspectives on Sport, Text and the Body*, London: Routledge.

Part I

Some transdisciplinary considerations

Chapter 1

Challenging the secular bias in the sociology of sport

Scratching the surface of Christian approaches to sociology

Tom Gibbons

Introduction

In an essay published in the *Sociology of Sport Journal* (one of the leading journals in the sub-discipline of the sociology of sport), Shilling and Mellor (2014: 350) argue that the topic of 'religion' has been 'marginalized' in sociological analysis of sport over the last two decades. Part of their argument is that 'studies focused purely on the secular dimensions of sport can be unhelpfully narrow' (ibid.: 352). The aim of the present chapter is to begin to address this void by identifying Christian approaches to sociology that are yet to be drawn upon by sociologists of sport (see also Parker and Watson, 2016).

While studies exist on the relationship between sport and various 'faiths' or 'religions', the interface between sport and Christianity is the fastest growing area of research within this field (see Watson and Parker, 2014). However, this area of scholarship appears to be dominated by sports theologians, philosophers, psychologists and historians and, at present, lacks examples of theoretically informed and/or empirically based sociological work.[1] While some scholars have attempted to adopt a more sociological standpoint on research into sport and Christianity,[2] there appears to be little, if any, serious reflection on Christian approaches to sociology within this literature or indeed within the sociology of sport per se (see for instance Horne, 2015). So far no purposeful attempts have been made to specifically discuss the connection between Christian approaches to sociology and the sociology of sport. In this exploratory chapter, I begin to address what appears to be a lacuna in the literature surrounding sports and Christianity in order to: (i) challenge the secular bias that has saturated the sociology of sport to date, (ii) initiate debate between Christian and non-Christian scholars, and (iii) stimulate further discussion on the potential connections between Christian approaches to sociology and the sociology of sport.

To this end, the chapter is divided into three sections. In the first, the paradox regarding the growth of Christianity (especially over the last century) and the claims made by advocates of the secularisation thesis are briefly discussed. In the second, further evidence is provided from Shilling and Mellor (2014) concerning the secular bias in the sociology of sport. The cause of this is attributed to the fact that the sociology of sport mirrors its parent discipline (sociology). In the third section of the chapter, the historical work of Brewer (2007) regarding the distinction between 'religious sociology' and 'the sociology of religion' is drawn upon and three main areas of what might be considered 'Christian approaches to sociology' are outlined with a view to encouraging sociologists of sport to explore these resources for themselves. The intention here is not to make definitive links between Christian approaches to sociology and the sociological study of sport but to open the door to a set of perspectives that so far remain largely unexplored by those undertaking sociological analyses of sport.

The growth of Christianity in a secular age

The term 'secularisation' refers to a process whereby identifications with 'religious' values and institutions decline and are replaced by 'irreligious' values and 'secular' institutions in a particular society. This occurred in Western societies following the seventeenth-century 'Enlightenment period' or 'scientific revolution' that resulted in what are known as the 'modernising revolutions' of the eighteenth and nineteenth centuries, including the American and French political revolutions and the British Industrial Revolution. In response to what became known as the 'modernisation' of Western societies, the 'secularisation thesis' – that the decline of religiosity would be one of the outcomes of the progressive modernisation of society – was conceived by classical social theorists such as Karl Marx, Max Weber, Émile Durkheim and others from the latter part of the nineteenth century onwards. According to one of its contemporary adherents, Bryan Wilson (1998), the core concerns of the secularisation thesis include 'religion' losing claims to 'authority' and therefore the legitimate production of 'knowledge' in all aspects of social life (Han, 2015).

The subsequent dominance of the secularisation thesis in Western societies meant that for much of the twentieth century 'religion ... tended to be restricted to the private sphere' (Brewer, 2007: 9). According to Berger (1999) we began to witness the 'desecularisation' of the world in the late twentieth century and there has been (and continues to be) a global resurgence in religious adherents. Yet Christianity has been expanding on a global scale beyond Europe since at least 1500 and at a particularly rapid rate since 1900 (O'Donnell, 2009). Indeed, Threlfall-Holmes (2012: 129) states that Christianity has grown significantly, 'from around 500 million adherents in 1900 to around two billion in 2000, nearly a third of the world's population'. She goes on to state:

Such growth has confounded the belief, increasingly frequently expressed over the course of the twentieth century until its final decade, that secularism was rapidly spreading and that Christianity, and indeed religion in general, was an outdated mindset that would soon be eclipsed or eradicated.

(Ibid.)

For example, despite secular claims that the Christian church in Britain is in decline, the contributions to Goodhew's (2012) edited text *Church Growth in Britain: 1980 to the Present* highlight clear signs of vitality and growth across various denominations since the 1980s. Current statistics indicate that the growth of the Protestant church is limited to Pentecostal/charismatic churches and/or those congregations emerging from immigrant populations in Britain (Davie, 2015; Gibbons, 2016). Another example is the rapid growth of the Pentecostal church that began in 1906 following the Azusa Street revival in Los Angeles. Jennings (2015: 62) argues that such expansion:

constitutes Christianity's most compelling response to secularisation theory. Here we have, beginning in the 20th century, a religious movement that grew from zero to half a billion – all in the midst of an era when religion was supposed to be in decline.

As is the case for other disciplines within the social sciences (including, for example, anthropology, history and psychology), even a cursory glance at the mainstream sociology literature outside of sport reveals a strong secular bias and this is something that is readily recognised by scholars within the sociology of religion (see, for example, Brewer, 2007; Fraser and Campolo, 1992; Perkins, 1987; Turner, 2014). Turner (2014: 774–775) states that there has been a 'revival of the sociology of religion in the late 20th and early 21st century' which is 'associated with growing recognition of the importance of religion in public life'. Moreover, the 'post-secularisation thesis' of the well-known contemporary social theorist Jürgen Habermas (2006 cited in Turner, 2014: 773) argues that 'secular and religious citizens have a duty to engage in dialogue within the public sphere in the interests of a liberal consensus' (Turner, 2014: 771–772) – a point that helps to underpin my own rationale for exposing the secular bias inherent within the sub-discipline of the sociology of sport.

The secular bias within the sociology of sport

In the introductory chapter of their edited text *With God on Their Side: Sport in the Service of Religion*, Magdalinksi and Chandler (2002: 1) claim that sport and 'religion' possess 'disparate philosophical foundations'.

Although this proposition sounds justifiable in relation to the hyper-commodified global sports industry of the twenty-first century, such a view ignores the history behind the genesis of those modern sports which owe much to the 'muscular Christian' values imbued in them via the Victorian English public schools and which were subsequently propagated throughout the British Empire and beyond by Christian athletic missionaries (see, for example, Mangan, 1984, 1986). According to Watson and Parker (2012: 28), these values (or virtues) include: 'teamwork, altruism, strength, self-control, justice, loyalty, wisdom, self-sacrifice, equality, courage, generosity, joy, honesty, tenacity, hard work, solidarity, peace, love (*Philia*, friendship love) and community spirit'. Thus, it can be argued that Christian values – rather than those of any other faith – are at the very core of some of today's global sports (see also Parker and Weir, 2012; Watson *et al.*, 2005).

During the twentieth century sports began to gradually lose these values and sociologists of sport have written about this from a variety of theoretical perspectives. In his 'historical-sociological' study based largely upon Weber's rationalisation thesis and Calvinist Protestantism, Overman (2011) demonstrates how American elite sport became riddled with ethical and moral problems over the course of the twentieth century as a consequence of its increasing professionalisation, commodification and commercialisation. The Marxist scholar Jean-Marie Brohm (1979) referred to modern sport as 'a prison of measured time' arguing that in the contemporary age athlete's bodies are treated as machines designed to produce entertainment and profit for others rather than fun and pleasure for themselves. Moreover, Lasch (1979) famously referred to 'the degradation of sport' in relation to the loss of the 'sacred dimension of play' in the pursuit of winning (as well as other aspects); and Walsh and Giulianotti (2007) have more recently referred to the ethical and moral problems in contemporary sport as 'the sporting mammon'.[3] In turn, Watson and Parker (2012: 28–29) list a number of research topics that have been pursued by sports sociologists, psychologists and philosophers around the ethical and moral problems that have become entrenched in sport as a consequence of its business focus. Examples of these topics include: the abuse of athletes, officials and others involved in sport; violence both on and off the field of play involving athletes, fans and others; political/national divisions; sectarianism; cheating; playing through pain and injury; overtraining; burnout; financial greed and corruption; use of performance enhancing drugs/doping, and others.

It has been argued that these problems are strongly related to the dissolution of Christian ethics in modern-day sport and have fuelled wider discussion (see, for example, Dixon and Gibbons, 2015). Nevertheless, Shilling and Mellor (2014: 350) state that although 'analyses of sport and religion, and various aspects of their relationships, exist … these tend to occupy a discrete corner in sports studies'. Horne (2015) has produced a comprehensive bibliography listing core readings across the entire area of the sociology of sport and nowhere is the topic of 'religion' given prominence, other than indirectly in relation to classic studies of sectarianism in Northern Ireland (Sugden and Bairner, 1993) and Scotland (Murray, 1984). In this sense it is fair to say that sociological analyses of sport and 'religion' do exist but they remain on the fringes of wider debate. Shilling and Mellor (2014: 350) state that: 'Sociological studies of sport have, during the last two decades, established their subject matter as central to a wide range of social and cultural, disciplinary and interdisciplinary, concerns.' However, they go on to recognise that: 'One area marginalized in most of these studies ... is religion' (ibid.). Furthermore, these authors posit that 'sociologists who focus on sport's secular impact often view religious adherence as a remnant of traditional practices. More frequently, they ignore religion altogether' (ibid.: 351). Shilling and Mellor go on to argue that 'analysing sport purely as a secular phenomenon, and marginalizing its religious significance, is potentially antagonistic to a broader attempt to grasp its societal importance' (ibid.: 351). Shilling and Mellor (ibid.: 352) develop what they describe as 'a novel theoretical account of sport's centrality to social life, attentive to its secular, religious and sacred aspects' by using what are widely considered to be two of the 'founding fathers' of sociology, Émile Durkheim and Max Weber. The former argued that 'religion' and the 'sacred' persist in modern societies playing a role in maintaining social order; whereas the latter suggested that the increasing rationalisation of modern societies diminished the significance of 'religion' and the 'sacred'.

While Shilling and Mellor (2014) should be commended for recognising the dominance of secular studies within the sociology of sport and advocating an approach that takes into account both secular and 'religious' viewpoints on the social significance of sport, their argument has one significant limitation. Despite aiming to highlight that a secular bias within the sociology of sport exists and subsequently calling for scholars not to divorce the 'religious' and the 'sacred', Shilling and Mellor unintentionally reinforce the secular bias within the sub-discipline of the sociology of sport by only drawing upon secularist theorists to guide their analytical framework. Both Durkheim and Weber were in fact atheists as are the majority of the social theorists utilised within the discipline of sociology and concomitantly it seems in the sub-discipline of sports sociology. There are four significant atheists who were the 'classical social theorists' involved in the development of the subject matter of sociology: Auguste Comte, Émile Durkheim, Karl Marx and Max Weber. Of these the "holy trinity' of Marx, Weber and Durkheim', are the most widely used within sociology (Shilling, 2011: 2) and correspondingly in sports sociology. Perhaps somewhat ironically, all three had much to say about the role of religion in modern societies (Turner, 2014: 772). Yet secular theorists are not the only ones to be involved in the establishment of the discipline of sociology.

Hidden and long forgotten? An outline of Christian approaches to sociology

> Sociologists and Christians have a good deal to say to each other. Unfortunately, what is said is often not encouraging.
>
> (Perkins, 1987: 13)

The above statement suggests that something of an impasse exists between Christianity and sociology. While this may be true today, it has not always been the case. There are some early social thinkers who wrote from a distinctly Christian perspective. One who pre-dates the establishment of the subject matter for sociology, let alone its institution as a distinct discipline, was Italian Catholic Giambattista Vico (1668–1744) who 'argued for the development of a new science that would unveil the laws governing the rise and fall of nations' (cited in Fraser and Campolo, 1992: 17). In the second edition of his book *Principles of a New Science Concerning the Common Nature of the Nations*, Vico (ibid.) posited that humans cannot be studied in the same way as nature is studied, i.e. by the natural sciences. Instead, Vico suggested that only God could fully understand the forces governing the physical world because He created it and that human beings could only ever gain a partial understanding of this world as they were merely created as part of it – and were not its creators. However, Vico suggested that humans may understand the social world more fully than the physical world given that they create the former and that it comprises their relationships with one another. Fraser and Campolo point out that Vico's work came well before that of Auguste Comte (1798–1857), the Frenchman often credited as the founding father of sociological thought and who famously argued that 'sociology was the new religion' (Brewer, 2007: 10). As Fraser and Campolo (1992: 17–18) go on to assert:

> Since Vico's idea for sociology was published a hundred years before Comte's, why is Vico not acknowledged as the founder of sociology? Is this a reflection of the bias of secularists who do not wish to acknowledge Christians at the very foundations of sociology?

Nor is Vico an anomaly in this respect. Other Christians from both the US and Europe were significantly involved in the beginnings of sociology yet their work is not readily referred to by modern-day sociologists. Examples include (in chronological order by birth): Frédéric Le Play (1806–1882), Eilert Sundt (1817–1875), Albion Small (1854–1926) and Paul Göhre (1864–1928). Le Play was a French Catholic who wrote the first major empirical sociological study entitled *The European Workers* (1855) (cited in Fraser and Campolo, 1992: 21), which was six volumes in length. Sundt was an ordained Lutheran minister who pioneered sociological research into the social and economic conditions of the poor in Norway (Reinertsen, 1969 cited in ibid.: 21–22). Small was the Chair and founder of the first graduate department of sociology in the world located at the University of Chicago in the USA and a theologically trained son of a Baptist preacher as well as being a Baptist deacon for much of his adult life (Brewer, 2007: 11). In turn, Small established the *American Journal of Sociology* in 1895 and was one of the only American sociologists of his era to have 'retained his Christian commitment' (ibid.: 12). In 1891 Göhre, a Protestant pastor and theologian, initiated empirical sociology in Germany when he conducted a participant observation study of German factory workers entitled *Three Months as a Factory Worker* in which he highlighted structural forces leading to the disintegration of the family. Göhre later went on to work with Max Weber on an empirical study of agricultural labour in Eastern Prussia (Oberschall, 1965 cited in Fraser and Campolo, 1992: 22). Along with Vico, these scholars appear to be largely ignored by secular sociology and one would be hard pressed to find any reference to them within the sociology of sport. Thus, one area worthy of further exploration by sociologists of sport is the work of early Christian sociological thinkers.

Second, it is important to consider the distinction that Brewer (2007) makes between what he terms 'religious sociology', (which, upon closer examination, appears to have been entirely Christian in nature) where 'sociology is put to serve faith', and the 'secular sociology of religion' where 'religion is studied scientifically'. Brewer argues that 'religious sociology' contributed significantly to the development of early sociology in Britain, France and the US (although its development within these countries differs somewhat), yet remains obscured and underdeveloped in modern-day sociological circles.

If one looks hard enough it is clearly evident that there have been attempts since the late nineteenth century to establish an essentially 'Christian sociology' or to at least consider the interface between Christianity and sociology from the perspective of the Christian faith. I will refer to this literature as 'Christian sociology' hereafter abandoning the term 'religious sociology' which I consider too broad. The earliest work in this area is somewhat helpfully entitled *Christian Sociology*. This text was originally published in the US in 1880 and was written by a theology professor at Wittenberg College in Springfield Ohio by the name of John Henry Wilbrandt Stuckenberg (see Stuckenberg, 1881).[4] Much of Stuckenberg's controversial book was written from a Liberal Protestant standpoint, which Brewer (2007: 11) states, 'has always been socially reformist and committed to social progress ... reflected in significant philanthropy and campaigning for social reform but also in the desire to make Christianity relevant to modern society'. Indeed, this seminal work is focused upon justifying the need for a Christian approach to studying society and defining the link between Christianity and sociology. Despite its focus on late nineteenth-century society, the following passage from Stuckenberg's (1881: 16) argument encapsulates what Christian sociology has the potential to do today:

> Social problems are constantly arising which should receive their solution from a Christian standpoint. Many of these problems are of vast importance, and present an inviting field for the application of the principles of the Gospel – an application that is much needed, and which promises to be fruitful of rich results. Why leave the most important civil and social questions of the day to the solutions of a worldly philosophy and of a godless political economy? Why not make the ethics of the New Testament the test of all social theories? The problems connected with education, with capital and labor, with the relations of employer and employé, problems connected with politics, and with the various social relations and social life – all should be discussed by Christians in the light of the Gospel, and should be settled according to its spirit. This is essential to social welfare.

Could the various sociological issues and problems that pervade modern-day sport be added to the list identified by Stuckenberg? Examples of similar texts from the early twentieth century include Moss's (1924) *Studies in the Christian Gospel for Society* and Penty's (1924) *Towards a Christian Sociology*. Both went against the 'secularism inherent in sociology' and were subsequently regarded as 'religiosity' which was 'a practice not acceptable to the guardians of the discipline' who only condoned 'religion' as a topic of 'serious' social scientific investigation (Brewer, 2007: 12).

An interesting example of a Christian (Lutheran) with an interest in secularisation and modernity who opted for significance within mainstream sociology rather than seeking to develop an explicitly Christian perspective is Peter Berger. Berger and Luckmann had a significant impact on the sociology of knowledge with their ground-breaking book *The Social Construction of Reality: A Treatise in the Sociology of Knowledge* (1966) in which, according to Turner (2014: 773), they regarded the 'study of religion as an inseparable component of the sociology of knowledge'. Turner states that alongside their subsequent (separate) works on the sociology of religion (see Berger, 1967 and Luckmann, 1967), this particular text led to a 'revival of the sociology of religion as part of the core curriculum of the sociological discipline' (Turner, 2014: 773). Yet, ironically, this acted as the main stimulus for the development of the secular sociology of religion rather than to the advancement of a distinctly Christian sociology.[5]

From the 1970s a number of sociological books written from a Christian (Protestant evangelical) perspective began to emerge in the US and there are now a growing number of such titles.[6] While space restricts how much can be said about these texts, their increase is evidence enough that the debate between Christianity and sociology is alive and well. Needless to say, such work represents a second area ripe for exploration by sociologists of sport.

In addition to the Christian sociology books referred to here, there have been a number of Christian contributions to early editions of the longest standing mainstream academic journals in sociology. Moreover, it is argued that some of the early presidents of the 'American Sociological Society' were Protestant ministers before becoming sociologists (Oberschall, 1972 cited in Fraser and Campolo, 1992: 21). Alas, this kind of sociology either became isolated, marginalised or succumbed to the mainstream secularised trend throughout much of the twentieth century. While the Catholic Church retained involvement in the social sciences and 'Catholic sociologists' remained active, they were ostracised by the secular sociological mainstream (Brewer, 2007).

In comparison to both France and the US, the trajectory was somewhat different in Britain (Brewer 2007: 16). Clergy of the Church of England were involved in the establishment of 'The Sociological Society' in Britain in 1903 and can be found to be contributing to the *Sociological Papers* (the forerunner to *The Sociological Review*) from its inception in 1904 and well into the 1920s (Brewer, 2007: 17). Yet 'as academic sociology developed in Britain in the 1930s, the Christian sociologists disconnected themselves from the mainstream as it secularized'. A distinct journal of Christian sociology called *Christendom* that ran from 1931 to 1950 acts as evidence of the partition (Brewer, 2007: 20). There have been other Christian sociology journals and organisations, some of which are still in existence. As Brewer (2007: 13–14) notes 'a Christian sociologists' prayer group' has long been active in the USA and 'eventually became the Christian Sociological Society in the 1970s. There is also the association of Christians Teaching Sociology [ACTS], founded in 1976'. The website of ACTS (2015) contains both a bibliography and a resources section listing a wealth of useful material that could be reviewed by sports sociologists. A more recent example of a Christian sociology journal is the *Journal for the Sociological Integration of Religion and Society* (JSIRS) that began in 2011 and publishes two issues per year. The mission of the Journal is 'to provide a forum for the latest research and inquiry relative to the sociological integration of the Christian religion and society' (JSIRS, 2015). To summarise, it would appear that Christian contributions to early versions of mainstream sociology journals, specifically issues of the journal *Christendom*, as well as more recent journals for Christian sociology, have yet to be used in any sociological analyses of sport. Added to the books cited above, such resources represent the second area of Christian sociology ripe for further investigation by sports sociologists.

Finally, the third area worthy of more thorough investigation by sociologists of sport is that which links sociology with theology. Brewer (2007: 21) argues that sociology and theology were eventually successfully combined in Britain in the late 1970s stimulating new 'sociological work by biblical scholars'. Robin Gill, an Anglican clergyman and Emeritus Professor in Applied Theology at the University of Kent (UK), has recently produced three volumes on 'Sociological Theology' in which he revisits three elements that make up the dialogue between theologians and sociologists (Gill, 2012a; 2012b; 2013). This developing area of research might be useful to sociologists of sport as Gill (2012a: 11) notes:

> It should not in principle be too difficult for the competent theologian to acquire a certain measure of expertise in sociological terms, or for the sociologist to acquire a similar expertise in theological terms.

It is hoped that this will encourage sociologists of sport to embark on a new journey of discovery of this burgeoning field of study. If it does, who knows what new gems might be found.

Conclusion

This exploratory chapter has argued for a challenge to be made to the supremacy of secular studies within the sociology of sport through the exploration of Christian approaches to sociology. First, I have suggested that excavations of the work of early Christian social theorists and thinkers would be beneficial in order to determine whether an alternative Christian theoretical toolkit exists for establishing a distinct Christian sociology of sport. Second, I have suggested that a systematic review of texts specifically written by Christians on the relationship between Christianity and sociology since the late nineteenth century would help to determine the full diversity of Christian approaches to sociological thought and, in turn, which (if any) might be meaningfully linked to the analysis of specific sociological issues in sport. It would be useful for the same reasons to perform a systematic review of the following: contributions to mainstream sociological journals written from a Christian perspective; the contents of the mid-twentieth-century journal *Christendom*; and, contributions to the publications emanating from the Association of Christians Teaching Sociology (ACTS) and the Christian Sociological Society (CSS), the most recent being the JSRIS. Third, the sociological theology that has been developed from the 1970s would be worth analysing with sociological issues inherent in sport in mind.

Finally, it is acknowledged that this chapter has not recognised all of the Christian approaches to sociology that are in existence. However, I hope that those interested in challenging the secular dominance outlined above will join me in this exciting process of discovery in an attempt to ensure that the voices of Christian sociologists are heard and no longer ignored within the sociology of sport.

Postscript

> The Christian and sociological parts of my thinking continue to glare at each other from opposite corners of my mind.
>
> (Perkins, 1987: 10)

I felt it important to provide the reader with the epistemological roots of my argument and thinking employed in what I have presented above, hence the following personal reflections that acts to contextualise my Christian faith with my sociological imagination.

I studied for my undergraduate degree in sports studies and my Master's degree in the sociology of sport as a non-Christian in what are secular universities – De Montfort University (Bedford, UK – now the University of Bedfordshire) for the undergraduate degree and The University of Leicester (UK) for the Masters. At Leicester I was based in what was the 'Centre for Research into Sport & Society' (CRSS) and I was taught the 'figurational' approach to sociology (and sport) originally established at Leicester by the German social theorist Norbert Elias. As part of this socio-logical training I was taught to take what Elias (1987: 6) termed a 'detour via detachment' and to attempt to make, as far as possible, 'value-free' rather than 'value-laden' judgements as a social scientist. I was taught to recognise that although complete objectivity is impossible in social scient-ific investigations where a degree of subjective involvement with the subject matter is unavoidable and usually necessary, it is essential to also take 'degrees of detachment' from the object of study in order to avoid clouding one's judgement in conducting valid and reliable research. I later went on to complete a PhD while working as a full-time lecturer at Teesside Univer-sity (UK) and engaged my figurational sociological training in a study into the relationship between English national identity and football fan culture, which was later published as a book (Gibbons, 2014).

Much to the surprise of my family, friends and work colleagues, I became a Christian in 2008 while studying for my PhD. Although this decision was nothing to do with the subject matter of my studies, my soci-ologically programmed mind significantly delayed my decision to come to faith in Christ. The decision process manifested as an internal dialogue between the sociologist in me on one side encouraging me to take a 'detour via detachment' in considering whether Jesus was real, and on the other, a 'still, small voice' (1 Kings 19:12) beckoning me to trust in Jesus Christ. This decision-making process began when I attended an evangelical Gospel crusade in a large marquee erected in a park in Teesside in the summer of 2008. A Christian colleague of mine had invited me to a number of events before and in the past I had always declined, but this time I went along as I had ran out of excuses! After six weeks of attending weekly meetings on Wednesday evenings and thinking seriously about whether it was even possible for a sociologist to have faith, I eventually concluded that I had no good reason not to give following Jesus Christ a try. No one was more surprised than me at my conversion and a decade on I am still discovering the ways in which my decision to follow Christ has impacted upon my professional occupation as a sociologist of sport.

Becoming a Christian and growing in faith in Jesus Christ has definitely altered my identity as well as what sociologists refer to as my 'habitus'. The term 'habitus' is closely related to the word 'identity' although it's meaning is more complex. Habitus refers to a kind of second nature or internal steering mechanism, a specific set of acquired dispositions of thought, behaviour and actions that are embedded in individuals through socialisation into particular cultures. Mennell (1994: 177) refers to habitus as

> closely related to the notion of *identity*. The difference is perhaps that 'identity' implies a higher level of conscious awareness by members of a group, some degree of reflection and articulation, some positive or negative emotional feelings towards the characteristics which members of a group perceive themselves as sharing and in which they perceive themselves as differing from other groups.[7]

Elias uses the phrase 'social habitus' which he contends exists within the personality structure of every individual human being (cf. Elias, 1978, 1991, 1996; Elias and Scotson, 1994). Hence, I now consider my identity and social habitus to be Christian and while I would still regard myself as a sociologist of sport, I have yet to fully explore the internal juxtaposition between being a Christian and a sports sociologist.

Notes

1 See for example the diversity of scholars mentioned in Watson and Parker's (2012; 2014) comprehensive reviews of literature on sport and Christianity.
2 See for example some of the recent research on the relationship between sport, Christianity and disability by Parker and colleagues, some of which contains sociological insight (Howe and Parker, 2012, 2014; Parker and Watson, 2014; Watson and Parker, 2015).

3 In the New Testament 'Mammon' is referred to as material wealth or greed, and is often personified as a false idol (see for instance Matthew 6:19–21).

4 I refer here to the version of the text published in London in 1881 in this essay.

5 As an aside, key contemporary scholars in the secular sociology of religion have paid scant attention to the social significance and impact of sport (see for example, Beckford and Demerath, 2008; Davie, 2000, 2013, 2015).

6 See for example: Campolo (1995); Fraser and Campolo (1992); Grunland and Reimer (1991); Hunter (2010); Perkins (1987); Poythress (2011); Schmidt and Heybyrne (2004); Wright (2010).

7 Although habitus is a term thought to have originated in the work of Aristotle, Bourdieu (cf. 1977) is most commonly associated with its modern usage in sociology (Scott and Marshall, 2009: 299). Yet it is important to clarify that the term 'habitus' was actually used in a sociological context prior to this by Elias (1939/2000) in *The Civilizing Process*, which was originally published in German in 1939 as two separate volumes, *The History of Manners* and *State Formation and Civilization*. English translations of the separate volumes were not published until 1978 and 1982 respectively. Both volumes were eventually published together in English in 1994. The revised edition (2000) of the 1994 version is the text referred to here.

References

Unless otherwise stated, all references to the Bible are taken from the New King James Version.

ACTS (2015) Homepage for the Association of Christians Teaching Sociology, available at: www.actsoc.org/ (Accessed 12 February 2015).

Beckford, J. A. and Demerath, J. (eds) (2008) *The Sage Handbook of the Sociology of Religion*. London, Sage.

Berger, P. L. (1967) *The Sacred Canopy: Elements of a Sociological Theory of Religion*. New York, Doubleday.

Berger, P. L. (1999) The Desecularization of the World: A Global Overview. In P. L. Berger (ed.) *The Desecularization of the World: Resurgent Religion and World Politics*. Grand Rapids, MI, W. B. Eerdmans, pp. 1–18.

Berger, P. L. and Luckmann, T. (1966) *The Social Construction of Reality: A Treatise in the Sociology of Knowledge*. Garden City, NY, Anchor Books.

Bourdieu, P. (1977) *Outline of a Theory of Practice* (originally published in French 1972, trans. Richard Nice). Cambridge, Cambridge University Press.

Brewer, J. D. (2007) Sociology and theology reconsidered: religious sociology and the sociology of religion in Britain. *History of the Human Sciences*, 20 (2): 7–28.

Brohm, J.-M. (1979) *Sport: A Prison of Measured Time*. London, Inklinks.

Campolo, T. (1995) *Partly Right: Learning from the Critics of Christianity*. Dallas, TX, Word Publishing.

Davie, G. (2000) *Religion in Modern Europe: A Memory Mutates*. Oxford, Oxford University Press.

Davie, G. (2013) *The Sociology of Religion: A Critical Agenda* (Second Edition) London, Sage.

Davie, G. (2015) *Religion in Britain: A Persistent Paradox*. Chichester, Wiley-Blackwell.

Dixon, K. and Gibbons, T. (eds) (2015) *The Impact of the London 2012 Olympic and Paralympic Games: Diminishing Contrasts, Increasing Varieties.* Basingstoke, Palgrave Pivot.

Elias, N. (1978) *What is Sociology?* London, Hutchinson.

Elias, N. (1987) *Involvement and Detachment.* Oxford, Basil Blackwell.

Elias, N. (1991) *The Society of Individuals.* Oxford, Basil Blackwell.

Elias, N. (1996) *The Germans.* Cambridge, Polity Press.

Elias, N. (2000) *The Civilizing Process* (Revised Edition). Oxford, Basil Blackwell.

Elias, N. and Scotson, J. L. (1994) *The Established and the Outsiders: A Sociological Inquiry into Community Problems.* London, Frank Cass.

Fraser, T. A. and Campolo, T. (1992) *Sociology Through the Eyes of Faith.* New York, Harper Collins.

Gibbons, T. (2014) *English National Identity and Football Fan Culture.* Farnham, Ashgate.

Gibbons, T. (2016) Christianity as Public Religion in the Post-Secular 21st Century. In J. F. Nussbaum (ed.), *Oxford Research Encyclopedia of Communication,* available at: http://communication.oxfordre.com/ (Accessed 16 March 2017).

Gill, R. (2012a) *Theology in a Social Context: Sociological Theology* (Volume 1). Farnham, Ashgate.

Gill, R. (2012b) *Theology Shaped by Society: Sociological Theology* (Volume 2). Farnham, Ashgate.

Gill, R. (2013) *Society Shaped by Theology: Sociological Theology* (Volume 3). Farnham, Ashgate.

Goodhew, D. (2012) (ed.) *Church Growth in Britain: 1980 to the Present.* Farnham, Ashgate.

Grunland, S. A. and Reimer, M. (1991) (eds) *Christian Perspectives on Sociology* (Reprint edition). Eugene, OR, Wipf & Stock Publishers.

Han, S. (2015) Disenchantment revisited: formations of the 'secular' and 'religious' in the technological discourse of modernity. *Social Compass,* 62 (1): 76–88.

Horne, J. (2015) Sports. In J. Baxter (ed.) *Oxford Bibliographies in Sociology.* Oxford, Oxford University Press.

Howe, P. D. and Parker, A. (2012) Celebrating imperfection: sport, disability and celebrity culture. *Celebrity Studies,* 3 (3): 270–282.

Howe, P. D. and Parker, A. (2014) Disability as a path to spiritual enlightenment: an ethnographic account of the significance of religion in Paralympic sport. *Journal of Disability and Religion,* 18 (1): 8–23.

Hunter, J. D. (2010) *To Change the World: The Irony, Tragedy, & Possibility of Christianity in the Late Modern World.* New York, Oxford University Press.

Jennings, M. (2015) An extraordinary degree of exaltation: Durkheim, effervescence and Pentecostalism's defeat of secularisation. *Social Compass,* 62 (1): 61–75.

JSIRS (2015) Homepage for the *Journal for the Sociological Integration of Religion and Society,* available at: http://religionandsociety.org/jsirs/ (Accessed 11 February 2015).

Lasch, C. (1979) *The Culture of Narcissism: American Life in an Age of Diminishing Expectations.* New York, W. W. Norton & Co.

Luckmann, T. (1967) *The Invisible Religion: The Problem of Religion in Modern Society.* New York, Macmillan.

Magdalinski, T. and Chandler, T. J. L. (2002) With God on their side: an introduction. In T. Magdalinski and T. J. L. Chandler (eds) *With God on Their Side: Sport in the Service of Religion*. Oxford, Routledge, pp. 1–19.

Mangan, J. A. (1984) Christ and the imperial games fields. *The British Journal of Sports History*, 1 (2), 184–201.

Mangan, J. A. (1986) *The Games Ethic and Imperialism*. London, Viking.

Mennell, S. (1994) The formation of we-images: a process theory. In C. Calhoun (ed.) *Social Theory and the Politics of Identity*. Oxford, Blackwell, pp. 175–197.

Moss, A. H. (1924) *Studies in the Christian Gospel for Society*. London, Student Christian Movement.

Murray, B. (1984) *The Old Firm: Sectarianism, Sport and Society in Scotland*. Edinburgh, John Donald.

O'Donnell, K. (2009) *A Pocket Guide to Christian History*. Oxford, Lion Hudson.

Overman, S. J. (2011) *The Protestant Ethic and The Spirit of Sport: How Calvinism and Capitalism shaped America's Games*. Macon, GA, Mercer University Press.

Parker, A. and Watson, N. J. (2014) Researching religion, disability and sport: reflections and possibilities. *Journal of Religion, Disability and Health*, 18 (2): 192–208.

Parker, A. and Watson, N. (2016) Spiritualized and Religious Bodies, in D. Andrews, M. Silk and H. Thorpe (eds) *Routledge Handbook of Physical Cultural Studies*, London, Routledge, pp. 209–217.

Parker, A. and Weir, J. S. (2012) Sport, spirituality and Protestantism: a historical overview, *Theology*, 115 (4): 253–265.

Penty, A. (1924) *Towards a Christian Sociology*. London, Allen & Unwin.

Perkins, R. (1987) *Looking Both Ways: Exploring the Interface between Christianity and Sociology*. Ada, MI, Baker Book House Company

Poythress, V.S. (2011) *Redeeming Sociology: A God-Centred Approach*. Wheaton, IL, Crossway Books.

Schmidt, C. and Heybyrne, B. (2004) *Sociology: a Christian Approach for Changing the World*. Marion, IN, Triangle Publishing.

Scott, J. and Marshall, G. (2009) *Oxford Dictionary of Sociology* (Third revised edition). Oxford, Oxford University Press.

Shilling, C. (2011) Series Editor's Introduction. *The Sociological Review*, 59 (s1): 1–4.

Shilling, C. and Mellor, P. A. (2014) Re-conceptualizing sport as a sacred phenomenon. *Sociology of Sport Journal*, 31 (3), 349–376.

Sugden, J. and Bairner, A. (1993) *Sport, Sectarianism and Society in a Divided Ireland*. Leicester, Leicester University Press.

Stuckenberg, J. H. W. (1881) *Christian Sociology*. London, R. D. Dickinson, available at: https://archive.org/details/christiansociol01stucgoog (Accessed 9 February 2015).

Threlfall-Holmes, M. (2012) *The Essential History of Christianity*. London, SPCK.

Turner, B. S. (2014) Religion and contemporary sociological theories. *Current Sociology Review*, 62 (6): 771–788.

Walsh, A. J. and Giulianotti, R. (2007) *Ethics, Money and Sport: This Sporting Mammon*. London, Routledge.

Watson, N. J. and Parker, A. (2012) Sports and Christianity: Mapping the Field. In N. J. Watson and A. Parker (eds) *Sports and Christianity: Historical and Contemporary Perspectives*. New York, Routledge, pp. 9–88.

Watson, N. J. and Parker, A. (eds) (2014) *Sport and the Christian Religion: A Systematic Review of Literature*. Newcastle upon Tyne, Cambridge Scholars Publishing.

Watson, N. J. and Parker, A. (eds) (2015) *Sports, Religion and Disability*. London, Routledge.

Watson, N. J., Weir, S. and Friend, S. (2005) The development of muscular Christianity in Victorian Britain and beyond. *Journal of Religion and Society*, 7 (1): 1–25.

Wilson, B. R. (1998) The Secularization Thesis: Criticisms and Rebuttals. In R. Laermans, Wilson, B. R. and Billiet, J. (eds) *Secularization and Social Integration: Papers in Honor of Karel Dobbelaere*. Leuven, Leuven University Press, 45–66.

Wright, B. R. E (2010) *Christians Are Hate-Filled Hypocrites ... and Other Lies You've Been Told: A Sociologist Shatters Myths From the Secular and Christian Media*. Minneapolis, MT, Bethany House Publishers.

Chapter 2

Sports in the biblical narrative

Jeremy Treat

Introduction

Whether in the pub or in the pew, there is one question one can always count on hearing: "Did you see that game?" Sports are prominent in culture and relevant to life, which is why the average sports show often spends as much time talking about ethics, racism, crime, and sexuality, as it does athletics. In many ways, sports are a microcosm of life. And yet, while sports have captured the hearts and minds of people across the globe, they have largely evaded the attention of theologians.[1] Finding a scholar who has thought deeply and critically about sports from a distinctly Christian perspective is as likely in the church as a triple play on the diamond. This is a surprising phenomenon considering not only the prevalence of sports globally but also that historically many sports began and developed in overtly religious settings.[2] Thankfully, there is a budding field of scholarship on religion and sports emerging today, and Christian theologians are finally getting into the game.[3] What is the meaning of sport? There seem to be two polar responses to this question: some dismiss sports as merely a game, while others worship sports as nearly a god. The first response minimizes sports as a childlike activity, good for passing time but largely insignificant for the deeper matters of life. The second deifies sports, expressing religious devotion and offering sacrifices of money and time at the altar of winning.

When viewed through the lens of Scripture, however, we will see that sport is more than a game, less than a god, and when transformed by the gospel can be received as a gift. Since the discussion of theology and sport is relatively new (for Christian theologians at least), this chapter aims to provide a broad overview of a theology of sport, grounded in the unfolding narrative of redemption as revealed in Scripture. But first, let us acknowledge that we are not the first to talk about faith and sports, and therefore locate ourselves within the broader conversation by surveying the history of the church's attitude toward sports.[4]

Faith and sports in the history of the Church

The church has always struggled to rightly understand the role of games in God's greater purposes. The Apostle Paul seemed to appreciate sports, or he was at least familiar with them, using athletic metaphors such as running the race (1 Cor 9:24), fighting the good fight (1 Tim 6:12), and training in righteousness (2 Tim 3:16).[5]

In the first few centuries of the church, however, Christians were largely against the sports of the day, albeit for understandable reasons.[6] The early Olympic games were dedicated to pagan gods like Zeus and Nike and athletes usually competed in the nude. Moreover, the most popular sporting event—the gladiator games—involved throwing Christians into the ring with wild bears and lions.

Broadly speaking, throughout history the church has had a negative or dismissive view of sports—the devil's workshop at worst and a secular means to an evangelistic end at best.[7] John Calvin played a bit of bocce ball, Dietrich Bonhoeffer a little tennis, but in the early years of America the serious-minded Puritans put sports almost completely outside of God's will (Ellis, 2014; Harvey, 2014).

Up until the late eighteenth century, sports were for the most part recreational. The industrial revolution, however, laid the railroad tracks for professionalization, with the train pulling into the station in the latter half of the twentieth century. With the popularization of sports today, Christians have jumped on board, to say the least, seeing sports as a potential classroom for morality and a platform for evangelism.[8]

How, then, ought followers of Jesus think of sports today? Athletes or fans regularly invoke the name of God as an expletive of frustration in sports, but rarely think about whether God has anything to do with the game at all. Does God care about sports? Does his word offer insights for athletics? The way one answers these questions is largely dependent upon their understanding of the broader narrative within which we live. The narrative of the American Dream that culminates in individual happiness offers a starkly different framework for sports than the story of God's kingdom as told by the Jewish messiah. To that narrative, we now turn.

More than a game

As a child growing up in the church, my pastor had a small rotation of canned jokes, his favorite of which went something like this: "The Bible does talk about sports, you know? It's actually in the very first verse of the Bible: 'In the *big inning* God created the heavens and the earth.'" The notable feature of this (bad) joke is that the punch line is dependent on the assumption that God's Word does not, in fact, address the world of sports, and especially not in the opening—and therefore very important—chapters of the Bible. No—the line of thought goes—certainly sports are "just a game" and part of the "secular world" which lies outside of God's eternal purposes. Scripture, however, presents a different story.

Created to play

The biblical story begins in the garden, where God placed Adam and Eve. But contrary to popular opinion, God did not give Adam and Eve a vacation, he gave them a task: God's image bearers were to work and keep the garden and to fill the earth and develop it on God's behalf (Gen 1:28; 2:15). This is often called the cultural mandate, because the command to work and keep the garden is essentially a command to create culture. As Stott (2009: 222–3) notes, "Nature is what God gives; culture is what we do with it." What, then, were Adam and Eve supposed to do with it?

First, God's stewards are called to *develop* his creation. God did not create the earth as a finished product but rather as an unfinished project. It was made with potential that needed to be developed. Adam's task as a gardener was a prototype for all culture-making: take the raw materials of the earth and cultivate them for the good of society. Furthermore, the son and daughter of the Creator-King were not only called to cultivate the garden, but also to extend the order of the garden and the blessings of God's reign to the ends of the earth. Eden was a lush and beautiful garden, but the rest of the earth was untamed and wild. Adam and Eve were called to Edenize the world.

Second, Adam and Eve were not only commanded to *develop* God's creation, they were also called to *delight* in it. God says, "You may surely eat of every tree of the garden, but of the tree of the knowledge of good and evil you shall not eat" (Gen 2:16–17). Unfortunately, many have focused so much on the prohibition of the one fruit that they have overlooked the invitation to feast upon all the other fruits. The God who abounds in love and kindness created a world of delights and placed his beloved image bearers in it with an invitation to enjoyment. Creation is not merely a resource to be used for productivity, it is a gift to be received and enjoyed.

This is where the idea of "play" comes in, which is implicit in humanity's calling to develop and delight in God's creation. To play is to creatively enjoy something for its own intrinsic good. Building upon Huizinga's classic definition of play, Thoennes (2008) says, "Play is a fun, imaginative, non- compulsory, non-utilitarian activity filled with creative spontaneity and humor, which gives perspective, diversion, and rest from necessary work of daily life."[9] At the core of the definition of play is that it is autotelic; it is for its own purposes. Play need not be justified by its effects, be it psychological (peace of mind), physical (better health), social (learning teamwork), etc.; it is simply creatively delighting in and enjoying God's good creation for its own sake.[10]

In short, we are created to play. Like a father who builds a sandbox for his children, God is honored and takes joy when his sons and daughters delight in his workmanship. The world is—as it has been said—the theater of God's glory (Calvin, 2006); but it is also the playground of God's goodness.

Play, sport, and competition

Of course, playing in the garden of Eden is a long way from the playoffs in Madison Square Garden. God did not give Adam and Eve a court and a ball, but he did give them a natural instinct to play that would inevitably develop into something more.[11] So while technically one does not find sport in Genesis 1–2, we can speak of play with the potential and even intention toward sport. We must remember that a biblical doctrine of creation is not merely about what happened in Genesis 1–2, but about the way the world was meant to be.[12] In other words, creation is not just about what God did "in the beginning," but also about what God intended from the beginning.

There is a trajectory to Genesis 1–2 and when we take that playful instinct, add competition and rules, then we have sport. However, we must be careful and precise with definitions of play, games, sport, and competition; and how one relates to the others.[13] Play, as noted above, is the unstructured, autotelic activity that creatively enjoys the gift of creation. Play turns into a game when rules are added and teams are formed (in some cases). Sport, then, is when the rules of a game are universalized and there is the added element of *agon*, moving it from a mere game to a contest.[14] Ellis (2014: 129) defines the jump from play to sport in the following way: "Sport gathers up elements of the definition of play and adds to it that it is a bureaucratized embodied contest involving mental and physical exertion and with a significant element of refinable skill." Clifford and Feezell offer a similar and yet more concise explanation: sport is "a form of play, a competitive, rule-governed activity that human beings freely choose to engage in" (Watson, 2013: 169).

Competition has often been one of the most difficult aspects of a Christian understanding of sport. Can one love their neighbor while trying to block their shot, tackle them behind the line of scrimmage, or check them into the boards? The etymology of the word "competition" is helpful, for the Latin *competito* literally means "to strive together," rendering sport a "mutually acceptable quest for excellence" (Weir, 2008: 113). As iron sharpens iron, competition enhances play. Goheen and Bartholomew (2008: 154) argue that it is cooperation, not rivalry, that is at the heart of competition: "In sports, teams or individuals agree cooperatively to oppose one another within the stated goals, rules, and obstacles of the game."[15]

In sum, God's image bearers are called to develop God's creation for the good of others and to delight in God's creation because of its intrinsic good. Within this context of playfully developing and delighting in God's creation we can say that sports are part of God's intention and design for creation.

The intrinsic good of sports

Building upon the above argument that sports are a part of God's intended design for his created order, I now argue more specifically that sports were intended as a good part of God's design. Claiming that sports were created good might not sound like a revolutionary statement, but it goes against the grain of the way most Christians think about sports. There are two common views that oppose the goodness of sports in God's design for creation, both based on dualistic thinking. First, an ascetic body/soul dualism portrays sport as bad. Second, a sacred/secular dualism portrays sport as merely neutral, neither good nor bad.

The ascetic view is based on a body/soul dualism that understands anything spiritual as good and anything physical as bad (or at least inferior). The word *ascetic* comes from the Greek ἄσκησις, which is often translated *exercise* or *training*. The ascetic mindset, generally speaking, seeks to abstain from worldly pleasures and to discipline the body for the pursuit of spiritual and heavenly fulfillment. The ascetic view rightfully emphasizes the call of Jesus as one of self-denial, but often wrongly confuses the denial of the sinful nature with the denial of God's good creational gifts. As we have seen above, God made the world good and is to be received for the enjoyment of his people (see Titus 1:15; Col 2:20–23). Denial of the "flesh" (σάρξ) is not a denial of our physicality, but a denial of our sinful nature. This dualism, rooted in Greek thought and inherited in part by the monastic movement of the early church, has endured into evangelicalism and often been the foundation for a view of sports as "worldly" or a distraction from religion.

The second enemy of the goodness of sports in God's design for creation is the type of dualism that divides God's creation into two categories: sacred and secular. According to this view, God cares about prayer, Bible studies and church but the activities of work, sports, and art are neutral and only matter to God if they are used for higher spiritual purposes such as evangelism. While common in Christian thought today, this way of thinking resembles a type of otherworldly Greek dualism more than God's will being done on earth as it is in Heaven.[16]

Scripture clearly says that after God finished his work of creation, he proclaimed that it was all very good (Gen 1:31). This declaration of goodness does not merely pertain to the physical matter of creation (dirt and trees) but also to the cultural fabric of creation (developing and delighting).

God cares about baptism *and* business, redemption *and* romance, Sabbath *and* sport. Playing sports was not meant to be a neutral activity, but was designed as a good part of the broader vision of humanity cultivating and cherishing God's creation. Although sin and the fall certainly have done their damage to sports, one thing is clear: sports were made good and were part of God's plan for human flourishing.

This leads to a significant point regarding whether and why God values sports. The common view is that sports are neutral in and of themselves but they have the potential to be good if they are used for higher spiritual purposes such as moral training or evangelism. This is the world where the be-all-and-end-all of faith and sports is thanking God after the game (usually only when they win). According to this view, sports only have *instrumental* value; they are good if they are used as an instrument for evangelism. But as we learned from the doctrine of creation, God's image bearers are called to develop God's creation for the good of others, but are also called to simply delight in God's creation itself. Sports can be used for many good things, but they are also made good in and of themselves. In other words, sports do not only have *instrumental* worth, they have *intrinsic* worth.

It makes sense that sports would be instrumentalized in cultures—like American culture—that assign value to something based largely on its productivity or utility. For this reason, Protestants in the West often have a great work ethic but lack a play ethic. When a culture identifies value with utility then it assumes that if something is not productive then it cannot be meaningful; it does not even have categories to talk about such an activity. But that is precisely the category that play fits into. As Huizinga (1955: 9) argues, play is "meaningful but not necessary." Play and sport matter to God and have value for society regardless of whether they meet a need or produce a cultural good.

This raises the important question of whether sports only have intrinsic good or whether there is also instrumental good. Harvey (2014) works hard to protect the intrinsic value of sport, but I would agree with Johnston (1997: 42), who argues for "non-instrumentality which is nevertheless productive."[17] Sports can be a platform for evangelism or a classroom for morality, but they are first and foremost a playground for receiving and enjoying the goodness of the Creator.

Less than a God

Sports are more than a game; they are a part of God's good design for the flourishing of his image bearers as they develop and delight in God's creation. But, of course, things are not the way they are supposed to be. In a world ravished by sin, sports are not outside of its devastating effects. Sin not only fractures our relationship with God, it shatters the goodness of

God's created order, including God's design for play and sports. But how does sin affect sports? The answer is twofold because all sin amounts to either taking a good thing and twisting it into a bad thing (sin as immorality) or taking a good thing and making it an ultimate thing (sin as idolatry).[18] Both aspects are crucial to understand how the fall affects sports.

The immorality of sports

First, the effects of the fall on sports can be seen through the destructive behavior of athletes. Sports are good, but when used for sinful purposes can become very bad. Ethical problems in sports seem to be more prominent each year. In a world marred by sin, sports become a playground for violence (bench-clearing brawls), cheating (corked bats, deflated footballs, etc.), injury (especially life-threatening and brain-damaging injuries), and performance-enhancing drugs (haunting whole sports such as baseball, cycling, and track).

The effects of sin, however, are not limited to the individual immorality of athletes, but also extend to the systemic brokenness of sports teams, cultures, and industries. Modern professional sports are a powerful engine in the machine of American consumerism, greed, and narcissism. In many ways, modern professional sports simply represent the cultural brokenness of the society at large, but they also further shape the society as well. Sin shapes sport culture in a variety of systemic ways, such as the win-at-all-costs mentality that leaves in its wake broken families, compromised integrity, and wounded friendships.

The idolatry of sports

Talking about immoral behavior, however, only scratches the surface. There is a deeper problem yet. Sin is not merely doing bad things, it is making a good thing an ultimate thing. The Bible calls this idolatry. People are made to love God, be satisfied in him, and find their identity in him. An idol is anything that seeks to take God's place in fulfilling those very needs, whether it be a physical object or an idol of the heart. As Calvin (2006) argues:

> Scarcely a single person has ever been found who did not fashion for himself an idol or specter in place of God. Surely, just as waters boil up from a vast, full spring, so does an immense crowd of gods flow forth from the human mind.

So how does idolatry relate to sports? As we have seen, the inference from Genesis 1–2 is that sports are a good thing. But in a fallen world, rather than enjoying sports as a gift from God, sports are often used to replace God or even, ironically, compete with God. In other words, many look to sports for what is meant to be found in God: identity, meaning, and even salvation.

The religious nature of sports

My claim is not that sports are an organized religion, akin to the major world religions. Rather, many today look to sport for that which people traditionally found in religion. Sports are religious in nature; they are a vestige of transcendence in what Taylor (2007: 308) has called "the malaise of immanence." Berger (1970: 20) argues that in the face of such a secularized, disenchanted society, play can function as a "signal of transcendence." When a player is "in the zone"—what psychologists and sociologists call "flow"—they are having a spiritual experience that begins with their physical body but connects them to something beyond the physical realm. And this is true not only for the athlete, but for the fan as well. As Guttman (1986: 177) states, "many sports spectators experience something akin to worship."

Ellis (2014) finds historical evidence for sports competing for religious fervor by observing that the year 1851 marked the decisive moment in both the decline of organized religion and the emergence of modern sport; a trend which has also been noticed elsewhere.[19] Surely there are more factors at play in these studies, but Hoffman (2010: 273) is right to conclude that "sports ... compete for our religious sensibilities." If not fully convinced yet that sin can turn sports into an idol—a God substitute—then one ought to consider the overtly religious overtones that pervade modern-day professional sports.[20] It is not figurative to say that fans today have a type of religious devotion to their favorite teams and players. It is easy to look back to the Old Testament and scorn Israel for worshipping a golden calf, but is contemporary society really that different? We would *never* worship a golden image with such religious fervor. Or would we?

Imagine a modern religion where people worship a golden image (in this case, the NBA Finals trophy). They gather regularly at the temple (the sports stadium), where they take up an offering (ticket purchases) and worship with emotive expression (cheering fans). Of course, as with any religious service, they make sacrifices (their time, their money, and often their families). The high priest (the coach) oversees the activities, and those involved have a series of rituals they perform to prepare (team huddles and chest-bumping), all beneath the icons of the saints of old (retired jerseys in the rafters). There are strict programs of discipleship, learning about the gods so they can become like them (which is why they wear their jerseys and buy their shoes).

Maybe, just maybe, it is not that far-fetched that sport can function as a religious idol, a God- substitute to which people turn for identity, meaning, and salvation.[21] The hard truth, however, is that sport is not a good god because, like all idols, it always lets its worshippers down. When a good thing becomes an ultimate thing it eventually turns into a destructive thing. Sports are more than a game, but they are certainly less than a god.

Transformed by the Gospel

There is hope for sports; God has not given up on his creation. Sports are more than a game and less than a god, but when transformed through the gospel can be received as a gift—a gift to be enjoyed for its intrinsic worth and stewarded for the glory of God and the good of others.[22]

To have a gospel-transformed perspective on sports, however, one must have the right understanding of the gospel itself. The good news is not merely that Jesus is saving souls but that he is renewing his entire creation as its king. Through his life, death and resurrection, Jesus is restoring his design for the world and his purposes for his people. Goheen and Bartholomew (2008: 153) demonstrate the relation between one's understanding of the gospel and their view of sports:

> If one embraces a narrow, world-negating view of the gospel, one will have little place for sports and athletic competition. But since the gospel is a gospel about the kingdom of God, sports and competition cannot so easily be jettisoned from a Christian view of things, for these too are gifts of God in creation, to be richly enjoyed with thanksgiving.

How, then, does the gospel relate to sports? The gospel will not necessarily increase one's batting average or vertical leap, but it will give the sportsperson a new purpose, a new identity, and a new ethic.

A new purpose

Why do people play sports? On the one hand, men and women play sports because they are created to play and want to use their gifts to glorify God. On the other hand, people often play sports as a way to justify themselves; to prove themselves to the world. Many can identify with the scene in *Chariots of Fire* where the Olympic runner Harold Abrahams, while preparing for the 100m dash, says that he has "ten lonely seconds to justify my whole existence." Just as sports were created good but can become twisted by sin, many people begin playing sports with a love for the game but then turn to using sports for a deeper love of fame, money, or accomplishments. Sports begin as a gift but can easily evolve into a god.

Thankfully, Jesus saves not only from forensic guilt but also from false gods. When sinners understand that they are justified by the blood of

Christ, this frees them from having to justify themselves through their accomplishments. Sports then become a gift; they no longer bear the pressure of being the way that we prove ourselves to the world. Because of grace, God's people are motivated not by guilt but by gratitude. Through the gospel, athletes can stop looking to sports to justify themselves and play sports as they were designed to be, as a gift to be enjoyed for their intrinsic good and to be stewarded for the good of others.

A new identity

Second, the gospel gives the sportsperson a new identity. Sports go deeper than what we do, they speak to who we are. The identity-shaping power of sports is evident, for the sport that a person plays often shapes the way they dress, the music they listen to, and the friends they spend time with. None of these are bad in and of themselves, unless they have worked their way into the center of a person's identity. It is fine for an individual to identify themselves by the sport they play, but a sport cannot bear the burden of defining our core identity. The core identity of a Christian is that he or she is "in Christ" by the work of the Spirit. This truth flows from the fountain of the gospel: the Christian's identity is based not on their performance but on God's grace. He or she is not a soccer player who happens to be a Christian, rather a Christian who plays soccer. The follower of Jesus does not need to build an identity through their accomplishments, for they have been given an identity because of Jesus's accomplishment. Sports matter, but they must be understood from the right perspective. Because of the gospel, we are not defined by our sin nor by our success, but by our saviour.

A new ethic

The gospel gives the sportsperson a new purpose, a new identity, and lastly a new ethic. The win-at- all-costs mentality of modern sports (where winning is an idol by which the athlete is willing to sacrifice anything else) comes at a high price to the integrity of sports. Sports ethics plays out both on and off the field.

On the field, steroids and performance-enhancing drugs have cast a shadow over the last two decades of baseball. In other sports, players have bullied their own teammates and even been paid by coaches to physically injure their opponents. Off the field, the stories are endless: dog fighting, sexual promiscuity, spousal abuse, and even murder. But the temptation to sacrifice integrity is not only true of players at the highest level. Bob Goldman, a physician from Chicago, asked 198 athletes if they would take a banned drug if they were guaranteed to win and not be caught; 195 said they would. Goldman then asked if they would take a performance-enhancing substance if they would not be caught, win every event they entered in the next five years, and then die from the side effects? Over half said they would (McComb, 2004).

The Christian must approach sports with a different ethic, and as O'Donovan (1986: 11) demonstrates, "Christian ethics must arise from the gospel of Jesus Christ." Those who are justified in Christ are called to seek justice and righteousness, on and off the field. And as O'Donovan emphasizes, the bodily resurrection of Christ is God's reaffirmation of his creation and his purposes for his people. Just as God intended play (and sport) to be in harmony with his design for human flourishing, the gospel restores God's people into those very creation purposes. The church does not need more athletes who cut corners so they can get to the top and thank God, but rather athletes with integrity who are unwillingly to compromise their conduct because they care more about what God thinks of them than what the world does.

Sports in the new creation

In the classic sports movie *Field of Dreams*, John Kinsella walks onto an idyllic baseball field and asks his son, Ray (played by Kevin Costner), "Is this Heaven?" "It's Iowa," responds the son. And John, still with a glimmer in his eye, retorts, "I could've sworn it was heaven." John's awe at the heavenliness of his sports experience not only made for a classic movie scene, but it raises an important question: will there be sports in the new heaven and new earth?

The answer to this question all depends on one's view of salvation. If Jesus is tossing his fallen creation and saving souls into a disembodied heaven, then the shot clock is winding down on our sport experience. But the story of redemption in Scripture is not one merely of rescuing souls from the fallen creation but rescuing embodied souls and renewing all of creation (Col 1:15–20; Rom 8:18–25). The final vision of salvation is the enthroned Jesus declaring "Behold, I am making all things new" (Rev 21:5). Salvation is the restoration of creation, and if creation included God's design for play and sport, then there will certainly be sport in the new creation. As Bavinck (2003: 380) says, "The whole of re-creation, as it will be completed in the new heaven and the new earth, is the fruit of the work of Christ." Certainly the re-creation will include recreation.

It is no surprise then that when Scripture wants to prophetically stir up the imagination of God's people for the consummated kingdom that it appeals to images of play. The prophet Zechariah says, "And the streets of the city shall be full of boys and girls playing" (Zech 8:5). Isaiah prophesies that when the earth is finally full of the knowledge of God, "The nursing child shall play over the hole of the cobra, and the weaned child shall put his hand on the adder's den" (Isa 11:8). Harvey (2014: 114) is perhaps right: "Though the heavenly city may have no temple, Christians can be confident that it will have a stadium where we can continue to chime. Sport is here to stay. We can enjoy it forever."

What will sports be like in the new creation? This is a question that can only lead to the most fruitful kind of speculation. Indeed, one can only begin to imagine a volleyball rally between players with glorified, resurrection bodies. Although it is somewhat speculative, 1 Corinthians 15:35–49 does provide some guardrails for such dreaming. Those raised to eternal life will receive a glorified, resurrection body that will have both continuity and discontinuity with their fallen bodies. The analogy of sowing a seed is appropriate. Play and sport as we understand them today will blossom in the new creation to be something beyond what we can imagination and yet will feel exactly the way it was supposed to be.

Sport foreshadows the playful joy of the consummated Kingdom

Moltmann (1972; 2) once asked whether it is appropriate for Christians to be playing games while war is ravishing the nations, children are starving, and the innocent are being oppressed. It is a weighty question, but I concur with Moltmann when he answers with a resounding "yes," because in playing we anticipate the eschaton, a time when there will be no war, a time when sin will not corrupt the goodness of which we are to delight, and a time when we our longing for freedom and childlike joy will be satisfied. Play foreshadows the joy of the kingdom when Christ reigns over all, and decay, disease, and death will be no more. This is not merely a glimpse of the future; it is the in-breaking of the future. As Witherington (2012; 57) argues, "The foreshadowing of better times is itself a foretaste of better times, and this is in part the theological function of play."

Conclusion

Dietrich Bonhoeffer once sat in a prison cell and wondered whether the church could regain its position of providing a robust understanding of activities such as play, friendship, art, and games. For far too long the church (and specifically its scholars) have passed on such an endeavor. Thankfully today Christian theologians are seeking to regain such a position. Hopefully, the church will be able to fulfill its theological task with the confidence with which Bonhoeffer (1971: 198) expressed, for he concludes that for such meaningful activities, it is "only the Christian" who has the resources to provide a robust view. I agree that Scripture and the Christian theological tradition provide an overwhelming set of resources for followers of Christ to think deeply and critically about God's intention for sports and their current role in society today. Sport is more than a game, less than a god, and when transformed by the gospel, can be received as a gift to be enjoyed forever.

Notes

1 According to Watson and Parker (2013: 9), there is "general agreement that academics outside the traditional social-science sports studies disciplines, such as theologians and philosophers of religion, have been slow to recognize the cultural significance of modern sports."

2 For example, the Mayans and Minoans played ball near their temples sites, tennis began in a French monastery, and a Presbyterian minister in the Young Men's Christian Association invented basketball. For an insightful and concise summary of the history of sports, see McComb (2004).

3 Novak's (1994) seminal work, first published in 1967, was the first systematic study of the sport-faith interface. For an excellent introduction to the field of sports and faith, and an overview of recent scholarship, see Watson and Parker (2013).

4 The arguments set out in this chapter first appeared in Treat (2015).

5 Scholars disagree whether Paul supported the sports of his day or whether he was merely using sports terminology as part of rhetorical tradition. For a brief overview of such debates, see Pfitzner (2009).

6 Tertullian, for example, was vehemently against the Games, claiming that they "are not consistent with true religion and true obedience to the true God."

7 According to Ellis (2014), while the ancients viewed sport as a vehicle for communion with the divine, Christians from the early church to the Reformation understood sport as a distraction from religion, and after that, as a mere instrument with potential for religious purposes.

8 The key moment in the coming together of faith and sports was when Christians began using sports for moral training, a movement that became known as Muscular Christianity. For an introduction to this movement, see Hall (2006).

9 Huizinga's work on play has been foundational for discussions on sport. He defines play as

> a free activity standing quite consciously outside 'ordinary' life ... but at the same time absorbing the player intensely and utterly. It is an activity connected with no material interest, and no profit can be gained from it. It proceeds within its own boundaries of time and space according to fixed rules and in an orderly manner.
>
> (Huizinga, 1955: 13)

10 While Huizinga (1955: 17) and others have made the anthropological point about play, Moltmann grounds it theologically. Humans are *homo ludens* because they are made in the image of *Deus ludens*. Moltmann points out that God did not create the world out of necessity or obligation, nor is there any purposive rationale for why something exists rather than nothing. Creation, therefore, must have its ground in the good will and pleasure of God. "Hence the creation is God's play, a play of groundless and inscrutable wisdom. It is the realm in which God displays his glory."

11 McComb (2004) calls this natural instinct the "athletic imperative."

12 Goheen and Bartholomew (2008: 39) demonstrate that

> "creation » had a much broader scope of meaning for Old Testament Israel than it often does for us today. Creation includes the cultural and social

endeavors of human beings and thus covers the whole of human life—personal, social, cultural.

13 In the following paragraph I am drawing especially from Ellis (2014: 125–9).
14 I need to clarify at this point that by "sport" I do not necessarily mean what we think of with modern professionalized sport. It is debated whether that counts as "play" by definition, and in many ways modern sport is more about entertainment and business than about playful delight. The complex issues of sport and economics, culture, and sociology are not easily disentangled from the games themselves, and engaging these aspects of the *professional* world of sports is beyond the scope of the present discussion.
15 Ellis (2014: 198–9) adds an important point regarding competition:

> If competition is an evil that Christians should avoid or discourage such a judgment would place a ban on a great deal more than our sporting activity. It would affect business (and the creation of wealth) and education very clearly, but its impact would have much wider reverberations.

16 Watson and Parker (2013: 17) argue that

> The Greek dualistic philosophy of Plato, as used especially in the writing of church father Origen (*c.*182–251), have been extremely influential in denigrating the worth/sacredness of the body and thus sport and physical education ... in the last two millennia.

17 Here I clearly disagree with Harvey's (2014: 96) thesis, "Sport is understood to be the only thing that is not worship."
18 I have benefited much in understanding idolatry as the root of sin from Keller (2009). Keller himself has been greatly shaped on the topic of idolatry by Luther and Calvin.
19 More recently, Beneke and Remillard (2014) have argued that there is a direct correlation between the decline of traditional religion in America and the rise of devotion in sports.
20 There is a vast amount of literature on sports as religion (see, for example, Price, 2001).
21 For a general explanation of the religious nature of "secular" liturgies, whether in the mall or the arena, see Smith (2009).
22 It is important here to acknowledge the distinction between common grace and saving grace, both of which apply to sports. I understand common grace as preserving in part the goodness of creation and restraining the effects of sin, whereas saving grace is the restorative grace that flows from the gospel and brings in advance the effects of God's renewal of creation.

References

Bavinck, H. (2003), *Reformed Dogmatics*, ed. J. Bolt, trans. J. Vriend. Grand Rapids, Baker Academic.

Beneke, C. and Remillard, A. (2014), Is Religion Losing Ground to Sports? *Washington Post*. Retrieved from www.washingtonpost.com/opinions/is-religion-losing-ground-to-sports/2014/01/31/6faa4d64-82bd-11e3-9dd4- e7278db80d86_story.html (accessed August 27, 2015).

Berger, P. (1970), *A Rumor of Angels*. New York, Doubleday.

Bonhoeffer, D. (1971), *Letters and Papers from Prison*, ed. E. Bethge. New York, Macmillan.

Calvin, J. (2006), *Institutes of the Christian Religion*, ed. J. McNeill, trans. F. L. Battles. Louisville, Westminster John Knox.

Ellis, R. (2014), *The Games People Play*. Eugene, Wipf & Stock.

Goheen, M. and Bartholomew, C. (2008), *Living at the Crossroads: An Introduction to Christian Worldview*. Grand Rapids, Baker Academic.

Guttmann, A. (1986), *Sports Spectators*. New York, Columbia University Press.

Hall. D. E. (2006), *Muscular Christianity: Embodying the Victorian Age*, Cambridge Studies in Nineteenth-Century Literature and Culture. Cambridge: Cambridge University Press.

Hall, D. E. and Fraser, R. (1996), 'Muscular Christianity: Embodying the Victorian Age.' *The Modern Language Review*, 91 (3): 704.

Harvey, L. (2014), *A Brief Theology of Sport*. London, SCM.

Hoffman, S. (2010), *Good Game: Christianity and the Culture of Sports*. Waco, Baylor University Press.

Huizinga, J. (1955), *Homo Ludens: A Study of the Play Element in Culture*. Boston, Beacon.

Johnston, R. K. (1997), *The Christian at Play*. Eugene, Wipf & Stock.

Keller, T. (2009) *Counterfeit Gods: The Empty Promises of Money, Sex, and Power, and the Only Hope That Matters*. New York, Dutton.

McComb, D. G. (2004), *Sports in World History*. New York, Routledge.

Moltmann, J. (1972) *Theology of Play*, trans. R. Ulrich. New York, Harper & Row.

Novak, M. (1994), *Joy of Sports: End Zones, Bases, Baskets, Balls, and the Consecration of the American Spirit*. Lanham, Madison Books.

O'Donovan, O. (1986), *Resurrection and Moral Order: An Outline for Evangelical Ethics*. Grand Rapids, Eerdmans.

Pfitzner, V. C., Hess, R., Preece, G. R., and Australian Theological Forum. (2009). 'We Are the Champions! Origins and Developments of the Image of God's Athlete,' *Sport and Spirituality: An Exercise in Everyday Theology*, 11 (1): 49–64.

Price, J. L. (2001), *From Season to Season: Sports as American Religion*, Macon, Mercer University Press.

Smith, J. (2009), *Desiring the Kingdom: Worship, Worldview, and Cultural Formation*. Grand Rapids, Baker Academic.

Stott, J. (2006), *Issues Facing Christians Today*, ed. R. McCloughry, 4th edn. Grand Rapids, Zondervan.

Taylor, C. (2007), *A Secular Age*. Cambridge, Harvard University Press.

Tertullian, *Spectacles*, 1, ANF 3:79.

Thoennes, E. (2008), 'Created to Play: Thoughts on Play Sport and the Christian Life,' in *The Image of God in the Human Body: Essays on Christianity and Sports*, ed. D. Deardorff and J. White, Lampeter, Mellen.

Treat, J.R. (2015) "More than a Game: A Theology of Sport." *Them*, 40 (3): 392–403.

Watson, N. J. (2013), "Special Olympians as a 'Prophetic Sign' to the Modern Sporting Babel," *Sports and Christianity: Historical and Contemporary Perspectives*, New York, Routledge: 167–206.

Watson, N. J. and Parker, A. (2013), "Sports and Christianity: Mapping the Field," *Sports and Christianity: Historical and Contemporary Perspectives*, New York: Routledge: 9–88.

Weir, S. (2008), "Competition as Relationship: Sport as a Mutual Quest for Excellence," in *The Image of God in the Human Body: Essays on Christianity and Sports*, eds. D. L. Deardorff and J. White. Lampeter: Mellen: 101–22.

Witherington III, B. (2012), *The Rest of Life: Rest, Play, Eating, Studying, Sex from a Kingdom Perspective*. Grand Rapids, Eerdmans.

Non-Western perspectives on sport and Christianity

Part II

New Western
perspectives on space and
Christianity

Chapter 3

Interreligious football
Christianity, African tradition, and the religion of football in South Africa

David Chidester

During the 2010 Fédération Internationale de Football Association (FIFA) World Cup in South Africa, many commentators observed that football was a religion. They noted that the sport was structured like a religion; that it functioned like a religion; and that it mobilized the collective effervescence, social cohesion, and intense contestation associated with religion. But football has had a long relationship with Christianity and indigenous religious traditions in South Africa. Introduced by the British military in the nineteenth century, football was adopted by African Christian converts at mission schools and churches, becoming a part of African Christian life like literacy, wage labor, and European clothing. As football developed to become the most popular African sport during the twentieth century, it was attended by indigenous rituals of strengthening and healing, drawing upon an African traditional religious heritage. During the World Cup in 2010, three religions were on display—Christianity, African indigenous religion, and the religion of football. By analyzing the Christian prayers, the ancestral rituals, and the contests over ownership of sacred symbols, such as the *vuvuzela*, in the religion of football in South Africa, this chapter identifies three important features of World Christianity—mediations with indigeneity; negotiations with local sovereignty; and transactions with a global economy.

Religion features prominently in histories of football in Africa. Acknowledging the role of Christianity, historians have linked football with the colonial Christian mission, recognizing that its nineteenth-century imperial advocates saw football advancing "the virtues of Christianity, capitalist commerce, and Western civilization" (Alegi 2010b, 1; see Couzens 1983). This formula—Christianity, commerce, and civilization—was commonplace in British imperial ambitions and colonial interventions throughout Africa. The *Christianity* in this formula eventually emerged as a "muscular Christianity," a religion of discipline, health, and morality (Alegi 2010b, 8). As the historian John Connell has observed, football merged "sport, muscular Christianity, and empire" (Connell 2014, 396).

By the twenty-first century, however, the role of Christianity in football had been largely reduced to the medium of prayer, with Christian prayers featuring as both text and team sport. Christian prayers featured prominently in the run-up to the 2010 FIFA World Cup in South Africa. The Anglican Archbishop in Cape Town, Thabo Makgoba, announced a simple prayer that he hoped would be embraced not only by Christians but also by people of other faiths. "It is a short and simple prayer which is easy to learn," Archbishop Makgoba explained. "I hope many people, of many backgrounds, will join me in praying it daily in the coming weeks." The text of this prayer called upon God to bless the event and everyone involved (Zendran 2010). The Catholic Church of South Africa designed the text of a prayer in the shape of a football invoking divine blessing but also praying that South Africans would be good hosts, especially by refraining from crime (Catholic Church of South Africa 2010).

More dynamic than these texts, prayer as performance preceded the World Cup. As the newly built stadium in Cape Town was being prepared for the festival, it was tested by a series of escalating events—a football match for 20,000, a rugby match for 40,000, and then the final test, a Christian evangelical prayer rally for 60,000 people. On May 29, 2010, a prayer rally was held at Super Stadium, in a suburb of Pretoria, to mark a national day of prayer for the World Cup and South Africa's national team, known as Bafana Bafana, "the boys, the boys." Reverend Mcebisi Xundu, president of the National Interfaith Leaders Council, prayed for strength, wisdom, and victory for the national team. "We are here to ask God to give our team Bafana Bafana strength and wisdom during this world cup," he explained, "and only through prayer can they really go far in the tournament" (BuaNews 2010). Dr. Mathole Motshekga, Chief Whip of the ruling African National Congress in Parliament, prayed for national unity. "We are of the view that through sports our nation can prosper," Motshekga declared, "and as we pray for Bafana we must appreciate how we have worked all of us black and white to bury apartheid so let's use this event to unite us behind the team" (BuaNews 2010). In these stadium events, Christian prayer was a kind of team sport as prayer rallies were performed as an integral part of the World Cup in South Africa.

Indigenous African religion has also played a significant role in the history of football in Africa. The historian of African football Peter Alegi has identified three modes of African religious tradition that have been evident in the sport: rituals of sport, such as competitive dancing, stick fighting, cattle raiding, cattle racing, and hunting, which echo in football (Alegi 2010a, 7–14); rituals of magic, empowering and cleansing (Alegi 2010b, 26–27, 2010a, 49–51); and rituals of spectatorship employing praise names and praise singing (Alegi 2010b, 30–31, 2010a, 51–52). While indigenous rituals of sport might provide deep background, rituals of magic and spectatorship have been thoroughly integrated into the game. Employing the services of traditional diviners, herbalists, and other ritual specialists, with their ancestral invocations and powerful medicines, rituals of magic have long been a part of football in South Africa. Studying these practices in the early 1960s, N. A. Scotch observed, "Even though players are Christians and have lived in towns for a long time, they do it, and believe in it" (Scotch 1961, 72). Rituals of spectatorship, which bear traces of traditional praise singing, were amplified during the World Cup in South Africa by the omnipresence of the *vuvuzela*, the plastic horn that produced noise that was compared to the buzzing of swarming bees, the moaning of distressed elephants, and the droning of airplanes, all at deafening volume. This instrument was celebrated as distinctively African, although Christian claims were also made on the meaning and power of the *vuvuzela* (Jethro 2014). In preparing for the World Cup, however, the primary indigenous religious ritual was sacrifice, the sanctification, killing, distribution, and eating of a sacrificial animal.

While Christianity and indigenous African religion have been in opposition, fusion, or counterpoint, both were related to a third religion that has often been identified in histories of football in Africa—"*Sportgeist*—the spirit of sport" (Alegi 2010b, 1; see Hardy 1990). Football might be a religion by analogy, as John Sugden and Alan Tomlinson found that FIFA was analogous to the nineteenth-century imperial Christian mission. For FIFA's leadership, "football, like Christianity was viewed as something that was good for the savages and as such it was FIFA's mission to develop the game in the farthest flung corners of the globe" (Sugden and Tomlinson 1996, 31; cited Darby 2002, 22). In the advent of the 2010 FIFA World Cup in South Africa, many commentators observed that football is a religion because it looks like religion and acts like religion.

Adopting a morphological analysis of religion by attending to characteristically religious forms, CNN National Editor, Dave Schechter, declared his devotion to the "religion of football." Schechter identified forms of religion operating in football: prayers, curses, hymns, vestments, transcendent gods and sacrificial rituals. "Deities will be implored," he noted. "Sacrifices will be pledged, some even offered." All of this religious activity, according to Schechter, must revolve around a sacred center, "a shrine that must be visited at least once in a lifetime" (Schechter 2010). For the "football worshipper," this sacred center, the holy of holies, is the FIFA World Cup, moving to a different location every four years, but retaining its structural role as the central shrine of the religion of football. In these terms, football is a religion because it looks like religion.

Adopting a functional analysis of religion, *Guardian* commentator Theo Hobson argued that football was a religion that was better than any institutionalized religion because it provided the world with a genuine ritual of social solidarity. In his article, "The World Cup: A Ritual that Works," Hobson (2010) implicitly drew on Durkheim's definition of religion as beliefs and practices in relation to the sacred that draw people into a unified community (Durkheim 1965, 62). In this respect, football is a

religion because it acts like a religion, making us "feel that we are participating in something huge and communal." In British society, Christmas or
royal events might achieve that religiously ritualized social solidarity,
according to Hobson, but conventional religions, which form communities
around churches, mosques, or temples, do not generate "a sense of solidarity with society in general." Accordingly, in functional terms, Hobson
can conclude that recognized religions are less "religious" than the religion
of football in forming social solidarity. Given the diversity of organized
religions, "religion divides rather than unites," as their religious festivities
disguise the demands of authoritarian religious leaders, although Hobson
acknowledges that conventional religious institutions can sometimes
approach the pure religion of football, noting that he is "impressed by
Catholic cultures in which holy days resemble big football events." Nevertheless, if we recognize the essential function of religion as creating a
sacred sense of social solidarity, then football religion is more religious
than any conventional religion. "The desire for society to be united in
common ritual expression, or worship, is basic to religion, and perhaps
politics too, but all actual realisations of this ideal should be viewed with
suspicion," Hobson concluded. "We should be grateful for a harmless
version of this deep-rooted instinct" (Hobson 2010). In these terms, football is a religion, better than most, because it acts like religion.

None of the commentaries on football religion that were framed outside
of South Africa, the sacred site of the 2010 FIFA World Cup, tried to relate
religion to economics. Within South Africa, where hosting the World Cup
required enormous capital investment in stadiums and infrastructure,
neglecting pressing needs for addressing poverty, crime, housing, health
care, and education, while ensuring record-breaking profits for FIFA, the
intersection between religion and economics, between rituals of solidarity
and financial calculations, could not be avoided. Accordingly, when one of
South Africa's leading social anthropologists, Steven Robins, defended the
religion of football, his article in the popular press was entitled, "World
Cup Ritual Worth Every Cent" (Robins 2010). As we will see, the cultural
officials of the 2010 FIFA World Cup drew on indigenous religious
resources to reinforce the religion of football, officiating over blood sacrifices in keeping with the religious practices of African religion.

Sacrifice

In December 2009, Zolani Mkiva, speaking on behalf of the Makhonya
Royal Trust, which was coordinating cultural events for the 2010 FIFA
World Cup, announced the plan to perform ritual sacrifices of cattle at each
of the ten stadiums that had been prepared for the tournament. "We must
have a cultural ceremony of some sort, where we are going to slaughter a
beast," Mkiva explained. "We sacrifice the cow for this great achievement

and we call on our ancestors to bless, to grace, to ensure that all goes well" (BBC 2009). In support of this proposal to perform ten sacrificial rituals, South African Minister of Cooperative Governance and Traditional Affairs, Sicelo Shiceka, argued that these ceremonies would not only sanctify but also Africanize the international event. "The World Cup will be on the African continent," Minister Shiceka observed, "and we will make sure that African values and cultures are felt by the visitors" (BBC 2009). Although the term, "sacrifice" is often used metaphorically in the religion of football, here was a proposal to perform actual blood sacrifices, rituals that required the killing of an animal, as an integral part of the cultural, spiritual, and religious significance of the World Cup. An international outcry erupted in the media and animal rights organizations mobilized petition campaigns against the ritual. FIFA remained silent about its policy regarding the sacrifice of animals. As *Guardian* correspondent Matt Scott reported, "The plan, which apparently involves slicing the throat of a cow with a knife or an assegai, reportedly has the support of South Africa's traditional affairs minister, Sicelo Shiceka." Despite attempts to get a response, Scott found that FIFA was not prepared to say "whether it will allow the slaughter rituals to go ahead" (Scott 2009).

During the previous month, ritual sacrifice had become the focus of controversy in South Africa as Animal Rights Africa went to court to stop the killing of a bull that forms part of the annual observance of *Ukweshwama*, the first fruits ceremony presided over by the Zulu King. In addition to Zulu King Goodwill Zwelithini, respondents challenged both hereditary traditional leadership and elected democratic leadership in South Africa to defend the ritual sacrifice of a bull at an annual celebration of Zulu royalty. As one aspect of the ceremony, young men catch and kill a bull with their bare hands. Characterizations of this ritual differed dramatically. "During the Ukweshwama ritual," according to Animal Rights Africa, "men pulled out the bull's tongue, stuffed sand in its mouth and also attempted to tie its penis in a knot." By stark contrast to this visceral account, defenders of the ritual consistently rendered it as religious symbolism, observing that "Ukweshwama is a symbolic way of thanking God for the first crops of the season" (Mthembu 2009; Sapa 2009). Accepting the argument that the ritual killing was religious symbolism, the judge in this case observed that "the activity was as important to the Zulu tradition as the Holy Communion was to Catholics" (BBC 2009). Furthermore, acknowledging the royal symbolism of the ceremony, the judge found that the bull was killed by Zulu warriors in order to transfer "symbolic powers" to the Zulu King. "If this is stopped, the symbolic powers would be stopped," he said. "In effect, you are killing the king" (Regchand 2009). Accordingly, religious freedom, guaranteed by the South African Constitution, allowed for the ritual killing of a bull that symbolized thanksgiving to God and the sovereignty of the Zulu King.

On the eve of the 2010 FIFA World Cup, a sacrificial ritual was performed at one stadium, Soccer City, where the opening and closing ceremonies of the World Cup were scheduled. Organized by Zolani Mkiva, the ceremony was officiated by 300 traditional diviners and healers, *sangomas* and *inyangas*, with about 2,000 people in attendance. The ceremony began at 6 am with the ritual killing of an ox by a 70-year-old "Xhosa warrior" who speared the animal at the back of its neck, between its horns, according to tradition. Burning the traditional herb, *impepho*, the ritual specialists invoked the ancestors, as Mkiva explained, calling on "the spirits of our African ancestors to usher in their wisdom and energy in setting the scene of what was to follow in the day" (Sapa 2010). Phepsile Maseko, national coordinator for the Traditional Healers' Organisation, described the ceremony as having three effects—unifying people, welcoming visitors, and appeasing ancestors. "We burnt incense and other medicines and we slaughtered a cow near the stadium," Maseko recounted. "The cow symbolizes strength ... it is a unifying cow." Dealing with foreign fans and indigenous ancestors, the ritual was both the way "we bless the stadium as a symbol of welcome to the nations that are coming," but also a way to alert the ancestors of the arrival of football fans from all over the world, because "We don't want our spirits to be scared of all the different languages" (Reuters 2010). Spiritually, the energy of this ritual was transmitted to all of the other stadiums throughout the country. As a result, despite abandoning the plan to perform sacrificial rituals at ten stadiums, Zolani Mkiva could conclude, "Our stadiums are now officially blessed according to our culture, for the tournament" (Sapa 2010).

Here we find different understandings of sacrifice, not merely in the rift between defenders of cultural traditions and defenders of animal rights, but in the contrasting interpretations of sacrifice by participants in the Zulu royal sacrifice and the World Cup sacrifice. On the one hand, the Zulu royal sacrifice during the annual observance of *Ukweshwama* was interpreted as a ritual of transcendence, invoking a transcendent deity, empowering the sovereign king, which reinforced the legitimacy of a traditional polity. As a ritual symbolizing the supreme power of God and king, this royal sacrifice was interpreted as re-establishing hierarchical relations of domination and subordination in Zulu society. Sacrifice, in this case, was understood as a religious ritual of political sovereignty. On the other hand, the World Cup sacrifice was understood by its officiants as a sacred event that generated a shared spiritual energy which effectively mediated relations among participants, strangers, and ancestors. Not a symbolic invocation of vertical transcendence, this sacrifice was understood to operate on a horizontal plane, extending spiritual energy to the ancestors in the earth, the stadiums throughout the country, and football fans all over the world. By contrast to the Zulu royal offering to the centralized, hierarchical power of God and king, the World Cup sacrifice radiated centrifugal force by transmitting spiritual energy everywhere and centripetal force by drawing everyone into the sacrificial space. Accordingly, this sacrifice was rendered as an act of ritual inclusion in a blessed community.

Festival

On June 11, 2010, Zolani Mkiva, the Poet of Africa (Mkiva 2015), began the opening ceremony of the 2010 FIFA World Cup at Soccer City with a performance of traditional African praise singing. Anticipating his appearance on the global stage, Mkiva said, "I am thrilled. It's a dream come true. I will be watched by more than three billion people from across world." Mkiva called upon all South Africans to come together, in prayer, in support of their national team. "We must keep on praying for our boys, Bafana Bafana," Mkiva urged. "We must see them going to the finals. We must create a vibrant team spirit. They are patriots who have the entire world on their shoulders" (Feni 2010). Like the sacrificial ritual he officiated at Soccer City before the World Cup, Mkiva's performance in the opening ceremony was intended to radiate sacred energy in larger and larger concentric circles of ancestral spirits, traditional royalty, national leadership, patriotic citizens, and a vast global community. Sixteen years earlier, Mkiva had been on a comparable stage, acting as the *imbongi*, the praise singer, at the inauguration of Nelson Mandela, the first democratically elected president of a new South Africa. His performance on that occasion had also mediated between local tradition, tracing Mandela back through heroic founders of the African National Congress, and global audience, with special attention to singing the praises of Fidel Castro, Yasser Arafat, and Muammar Gaddafi (Kaschula 2004). Now he was opening the festival of the 2010 FIFA World Cup in South Africa.

In his defence of the World Cup, anthropologist Steven Robins emphasized the spectacularization of sports as festival, as carnival, as an "ecstatic experience of solidarity and belonging." Individuals, in ecstasy, found themselves "losing one's self in the collective spirit of the carnival" (Robins 2010, 13) The World Cup provided an occasion for individuals to find their ecstatic sovereignty by abandoning the world of things, utility, projects, and economic calculations. During the World Cup, as the everyday, ordinary, and mundane world was "temporarily cordoned off," South African society was transformed into a community. As Robins concluded, we should appreciate the World Cup for the "benign social solidarity that occurred during this hyper-transient, yet wondrous, collective ritual" (Robins 2010, 13). Ecstasy and solidarity, as other analysts have observed, were the essence of the religion of football presented at the 2010 FIFA World Cup. For example, according to political philosopher Achille Mbembe, football at the World Cup was "an act of communion that offers its members the opportunity to share, with countless pilgrims from around the world, the moments of a unique intensity" (Devriendt 2010). Durkheim's notions of ecstasy and solidarity—collective effervescence, unified moral community—provided the template for these analyses of the World Cup festival.

However, the sacred ecstasy of the festival takes place in tension with the profane world of utility, economic calculation, and political authority that it can only temporarily disrupt. Although festival, with all of its sacrificial and celebratory giving, loss, waste, and destruction, might break through the limits of profane regularity into sacred immediacy, festival is inevitably limited by the demands of the profane. The profane, in at least two instances, was asserted by Christians in relation to the central aural icon of the World Cup, the *vuvuzela*.

Certainly, this festive horn, celebrating football, transgressed conventional standards of the profane world by breaking the rules of music and producing senseless noise. Although it was frequently defended as a necessary part of African football culture, even by Sepp Blatter on behalf of FIFA, the *vuvuzela* was entangled in the profane world of property when its manufacturer was sued by the Nazareth Baptist Church. Founded in 1910 by the Zulu prophet Isaiah Shembe, the church had used such a horn in its worship services to invoke the Holy Spirit. As one follower of Shembe complained, the appropriation of their sacred horn by football meant that their Holy Spirit, rather than the spirit of the game, was being showered in the stadiums. As this dispute was settled out of court, the Nazareth Baptist Church secured a percentage of profits from the sale of *vuvuzelas* (Fisher 2010; Madlala et al. 2010). But Christian claims on the sacred horn extended further. Moving from the local to the global, the president of the South African Council of Churches, Tinyiko Maluleke, described the *vuvuzela* as a "missile-shaped weapon" that was loud enough to awaken the rest of the world to Africa. Against the background of European colonization of Africa, Maluleke argued, the *vuvuzela* was an African rejoinder to imperial oppression, dispossession, and neglect. "Now," he asserted, "we have created the vuvuzela, which is one of the most obnoxious instruments: very noisy, very annoying. It will dominate the FIFA World Cup. I see the vuvuzela as a symbol, as a symbol of Africa's cry for acknowledgement" (Maluleke 2010). Even the festive noise of the *vuvuzela*, therefore, could become property in legal disputes and a weapon in global politics during the World Cup.

The reconciliation of sacred and profane, the negotiation between festival and cost-accounting, was difficult to adjudicate when dealing with the World Cup in South Africa. Acknowledging the ecstatic enthusiasm and social solidarity generated by football, South African political philosopher and social activist Richard Pithouse ultimately found that the World Cup festival was an indictment of the ANC government that had abandoned the needs of the poor to offer "a mix of empty spectacle, participation in empty rituals like 'Football Friday,' and the fantasy of belonging in a society that is increasingly predicated on active and at times violent exclusion" (Pithouse 2010). By any rational cost-accounting, the festival of the World Cup represented a substantial financial loss to South Africa. Although the precise numbers remain in dispute, enormous local resources were directed into expenditure for the World Cup. Although the anticipated financial benefits to South Africa in the form of tourism and job creation turned out to be negligible, the profit to FIFA, estimated at R24 billion ($3 billion), was substantial (Bond 2010). Clearly, FIFA was the winner of the 2010 FIFA World Cup in South Africa.

Sovereignty

On November 5, 2009, Zolani Mkiva, president and director general of the Institute of African Royalty, convened a gathering of dignitaries at South Africa's Freedom Park, the central shrine of the nation (Jethro 2013), to bestow the first African Royal Award upon Nelson Mandela, who was praised as the Lion, the "king of the jungle," the icon of the nation. On the eve of the 2010 FIFA World Cup in South Africa, Zolani Mkiva presided over the second ceremony of the Institute of African Royalty, held in a Johannesburg hotel, at which the African Royal Award was presented to FIFA President Sepp Blatter (Makhonya.com. 2010). Ironically, South African critics and cartoonists were fond of representing Blatter as a king, as in Jabulani Sikhakhane's indictment of the World Cup, "The Shame of Being Colonised by King Sepp" (Sikhakhane 2010), or as a Pope, the head of "an organization that seems a bizarre cross between the Vatican and the IMF" (Singh 2010). During the World Cup, FIFA enjoyed sovereignty over all the stadiums and their precincts, tax-exempt status, freedom from exchange controls, police escorts and security, enforcement of brands and trademarks, restrictions on media reports bringing FIFA into disrepute, and indemnity from any legal proceedings. As Sophie Nakueira observed, "The traditional notion of national sovereignty is irrelevant when bodies like Fifa ... use governments to advance their own objects, which in Fifa's case is to further its profits" (Tolsi 2010). During the World Cup, FIFA was sovereign and Sepp Blatter a king, honored with the African Royal Award by the Institute of African royalty.

While celebrating the global sovereignty of FIFA, African traditionalists took the opportunity of the World Cup to revitalize their own royal claims on political sovereignty. Since 1994, South Africa has been a unified, nonracial democracy, under the sovereignty of one of the most progressive constitutions in the world, but governance has been shared with over 2,400 kings, queens, chiefs, and headmen, presiding over 774 chiefdoms that have maintained the same boundaries that were established under apartheid. Approximately 30 percent of the population live under the authority of a chief. Responsible for security, dispute resolution, and allocation of land, these traditional leaders are also custodians of ancestral rituals, especially sacrifices, which link traditional sovereignty with the spiritual realm of myths, gods, and ancestors (Williams 2010, 5–9). During the World Cup, the AmaGcaleka Xhosa King Zwelonke Sigcawu, whose predecessor had died in 2005, was installed in a traditional ceremony. Anticipating the coronation, Prince Xhanti Sigcawu asserted,

> The build-up towards the coronation of the next Xhosa King will be an exciting activity that presents an opportunity to educate the general public about customs, rituals, norms, values, traditions and protocols of the cultural dynamics of our African Royalty.

Besides educating the South African public, the organizers of the coronation also hoped to attract foreign dignitaries, journalists, and tourists who would be in the country for the World Cup. In a statement issued by the chief executive officer of the Xhosa Royal Trust, Zolani Mkiva, the link between royal ritual and World Cup was important. "This event will take place at a time when the eyes of the entire world will be focused in South Africa given the 2010 Fifa World Cup," Mkiva declared. "Surely the coronation of His Majesty, King Zwelonke, will not only attract the local viewership and listenership but the whole world" (Maqhina 2010). Asked about the costs of the coronation, which journalists estimated at around R10 million, Zolani Mkiva refused to answer any questions about money because "heritage is priceless" (Anonymous 2010).

   Although traditional heritage might be priceless, it nevertheless operates in a market economy. Accordingly, Makhonya Investments, on behalf of the Congress of Traditional Leaders of South Africa (CONTRALESA), was formed as a broad-based black empowerment company designed to advance the financial interests of traditional leaders. Under the leadership of its chairman, Zolani Mkiva, national executive director of CONTRALESA, Makhonya Investments was committed to providing financial support for South African royalty. In its mission statement, Makhonya Investments declared, "We take pride in having ensured that Kings and Queens together with senior Royals of our country are also direct beneficiaries of this investment initiative" (Makhonya Investments 2010). This initiative secured lucrative tenders from government, such as a five-year R3 billion contract to manage the vehicle fleet of the Eastern Cape Province, which caused critics to wonder how a poet such as Zolani Mkiva could have the necessary experience to run such an operation (Jika 2009).

   However, as we have seen, Zolani Mkiva has had extraordinary experience in the sacred as Poet of Africa and praise singer to Nelson Mandela, as officiator of the World Cup sacrifice and performer in the World Cup opening ceremony, as chairman of the Makhonya Royal Trust, president of the Institute of African Royalty, chief executive of the Xhosa Royal Trust, executive director of CONTRALESA, and chairman of Makhonya Investments, which presents him on its website as "HRH Zolani Mkiva," His Royal Heritage, royalty in his own right (Mkiva 2015).

Football, Christianity, and the political economy of the sacred

The 2010 FIFA World Cup in South Africa placed Christianity in complex relations—mediating with indigeneity, negotiating with local sovereignty, and transacting with a global economy—that are suggestive for how we might understand any notion of World Christianity.

The World Cup brought Christianity into new relations with African indigenous religion in South Africa. While Christian prayer was composed as text and performed in rallies, African indigenous ritual was given official sanction in sanctifying the event. Against the background of a long history of opposition between Christianity and indigenous religion, recalling the ways in which the nineteenth-century mission defined Christianity in opposition to sacrifice, healing, polygyny, initiation, and other indigenous religious practices, we should expect conflict. Instead, football mediated relations between Christianity and indigenous religion. This mediation was not a fusion of religions, which is often expected in African indigenous churches, such as the Shembes, which have been characterized as a syncretism of Christianity and African indigenous religion. Rather, as indigenous rituals alternated with Christian prayer rallies, Christianity and African traditional religion were in counterpoint, in melodic and rhythmic exchanges and interchanges, with religious resources playing off each other while playing with each other.

Some Christians saw the World Cup as an opportunity for evangelizing, with interreligious implications, because a "genuine revival," according to Ashley Cloete, "would impact both Judaism and Islam." As leader of a longstanding evangelical organization, Friends from Abroad, Cloete celebrated efforts "to use soccer as an evangelism tool in the run-up to the 2010 World Cup." This initiative in Christian revivalism, "The Ultimate Goal (TUG)," featured a campaign, "Eternal Goal," specifically directed toward converting Muslims to Christianity. Not content with composing Christian prayers or attending Christian rallies associated with the World Cup, these evangelists undertook "around the clock prayer for the duration of the global sports event," hoping to inspire a revival that would reach the unreached and in particular bring Muslims and Jews to Christianity (Cloete 2010). In a country with a Christian majority, an African Christian majority, accounting for the religious affiliation of perhaps 80 percent of the population, the "unreached" is a small minority. While evangelizing Muslims and Jews, Friends from Abroad did not seem to direct similar attention toward adherents of African indigenous religion. Against a background of conflict, there is also a long history in South Africa of practicing both Christian and traditional religion. As Nelson Mandela recalled in his autobiography, he saw no conflict in his childhood between attending the mission church and observing ancestral rituals (Mandela 1995, 12, 25; Chidester 2000, 431–433). Although some advocates of traditional religion object to this religious counterpoint, Christians also participate in African religious rituals of the home, the diviner, and the polity. The World Cup provided an interreligious occasion for mediating between Christianity and ancestral tradition.

During the 2010 World Cup, as we have seen, indigenous rituals of the polity were prominent. In the years before the event, a compelling television advertisement in South Africa featured a ritual of the traditional polity, formal praise singing, by Zolani Mkiva, invoking the ancestors and urging all South Africans to go forward to the World Cup (Mkiva 2008). The World Cup provided an opportunity for a range of actors to assert claims on sovereignty in South Africa. Essentially political claims to sovereignty—democratic and traditional—were adjudicated in relation to FIFA's global mission for the religion of football.

Since 1994 South Africa's post-apartheid polity has observed a balance between democratic constitutionalism and African traditionalism, with weight shifting toward traditionalism under the presidential administration of Jacob Zuma, who was simultaneously a Christian and a Zulu traditionalist. Openly aligning with Christianity, in 2009 Zuma formed a new National Interfaith Leaders Council, chaired by the charismatic Christian pastor Ray McCauley, to replace the National Religious Leaders Forum, which under the previous administration had been dedicated to promoting interreligious dialogue, understanding, toleration, and respect. In this new council, religious leaders were urged to support the government but also to challenge any legislation that went against what President Zuma called "the teachings of the Lord" (Rossouw 2009). As this council was charged with the responsibility of World Cup prayer rallies, the potency of a new kind of predominantly Christian legitimation in South African politics was being asserted. However, another leading figure in the council, Mathole Motshekga, was a prominent advocate of African indigenous religion, which he traced back to ancient Egypt (Chidester 2012, 152–175). Calling for a restoration of African traditional theocracy, Motshegka also participated in the World Cup prayer rallies. As we have seen, the most active advocate of indigenous sovereignty during the World Cup, Zolani Mkiva, used traditional religious resources of praise singing, sacrifice, and royal ritual in relation to both national and global politics. Therefore, while Christianity and indigenous religion might have played in counterpoint during the World Cup, they were also synchronized as complementary sources of religious legitimation for political sovereignty in a changing South Africa.

Transacting with the global economy during the World Cup, South Africans were urged to participate in a "millennial capitalism," an anticipation of extraordinary wealth arriving soon, produced by mysterious means, but bestowing sudden prosperity with the advent of FIFA (Tayob 2012; see Comaroff and Comaroff 2001). Like the prosperity gospel often associated with Pentecostalism, the World Cup raised an economic dilemma shared by World Christianity (see Meyer 2007; Gifford and Nogueira-Godsey 2011). What is the engine that generates wealth? Is it disciplined labor or miraculous gift? Clearly, even when acknowledging the discipline of the sport, FIFA and the South African organizers found common cause in celebrating the gift of the sport, the *Sportgeist* of abundant prosperity. Although this prophecy failed and the capitalist millennium did not arrive, the spirit of the global economy survived. In a reprise of his performance for the World Cup, in 2012 Zolani Mkiva appeared in a dramatic television advertisement for First National Bank, celebrating a kind of magical banking, by calling all South Africans back to origins, under the Baobab tree (the corporate logo of the bank), with its roots in the African soil and its branches bestowing bounty (Mkiva 2012). As the 2010 World Cup in South Africa demonstrated, many religious resources, whether derived from Christianity, indigenous tradition, or the religion of football, could be drawn into the promise of prosperity in the global economy.

The World Cup in South Africa was a matrix for producing the sacred: the sacred space of a stadium; the sacred time of a festival; the sacred solidarity of social cohesion; the sacred energy of collective effervescence; the sacred objects, like the *vuvuzela*, of mass, egalitarian participation; and the sacred offices, like kingship, of elite, hierarchical authority. As demonstrated by the World Cup, the sacred might be "that which is set apart," as Durkheim held, but it is set apart at the center of personal subjectivities, social formations, political power, and economic exchanges (Chidester 2005, 119–120, 2008, 2011). As we have seen, Christians, African traditionalists, and enthusiasts for the religion of football found different ways to interpret and ritualize the sacred during the World Cup. In the political economy of the sacred, interpretations and ritualizations serve to underwrite competing and inherently contested claims on the legitimate ownership of the sacred. Since no claim to the ownership of the sacred can ever be final, the contest continues, the games go on. For the next World Cup during 2014 in Brazil, the Church of England published a prayer that was certainly open to multiple interpretations, evoking either exultation or despair, "Oh, God ..." (Baines 2014). Although this simple Christian prayer might have spoken to the hearts of many football fans, FIFA continued to maintain the strongest claim on the global ownership of the sacred in the religion of football.

References

Alegi, Peter. 2010a. *Laduma! Soccer, Politics, and Society in South Africa, from its Origins to 2010*. Second edition. Scottsville, South Africa: University of KwaZulu-Natal Press; orig. edn. 2004.

Alegi, Peter. 2010b. *African Soccerscapes: How a Continent Changed the World's Game*. London: Hurst.

Anonymous. 2010. "King Xolilizwe [*sic*] Sigcawu Coronation," *MyPE.co.za* (May 7, 2010), http://budget-accommodation-port-elizabeth.com/king-xolilizwe-sigcawu-coronation/, accessed January 29, 2015.

Baines, Nick. 2014. "Church of England World Cup Prayers," *Episcopal Café* (June 17, 2014), www.episcopalcafe.com/church_of_england_world_cup_prayers/, accessed January 29, 2015.

BBC. 2009. "World Cup Stadium 'Cow Sacrifice' Plan Sparks Row." *BBC News* (December 1, 2009), http://news.bbc.co.uk/2/hi/africa/8388001.stm, accessed January 29, 2015.

Bond, Patrick. 2010. *A Political Economy of the 2010 World Cup in South Africa, Six Red Cards for FIFA*. Durban: Centre for Civil Society, University of KwaZulu Natal, http://ccs.ukzn.ac.za/files/Bond%20%20A%20Political%20Economy%20of%20the%20 20Soccer%20World%20Cup%202010%20ver2.pdf, accessed January 29, 2015.

BuaNews. 2010. Prayer for Bafana Bafana," *2010 FIFA World Cup South Africa* (May 31, 2010), www.sa2010.gov.za/node/3130, accessed January 29, 2015.

Catholic Church of South Africa. 2010. "2010 World Cup: Church on the Ball!" *South African Catholic Bishop's Conference*, content&task=view&id=292&Item id=29, accessed January 22, 2011.

Chidester, David. 2000. *Christianity: A Global History*. San Francisco: HarperCollins.

Chidester, David. 2005. *Authentic Fakes: Religion and American Popular Culture*. Berkeley: University of California Press.

Chidester, David. 2008. "Economy." In *Key Words for Religion, Media, and Culture*, edited by David Morgan, 83–95. London: Routledge.

Chidester, David. 2011. "Sacred." *Material Religion* 7 (1): 84–91.

Chidester, David. 2012. *Wild Religion: Tracking the Sacred in South Africa*. Berkeley: University of California Press.

Cloete, Ashley. 2010. *Seeds Sown for Survival*, http://isaacandishmael.blogspot.com/2008/11/seeds-sown-for-revival-personal.html, accessed February 12, 2015.

Comaroff, Jean, and John L. Comaroff. 2001. "Millennial Capitalism, First Thoughts on a Second Coming." In *Millennial Capitalism and the Culture of Neoliberalism*, edited by Jean Comaroff and John L. Comaroff, 1–60. Durham: Duke University Press.

Connell, John. 2014. "At Play on the Football Fields of Empire?" In *The Routledge History of Western Empires*, edited by Robert Aldrich and Kirsten McKenzie, 396–408. London: Routledge.

Couzens, Tim. 1983. "An Introduction to the History of Football in South Africa." In *Town and Countryside in the Transvaal*, edited by Belinda Bozzoli, 198–214. Johannesburg: Raven Press.

Darby, Paul. 2002. *Africa, Football and FIFA: Politics, Colonialism and Resistance*. London: Frank Cass.

Devriendt, Tom. 2010. "Vuvuzelas All Around," *Africa is a Country* (July 11, 2010), http://africasacountry.com/the-vuvuzela/, accessed January 29, 2015.

Durkheim, Emile. 1965. *The Elementary Forms of the Religious Life.* Trans. Joseph Ward Swain. New York: Free Press.

Feni, Lulamile. 2010. "King's Voice Fulfils Dying Father's Wish," *The Herald* (June 14, 2010), www.epherald.co.za/article.aspx?id=573036, accessed November 20, 2010.

Fisher, Jonah. 2010. "Unholy Row Over World Cup Trumpet," *BBC News* (January 16, 2010), http://news.bbc.co.uk/2/hi/8458829.stm, accessed January 29, 2015.

Gifford, Paul, and Trad Nogueira-Godsey. 2011. "The Protestant Ethic and African Pentecostalism: A Case Study." *Journal for the Study of Religion* 24 (1): 5–22.

Hardy, Stephen. 1990. "Entrepreneurs, Structures, and the Sportgeist: Old Tensions in a Modern Industry." In *Essays on Sport History and Sport Mythology*, edited by Donald G. Kyle and Gary D. Stark, 45–82. College Station, TX: Texas A&M Press.

Hobson, Theo. 2010. "The World Cup: A Ritual that Works." *Guardian* (June 12, 2010), www.guardian.co.uk/commentisfree/belief/2010/jun/12/world-cup-ritual-religion, accessed January 29, 2015.

Jethro, Duane. 2013. "An African Story of Creation: Heritage Formation at Freedom Park, South Africa." *Material Religion: The Journal of Objects, Art and Belief* 9 (3): 370–393.

Jethro, Duane. 2014. "Vuvuzela Magic: The Production and Consumption of 'African' Cultural Heritage during the FIFA 2010 World Cup." *African Diaspora* 7 (2): 177–204.

Jika, Thanduxolo. 2009. "BEE Shock in R3bn Bisho Fleet Contract," *Daily Dispatch* (October 3, 2009), www.dispatch.co.za/article.aspx?id=349332, accessed November 20, 2010.

Kaschula, Russell H. 2004. "Praise Poetry: Xhosa Praise Poetry for President Mandela." In *African Folklore: An Encyclopedia*, edited by Phillip M. Peek and Kwesi Yankah, 362–364. London: Routledge.

Madlala, Mpume, Kanina Foss and Sapa-AFP. 2010. "Vuvuzela Deal for Shembe Church." *IOL News* (June 22, 2010), www.iol.co.za/news/south-africa/vuvuzela-deal-for-shembe-church-1.487721, accessed November 20, 2010.

Makhonya Investments. 2010. "Welcome: Creating Wealth and Sustainable Growth for Rural Communities." *Makhonya Investments*, www.makhonyainvestments.co.za/, accessed January 29, 2015.

Makhonya.com. 2010. "Our Team Visited the Royal African Awards," *Makhonya.com: Prosperity through Unity*, www.makhonya.com/?page_id=134, accessed January 29, 2015.

Maluleke, Tinyiko Sam. 2010. "South Africa, Christianity, and the World Cup," *Ekklesia: A New Way of Thinking* (June 5, 2010), www.ekklesia.co.uk/node/12326, accessed January 29, 2015.

Mandela, Nelson. 1995. *Long Walk to Freedom: The Autobiography of Nelson Mandela*. Randburg, South Africa: Macdonald Purnell.

Maqhina, Mayibongwe. 2010. "Government to 'Assist' with King's Coronation," *Daily Dispatch* (May 10, 2010), www.dispatch.co.za/article.aspx?id=400264, accessed November 20, 2010.

Meyer, Birgit. 2007. "Pentecostalism and Neo-Liberal Capitalism: Faith, Prosperity, and Vision in African Pentecostal-Charismatic Churches," *Journal for the Study of Religion* 20 (2): 5–28.

Mkiva, Zolani. 2008. "What Kind of Country Do We Want SA to be in 2010 ... and Beyond?" www.youtube.com/watch?v=zFPNjGhJd9Q, accessed January 29, 2015.

Mkiva, Zolani. 2012. "Zolani doing ad for FNB," *Poet of Africa: His Royal Heritage*, www.poetofafrica.com/new1/, accessed January 29, 2015.

Mkiva, Zolani. 2015. *Zolani Mkiva: His Royal Heritage, The Poet of Africa*, http://poetofafrica.com/, accessed January 29, 2015.

Mthembu, Bongani. 2009. "Bull-Killing Ritual to be Debated in Durban," *Mail & Guardian* (November 24, 2009), www.mg.co.za/article/2009-11-24-bullkilling-ritual-to-be-debated-in-durban, accessed January 29, 2015.

Pithouse, Richard. 2010. "On the Path to Crony Capitalism," *Daily Dispatch* (September 25, 2010), www.dispatch.co.za/article.aspx?id=436143, accessed 20 November 2010.

Regchand, Sharika. 2009. "Bull-Killing Ritual Compared to Communion," *The Star* (December 2, 2009), www.iol.co.za/news/south-africa/bull-killing-ritual-compared-to-communion-1.466461#.VMn7aWccQeg, accessed January 29, 2015.

Reuters. 2010. "Cow Slaughtered at World Cup Stadium to Appease Spirits," *National Post* (May 26, 2010), http://sports.nationalpost.com/2010/05/26/cow-slaughtered-at-world-cup-stadium-to-appease-spirits/#ixzz0pAGwG3dK, accessed January 29, 2015.

Robins, Steven. 2010. "World Cup Ritual Worth Every Cent," *Cape Times* (October 25, 2010): 13.

Rossouw, Mandy. 2009. "Zuma's New God Squad Wants Liberal Laws to Go," *Mail and Guardian Online* (September 11, 2009), www.mg.co.za/article/2009-09-11-zumas-new-god-squad-wants-liberal-laws-to-go, accessed January 29, 2015.

Sapa. 2009. "Mkhize: Bull-Killing Ruling Promotes Cultural Tolerance," *Mail & Guardian* (December 4, 2009), www.mg.co.za/article/2009-12-04-mkhize-bullkilling-ruling-promotes-cultural-tolerance, accessed November 20, 2010.

Sapa. 2010. "Sangomas Sacrifice Ox to Bless the World Cup Stadiums," *Cape Times* (May 26, 2010), www.capetimes.co.za/index.php?fArticleId=5486198, accessed November 20, 2010.

Schechter, Dave. 2010. "The Religion of Football," *CNN Belief Blog* (June 4, 2010), http://religion.blogs.cnn.com/2010/06/04/the-church-of-football/, accessed January 29, 2015.

Scotch, N. A. 1961. "Magic, Sorcery, and Football among Urban Zulu: A Case of Reinterpretation under Acculturation." *The Journal of Conflict Resolution* 5 (1): 70–74.

Scott, Matt. 2009. "Fifa in a Stew over Ritual Slaughter of Cows in World Cup Stadiums," *Guardian* (December 23, 2009), www.guardian.co.uk/sport/2009/dec/23/fifa-world-cup-stadium-cow-slaughter, accessed January 29, 2015.

Sikhakhane, Jabulani. 2010. "The Shame of Being Colonised by King Sepp," *Sunday Tribune* (May 2, 2010), www.highbeam.com/doc/1G1-225354713.html, accessed January 29, 2015.

Singh, Nikhil Pal. 2010. "World Cup 2010," *Social Text: Periscope* (July 20, 2010), www.socialtextjournal.org/periscope/2010/07/introduction-south-africas-world-cup.php, accessed November 20, 2010.

Sugden, John, and Alan Tomlinson. 1996. "Football and Global Politics: FIFA, UEFA, and the Scramble for Africa," Unpublished paper, British Sociological Association (April 1996).

Tayob, Shaheed. 2012. "The 2010 World Cup in South Africa: A Millennial Capitalist Moment." *Journal of Southern African Studies* 38 (3): 717–736.

Tolsi, Niren. 2010. "Fifa Called the Shots—And We have Said 'Yes.'," *Mail & Guardian* (June 4, 2010), http://mg.co.za/article/2010-06-04-fifa-called-the-shots-and-we-said- yes, accessed January 29, 2015.

Williams, J. Michael. 2010. *Chieftancy, the State, and Democracy: Political Legitimacy in Post-Apartheid South Africa*. Bloomington: Indiana University Press.

Zendran, Delaine. 2010. "2010 FIFA World Cup: Unity in Diversity," *Interfaithing* (26 May 2010), www.interfaithing.com/2010-fifa-world-cup-unity-diversity-317/, accessed January 7, 2011.

Chapter 4

Soccer fandom as catechism

Practices of the sacred among young men in Argentina

Eloísa Martín

Introduction

The presence of the sacred in everyday life is broadly viewed as a trend that unifies working class cultures in Latin America; it is visible in rituals, feasts, devotions and miracles, as well as in daily activities. One's relations with the sacred are part of daily life, developed in and through "secular" practices. The fact that elements from the secular world—in this case, soccer and fandom—are included within the sacred denotes a specific way of being-in-the-world, a different logic by which heaven, earth, nature and human beings are intimately connected (Duarte 1986; Parker 1996; Semán 2001). The sacred is recognized, but not as something distant or "radically other," as in Durkheimian definitions of religion but as textures of the sacred (Martín 2009). Religious practices, in this sense, are one of many possible practices of the sacred.

The approach I am adopting in this chapter is not a classical way of examining the intersection between religion and popular culture (Scholes and Sassower, 2014), or the sport-religion interface (Snyder and Spreitzer, 1983), nor of understanding religion as a template for fan practices (Sandvoss, 2005). As Watson and Parker (2014) have shown, different theoretical and methodological approaches have been used to explore the relationship between sports and religion, and sport fandom and religion. The most recurrent perspective in the academic literature is considering popular culture as religion. I propose a new approach: not understanding sport as a civil religion but rather understanding soccer fandom as a practice of the sacred and, ultimately, as a form of "religious" socialization.

Literature on fandom tends to analyse its subject matter using religious metaphors, as if behind a secular form beats a sacred heart. So for Jindra (1999: 246) and Bickerdike (2016), a fan club is a modern and secularized version of a religious group, and Porter (1999) considers attendance at a fan convention as the secular heir of religious pilgrimage. In the case of Madonna, Hulsether (2000) identifies "religious content" in her performances and Coralis (2004) also refers to an almost religious worship of fans for the singer. Aden (1999) makes a strong homology between fandom and religion, stating that being a fan is like being a devotee or a believer, while Rodman (1996) claims that Elvis fandom is "almost religious," not only because of the rituals that take place in Graceland, where fans behave like devotees, but due to the connotations with which the singer has been invested. Here, fan and devotee are not interchangeable, one is not a metaphor for the other. Sport is not understood as a "quasi-religion," or a "pseudo-religion," nor is it my intention to highlight the similarities between sport and religion (Grimshaw, 2000). Religion and soccer, I argue, are two different types of practices of the sacred and are therefore related. In this sense, soccer fandom is not understood as a product of secularization or, in a functionalist fashion, as a result of the absence of proper churches, in the same way it is sometimes considered as part of the presence of folk practices and superstitions in the working class (Martín, 2010). Soccer works as a specific path to join a religion and a more traditional devotional engagement through practices that perform the sacred using a peculiar stock of resources, all of them learned within the values, morals and ideals of masculinity of soccer fandom.

As presented here, sacred does not indicate an institution, a sphere or a system of symbols. Instead, it refers to several recognized heterogeneities where human agency plays a central role, in a way similar to what Latour (2002) calls *fetish*. According to Latour's concept, it is necessary to acknowledge the human origin of sacred beings, places and times, pointing out the direct, active and constitutive human agency at work and the potentially transitory nature of the status of the "sacred," regardless of the specific content it is assigned. At the same time, understanding the sacred as an adjective for practices and textures, means also considering its autonomous nature. According to the dynamic relationship between devotees and the sacred forces (including God, saints, the deceased and other extraordinary beings, without distinction), both parties are defined and re-signified, along with their morals and values. Ideas of passion, attachment, loyalty and strength, among others, define notions of identity for the humans and the sacred forces.

In this chapter, I analyze a specific configuration of practices of the sacred in which soccer becomes a particularly pertinent matrix. Using an ethnographic case study in Argentina, I show how gestures, practices and meanings originating from soccer and more specifically, among soccer fans, are used to create and experience the sacred. This does not mean understanding soccer fandom as a lower form of religiosity, a pseudo-religion, or even a metaphor of the sacred, but as specific forms of practicing the sacred, that could also shift onto other areas of the sacred, including religious practices. Interestingly, practices of the sacred originating in soccer are now part of a recognizable and generalized spectrum of devotional resources (Martín, 2017).

The case presented in this chapter is that of Mario, a fan of the San Lorenzo soccer team and president of the fan club *No Me Arrepiento de este Amor* (I'm not sorry for loving you), which he founded to honour Gilda. Gilda is the stage name of Miriam Bianchi. She was an Argentine *cumbia* singer who died in a car accident in 1996 and was buried in the cemetery of Chacarita in Buenos Aires, becoming an icon of popular culture in Argentina. Hundreds of people visit her grave or the sanctuary built at the crash site every year at the anniversary of her death, others (either fans or devotees) visit her grave every week. Some of them make her promises and fulfil them in order to have a miracle come true, and some pray for protection, help or comfort, in the same fashion as to other popular saints in Latin America. And some of them just gather, "to remember her."

My analysis is based on more than two years of continuous ethnographic fieldwork among Gilda's fans, in different settings. I visited different fan clubs in the city of Buenos Aires and its suburbs; cooked at *Gilda's little hearts*, a soup restaurant for children founded by the president of another Gilda fan club in one of the most dangerous slums in Argentina;[1] spent every weekend at the cemetery, near her grave; joined the fans in their visits to TV channels and celebrations for Gilda; and little by little I was invited into their private homes and family parties, as a fellow fan. To cover aspects of the subject matter that ethnographic fieldwork and in depth interviews could not address, I also performed an online survey— posted in the most popular site of cumbia at that time—which generated more than 400 responses. Even though this data is not directly utilized here, it has helped me to better understand the phenomena. I also collected and analyzed dozens of articles published in newspapers and magazines regarding Gilda's life and death, and all videos and popular books released in the ten years after her death.

Gilda's fans have an ambiguous relationship with the media. On the one hand, they know they are an object of interest for journalists and that their stories are used to sell media products. Thus, they complain about being used as a news story or a media scandal, they dislike that their opinions and are cut or censored when they say something that deviates from what the media want to publish. On the other hand, they recognize that the media has an irreplaceable role in achieving the goal of keeping the memory of the singer alive in the public space and they tend to offer what they know the media expects of them. In this sense, as proposed by Auyero and Grimson (1997: 90), among the working class sectors in Buenos Aires, there is an instrumental relationship with journalists and the media in general, as these are part of everyday reality as institutions of everyday life and a potential access channel to the public space. Gilda's fans are not only an active and critical audience of media products but also key protagonists. I became aware of this and the fact that fans developed skills to deal with journalists (something that I observed during the fieldwork): they have learnt about the typical questions journalists ask and how to deal with radio and TV timings. They have learnt how to deliver standardized answers, and to "give them what they are looking for," while trying to include ideas and values regarding Gilda's "real" story and its true meaning.

When warning about the fallacy of internality that permeates most of the work based on interviews, Hills (2002: 67–68) states that the fan cannot be taken as an unproblematic source of meaning about their own consumption. Hills argues that questions about the reasons of fandom introduce a cut-off in the flow of experience, and produce a discursive kind of affection-free justification, because any conduct considered "normal" does not need to be explained. However, I did not want the standardized stories offered to journalists, so it was only during the final six months of fieldwork, before I left Buenos Aires, that I started in-depth interviews. Despite the fact that most of the topics I raised during the interviews were already covered by my ethnographic fieldwork, I expected that the answers would help illuminate the key elements that gave meaning to fan experiences but would not function as a demonstration of any "internal" truth.

Thus, when I proposed to do interviews, Mario agreed. In addition to asking for an individual interview in his capacity as fan club president, he strongly suggested a group conversation: to control the answers other fans could offer and to intervene in their interpretations. The group interviews (completed on two separate occasions) worked less as focus groups and more as a recorded get together. Since I knew them all very well, the limits of what should be on the record and off the record worked without any conflict. After more than 18 months of hanging out with fans, I already knew the subtleties of the intimate narratives, the limits of what could be publicized and what should be kept in the inner circle of the fan club and the deeply conscious reflexivity (almost a Giddensian double hermeneutics) of their discourses in the public sphere and impact it could have on Gilda's memory.[2]

The devil inside

Mario never got along very well with institutionalized Catholicism; after receiving a scholarship to Catholic school, he was expelled in first grade for stealing. "Instead of saving me, they threw me out! They thought I had the devil inside," Mario would say years later, laughing. Similarly, he had almost no socialization in the devotional practices so commonly described among working class sectors, since none of his family members are saint devotees. From a young age he was involved with the San Lorenzo *barra brava*.[3] As Toledo (1996) and Monteiro (2003) have shown, joining a *barra brava* it is not just about leisure and male sociability, but implies particular obligations and responsibilities. The practices and meanings Mario developed as a diehard fan inform his experiences of masculinity, morality, and also his relationship to the sacred. We will see how Mario uses the resources obtained from practices learned from the San Lorenzo *hinchada* to relate not only to Gilda but also to his devotion to Our Lady of the Miraculous Medal, to whom he was introduced to as a young adult through fellow soccer fans.

According to Mario, "you can ask Gilda for miracles," but he does not believe that these miracles are what attract followers to Gilda, and instead focuses on the passion and the *aguante*[4] that the singer embodies. Although he does admit that Gilda is his "guide" who "helped" him get custody of his daughter after he separated from her mother, in addition to "rescuing" him from drugs and being the one who puts people in his path and also removes them to help him and make his life easier. In the case of Gilda, fandom which slips toward religious devotion becomes enticingly simple, not only because she already has devotees but because fans often seem to act as such, asking for miracles, making promises, praying—including Mario. However, in emic terms, a fan and a devotee represent different attachments, whose specificity can be occluded by the use of the metaphor. To perform its function effectively, the metaphor requires two separate and distinctive entities that can be used interchangably. The separation between devotion and fanaticism among Gilda's followers, is far from clear-cut. It is what Velho (1995: 81) identifies as a "theology of harmony," a perspective that instead of operating by the principle of contradiction (either/or), uses the principle of inclusion (and/and). Gilda is an extraordinary being[5] beyond her capacity to peform miracles. And Gilda's miracles do not make her a saint, as Catholic dogma may understand. Any deceased person, fans agreed, could perform a miracle": "your dead grandma, if you ask her," Mario explained, "could help you." That's why, fans could identify themselves as such, and not as devotees, while asking her for help. Someone who identifies his/herself as a Gilda fan, does not preclude asking her for a miracle.

Mario signifies his experience of the sacred and his relationship with Gilda using concepts, feelings and values coined in his experience as a soccer fan. To Mario, passion is not a synonym of devotion nor is sacrifice a synonym for *aguante*. Soccer is more than just a metaphor for religiosity or a sort of "secular religion." Soccer, fandom and religion are three of a kind, deeply related as practices of the sacred.

Here I analyze soccer through native practices and meanings: *aguante*, passion, fighting, fandom and flag. This is not about soccer as a sport or a performance: it is an anchored matrix made unique by a "club," a "team" and "colours," all of which embody a specific morality that allows the fans to construct and signify their practices of the sacred.

The Gilda flag

Many years before the events that I describe in this section, Mario started thinking about make a giant flag in honour of Gilda. It took him a decade to raise the money. It was January in a particularly torrid summer when the preparations began. At the end of July, when a neighbour had sewed together the patches of cotton canvas into a single rectangle measuring 17×7 m, the drawing and painting began. The flag had Gilda's name with a heart on either side and down below, in smaller text, "*Fan's club oficial, No me arrepiento de este amor. La leyenda continúa....*"[6] Gilda's face had been painted in the middle of the flag and surrounded by stars.

On the last Sunday of August, when the flag was finally finished, those of us involved in its final stage—the painting—stood applauding before the canvas, which had been rolled out onto the floor of the neighbourhood center where we had gathered a few weeks earlier to begin the work. After reflecting on the image in silence for a few minutes, Mario began to sob and embraced one of the other participants. A few minutes later, after the wave of emotion had passed, he opened the door for Raul, a fan club member who lived too far away to afford to come and help make the flag. Mario stood alongside Raul, anxiously awaiting his reaction.

Raul entered the room, glanced at the flag and murmured, "Nice job!" Then he turned his back on it to join the circle of people drinking *mate*. Mario, clearly hoping he would be more impressed, started telling him about what it had taken to make the Gilda flag a reality: the many meetings of the fan club members, the long hours of work and dedication, the small mistakes on the canvas and the crafty ways they had resolved them. Raul interrupted him, a little annoyed: as he remembered it, the flag did not respect the original design that several fans had come up with during the previous summer. Mario insisted that it was a faithful replica of the model. Shaking his head emphatically, Raul contradicted him. It wasn't "exactly the same," he said, and a heated argument ensued. Immediately, Mario asked Adriana for the model, which had been drawn on graph paper and kept under a plastic report cover so that it would not get ruined. When Adriana gave Raul the paper, he claimed this too varied from the version he had seen several months ago. "Didn't you tell me that *La leyenda continúa* was going to be in blue and yellow?" Blue and yellow are the colours of the popular Boca Juniors soccer team. Mario told him they were, but that Carlos—who "is a Boca fan too"—had proposed going with black because otherwise there were just going to be too many colours. Mario didn't say that the blue and red letters of the fan club's name—the same colours as his soccer team, San Lorenzo—were part of what made it impossible to add blue and yellow letters to the flag as well. Raul continued insisting that Mario had promised that the flag would feature the Boca team colours and Mario countered that the stars around the singer's head were yellow. Raul remained unconvinced and barely glanced at the flag for the rest of the afternoon.

Raul is a Boca fan but unlike Mario he is not a member of the soccer club's *hinchada*, or fan group. However, like his friend, he refers to his two great loves—his soccer club and Gilda—as a passion. "I talk to Gilda and she understands me because she's a fan of the same team as me," he explains. Raul often puts a picture of Gilda on the Boca jersey and asks her to let the team win. In the most important matches, he repeats the same ritual to ensure that all goes well: he does not go to the match or even listen to it on the radio. Instead, he spends the day at the cemetery next to Gilda's grave and does not even find out how the game went until the cemetery closes. Boca always win whenever he does this, Raul explained: the singer makes sure his team won.

After the flag had been rolled up and put away, we went walking toward the bus stop. Mario again asked Raul what he thought of the flag, because "you haven't said a word about it." Raul countered, "Yes I did! I said, nice job." Mario wanted more; he reiterated the amount of work involved, the time, the money. "You don't make a flag like this every day." And then he concluded, "You've got no passion." Offended, Raul came back at him with, "What do you want me to do? Jump up and down? Shout?" Adriana murmured, "We all applauded when the flag was finished." Mario nodded in agreement. Exasperated, Raul continued: "Well then let me applaud," and clapping his hands together, he sarcastically added, "Bravo!" Mario, annoyed, repeated his verdict: "You've got no passion." Raul responded, "My passion ran out when you took out the yellow and blue!" Mario, now angry but calm, countered, "I already explained why!" No one else exchanged a word with Raul until his bus arrived.

This argument reveals how for a group of young men the relationship with sacred beings is sustained by a logic embedded in soccer meanings. Their relationship with Gilda is built on practices, feelings and meanings created in a context of football and *hinchadas*. The argument over the colours chosen for the words on the flag goes back to a dispute over "the colours of passion"; for Mario, these are blue and red (the San Lorenzo colours) and for Raul, blue and yellow (Boca). These colours are key components of their relationship to the sacred and specifically, as we will see below, of Gilda's own consecration.

The colours of passion

Mario had based the flag's design on a San Lorenzo fan flag: the wording, the final phrase, the hearts in the place of crows the San Lorenzo mascot. Since I imagined that the colours chosen for the flag were no coincidence, I intentionally suggested using green or pink on the flag when Mario first told me about the project. But Mario was adamant on this point: "The Gilda flag has to have the Cyclone's colours"[7] he exclaimed, as if there were no other option.

Using the club's colours goes way beyond a mere insignia. Mario wears sports apparel with his club's colours almost every day. The room at his parent's home where he resides is filled with the warm presence of both Gilda and San Lorenzo. Mario and his daughter share the room in the well-built but shabby house where his father, his younger brother, a friend of the brother, his older brother and wife and two young daughters also reside. The kitchen serves as a communal area, where the family comes together to watch TV, drink *mate* or cook, while each of the four bedrooms serves as a separate family abode. Mario's room is neat and orderly. The closet, the door and the window are painted blue and red. Above the bed, a shelf displays a series of objects associated with Gilda: a framed picture of Gilda dressed in blue smiles down, with a smaller photo of his daughter tucked into a corner of the frame. There is a plethora of prayer cards, tiny grottos with virgins inside, medallions, cards, old cassettes. These objects come together like an altar with a blue and red rosary and a plaster statuette of Our Lady of the Miraculous Medal. And the blue of Gilda's dress in countless copies of the picture match the San Lorenzo colours that predominate throughout the room. Analysing the use of Christian objects in everyday life, McDannell (1995) argues that they collaborate in establishing and maintaining relationships between supernatural beings and devotees, including their family and friends. Objects help to create a religious landscape that tells the devotees and the world who they are. In this sense, the objects exposed in Mario's home are not just decorations or an external reflection of intimate experiences, but a way to experience the sacred—through Gilda, the Virgin Mary and San Lorenzo colours—in continual interaction with and through those objects.

Mario has a tattoo of his daughter's name on one forearm and Gilda's name on the other. He did his own tattoos, piercing himself with a needle dipped in blue and red ink. These tattoos are self-inflicted scars that show his connection to these two women; they display his bravery and his ability to take the pain. The chosen colours reinforce these meanings as they represent the feeling of "passion" that his daughter and Gilda inspire and, at the same time, reveal the *aguante* necessary to sustain the passion.

One afternoon, as we drew the letters of the fan club's name with a pencil on the canvas, Adriana complained that she was tired and that it was difficult to draw some of the letters. Carlos, who was nearby pouring *mate*, said that the fan club's name was too long and Adriana jokingly proposed they change it. Mario understood that she was joking but nonetheless clarified that a name was a name. Plus, he added, it expressed what he felt: "because what it says is true: I'm not sorry for loving Gilda." I joked that maybe he could find another way to say it, since the letter "r" was one of the hardest to draw. Mario reflected for a moment. "Well, it could say 'passion'—'I'm not sorry for this passion,' which is the same thing ..." because "she worked herself to the bone to get to where she got. That's why we're passionate about her." Then he added, "In music, things didn't always go her way, it's not just about the miracles."

> My family always listened to *cumbia*. I was one of those kids who was never at home—I didn't even come home to sleep. I'd go to the *bailanta* instead.... And one day at the *bailanta*, this woman was singing and someone told me her name was Gilda. Then I saw her on that program on Channel 2 and they mentioned where she'd be playing. *So I went to see her and I liked what she did. So little by little, I became a follower. You know, it was like becoming a San Lorenzo fan, just like that, you see, just like I'm a San Lorenzo fan, I gradually became a follower. That's the way the passion comes together....* Like, that day the TV program announced where she'd be playing and I went there and was there all night. Then, well, what happened, happened. She died." (emphasis added)

The "passion" is the expression of the feeling that Gilda awakens in many of her followers: indescribable, it manifests itself and is shown through very specific gestures. There is no "passion" without *aguante* and *aguante* is driven by passion. *Aguante* is a call to action, a battle cry; it demands a response. *Aguante* is about not turning and running, not complaining, holding one's ground. It is about confronting risky situations and bearing the pain if necessary. It also refers to loyalty and fervor for the team one is rooting for. Yet the concept of *aguante* is not limited to the *hinchadas*. In this regard, Garriga Zucal and Moreira (2006) propose understanding *aguante* as a capital that the fans possess and which allows them to establish interactions with other actors in spaces outside of soccer. *Aguante* configures a category that criss-crosses the world of working class men. In this sense, *aguante* is a fundamental value for those who worship Gilda. While in the stadium, *aguante* manifests itself through chanting and fighting with rivals, in the case of Gilda it requires *following her*, that is, being with her, making her presence noted, sharing and preserving her memory. Going to the cemetery and spending the day with her, regardless of whether it is raining or frightfully hot; making flags (the bigger, the better); being the first to arrive and the last to leave the cemetery on the dates when she is commemorated; and tattooing her name or face on one's body are proof of *aguante*.

If it is possible to understand the relationship of some of Gilda's followers in terms of sacrifice, as traditionally argued by ethnographers who study popular religion in Latin America, for a group of young men, the relationship with Gilda—and also with other saints and the Virgin

Mary—is all about *aguante*. They define their relationship and feeling for Gilda not as a devotion but as a passion. This goes beyond a semantic difference: the content of each concept is not the same, creating distinct patterns and configurations of everyday contexts.

The *Trapo*[8]

One of the afternoons we worked on the flag, Mario, Adriana and I painted the red letters of the phrase "I'm not sorry ..." while Carlos and Jorge talked and passed the *mate* around. Every time Mario finished a letter, he would stand up to grab a smoke or drink a *mate*, and he'd take another look at the flag and exclaim how well it was coming along. He brought over Jorge to show him how perfect the letters were and how nice the red looked on the white background. He argued with Carlos as to what colour blue would work best for the rest of the letters needed to spell out the fan club's name and he mentioned, as he had repeatedly over the past few days, how envious other Gilda followers would be, especially Gabriel.

Then he again told the story of that Sunday afternoon when Gabriel—at the time, a friend of Mario's and vice-president of the fan club—had gone to the cemetery with his brothers and mother, to cut in half the flag the two of them had made together. Gabriel had been asking Mario to pay him back for half the cost of the fabric, a total of ten pesos. Mario told him he needed more time to get the money together. But Gabriel did not want to wait any longer: "He went right on in with the scissors to cut it in half." And that's what he did, with his brothers and mother alongside him because Gabriel alone was incapable—too much of a coward—to do it on his own. Mario's story always ended the same: "How can you cut a Gilda flag? You don't cut Gilda's flag.... It just shows how much he loves her.... He doesn't care about her at all if he's capable of cutting her flag!"

Jorge and Adriana interjected throughout the story, always to agree with Mario, who seemed at some points angry and at others, hurt and upset. In his research on San Lorenzo's diehard fans, Garriga Zucal (2007: 104) describes the *trapos* as though they were money. Transferring the flags from one place to another by car requires the organization of a "special operative similar to the ones cops perform when watch cash in and out of a bank." Cutting the flag, then, can be understood as ripping up money: simply insane.

Although I had heard the same story a dozen times, that day I realized how important the flags are. They are more than just an insignia or a banner and they communicate much more than a message or a belonging: they are imbued with the aura of whoever inspires them. They are both an offering (it's "a flag FOR Gilda") in which one invests money, work and effort as well as an icon or sacred representation similar to a statue of a saint (it's "Gilda's flag,") that cannot be damaged or destroyed without harming Gilda herself. The flag must thus be preserved and maintained. The enormous size of the *trapo*, on the other hand, reveals the love for Gilda, the hard work Mario is willing to do for her and how important she is for him. This flag was Mario's dream: "Since the day she died, I've been thinking about making her a flag." That's why, Mario noted, it was the biggest Gilda flag ever made, a logic shared by others who make smaller but more elaborate flags, embroidered with sequins, meticulously and colourfully painted, getting her face just right. On the other hand, there was the size of the letters of the singer's name (2 × 2 m), which took up a third of the canvas. The message that included the name of the fan club, as Mario had noted, "I'm not sorry for this love." The picture of Gilda in the middle and the final phrase, "The legend lives on," which, as Mario emphasized, indicated that not only had the fan club been following her for a decade but that Gilda was still with them, something that the flag corroborates. That is when I realized the extent to which Mario's insomnia for the past few weeks—an insomnia he always attributed to the flag—denoted the importance of this *trapo*. It wasn't just enthusiasm, it wasn't just feeling nervous because of the difficult task before him, it wasn't only his sense of owing it to her or needing to finish it for the anniversary of her death on September 7. It was also Mario's dream—as a wish, a feeling that it was nearly impossible to finish, a project to be completed at some future date. But now it was coming true, "just the way I imagined it." It was once again making Gilda visible at a point where the media no longer wrote about her and the radios no longer played her songs. It was an offering *for* and a representation *of* Gilda and, in both respects, part of a different sphere of the world, one that was in a very specific way, sacred.

Pride

To express what he feels for Gilda, Mario utilizes a vocabulary more associated with soccer than with religion. He himself makes the comparison, which is based on specific practices stemming from his experience as a San Lorenzo fan:[9]

MARIO: Gilda is like soccer... she's my passion! It's passion! It's like this: if the gang isn't out there among the fans, the fans don't say a word. They don't yell. They aren't proud of their colours …

ELOÍSA: Who's the gang?

MARIO: The gang, you know, the *barra brava*.... When the gang's not there yelling, causing a ruckus, the bleachers are dead, just like in Spain. Spain doesn't have *barras bravas*: the fans just sit there, not moving, applauding. *They're not passionate about their team colours.* Here [in the Gilda fan club] it's pretty much the same: *we're Gilda's gang, we make noise, we're passionate. (…) If it weren't for us, Gilda would be dead and forgotten"* (emphasis added).

Thus, Gilda and the fan club are what make Mario proud:

M: [Gilda] makes me feel more confident in terms of my own life…. While I think about her or do things for her, I grow, I mature, I learn things about life … I find a reason for doing everything I have to do … It's like something that lifts me up, you know, something lifting you up, and you say, "OK, I'm going to do this." That's what she does for me: she lifts me up. I may fall, you know, but when I get up, I'm stronger for it. When it comes to love, to work, to health … because when you don't have a job, it's a *bajón* and you don't even want to talk to anyone. You close yourself off and suddenly you hear her or you think of her and sometimes I can feel her words inside of me…. And that lifts you up. And then the *bajón* passes. I start doing things or I go out … and *that's when you start feeling proud….*

E: So it's about pride?

M: Yes. *That's what I feel. Pride* (italics mine).

Gilda and his relationship with Gilda allow Mario to create a place for his inner life, a place for reflection. This doesn't necessarily mean finding his inner divinity but rather recovering a more profane feeling of dwelling within a sacred order that contains this divinity. In the quote above, Mario does not claim that Gilda solves all his problems; he has not gotten a job or found love thanks to Gilda. Instead, he claims that by appropriating her words ("I can feel her words inside of me,"), he is better able to deal with his problems.

In such moments of reflection, Mario is not praying or asking for anything. Many times, he is not even "talking" with Gilda. Yet it is through Gilda and her words that he achieves "some degree of reflexivity about themselves and their desires, and … some 'penetration' into the ways in which they are formed by circumstances," (Ortner, 2005: 34) thus allowing him to take a step back and react, "start doing things." He is thus able to recover from the *bajón* (a mixture of sadness, lack of desire and desperation that was originally used to refer to the cocaine comedown) and find strength, but also mature, and recover his sense of pride, making him a man.

Conclusions

Similar to other popular (not canonized) deceased persons who perform miracles and become saints, Gilda's following can be analyzed as a devotional relationship, according to literature on the sociology of popular religions. This triangular relationship involves a request, a miracle and a promise: Gilda is asked for a broad range of favors, which she often grants, and the recipient returns the favor with different shows of his or her appreciation. If a more limited definition of popular religiosity is used, Mario's case might not be included, as his relationship with Gilda does not exactly fit the model of devotional gestures as they are commonly described. This is because even when Mario makes requests and then fulfils his promises when Gilda works miracles for him, his connection to the singer is established through a wide range of resources that exceeds the "religious." Mario, who is by no means exceptional, illustrates the limits of using the modern conceptualization of religion as the sphere[10] for discussing experiences of the sacred among working urban sectors in Latin America and of approaching the sacred as "radically other," as seen in the very definition of popular religiosity and a number of works on this topic (Parker, 2006; Martín, 2009; Possamai, 2015).

However, Gilda meets other conditions that could perhaps allow her to be considered part of a texture of the sacred; because her exceptional features go beyond miracles "that any dead person could do," and because she is in fact so exceptional that she instils "passion." Mario, like many of the singer's followers, does not overlook the fact that Gilda has the power to act in the world of the living and perform miracles. However, in order to understand what Gilda is really about, her followers say, it is necessary to remove her from the sphere of "religion." At a glance, Mario could be interpreted as a devotee of Gilda, who would thus be considered a saint. However, he rejects this definition and instead affirms that his relationship with Gilda "has nothing to do with religion."

For Mario and his friends, excluding Gilda from the sphere of "religion" should not be interpreted either as an attempt at secularization or as a strict appropriation of Catholic orthodoxy. Instead, this very exclusion allows us to observe how different resources contribute to making Gilda into an extraordinary being, a part of the world's sacred texture that exceeds religion. In this chapter, I have approached a specific configuration of practices of sacralization, a configuration where soccer fandom becomes a privileged matrix. In Mario's practices of sacralization, resources are brought into play, that stem less from saint devotions than from lessons learned from the *hinchada*: colours, passion, *aguante*, *trapos*. San Lorenzo was thus his Catechism.

Notes

1 Perhaps because they are organized around a deceased, one of the main activities of fans' clubs dedicated to Gilda or Elvis Presley (cf. Doss, 1999: 56) are the fundraising and goods donation. This is the case also for Star Trek fans, as shown by Jindra (1999) and McLaren (1999), though charities are performed according to the "philosophy" of the series.

2 Unless otherwise indicated, all quotations in the following pages are from my field notes, taken over the months that I spent with respondents in informal gatherings. Most of the quotes are things that were repeated, over and over, across different discourses and contexts. These narratives helped me better understand respondent experiences of fandom and, in particular, their articulation of *passion*.

3 The *barras bravas* or *hinchadas* are the groups of diehard fans with tight yet complex ties to their soccer club. A *barra brava* is an organized group, which has a recognizable hierarchy. There is a section in the stadiums reserved for them; they generally get free tickets and even a "kickback" from concessions and other club revenues. Most importantly, their members are usually the ones involved in violence against rival fans both inside and outside the stadium.

4 *Aguante*, a native concept to members of soccer *hinchadas* refers to courage, strength and physical and mental resistance (Alabarces, 2002, 2004; Alabarces, Garriga Zucal and Moreira, 2008, Elbaum, 1998; Garriga Zucal, 2005, 2007 among others), which has also been appropriated as a moral category by the youths, not necessarily linked to *hinchadas*, in urban popular sectors (Martín, 2004).

5 Similarly to Latour's *"factish"* (Latour, 2002), the concept of *extraordinary beings* (Martín, 2008) acknowledges the human origin of consecrated persons, places and times, pointing out the direct, active and constitutive human agency and the possible transitory nature of the status of "extrarodinarity."

6 Official Fan Club. I'm not sorry for loving you. The legend lives on....

7 "Cyclone" is the nickname of the San Lorenzo club.

8 Literally translated as rag, *trapo* is the soccer term used to affectionately refer to the team flag.

9 These data are taken from individual interview with Mario conducted at his home and tape-recorded.

10 If religion as a separate sphere of differentiated practices—far from being a self-evident object in "modern" societies—is a historically dated epistemological construction that requires perspective and analysis in each empirical context, that is because the modern ideology of division into spheres upon which it is based should also be questioned (cf. Latour, 1994).

References

Aden, R. (1999), *Popular Stories and Promised Lands. Fan Cultures and Symbolic Pilgrimages*. Tuscaloosa, London: The University of Alabama Press.

Alabarces, P. (2002), "'Aguante' and repression: football, politics and violence in Argentina," in: E. Dunning, P. Murphy, I. Waddington and A. Astrinakis, eds. *Fighting Fans. Football Hooliganism as a World Phenomenon*. Dublin: University College Dublin Press, 23–36.

Alabarces, P. (2004), *Crónicas del aguante. Fútbol, violencia y política*. Capital Intelectual: Buenos Aires.

Alabarces, P. Garriga Zucal, J. and Moreira, M (2008), "El 'aguante' y las hinchadas argentinas: una relación violenta" *Horizontes Antropológicos* 14(30): 113–136.

Auyero, J. and Grimson, A. (1997), "Se dice de mí.... Notas sobre convivencias y confusiones entre etnógrafos y periodistas" *Apuntes de Investigación* 1 (1): 81–93.

Bickerdike, J. (2016), *The Secular Religion of Fandom*. London: Routledge.

Coralis, P. (2004), *Nunca te Vi, sempre te Amei: Uma análise antropológica da idolatria a Madonna em um fã-clube virtual*, Unpublished MA thesis. Social Sciences, State University of Rio de Janeiro.

Doss, E. (1999), *Elvis Culture: Fans, Faith, and Image*. Kansas: University Press of Kansas.

Duarte, L.F.D. (1986), *Da Vida Nervosa em as Classes Trabalhadoras Urbanas*. Rio de Janeiro: Graal.

Elbaum, J. (1998), "Apuntes para el 'aguante'. La construcción simbólica del cuerpo popular," in: P. Alabarces, R. Di Giano, and J. Fridenberg, eds. *Deporte y Sociedad*. Buenos Aires: Editorial Universitaria de Buenos Aires (Eudeba), 327–344.

Garriga Zucal, J. (2005), "'Soy macho porque me la aguanto'. Etnografías de las prácticas violentas y la conformación de las identidades de género masculinas," in Alabarces, P. et. al. eds. *Hinchadas*. Buenos Aries: Prometeo.

Garriga Zucal, J. (2007), *"Haciendo amigos a las piñas." Violencia y redes sociales de una hinchada de fútbol*. Buenos Aires: Prometeo.

Garriga Zucal, J. and Moreira, M.V. (2006), "El aguante. Hinchadas de fútbol entre la pasión y la violencia," in: D. Míguez and P. Semán eds. *Entre santos, cumbias y piquetes. Las culturas populares en la Argentina reciente*. Buenos Aires: Editorial Biblos.

Grimshaw, M. (2000), "I can't believe my eyes!!! The religious aesthetics of sport as postmodern salvific moments" *Implicit Religion* 3(2): 87–99.

Hills, M. (2002), *Fan Cultures*. London: Routledge.

Hulsether, M. (2000), "Like a sermon. Popular religion in Madonna videos," in: B. Forbes and J. Mahan eds. *Religion and Popular Culture in America*. Berkeley and London: University of California Press, 77–100.

Jindra, M. (1999), "'Star Trek to me is a way of life' fan expressions of Star Trek philosophy," in: J. Porter and D. McLaren eds. *Star Trek and Sacred Ground. Explorations of Star Trek, Religion, and American Culture*. New York: State University of New York Press, 217–229.

Latour, B. (1994 [1991]), *Jamais fomos modernos*. Rio de Janeiro. Editora 34.

Latour, B. (2002 [1996]), *Reflexão sobre o culto moderno dos deuses fe(i)tiches*. Bauru/SP: EDUSC.

Lever, J (1983), *Soccer Madness*. Chicago and London: The University of Chicago Press.

Martín, E. (2004), "'*Aguante lo' pibe*!': Redefinitions of 'youth' among popular sectors in an impoverished Argentina" *Sephis e-magazine*, 1(2): 5–10.

Martín, E. (2008), "Seres extraordinarios. Más allá de la devoción y de los fans, *Revista Todavia* n. 20. www.revistatodavia.com.ar/todavia27/20.sociedadestxt.html, accessed September 19, 2015.

Martín, E. (2009), "From popular religion to practices of sacralization: approaches for a conceptual discussion." *Social Compass* 56 (2): 273–285.

Martín, E. (2010), "Religion in the practice of daily life in Latin America," in: R. D. Hecht; Vincent F. Biondo. (Org.). *Religion and Everyday Life and Culture. Religion in the Practice of Daily Life in World History*. Santa Barbara, CA: Praeger, v. 1, 451–480.

Martín, E. (2017), "God is Argentinean, and also the Pope! Catholicism, popular religion and the national imagination," in: A. Possamai, B. Turner, and P. Michel, eds. *Religions, Nations and Transnationalism in Multiple Modernities*. London: Palgrave Macmillan.

McDannell, C. (1995), *Material Christianity*. *Religion and Popular Culture in America*. New Haven and London: Yale University Press.

McLaren, D. (1999), "On the Edge of Forever. Understanding the Star Trek Phenomenon as Myth," in: J. Porter and D. McLaren, eds. *Star Trek and Sacred Ground. Explorations of Star Trek, Religion and American Culture*. Albany, NY: State University of New York Press.

Monteiro, R. (2003), *Torcer, lutar, ao inimigo massacrar: Raça Rubro-Negra! Uma etnografia sobre futebol, masculinidade e violência*. Rio de Janeiro: FGV Editora.

Ortner, S. (2005), "Subjectivity and cultural critique," *Anthropological Theory* 5(1): 31–52.

Parker, C. (1996), *Popular Religion and Modernization in Latin America. A Different Logic*. New York: Orbis Books.

Parker, C. (2006), "'Magico-popular religion' in contemporary society: towards a post-western sociology of religion," in J. Beckford and J. Walliss, eds. *Theorising Religion Classical and Contemporary Debates*, Aldershot and Burlington: Ashgate, 60–74.

Porter, J. (1999), "To boldly go. Star Trek convention attendance as pilgrimage," in: J. Porter and D. McLaren, eds. *Star Trek and Sacred Ground. Explorations of Star Trek, Religion, and American Culture*. New York: State University of New York Press, 245–270.

Possamai, A. (2015), "Popular and lived religions" *Current Sociology* 63 (6): 781–799.

Rodman, J. (1996) *Elvis after Elvis. The Posthumous Career of a Living Legend*. London and New York: Routledge.

Sandvoss, C. (2005), *Fans: The Mirror of Consumption*. Malden: Polity Press.

Scholes, J. and Sassower, R. (2014), *Religion and Sports in American Culture*. New York: Routledge.

Semán, P. (2001), "Cosmológica, holista y relacional: una corriente de la religiosidad popular contemporánea" *Ciencias Sociales y Religión/ Ciências Sociais e Religião* 3 (3): 45–74.

Snyder, E. and Spreitzer, E. (1983), *Social Aspects of Sport*. New Jersey: Prentice Hall.

Toledo, L. (1996), *Torcidas organizadas de futebol*. Campinas, SP: Autores Asociados/ ANPOCS. Coleção educação física e esportes.

Velho, O. (1995), "Religião e modernidade: roteiro para uma discussão," in: O. Velho *Besta Fera: recriação do mundo*. Rio de Janeiro: Relume Dumará, 207–219.

Watson, N.J. and Parker, A. (2014) *Sport and the Christian Religion: A Systematic Review of Literature*, Newcastle upon Tyne, UK: Cambridge Scholars Publishing.

Chapter 5

Soccer victory authorized by the gods

Prophecy, popular memory and the peculiarities of place*

Olutayo Charles Adesina

Introduction

> Manchester United is my English team. But, I support Real Madrid—
> Tomisin Adewole, 7-year-old Nigerian boy.
>
> (Ojeikere, 2016)

> The African Cup of Nations will be upon us soon; 16 nations will hold
> their breaths, pray to ancestors and pay their chosen marabout or juju
> man—to bestow their strongest magic on their heroes. Charms,
> amulets, spells and even animals buried in the vicinity of a stadium
> have all been used by African teams to bring them success on the field.
> Rituals on show during the tournament, and in football leagues the
> breath of Africa, are based in Africans' deeply held religious beliefs....
>
> (Sulaiman, 2015)

The heady days of soccer provincialism of the 1980s and 1990s are long
dead and buried. The twenty-first century, regarded as the age of soccer
globalism is well into its second decade. While the Yoruba Nigerian soccer
enthusiasts of the last decades of the twentieth century accommodated and
valorized traditional and modern cultural mixtures, those of the present
century appeared enamored by the seemingly modern and global. But the
two share something in common. Both periods simultaneously affirm their
love of soccer on one hand and deny the fact that victories in soccer may
not entirely be based on any informed understanding of the game of soccer.
While some believe it is luck, others affirm the presence of certain cosmic
powers at play. How do two generations that share the same geographic
space perceive and apprehend the beautiful game? This chapter discusses
the way in which these generations of Yoruba Nigerians engage the game
of soccer. The chapter analyzes how traditional religious credo, values and
ideas have also come to incorporate a multitude of perspectives that question and at the same time reinforce old ideas of winning soccer matches.
Taking its cue from the antics and enthusiasm of Ganiyu Elekuru (a.k.a.

Baba Eleran) the head of the supporters' club of the Ibadan-based Industrial Investment and Credit Corporation (IICC) soccer club fame and his rumored love for the occult, the narrative juxtaposes the past image of soccer enthusiasm with the glory of modern soccer. It highlights the "corrupting" strains of the past available in the present. Finally, it establishes a dialogue that shows the significance of place, space and time in the game of soccer. The chapter, adopting the historical and empiricist traditions expresses the complex relationship between culture, memory, reality and the senses.

The transnational status of soccer is no longer in doubt. Many sports historians have indicated the extensive interconnections of sports and global processes (Giuliannoti and Robertson, 2007). In this day and age, therefore, should African soccer continue to be defined by traditional cultural practices in the global age? Will this attachment to cultural practice now end, most especially with the massive exposure to, cultivation, diffusion and consumption of modern cultural practices and values in the game of soccer? This is predicated on the fact of tangible points of contact between soccer practices in the Western world and Africa. Diffusing practices have received the attention of scholars in the sporting field. Kaufman and Patterson averred that "diffusing practices are most likely to be adopted when they are first made congruent with local cultural frames and understanding" (Kaufman and Patterson, 2005:82). Such was the frame of mind where it relates to soccer. Of course, it will also not be out of place to mention what Bromberger referred to as the "intensity of the passions it arouses" in people (Bromberger, 1995:293).

The most enduring aspects of such "passions" in African soccer are the beliefs in and uses of rituals, incantations, charms and amulets as tools for winning games. These have over time been very popular and powerful cultural practices in African soccer. In recent times, however, several developments have begun to shape the human mind in very different ways. The love for foreign clubs and their cultures have radically altered the soccer space in Africa and for Africans. Foreign soccer clubs and practices are now appearing as dominant cultural forces. It could be in the light of the foregoing that Giulianotti and Robertson have argued that "football's globalization must be understood in terms of the highly complex interplay of the local and the global, or the particular and universal" (Giulianotti and Robertson, 2009:xv).

The epigraphs above show two worlds and two generations that occupy the same space in contemporary Africa. Whereas the pre-1990s generations of footballers, fans and spectators were socialized in the dynamic relationship between sports, religion and culture, the younger post-1990 generation became more globalized and more enamored with the foreign than the local. But do the two different generations meet and can they ever meet? That is a question that may baffle a foreign pundit but may not necessarily trouble an African. This is because "Like all narratives of identity, stories of place take shape and drive meaning in and through a system of differences. This is who we are, and more importantly perhaps, this is who and what we are not" (Cameron, 2002:411). The modern Yoruba, just like any other African society, belong to diverse religious communities and owe allegiance to different religious institutions and creeds. These cannot be divorced from their cosmological beliefs. The views of Africa as a pluralistic multi-religious society with three religions competing for allegiance and supremacy had survived in the literature. In some of the Yoruba communities, traditional religious beliefs take precedence over Christianity and Islam, while in others, Christianity and Islam jostle for supremacy. No matter their level of exposure to modernity, however, religion, religious credo and religious practices do define a set of behaviors and perspectives—from the sacred to the mundane, politics and even sports. The commitment to and the retention of beliefs in the efficacy of invisible forces and entities and their effectiveness in human affairs is part of the ritual behavior of Africans that has survived in attenuated or mutated forms (Hoffman, 1992). This has become one of the enduring perspectives in the history of sports in Africa. A major question in this regard is, is religion compatible with modern sporting activities, notably soccer? In contemporary African societies, there seemed to be a fusion of religion and soccer not as a way of saving souls but as a pathway to soccer glory.

In spite of the influences of Christianity and Islam, traditional beliefs had remained extremely strong and influential. Although with Western and Islamic education, not many people now openly declare themselves animists or adherents of traditional religions, a significant percentage of Africans retained traditional religious beliefs and practices. In an estimate provided by Baur (1994:526–527), he revealed that by 1990 the number of the continent's people claiming to still belong to traditional African religions had dwindled to 14 percent. Notwithstanding that, however, and much into the twentieth century, a significant proportion of Africans frequently held traditional beliefs that remained extremely strong even after many attempts at so-called Islamic reforms and the growing importance of Christianity of the Pentecostal hue.

Over time, there had remained talk about "witchcraft" and "rituals" in African soccer, just like in other facets of life. As Ian Lawrence noted, this is "an inherent part of the mental and physical preparation that facilitate an important emotional and spiritual link to a player's indigenous culture" (Lawrence, 2010:85). In reference to this, this empirical and historical narrative on soccer in Yorubaland of Western Nigeria places emphasis on the complex structure of place, time and imagination.[1] This provides a significant understanding of change and continuity in African soccer world. As a result of the foregoing, the socialization process in Africa based on active instruction—a very deep, significant and thorough process—has succeeded over time in producing an all-embracing ritualized space.

Myths, rituals and festivals as well as religious experiences and expressions, have continued to play significant roles in the life of the average Yoruba person. "Rituals and rites constitute some kind of religious expression. They are a means of concretizing one's belief systems" (Adelowo, 2014:148). Africans have therefore imbibed their values and practices from the cradle and this goes on through life irrespective of their religious or educational status. The influence of faith and the intersection of the religious, moral, cultural, linguistic and metaphysical are on-going processes. The Yoruba believe that the powers of their traditional rulers (*Oba*), ancestors, elders, witches, herbalists, medicine men, diviners are all related. They believe that all good and bad take their origins from the same source—*Olodumare* (the Supreme being) (Idowu, 1962:40–41; Hallen and Sodipo, 1986). The introduction of Christianity and Islam notwithstanding, the belief in traditional gods and deities have remained strong. Bewaji's testimony reveals the impulses that ruled Yoruba society:

> When the Christian God is introduced, it becomes easy to sin all morning and afternoon and repent in the evening and have all your sins forgiven through a special dispensation of grace. This introduction created room for permissiveness that has never been witnessed in Yoruba society before. A chasm was created over which no bridge was erected. Hence people swear on the Holy Bible and Holy Qúran without qualms, while they balk when called upon to do the same for *Ogun, Sango* or some other divinities....
>
> (Bewaji, 1998: 11–12)

The attachment to tradition and indigenous religious values have remained extremely strong and potent. It was therefore not strange to understand why the field of African soccer is filled with superstitious competitors, supporters and spectators. This is as prevalent among the Yoruba people who form the focus of this study as the other ethnic groups in Nigeria; Africa's most populous country. The Yoruba who populate the Southwestern part of Nigeria are a highly urbanized and westernized group. While the former had been part of the traditional Yoruba social structure, the latter can be attributed

> to their early contact with and benefits from Western European civilization, particularly the establishment and widespread acceptance of Western education by the people. Beginning from pre-colonial times, under the tutelage of European Christian missionaries, through the colonial period till the present day, the Yoruba people accepted and employed Western education as an ideology of development....
>
> (Babalola, 2006:102)

In spite of the foregoing, the Yoruba people who today occupy the present Ekiti, Lagos, Ogun, Ondo, Osun, Oyo, and parts of Kogi and Kwara States, have retained their beliefs and traditional practices almost intact. So, when some Africans shun African cultures and traditions, others relate to them proactively. "African ideas, concepts, and norms are of value to them, no matter their level of education and wherever they are. They are the ones upholding and keeping the traditions, and they are the custodians of the autochthonous customs" (Kehinde, 2009:313). In Yoruba cosmology and imagination, the cosmos comprises several layers comprising diverse beings with sacred powers entrusted to them. "Within each layer of the cosmic sphere, several activities take place to connect the layers vertically" (Olupona, 2011:32). A personal narrative will give more significance to this (Adesina, 2016).

At Origbo Community High School (OCHS), Ipetumodu, a small community school in an area populated by the Yoruba people (now in Ife North Local Government Area of Osun State, Nigeria), an event happened in 1978 that brought to light how the supernatural was viewed in soccer. The day was supposed to be an evening of display of soccer skills between the home institution (OCHS) and the visiting Oduduwa College (OC) from Ile-Ife, a much older school located about 15 kilometres away. There was one problem, though. OC had never been beaten home or away. People had usually put this down to OC's proficient use of juju in soccer. The kick-off time was fixed for 4.00 p.m. that sunny afternoon. The whole school was excited by the prospect of OCHS beating OC for the first time in their soccer career. The expansive lawn facing the classrooms had just been mown and the distracted students viewed the well-mown lawn with keen eagerness and a high sense of anticipation. Every student had their eyes on the field while listening with one ear to the equally worried teachers. By 1.00 p.m. there was bedlam in the school. A big black bird had alighted at the center of the field, right where the ball will be placed for the kick-off at 4.00 p.m. The entire school witnessed this in horror and in one great accord, all students trooped out of the school with their teachers in tow to catch and skin the black bird alive. The bird escaped. The visiting team arrived, the game kicked off at exactly 4.00 p.m. and the home team lost. Nobody expected anything less. Not with that black bird "sent ahead" by OC. That for all times socialized an entire generation of youngsters to the "reality of juju in soccer."

A cosmology defined by culture

The belief that something supernatural—a deity or some power—definitely increases soccer wins is prevalent among modern Yoruba. Skills and dexterity are not always adequate. You need some "fortification." The belief has been widespread. This was firmly lodged both in the consciousness and memory of many Africans. How does this play out in reality? How significant is the traditional belief system in African soccer? Religion permeates all aspects of social life (Botchway, 2009). Chief Olisa Agbakoba (SAN), a former President of the Nigerian Bar Association had reaffirmed the beliefs and perspectives of Nigerians in a modern world:

> Our DNA is highly cultural and traditional. So if you look into very many families and scratch deep, you will find traditional practice masquerading as the context of Christian and Muslim worship....
>
> (Adeoye, 2015:14)

Supernatural and mystical interpretations of events on the field of play are therefore not strange to Africans (Otubusin, 2015). What usually drives supporters of particular clubs to the extent of looking for ways of winning at all cost? Animashaun (1973:10), an official of the Housing Corporation Football Club of Ibadan, Nigeria in the 1970s puts this down to fanaticism. For him, fanaticism not only breeds a desire to win at all cost, it also becomes "a way of life." But just how different is the Christian values of praying, making the signs of the cross, and singing of hymns before matches in the West from the use of juju (charms, artifacts), magic (incantations, talismans) and witchcraft by Africans on and beyond the field of play that supposedly help them to win games? Superstitions are prevalent in soccer in many parts of the world. Several African teams and their supporters have been weaned by the use of magic, totems and the esoteric in the game of soccer.

The IICC Shooting Stars (now 3SC) Football Club of Ibadan, Nigeria presented the most well known of this attachment to the deeply traditional and supernatural. In 1984, the finals of the African Champions Club Cup was held at the National Stadium in Lagos. The IICC, having lost to the Zamalek Football Club in Egypt two weeks earlier, had a return leg scheduled as part of the finals. The passion this match generated has been well captured by Adesokan (2010:59):

> The most memorable, for me, was this jingle in Yoruba, a cross between wish, incantation and malediction, a gnomic *Ase* on the airwaves, periodically played by the culture-conscious official broadcast organ, Radio O-Y-O based in Ibadan like the football team:
> *Egibiti o ri'ranosan o* (May the Egyptians be blind this day)
> *Balubalu ntáfin o* (Blurry-blurry does the albino glimpse)
> It was rumoured that the high-spirited supporters' club, headed by Mr. Ganiyu Elekuru (aka *BabaEleran* because he was a professional butcher) had even paid witchdoctors for charms and fetishes ... Mr. Elekuru would go to any length to demonstrate his support for the team, which was so total and frightening it attained the condition of

fanaticism. Two years before, during a match in Tanzania, it had taken the personal intervention of the Nigerian High Commissioner in Dar es Salaam to rescue Elekuru from a mob which suspected him of being a witchdoctor and would have lynched the daylight out of him....

Even though the IICC soccer club lost the match to Egypt and people began to scoff at the idea of the use of the supernatural in soccer, the more things change, the more they remain the same. The question that comes to mind in the light of the above is, how vulnerable are the younger generations of Africans to this old belief that some forces exist specially to help soccer career along a particularly desired path?

Soccer and the "New World Order"

The world is flat. That was the conclusion of Thomas L. Friedman (Friedman, 2006), the American journalist, columnist and author in the aftermath of the great advances in technology and communications that have put people all over the world in touch more than ever before. But how "flat" it has become is clearly revealed by the game of soccer. In the 1970s and 1980s, there were teams with immense followership in Southwestern Nigeria. But by the 1990s and 2000s they had fizzled out. A new consciousness had developed to push the old Nigerian soccer teams out of relevance. The statement from the seven-year-old boy at the beginning of the chapter is symptomatic of the new reality. The old clubs included the IICC Shooting Stars (Ibadan), Stationary Stores of Lagos, Water Corporation FC (Ibadan), Leventis United (Ibadan) and Abiola Babes (Abeokuta). The clubs in the 1970s and 1980s had a cult following. Their players walked onto the fields of play with adulation from their supporters. Their fans stormed the stadium of play in droves and hours before kick-off time. Each of the teams had its overzealous fans. There were those who were moderate and ardent. Soccer (i.e., soccer in Nigeria) with its huge following in the country and the soccer stars venerated, has over the years been embraced as a veritable avenue for making money, socializing and a major tool for display of patriotism.

By the beginning of the twenty-first century, Arsenal, Manchester United, Tottenham, Liverpool, Chelsea and Southampton had become as familiar to the Nigerian soccer enthusiast as the English crowd. They developed the same kind of enthusiasms for the clubs in the Spanish, German and the Italian Leagues. The end of the terrestrial television and the arrival of the satellite TV, structural adjustment and the expansion in global travels and government inactions have all conspired to change the orientation of Nigerian soccer fans to the global rather than the local arena. According to Foer (2005:3),

Everywhere you looked, it suddenly seemed, national borders and national identities had been swept into the dustbin of history. The best clubs now competed against one another on a near-weekly basis in transnational tournaments like the European Championships League or Latin America's Copa Libertadores. It was easy to be wildly enthusiastic about the new order.

Understanding why the ball failed to go into the net

In Africa, the game of soccer is more than just a game (Sellstrom, 2010:32). In Nigeria, it became a war that must be won by any methods—fair and foul (Solarin, 1992:4). The passion with which many people on the continent follow and consume the game of soccer is ethereal. Many live by it and for it. It is like a religion. The cultic following and its significance for Africans have bred in them a tenacity that has pushed people to certain desperation and excitement. It was therefore not strange to hear stories of witchcraft, witchdoctors and sorcery in the game (Botchway, 2009). The use of mallams, marabouts, sorcerers and witchdoctors had for long defined whether a goal goes into the net or misses the net. Human agency was as important as the intervention of any spiritual agency. But to many authorities, African belief in magic was either a superstition or a heresy. J. G. Frazer (1922) had earlier in the twentieth century described superstitious belief as a menace to civilization that needed to be eradicated. This position obviously did not find wide acceptance in Africa. Younger soccer enthusiasts interviewed seemed to agree that there are forces beyond the ordinary at work in the field of play. Even now in their sitting rooms and the viewing centers where Africans have continued to subscribe to the feelings of excitement that is explained away by the desire for a consumption of the foreign leagues, they have continued to explain soccer in terms beyond skills and perfection.

What determines African reality? It was definitely not all about the scientific standards of play. The existence of indigenous practitioners, charlatans and syndicates has done a lot to taint the game of soccer in Nigeria. On Saturday, June 13, 1970, the African Clubs Cup Soccer competition between the Stationery Stores of Lagos, Nigeria and Ashanti Kotoko of Ghana was disrupted for 15 minutes at the Liberty Stadium in Ibadan. The reason for this was that a Stationery Stores supporter had suspected that the Fez cap worn by the Ghanaian goalkeeper was a magic wand that could ward off goal-bound shots. The Ghanaian goalkeeper seemed to lend credence to this belief by protesting the removal of the cap from where it was placed on the net. The goalkeeper even ended up slapping a Nigerian soldier that had gone to remove the cap from where it was placed (Oyed, 1970: 4).

Botchway (2009) has demonstrated that in spite of the prevalence of religion and magic in African soccer, "there are counterfeit clerical agents and swindlers parading as magicians, sorcerers, juju men and witches, whose evil practices are dreaded by people, including footballers, fans and club officials." In spite of this, several soccer fans have continued to share their belief in the existence of a "force" that directs the affairs of men. Ibadan and Lagos, two of the most cosmopolitan cities in Nigeria have been home to the huge industry in the esoteric as far as soccer is concerned. The modern African in this part of the world carries with him the transgenerational supernatural dimension and the idea of the sacred in analyzing the game of soccer. Segun Odegbami (2016), a foremost soccer Nigerian striker and sports commentator has provided a creative avenue for seeing the sacred in the affairs of the game of soccer. In his criticism of Manchester United FC, he claimed:

> Take the case of Manchester United FC for example. Why is Luis Van Gaal still in charge? Under normal circumstances he should have been history by now following his monumental disappointment as the anticipated *messianic* (emphasis mine) successor to Sir Alex Ferguson. He has turned out not to be the coach that Manchester United FC were looking for when they hired him to return the team to its old winning ways and playing style established under the *legendary* (emphasis mine) Sir [Alex] Ferguson. Even the great man thought he could deliver and endorsed Van Gall for the position. Unfortunately, the experiment is a monumental failure. The old Manchester United is unrecognisable in the new team assembled by Van Gaal.

Omooba one of those who reacted to Odegbami's article online could also not refrain from bringing in the "God" factor into his comments. Odegbami had suggested that perhaps, Jose Mourinho might be hired to coach Manchester United. He asserted:

> Jose [Mourinho] that was shown the exit door on 19th of December, 2015 having been on the road to Golgotha with the blues. Only *God* (emphasis mine) arrested the calamity and the blues' fortune would have been much better now if he had been kicked out much earlier. I am not *Nostradamus* (emphasis mine), but I believe if Man U. insists on Mo, they would be heading for a disastrous season come August to December 2016. He has outlived his usefulness because he is bereft of new ideas and currently runs an easily decoded formula by the smallest BPL opponents....
>
> (Omooba's comments in Odegbami, 2016)

The spiritual dimension is sometimes present in the analysis of the beautiful game of soccer. A supporter of Manchester United believes that the erstwhile coach, Sir Alex Ferguson is an *akandaeeyan* (a strange or exotic being). The use of such words to describe a coach and his invincibility is a key recognition of that unknown force ruling the affairs of soccer. This is interpreted as a sign that he is imbued with supernatural potentials. The foregoing signified a fusion of the traditional and the modern. This clearly demonstrated a weakening of the global (best) practices in the face of local realities. Predicting the outcome of matches had sometimes rested on spiritual assumptions and the sacred source of knowledge rather than training and skills, in predicting soccer events more accurately. Taribo West, former Super Eagles of Nigeria player and an international superstar from Rivers State who grew up among the Yoruba in Shomolu, Lagos not only confirmed the existence of charms and superstitious beliefs in African soccer but his own keen involvement in the practice. He affirmed:

> Of course yes (I was involved). I don't know why people decline to talk about their involvement with charms. Football has to do with a lot of powers. When there are big events, you look at the stadium, you see people, fans invoking all kinds of things; magicians are there, voodooists are there…. In my playing days, when I was ignorant, I used to get some Mallams and *Babalawos*(traditional doctors) to make charms for us, which we took to (national) camp. Sometimes it worked, sometimes it didn't.
>
> (Aiyejina, 2015:60)

He also confirmed the widespread acceptance of the practice by club officials—from the use of magic and talismans to dependence on soothsayers:

> In some clubs, before every game, the president or leader of the club will give you a lucky charm to play with. They will tell you to put it in your boots or socks and play. It's their superstitious belief; that it can help win matches. There are some coaches who are connected to African magicians and soothsayers from Senegal, Burkina Faso, Zaire or even Nigeria. These people are consulted to give these coaches results of games even before the matches are played. These people see strange things and they can tell you with their magic and charms, what the outcome of a match will be. People believe and used it and I used it. So, why are people denying it? There are charms and rituals in football. It still exists.
>
> (Aiyejina, 2015:16)

Taribo West's testimony seemed to confirm for all times the reality of charms and rituals in African soccer. The intermingling of soccer, myths, religion and rituals has therefore remained constant in African soccer. It is a deep manifestation of the people's love for the game.

But if club officials and players routinely consult marabouts and perform rituals, there were also those who engaged in the "Metaphysical assessment" of players and matches. One of those who specialized in this in the 1980s was a well-known parapsychologist, G. O. Okunzua. He believed that picking a winning team depended not on coaching but also on "the application of extra sensory perception." For instance, seven days before the Nigeria versus Algeria World Cup match of October 10, 1981, Okunzua had written that "if Segun Odegbami captained the team Nigeria would not win the match" because "his vibrations were not synonymous with victory." He then went ahead to list the players whose aura would help Nigeria to win the second leg of the match more convincingly. He explained this further:

> On the whole it is not sufficient to choose a team because you coach the players or watch them play; it is more important to perceive what the outwardly invisible side of the player is contributing to his game. The ideal thing is to sum up and pick the team on that basis.
>
> (Okunzua, 1981:23)

Although there were no indications or confirmations that Nigerian coaches depended on the suggestions of the parapsychologists, there was no doubt that African soccer depended on both the physical and the esoteric.

Interfacing the local and the global

National honor and pride are crucial in the game of soccer but things are changing. Satellite television has indeed caused a revolution in soccer. Many soccer enthusiasts in Nigeria are hardly satisfied with the marginal improvements in the Nigerian Premier League in particular and the game of soccer in general. Efforts by the National Association of Nigerian Professional Footballers to ensure that clubs paid their players and take players' welfare more seriously have proved abortive. Virtually all Nigerian club players are being owed salaries, match bonuses or sign-on fees (Okpi, 2016). Many of the fields sighted by fans on satellite television evoke a feeling of aura and satisfaction. Not the same with Nigerian stadia.

In the 1970s, 1980s and 1990s, four of Nigeria's most popular stadia were located in the Southwest: National Stadium in Lagos; Onikan Stadium in Lagos; Teslim Balogun Stadium in Lagos; and Liberty Stadium in Ibadan. By the early 1990s, the stadia had become derelict and abandoned. By the 2000s, how difficult it has become to sever the local from the global manifested in the commentary of a sports enthusiast, Ade Ojeikere (2016). In comparing the local stadia with the global, he noted:

> Good old Onikan stadium [in Lagos, Nigeria] is still looking derelict. The management and members of the Ikorodu United FC Lagos

tried to repair the edifice ahead of its Nigerian Premier League matches [in 2016]. But the repair works could not cover the fact that it had been long abandoned. There were still structural defects but Ikorodu FC's management should be congratulated for bringing life to [the] stadium. The scruffy dressing rooms have been cleaned. The sanitary systems are functional. There is hope that the place could be better as the matches hold weekly. The drainage has been dug but not tested because the rains are not here yet. Onikan Stadium's pitch is notorious for its waterlogged conditions when it rains. In fact, I kept pinching myself at half time when I saw several sprinklers watering the pitch. It meant that there was sufficient water for the players and match officials to wash up and, perhaps, make a decent appearance at the post-match conferences *like we see in most European matches.* (emphasis mine)

How prominent the foreign soccer clubs had become in Nigeria is revealed by Mike Awoyinfa (2015), one-time editor of Nigeria's tabloid, the *Sun* newspaper. Writing on the fate of Chelsea football club on November 21, 2015, and the need to prevent his health from slipping due to the fate of the club, he affirmed:

Today, I could also have written on Jose Mourinho and how my wife barred me from watching Chelsea matches. For diehard Chelsea fans, watching Chelsea live is the easiest way to die. She doesn't want me to die with Chelsea now languishing at the bottom, threatened with relegation. Ah, life!

How difficult it has become to sever the local from the global further manifested in Ade Ojeikere's comments:

But my star attraction of the day ... [was] little Tomisin Adewole, the seven-year-old, who awed me with his faultless understanding of the trend of the [soccer] game.... His receptive knowledge of the game was stunning. Tomisin spotted a Manchester United shirt number 7. And I asked him why. Tomisin said: "I wanted to wear this shirt. You can see that my brother has his (touching his brother, Tomilola, who wore shirt number 9 but was also engrossed in the game). Manchester United is my English team. But I support Real Madrid." Tomisin's, Tomilola's and their elder brother's presence at the Onikan Stadium last Sunday [February 21, 2016] represents the new dawn of the domestic game.

(Ojeikere, 2016)

The question is, how much of the local and how much of the global will the youngster grow up to radiate? The contexts of the boy vouchsafing his support for the two foreign clubs and his father taking him to the stadium to watch local soccer develops an analytic category of the contest for the minds of young people by global and local forces. The affirmation of the foreign over the locals also came from telecommunication companies that provide Global System for Mobile (GSM) communications in Nigeria. Globacom (Glo) Nigeria limited, a Nigerian telecommunications company that started operations in August 2003 as part of its services to people also got involved in sports advertisement. Glo in one of its numerous short messages (SMS) to its customers in December 2015 had announced: "The fight for glory begins. Who do you support? The Gunners, Red devils, Blues or City? Latest Team news and more. Dial *50000*3# at just N40 for 7 days" (Glo, 2015). It never did the same for local leagues.

The enthusiasm displayed by local fans in support of their European clubs sometimes went overboard. Fans began to exhibit an uncanny attachment to European clubs. On April 27, 2016, one Toheeb Afolabi (20 years old) appeared before a court in Lagos, Nigeria for punching off a man's teeth. The accused and his neighbor were fighting over soccer matches involving two rival clubs in Europe. Afolabi was later charged to a Surulere Chief Magistrate's Court for the offence he committed contravened Section 171 of the Criminal Law of Lagos State, 2011 (*Guardian*, 2016:7).

Ayinor (2016:61) has given a roadmap to unlocking one of the knottiest questions of soccer in Nigeria. He also looked towards Europe for the sustainable solution to the concept of "victories ordained by the gods":

> I do hope that we continue to see more goals irrespective of where teams are playing. The European leagues do not understand the concept of home and away as you can win or be beaten anywhere. That's the dream for the Nigerian league too.

Conclusion

While globalization has made tremendous inroads into African consciousness and practices, the people have also increasingly asserted their place in the emerging global cultures and social spheres that have threatened to swamp them. Indigenous peoples in the modern world "have made tremendous strides in gaining recognition and respect for their cultural norms and traditions. Their agenda and strategies have evolved over time" (Cordova, 2014:29). The tensions that have emerged from the interface of the global and the local have resulted in a form of hybridization that both contribute to and contradict what it means to be a modern African. Upon analyzing this, however, it is quite obvious that a significant percentage of Nigerians have continued to live with their superstition, religious practices and beliefs, and mystic rituals. The future of the Nigerian soccer scene is, therefore, likely to remain an admixture of the local and the global.

Notes

* This is the revised version of a paper presented at the conference on "Soccer as a Global Phenomenon" organized by the Weatherhead Initiative on Global History, Harvard University, Cambridge, Massachusetts, U.S.A., April 14–16, 2016. I thank the Conference Conveners for their support and the participants, for their incisive comments on an earlier draft of the paper.

1 Interesting works on African soccer include: Ian Hawkey, *Feet of the chameleon. The story of African football* (2009); Peter Alegi, *African soccerscapes. How a continent changed the world's game.* (2010); and, Steve Bloomfield, *Africa united. How football explains Africa.* (2010).

References

Adelowo, Dada E. (2014). "Rituals, Symbols and Symbolism in Yoruba Traditional Religious Thought." In S. Oyin Abogunrin and I. Deji Ayegboyin (eds) *Under the Shelter of Olodumare: Essays in Memory of Professor E. Bolaji Idowu*, Ibadan, John Archers (Publishers).

Adeoye, Gbenro (2015). "When Politicians Fight, It's for Their Pockets – Agbakoba," *Saturday Punch*, (Lagos), November 21, p. 14.

Adesina, Olutayo Charles. August 2016. Personal Account.

Adesokan, Akin. (2010). "Ibadan, Soutin and the Puzzle of Bower's Tower." *African Cities Reader*, Available at: africancitiesreader.org.za, pp. 59–72, accessed March 15, 2016.

Aiyejina, Tana. (2015). "Taribo Finds Shelter Amidst Storms of Life," *Sunday Punch* (Lagos) newspaper, September 20, p. 60.

Animashaun, Bayo. (1973). "This Constant Rot Must Be Halted," *Nigerian Tribune* (Ibadan) newspaper, October 29, p. 10.

Awoyinfa, Mike. (2015). "Mike Enahoro's Swan Song," Saturday Sun (Lagos), November 21. Available at http://sunnewsonline.com/new/mike-enahoros-swan-song/, accessed on November 21, 2015.

Ayinor, Pius. (2016). "Awka United, Leicester and Our League," *Saturday Punch* (Lagos), February 20.

Babalola, Ademola. (2006). "Yoruba Ethnicity and the Pursuit of Western Education in Southwestern Nigeria." In Toyin Falola and Ann Genova (eds) *The Yoruba in Transition: History, Values, and Modernity*, Durham, NC, Carolina Academic Press, Chapter 6.

Baur, John. (1994). *2000 Years of Christianity in Africa: An African History, 62-1992*. Nairobi, Pauline Publications.

Bewaji, Ayotunde Isola (1998). "Olodumare: God in Yoruba Belief and the Theistic Problem of Evil." *African Studies Quarterly*, Vol. 2, Issue 1, pp. 1–17.

Botchway, Francis J. (2009). *Juju, Magic, and Witchcraft in African Soccer: Myth or Reality?* Accra, Ghana, Centre for Christian Communication and Media Research, 238pp.

Bromberger, Christian. (1995). "Football as World-View and as Ritual." *French Cultural Studies*, October 1, 6, pp. 293–311.

Cameron, Ardis. (2002). "When Strangers Bring Cameras: The Poetics and Politics of Othered Places." *American Quarterly*, September, Vol. 54, Issue 3, pp. 411–435.

Cordova, Fabiola. (2014). "Weaving Indigenous and Western Methods of Conflict Resolution in the Andes." In Akanmu G. Adebayo, Jesse J. Benjamin, and Brandon D. Lundy (eds) *Indigenous Conflict Management Strategies*, Lanham, Lexington Books, Chapter 3.

Foer, Franklin. (2005). *How Soccer Explains the World*. New York, HarperCollins.

Frazer, Sir James George. (1922). *The Golden Bough: A Study in Magic and Religion*. New York, Macmillan.

Friedman, Thomas L. (2006). *The World is Flat. A Brief History of the Twenty-First Century*. New York, Farrar, Straus & Giroux.

Giulianotti, R. and Roland Robertson. (2007). "Introduction: Sport and Globalization: Transnational Dimensions." *Global Networks*, Vol. 7, Issue 2, pp. 107–112.

Giulianotti, Richard and Roland Robertson (2009). *Globalization and Football*. London, Sage Publications, 2009.

Glo, Sender 50000. Sent: 14 December 2015. 11:42:55 am.

Guardian (Lagos). (2016). "European Football League: Man, 20, Docked for Punching Off Man's Teeth," Saturday, May 7.

Hallen, Barry and John Olubi Sodipo. (1986). *Knowledge, Belief and Witchcraft*, London, Ethnographica.

Hoffman, Shirl James. (1992). *Sport and Religion*. Champaign IL., Human Kinetics Publishers.

Idowu, Bolaji E. (1962). *Olodumare: God in Yoruba Belief*, London, Longmans.

Kaufman, Jason and Orlando Patterson, (2005). "Cross-National Cultural Diffusion: The Global Spread of Cricket." *American Sociological Review*, Vol. 70, Issue 1 (February), pp. 82–110.

Kehinde, Ayo. (2009). "Globalizing the Local, Localizing the Global: Troping Cultural Miscegenation in Recent Immigrant Nigerian Novels." In Akanmu G. Adebayo and Olutayo C. Adesina (eds), *Globalization and Transnational Migrations: Africa and Africans in the Contemporary Global System*, Newcastle upon Tyne, Cambridge Scholars Publishing.

Lawrence, Ian (2010). "The Place of Ritual in South African Professional Soccer." *International Journal of Religion and Sport*, 2, pp. 85–111.

Odegbami, Segun (2016). "The Coach Manchester United May Have Been Looking For," *Guardian* (Lagos), February 20. Available at: www.ngrguardiannews.com/2016/02/the-coach-manchester-united-may- have-been-looking-for/, accessed on February 21, 2016.

Ojeikere, Ade (2016). "New Dawn for the Local League," *The Nation Newspaper*, (Lagos, Nigeria), February 27. Available at: http://thenationonlineng.net/new-dawn-for-the-local-league/, accessed on February 27, 2016.

Okpi, Allwell. (2016). "Nigerian League Resumes With Unanswered Questions," *Saturday Punch* (Lagos), February 20, p. 59.

Okunzua, Gabriel Omotoye (1981). "Odegbami's Vibrations are Not Synonymous with Victory," *Sunday Punch* (Lagos), October 25. p. 23.

Olupona, Jacob. K. (2011). *City of 201 Gods. Ile-Ife in Time, Space, and the Imagination*, Berkeley and Los Angeles: University of California Press.

Otubusin, Idowu. (2015). Oral Interview. Otubusin was a star with the IICC Shooting Stars Football Club of Ibadan in the 1970s and 1980s, December 19.

Oyed, Izzy. (1970). "Why Blame Failures on Juju?" *Nigerian Tribune*, (Ibadan), Thursday, June 18. p. 4.

Sellstrom, Tor. (2010). "Beyond the Big Stage: Football, Reconciliation and Social Development in Africa." Accord: The African Centre for the Constructive Resolution of Dispute. *Playing for Peace*, Special Issue, June. pp. 32–47.

Solarin, Tai. (1992). "The Vain Gloriousness of Footballing," *Sunday Tribune* (Ibadan), February 2.

Sulaiman, Phillip. (2015). "African Footballers Call on Their Juju Men," 7 January. Available at: www.mediaclubssouthafrica.com/africa/4111-african-footballers-call-on-their-juju-men, accessed November 10, 2015.

Chapter 6

The church and FIFA World Cup in Ghana

A gender perspective

Rose Mary Amenga-Etego

Introduction

Soccer, known in Ghana as football, is the most popular sporting activity, both locally and internationally. Introduced to Ghana (Gold Coast) at the latter part of the nineteenth century, football was one of the leisure sports of the European merchants and colonial administrators. However, in 1903, Mr Briton, a Jamaican-born Briton and Head Teacher of the Philip Quaicoe Government Boys School in Cape Coast, introduced the game to his pupils. This led to the formation of the first football club in Ghana. This club was known as Excelsior. Since its inception, first as a leisure-time game and second as an academic (school) sporting activity, football has developed into a comprehensive and structured national game, with various national teams and a national governing body, the Ghana Football Association (GFA).

Governed by the GFA, the local clubs have been organised according to the international structure with their various divisions both for friendly and competitive matches, including the Ghana Premier League. Some of these clubs also participate and compete in African Club games. Above all, these local clubs form the resource base for the various national male teams: Black Stars (Senior team), Black Meteors (Under 23 team), Black Satellites (Under 20 team) and Starlets (Under 17 team), and the national female teams: Black Queens (Senior women's team), Black Princesses (Under 20 women's team) and Black Maidens (Under 17 women's team). Representing the nation in international matches and winning awards, these national teams have attracted the attention of the nation in terms of support and sponsorship.

Despite its development in popularity and gender inclusiveness, football remained an exclusively male game in Ghana until the late 1990s. Women's football came into the limelight in 1999 when the Black Queens participated in the 1999 FIFA Women's World Cup. Even so, women's football in Ghana was not formally launched until 2006. It was not also until 2012/2013 that the women's football Premier League was first organised. This is because, unlike their male counterparts, the female national team was formed before any serious development of women's football started at the ground level. Notwithstanding the GFA's efforts to strategically organise, promote and develop women's football, it is still bedevilled with many problems including support (fans) and sponsorship. In his response to questions before the Commission of Enquiry into the 2014 World Cup, Mr Kwesi Nyantakyi, President of GFA, underscored this when he said '[t]hough there is no sponsorship for the Women's game, for the first time, we have a well structured women's league and that is positive' (Ampaw, 2014, para. 7). Despite these loopholes, the nation currently has a growing number of women and girls football clubs in addition to the three steadily developing national women's teams.

Theory and method

Writing on 'Querying Sport Feminism: Personal or Political', Jennifer Hargreaves (2004, p. 187) made three observations that underscore the importance of this contribution. First, she noted that there is a link between sport feminism and the development of mainstream feminism hence the need to 'expose, challenge and eliminate gender-based dominant policies and practices' in sports. Second, with reference to cultural studies and cultural feminism, Hargreaves recognised the crucial role of hegemony in placing women's sports at a disadvantage. At the same time however she also argues that hegemony 'recognises that women are active agents struggling creatively for better opportunities in sport' (Hargreaves, 2004, p. 188). Her third and final significant observation for this contribution is her view that the ubiquitous treatment of women as a homogenous group with its embodied specific underpinnings is problematic. Quite similar to Hargreaves' (2004, p. 189) views on postmodernist feminists, postcolonial African feminists are intrigued with the issues of religion, patriarchy, gender, sexuality and the body as they continue to emerge in different forms of sports depending on the context. In this regard, the need to understand the nature and form of gender discrimination in Ghanaian football is an essential component of paving the way for an improved and equal opportunity for all players of the game.

Using the 2010 FIFA World Cup in South Africa as a reference point, the chapter describes how the exponential growth in the popularity and support for football in Ghana and especially among Christians is not gender inclusive. In the first place, football in Ghana is a man's game but this is not an exception, this observation is applicable to other nations (Hartmann-Tews and Pfister, 2003, p. 272; Matheson and Congdon-Hohman, 2011, p. 4). This may be partly because of women's late entrance into the game. In view of this, even though the nation currently has male and female football teams, it is still quite early to draw any meaningful gender analysis from the available data. Notwithstanding the above, there is some acknowledged inequality in the allocation of funding towards women's football in Ghana. For instance, writing on 'The Ugly Truth of Women's Football in Ghana', Akosua Addai Amoo (2016, para. 2–3) explained that apart from owing the Black Queens in unpaid bonuses; when in camp, the women receive a weekly allowance of only '30 Ghanaian cedis' while the men take '280 Ghanaian cedis'. The same thing applies to media coverage and general support in terms of moral and patronage of women's matches or other events. This disproportionate support for women's football and footballers in contemporary Ghana is not simply an endeavour to maintain hegemony and patriarchy, but rather, a despicable attempt to erode all the efforts these women's teams have put into the game as well as all the strides made on gender awareness and inclusiveness in the country.

Therefore, the need to examine some of the available data on the subject is essential in providing insights into the situation in women's football in Ghana. Besides, as the largest religious tradition in Ghana with influential public opinions, understanding the role of the church in this context vis-à-vis men's football may provide significant strategies to the development of women's football in the nation. This qualitative contribution depended on heavily on secondary data. According to Harry F. Wolcott (2001, pp. 72–75), the review of literature in a given research should not be seen as an independent synthesis of previous works. Rather, it should be integrated into the text to help situate the specific subject of research within its wider field of study. Thus in response to Wolcott's views the literature gathered in this study has been integrated into the text.

Football in Ghana

In Ghana, football is, more or less, synonymous to sports. Other sporting activities like boxing and athletics become prominent and are able to generate public interest only when competitors or athletes have made strides in international competitions. The rest, including boxing, hockey, tennis, basketball and volleyball, do not seem to attract much attention to nurture as much popular support, enthusiasm and patriotism from the Ghanaian populace. Various reasons haven been given for this disparity. However, the most common reasons centred around: easy access and less expensive [for learning and participation], adaptability and easy manoeuvring [skills], competitive display of individual skills even within the spirit of teamwork, frequency and financial gains as well as its global popularity and competitive nature.

Even so, it is difficult to understand the emotional attachment Ghanaians exhibit when the men's senior national team is playing in FIFA-organised tournaments. For instance, workers leave their offices or workplaces early to enable them go home or move to the nearest place with a good or large TV screen to watch the matches. Restaurants, drinking spots, TV repair places as well as shops become favourite gathering places for football fans to meet and watch matches together. Similarly, friends with big TV screens organise home gatherings with their peers and neighbours where they watch the matches and run their own commentaries, sometimes, alongside drinks, meals or both.

While the above deals with access (the ability) to watch the games, the 2010 FIFA World Cup in South Africa brought a paradigm shift to the way Ghanaians publicly and emotionally exhibited their sense of nationalism and patriotism through football. The Ghanaian scene was saturated with the sale of both national and football paraphernalia. Different sizes of the national flags were sold in town, market centres and on streets. Some individuals also showed their patriotism through body paintings while others clothed themselves in garments made with the national colours. Another area was the display of the national flag in people's cars, offices, homes and public buildings. Referred to in various ways as the show of support, solidarity, patriotism and nationalism, some also wore scarfs and plastic bands with the national colours around the period.

Apart from these the nation also saw an unprecedented rise in public football sponsorship. It was the first time that football in Ghana received so much sponsorship from the government, corporate bodies, industry and other channels (GNA, 2010b, para. 5). The media [TV] also received a fair share of sponsorship to telecast the matches to the Ghanaian population. Most of these sponsorship deals were however packaged with adverts and this created problems for some of the media houses because the length of time spent on adverts interfered with some of the matches.

One other area that was affected during the period was religion. Although religion and football in Ghana has a long history, the 2010 FIFA World Cup marked a new phase in the relationship between religion and footfall in the nation. To foster understanding of the latter, a brief overview of religion and football in Ghana is provided below before the discussion on church and football.

Meanwhile, significant to this section is the nature in which this growth in popular support and sponsorship continue to be one-sided and not gender inclusive. One would assume that such an excitement and support would be extended to the women's football to enable them to develop and compete favourably with their counterparts on the world stage, unfortunately, this is not so.

Religion and football in Ghana

Generally, religion and football are bedfellows in Ghana. Any reference to religion in/and football conveys some form of understanding, individually and collectively. The issue at stake, however, relates to an observation that the 2010 FIFA World Cup in South Africa marked a new phase in this relationship. The questions arising from this view include: What was the old phase of religion and football in Ghana like? How different was that from the new phase and what has that got to do with the 2010 FIFA World Cup tournament?

From popular rumour to serious allegations, many Ghanaians have come to view the nation's beloved game of football and its relationship with religion as occultic (see Ter Haar and Ellis, 2009, pp. 406–409).[1] In his dissertation on 'Football as "Quasi" Religion', Kwaku Onyina (2015, p. 59) provided a quotation that can be used to exemplify the allegations that football and religion in Ghana is occultic. The quotation by Onyina, which was extracted from a statement made by an executive member of the Accra Hearts of Oak club concerning his childhood, involved the club and its purported rituals (practices) involving youth perceived as virgins.

Besides serving as an example, this reference to Onyina's research indicates that one has to be mindful of the fact that football as a sport has both collective and individual dimensions. In a subsequent discussion with Elizabeth Amoah,[2] she observed that the notion of collectiveness should not be limited to the club or team level. She was of the view that in a study such as this, it is important to see within these broad categories, different individuals as well as groups of people. While the individuals include the individual players, managers, technical team members and fans, the category of groups may be dealing with the players, managers, technical teams and fans. In this case, whether or not each of these individuals and groups adhere to the doctrines prescribed by their own religious traditions or those of the World Religions paradigm (which prescribes devotion to one God), is an area of concern. This form of concern is however not only for football observers, but also, for its critics, who are often quick to draw a connection as to whether it is good or bad.

Notwithstanding Amoah's views on individual or group religious allegiance, it is not clear whether or not the observers and critics understand the religio-cultural context in which they find themselves. This creates another dimension to these allegations of occultism. That is to say, Ghanaians live within a context in which the indigenous worldview is still a vital component in many people's lives, instilling either fear or honour depending on one's spiritual disposition. Described variously by scholars as accommodative, adaptive, transformative and innovative (Nadel, 1954, pp. 207–229; Horton, 1971 and Olupona, 1999, pp. 31–32), it indicates the indigenous worldview's ability to survive and respond to the needs of every age. Additionally, this indigenous worldview is also called the religio-cultural heritage or simply, our culture or heritage; creating a complex link with one's identity. But it is also within this backdrop that some Ghanaians with the historically engrained tabula rasa principles and the current ambiguous stands of Charismatic/Pentecostal on indigenous religions operate. Although this contribution cannot delve further into the above outline, this background is quite essential for the understanding of the arguments in this chapter.

Interestingly, although allegations of occultism abound they are neither situated within the above discourse nor are they clearly distinguishable between the individual and the team. On the whole, Ghana's football's relationship with religion is perceived as one that is steeped in some form of occult practices. Writing on these issues, Asamoah-Gyadu (p. 240) stated that:

> Africans also generally believe that lobbying, skill, talent, ability and the right connections are by themselves not sufficient to accomplish much. They are not unimportant, but a person needs an extra push and cover to forge ahead, and the search for these advantages from the religio-theological realm is common.

This statement indicates the individuals attempt to excel in their respective roles within the team. Although an individual issue, there is no doubt such an effort can contribute to a team's performance.

At the club level, allegations that every football club, if not, most football clubs in Ghana are involved in 'ways and means' are widespread (Asamoah-Gyadu, 2015, p. 244). The phrase 'ways and means' has different interpretations. One form of interpretation is that 'ways and means' relates to some form of unconventional practices and methods used by footballers and their managers to secure successes for their clubs. Another way of interpreting the phrase is 'whatever means necessary' for success, without necessarily outlining what those are. This lends itself to all forms of unconventional relationships with ritual specialists in the various religious traditions for spiritual favour. In short, it is the context, content and outcome of these efforts that are classified as 'ways and means'.

These so-called unconventional practices are said to include prayers and the provision of concoctions (herbal or other forms of ritual preparations), powders, oils, candles, formulas and chants, as well as a variety of other spiritual items or symbols to be disposed off on the field of play. Others are rings and handkerchiefs for use by the players. At another level, the practices may involve special washing of jerseys, baths and sacrifices. It is alleged that for these practices to take place, there must be willing participants like fans, footballers and/or managers as reported by Onyina (2015, p. 59). This notwithstanding, it is the ritual specialist who determines the approach or method of assistance. Thus, it was said that even though footballers can be taken to the Mallams,[3] fetish priests (traditional priests or medicine men/women, also referred to as 'juju men') or prophets[4] (Christian leaders belonging to the AICs), their managers might decide to stand in for the players (Bonsam, 2013, p. 21).

In an attempt to identify and classify some of these ritual specialists, Nana Agyemang (2003, para. 7), once head coach of Okwawu United, was of the opinion that:

> Football and the Mallam in football, Witches, Wizards or Fetish Priests are known as Mallams. There is no difference in performance except to say that these witches are so called specialist in determining the winners and losers in a game of football.

This conceptualisation is however problematic and misleading. Although the expected result may be the same, it is erroneous to classify these different categories of actors as Mallams. Besides, the Mallams and traditional priests are not generally perceived as witches and wizards. Unless Nana Agyeman is saying that as long as the desired goal is one-sided and at the disadvantage or expense of the other, it is tantamount to the practice of witchcraft, it is quite problematic; if not, challenging to refer to the traditional priests, witches and wizards, as Mallams.

Again, even though it is possible that some of the Mallams, traditional priests and prophets may be witches and wizards; that is, in addition to the other powers and knowledge systems they possess; not all witches and wizards are Mallams, traditional priests and prophets. Hence, it is problematic to generalise all these different categories of specialists. Whatever the case may be, more information is needed to substantiate this merger. This notwithstanding, the perception that witchcraft and witch doctors are also associated with African football is wide spread. Frieder Ludwig (2015, p. 209) reports how Benjamin Koufie, a former president of the GFA and technical director of the Confédération Africaine de Football confirmed this allegation.

Notwithstanding their identity, the problem stems from the fact that these specialists are neither coaches nor technical members of clubs. It is for this reason that it is feared that their physical presence in any club or open alliance with a club could generate questions and suspicion. Yet because their services are required, it becomes paramount that they remain hidden (out of sight) and quiet even as they render the much-needed 'backdoor' services in exchange for payment. In other words, they can be described as the unseen tactical members of the clubs, whose job description is labelled 'ways and means' because they are capable of using any way or means necessary to help their clubs secure victory. So although these spiritualists apply unconventional methods, which may be referred to as spiritual performance-enhancing systems, they are free from sanctions from the sport authorities. Perhaps, this is because they are neither on the field of play or on the bench.

In line with 'ways and means' is a further allegation that some forms of budget allocations, salaries or honorarium are made available for spiritual consultations or ritual specialists who are clandestinely attached to football clubs. Thus the 'ways and means' budgets are used to pay the religious or spiritual specialists for the services they render to the clubs. With the current involvement of Pentecostal/Charismatic religious leaders, we could also argue that they would be beneficiaries of this 'ways and means' budget, that is, if they are not already doing so.

Apart from the clandestine magico-religious practices tabled above, other overt forms of religiosity are present among footballers and their fans. On the field of play, players display collective and individual religiosity when they are on the field of play. Examples include, praying together before the start of a match and when a goal is scored. Varied expressions of gratitude to God can be seen in the form of Muslims prostrating towards Mecca on the field while Christians kneel or look up as a sign of thanksgiving to God. Others also touch their forehead, chest, and shoulders to signify the cross or gratitude to the Father, Son, and the Holy Spirit. Joseph L. Price (2009, pp. 60–61) extensively discussed some of these in his article 'Playing and Praying, Sport and Spirit'.

Despite the involvement of Ghanaian footballers in the above, some Ghanaian Christians continue to view the game as evil. But this is partly due to earlier Charismatic/Pentecostal views that football and footballers are 'caught in Satan's trap through the lure of money and fame' (see Fumanti, 2013, p. 135). This perspective was however in view of the game's alleged association with Mallams and traditional priests, discussed above. By extension, in the past, born-again Christians frowned upon commercial football and its supporters. Therefore, what is new is the overt involvement of the church, especially, those in the Pentecostal/Charismatic denominations and their leaders. It is this involvement that has introduced the alleged paradigm shift in the religion-football discourse in Ghana in recent times. What is however interesting is the desire to label this new phase of Christianity or the church and football in Ghana. Therefore, unlike the former, the latter is preferably presented as the church and football in Ghana.

One other interesting discovery in this area of the study was the ability to sometimes disassociate footballer's collective religiosity, as if to say that is part of the profession, from 'the individual footballer's personal religiosity'. Although this detection is within the so-called new phase of church and football, it is of essence to our understanding of the Charismatic/Pentecostal perspective of the game in Ghana as a whole. In this context, any relationship with the alleged dislikeable practices is understood as a professional hazard, hence, the need to concentrate on the footballer's personal religiosity.

The church and football in Ghana

As stated above, the church is not left out when it comes to the game of football in Ghana. The church, both as an institution and a collection of individuals, has always been involved with football in Ghana. This is not only in terms of individual negative criticism or support for the games; but also, within its congregation and church programmes. As an institution, the church can sometimes make policies or declarations concerning football. As a church it can organise institutional prayer sessions, fasting and vigils to support specific international football games like the African Cup of Nations (CAN 2008), 2006 FIFA World Cup in Germany and 2010 FIFA World Cup, Confederations cup, inter-club games or premier leagues. Again, it may also promote football games as congregational, inter-church or youth games. On the other hand, as a collection of individuals, some church members are footballers, managers, promoters or supporters of football clubs (Roberts, 2016). In the same vein, some individual members may admire and enjoy the game, while others either dislike or are ambivalent about it. Those who like it may encourage their family members to join in and perhaps play while others may not. All these have an effect on Ghanaian football as a game.

With the involvement of Christians and churches in prayers, blessings, deliverances, predictions of scores and thanksgiving services, especially by the Charismatic/Pentecostal denominations, Ghanaian popular Christian views of football have changed tremendously within the last two decades.[5] For instance, preaching at the national thanksgiving service after the 2010 FIFA World Cup, Rt. Rev. Dr Charles Agyin-Asare, Bishop of the Word Miracle Church and Vice President of the Pentecostal Council, stated that 'the gallant success of the Stars was parallel to the exploits of David who as an underdog defeated Goliath the giant' (GNA, 2010a). Besides this, his view that 'the Black Stars achieved their success through regular prayers …' shifted the focus from allegations of occult practices to the acceptable form of prayers engineered by the Charismatic/Pentecostal churches. This is not to say that all Ghanaians have abandoned the allegations of 'ways and means' or the occult. It is only a new notion that has been added to indicate that Ghanaian football and its footballers are being rescued. In this respect, the Black Stars are abandoning the occult way for 'regular [Christian] prayers' through the interventions of Christian prayers and some powerful men of God. Agyin-Asare in this statement also implied that success only comes from Christian prayers and nothing else.

Underlying these undifferentiated allegations is the possibility that some footballers were not or are not personally involved or interested in occult practices. These others consult Charismatic/Pentecostal pastors for their personal spiritual needs and support. Pastor TB Joshua and Mensah Otabil are among these powerful men of God that are gaining the attention of some of the footballers from the national teams (Osaremen, 2016). This new form of individual church-based relationships may be expressing a need for a transparent spiritual support for footballers and their clubs. In other words, the lack of chaplains for football clubs in Ghana is a problem. It has created a void for the teams as collective bodies and for the individuals who undisputably need the spiritual succour and nourishment for the various trajectories of their football lives (Soccer News, 2016).

In as much as the church is transforming the religious dimension of football on the Ghanaian scene, so also is football changing the church, especially in the Charismatic/Pentecostal churches. For instance, church programmes in some of these churches have been re-arranged for members to either come in early for church services or activities before the start of important matches or after such matches. This started with the 2010 FIFA World Cup when members stopped attending church programmes to enable them watch football matches. To circumvent the emergent problems the churches were facing, some churches provided large TV sets within their church premises and adjusted their programmes to accommodate their members' football desires. Additionally, church programmes either ended before the start of a match or immediately after the match. This encouraged church attendance and more churches eventually adopted the approach. Since the 2010 FIFA World Cup in South Africa, many churches now have TV sets in their church premises and programmes are continually rescheduled to make room for football matches that are considered important. This is a significant shift from the past when the church would have preached against it as worldly desires.

With the exception of a few key matches in the National Premier League, however, the above argument of rescheduling programmes in churches in favour of football matches does not apply to local club or friendly games. Thus apart from major international games, in which Ghanaian national teams are participating and performing well, it is the English Premier Leagues (EPL) that has taken over this area of popular church-football discourse in Accra. Speaking to Ike Baffour, a member of the Action Chapel International and student of the Department for the Study of Religions, University of Ghana, he affirmed the practice as a phenomenon known as the Premier League Services. He explained how the approach has attracted some 'football lovers' (football fans as new members) to some churches. Baffour however explained that the phenomenon is not limited to the newer Charismatic/Pentecostal churches. He named the Calvary Baptist Church at Adabraka, Accra as a concrete example where the practice is quite effective in drawing new members to the church.

It is quite clear that in as much as some of the earlier involvement of the church (with reference to the AIC churches and their prophets) in football is criticised as part of the occult, the current relationship between the church and football in Ghana is also unsettling. To understand this polarisation of the church and football in Ghana, however, a short historical reference is necessary. That is to say, the church's historical identity in Africa as a civilising religion to a continent whose religion it derogatorily described as pagan, idolatry and fetish, and its subsequent attempt to delink the people and their religion, is crucial in providing the foundation for this discourse. Arguably, the difficult task of cleansing and disconnecting the inhabitants with their indigenous religions resulted in the application of tabula rasa in some communities. This effort by the church eventually produced the dual Christian worldview in which the AICs and Charismatic/Pentecostals currently operate. That is, the AICs with their indigenous inclination on the one hand and the Charismatic/Pentecostals with their overt dissociation with the indigenous religions on the other.

As part of the society, however, the church must be interested, if not involved in, its (national) activities. This notwithstanding, it must not allow itself to be pulled along. The emerging criticism is that the church must remember that even though it is in the world, it is not of the world; hence, it must remain strong and not give in to some of these influences. The other strand of the argument is centred on the view that football is a kind of religion, consequently, a force to reckon with. Therefore, bringing it into the church space and allowing it to influence church programmes is quite problematic (see Fitzgerald, 2000, pp. 103–104). In other words, using TV sets in church premises for football matches and organising EPL Services is appalling. Perhaps, like Robert J. Higgs and Michael C. Braswell in their book *An Unholy Alliance* (2004, p. 29), '[o]ne symbolic purpose of the sacred is to remind us of the holy, not with pride allied with nationalism, ethnicity, or gender but with humility before the everlasting and the inconceivable', hence, the church and football, especially on church premises is an unholy alliance.

Despite these developments, it is argued that the turning point in the popular religion-football discourse in Ghana started with the 2008 African Cup of Nations (CAN 2008) that was hosted in Ghana. That was the time the church in Ghana started to pray for the national team, the Black Stars to excel in the competition. It is alleged prayers were said both in official Sunday church services as well as auxiliary church programmes. It is believed that, even though the national team did not win, it set the tone for further future involvement. For instance, in an article entitled 'Football [Soccer] and Nationalism: the Ghanaian Experience', the author, an unidentified high commissioner, writing after the CAN 2008 stated:

> Football, or soccer has always been a unifying force and this year's games played just that role. The tournament served as a rallying point of nationalism not only for Ghana but for all countries which participated. Love for one's country showed through frenzied support for

national teams with incredible display of national symbols and colours. The Ghana national flag, exhibiting our national colours, adorned nearly every vehicle, home, office, street and building. These colours were worn as attires either fully or partially and decorated nearly every piece of architecture. The national flag flew everywhere! Ghanaians dressed in national colours to their places of worship and some churches sang the Ghana national anthem as though it was an item in the church hymnal! Such was the passion and nationalism that, for once, the entire country was united – unified in support of the Black Stars![6]

In addition to CAN 2008 there is the media. It is good to acknowledge that the 2010 World Cup received prominence in Ghanaian popular life and football discourses because of the national team's efforts, the Black Stars' advancement to the quarter-final stage, even so, one cannot deny that the explosive nature of the 2010 World Cup was enhanced because of the growth and development of the media (Maguire, 2006, pp. 435–446). The constant broadcast of news, reviews and replay of football matches got people interested and involved. Besides, the 2010 games did not only interrupt church programmes but businesses as well. For these reasons, discussions on the church and football in Ghana need to include the role of the media. This notwithstanding, the current study cannot fulfil this aspect.

Women's football in Ghana

The emergence of women in the Ghanaian football scene was quite a surprise. This was because women's football was not nurtured or developed from the ground (grass-root-school or regional level) in the country. Their presence in the country came to the limelight when they were participating in the FIFA Women's World Cup in 1999. Notwithstanding their background, their performance bewildered many in the nation.

With regards to the church as an institution, not much is heard concerning women's football. As such, it is not clear if this is part of the church's own stereotyping of gender roles, or it is simply a reflection of what is going on in the Ghanaian society. Besides, one is not sure if this lack of interest or silent treatment is because of the current absence of the saviour complex in female football. By this, I am referring to the lack of popular allegations of occult practices, as it is the case with men's football.

Generally, there is no serious national interest in the women's game in all levels at the moment. They have not yet captured the attention of the public; hence, their games do not affect church attendance in anyway. Consequently, the church has not made provisions for them or their fans, even though there may be occasional prayers for their success in some churches; that is, if the public is made aware of their matches. Institutionally, church committees generally organise football matches for men and male youth and picnics with other games for women, girls and children. In other words, these institutional (church) structures are yet to overcome the prevailing gender boundaries in the church and society (Thompson, 2007).

As indicated by the above respondent, one of the problems surrounding the relationship between women's football and the church in Ghana is partly influenced by the media, the nature of media coverage. In a caption 'Queens host Egypt, Meteors off to Congo' by Selorm Yaw Dovia (2015), I was quite surprised to read that Ghana's Black Queens drew 1–1 with Egypt on their last leg in Egypt and were waiting for their return match at home. Although this match was crucial, their last match to advance into the qualifiers, the Ghanaian population was oblivious about such a major tournament on home soil, the same with their previous away match. The manner with which the GFA and Ghanaian media gave that important match a low key was quite shocking because it would have been very different if it were the Black Stars.

In an article on 'A Piece on Women's Football in Ghana', the *Sports Crusader* enumerates a number of pertinent problems confronting women's football in the nation. In addition to sponsorship, the *Sports* Crusader states the following:

> The major challenges facing women's football in the country has got a variety of angles as both the government and the football associations are doing little to help. Women football is seen as an alien sport in the country as a lot of people even kicked against it when it was introduced in the country. Many were those who kicked against it on traditional grounds branding football as a game for men hence women who showed interest in the game were discouraged. Again, the traditions – norms and values – of the country which doesn't endorse women's football, has made it difficult for good and qualified football administrators to take over the administration of women's football. Only few people with interest in the sports do it with or without any technical know-how. This has made the development of the sport difficult in Ghana. Of course, fans play a key role in the development of any sport, but the patronage of women's football in Ghana by fans is very slowly killing the enthusiasm and the zeal the players will require to peak.[7]

Perhaps, one might excuse the private sector and general public on certain grounds but not the government, especially, on the payment of bonuses. On 25 September 2015, some Ghanaians were appalled to hear that the government had refused to pay the Black Queens their winning bonuses even after they had won gold at the All African Games. As though that was not enough, the hotel they were put in after their return sacked them from their premises. If one considers the fact that the Black Stars threatened the nation during the 2014 FIFA World Cup in Brazil and the government paid them their money while the tournament had not ended and when it did, they did not win a medal, it is just unimaginable that the Black Queens were treated in such a shameful manner. There is no doubt in this case that their gender was a crucial factor in this unequal treatment (Al-Smith, 2015).[8]

Although culture has had an enormous influence on football in Ghana, I wonder if the problems with women's football are simply cultural. Yet, this is not surprising, Gertrud Pfister and Ilse Hartmann-Tews (2003, p. 1) made a similar statement in the chapter entitled 'Women and sport in Comparative and international perspectives: Issues, aims and theoretical approaches':

> Physical activities are always intertwined with the structures, norms and ideals of a society, and they always mirror that society's gender order and gender hierarchy. Therefore, in many countries all over the world and in all phases of history, women have played a specific, but often marginal, role in traditional games, dances and physical activities.

This notwithstanding, the Black Queens have taken part in most FIFA Women's World Cup Championships since their debut in 1999. In a similar way, both the Under 20 and Under 17 women's teams have participated at these levels of FIFA Women's World Cups. They have also performed creditably at the African Women's Championships. Although they have not yet won the coveted trophy, these are said to be great achievements, considering the fact that women's football has no strong grounding in the nation.

Conclusion

Discourses on the church and football in Ghana are still simmering. As indicated above, this is not to say that the involvement of the church in football in the country is new. Rather, it has to do with the nature of its involvement. While the former was clandestine and associated with the AICs and its prophets, the latter is public and aligned with popular Charismatic/Pentecostal churches and their pastors. It is this nature of the church's involvement that has produced the polarised discourse in which the former is included in the allegations of the occult while the latter is linked with the church; this polarisation is deeply rooted in the nature and history of the church in Ghana.

Additionally, the late entry of women and girls into the nation's favourite game alongside the slow development of the sector and lack of popular appeal and support has placed women's football in the nation in an unequal footing. This has an effect on any meaningful gender analysis on the topic. However, with the gradual development of female football clubs and the emergence of the National Women's Premier League as well as the continuous qualifications of the women's national teams for international competitions, they may soon win the hearts and minds of Ghana's football fans and sponsors. This might not only raise their game and status in relative comparison to the men but may gradually enable them to make their way into the church. That is, not simply as members of congregations because some already are, but as a collective body engaging the institution's (church) attention with pride and accompanied by prayers. It is through this that women's football can also influence the structure of church programmes.

Apart from promoting good health and creating wealth, fame, power and prestige for the players and members of the team, Ghanaians cannot deny the fact that football has contributed immensely to their national pride, identity, unity, nation building and development. With the public involvement of the church, especially the Charismatic/Pentecostal churches, and the compromises that are taking place in the church's stance in favour of football and membership, there is no doubt that the church is entering into dialogue with football as a sport. Whether this is done consciously or unconsciously, Ghanaian football has already started wrestling with the church for attention, space and time through its programmes and attendance.

Notes

1 It is important to note that the use of the word occult or occultic in this study is more or less a descriptive term for the clandestine ways in which these relationships and practices are negotiated and/or carried out. It should also be noted that the study was conducted in a university setting; hence, respondents are influenced by their education and other belief systems including contemporary Ghanaian Pentecostal/Charismatic Christianity. This notwithstanding, these popular perspectives of the occult do not engage any of the critical analysis established by Ter Haar and Ellis.

2 Elizabeth Amoah is an Associate Professor of Religious Studies in the Department for the Study of Religions, University of Ghana. With over 30 years' teaching experience in African Indigenous/Traditional Religions and West African Church History, she was interviewed at the Main Campus.

3 The Mallam is a corruption of the Islamic *Mu'alim*, which means teacher. However, the popular understanding of the Mallam in Ghanaian football relates to those Islamic clerics involved in magico-religious practices.

4 This refers to prophets/prophetesses belonging to the African Independent Churches. However, caution is needed with the contemporary use of the term because some leaders of the Pentecostal/Charismatic churches also use the term.

5 Sports News, 'Nigerian Pastor TB Joshua Predicts Draw in Ghana–Egypt Clash', *Modern Ghana*. 15 October 2013. www.modernghana.com/sports/496650/2/nigerian-pastor-tb-joshua-predicts-draw-in-ghana-e.html.

6 'Football [Soccer] and Nationalism: the Ghanaian Experience'. www.ghc-ca. com/newsletter/news-jan-feb-2008.pdf.
7 'A Piece on Women's Football in Ghana', *Sports Crusader*. www.sportscrusader. com/a-piece-on-womens-football-on-ghana/.
8 Admin, 'Government refuses to pay bonuses to Black Queen after winning gold at AAG', Ghana News. 25 September 2015. www.newsghana.com.gh/ government-refuses-to-pay-bonus-to-black-queens-after-winning-gold-at-aag/. See also, Gary Al-Smith, 'Black Queen bonuses still unpaid', *Super Sports*. 25 September 2015.

References

A piece on women's football in Ghana. *Sports Crusader*. www.sportscrusader.com/ a-piece-on-womens-football-on-ghana/, accessed 28 May 2015.

Admin. (2015, 25 September). Government refuses to pay bonuses to Black Queen after winning gold at AAG. *Ghana News*. www.newsghana.com.gh/ government-refuses-to-pay-bonus-to-black-queens-after-winning-gold-at-aag/, accessed 28 May 2015.

Agyemang, N. (2003, 15 October). Is there football after juju? The Ghanaian experience. *Sports News*. www.modernghana.com/sports/42663/2/is-there-football-after-juju-the-ghanaian-experien.html, accessed 25 May 2015.

Al-Smith, G. (2015, 25 September). Black Queen bonuses still unpaid. *Super Sports*.

Amoo, A. A. (2016, April). The ugly truth about women's football in Ghana: Its an open truth that women's football will always play second fiddle to men's. http:// pulse.com.gh/sports/features/opinion-the-ugly-truth-about-womens-football-in-ghana-id4888643.html, accessed 7 January 2016.

Ampaw, M. O. (2014, October). Ghana has excelled in women football. *GhanaWeb*. http://ghanaweb.com/mobile/wap/article.php?ID=328640, accessed 8 January 2016.

Asamoah-Gyadu, J. K. (2015). Christianity and sports: Religious functionaries and Charismatic Prophets in Ghana soccer. *Studies in World Christianity*, 21(3), 239–259.

Bonsam, K. (2013, 21 October). TB Joshua should not be thanked for Ghana's win over Egypt. http://ghanasoccernet.com/tb-joshua-thanked-ghanas-win-egypt-kwaku-bonsam, accessed 28 May 2015.

Dovia, S. Y. (2015) Queens host Egypt, Meteors off to Congo. Graphic Online. www.graphic.com.gh. Accessed on 28 May 2015.

Fitzgerald, T. (2000). *The Ideology of Religious Studies*. New York and Oxford: Oxford University Press.

Football [Soccer] and nationalism: The Ghanaian experience. www.ghc-ca.com/ newsletter/news-jan-feb-2008.pdf, accessed 8 January 2016.

Fumanti, M. (2013). Blank chicken, white chicken: patriotism, morality and the aesthetics of fandom in the 2008 African Cup of Nations in Accra. In Baller, S. Miescher, G. and Rassool, C. (eds) *Global Perspectives on Football in Africa: Visualising the Game*. 126–138. London and New York: Routledge.

GNA [Ghana News Agency]. (2010, 11 July). National thanksgiving service offered Black Stars.www.ghanaweb.com/GhanaHomePage/religion/National-Thanksgiving-Service-offered-Black-Stars-185886, accessed 29 May 2015.

GNA [Ghana News Agency]. (2010, 30 July). $US15 Million Spent of 2010 World Cup – Minister. GhanaWeb. www.ghanaweb.com/GhanaHome Page/NewsArchive/US15-million-spent-on-2010-World-Cup-Minister-187178, accessed February 2016.

Hargreaves, J. (2004). Querying sport feminism: Personal or political. In R. Giulian-otti (ed.). *Sport and Modern Social Theorists.* 187–205. Basingstoke: Palgrave.

Hartmann-Tews, I. and Pfister, G. (2003). Women's inclusion in sport: Inter-national & comparative findings. In I. Hartmann-Tews and G. Pfister (eds). *Sport and Women: Social Issues in International Perspective.* 266–280. London and New York: Routledge.

Higgs, R. J. and Braswell, M. C. (2004). *An Unholy Alliance: The Sacred and Modern Sports.* Macon, GA: Mercer University Press.

Horton, R. (1971, April). African conversion. *Africa: Journal of International African Institute,* 41(2), 85–108.

Ludwig, F. (2015). Football, culture and religion: Varieties of intersections. *Studies in World Christianity,* 21(3), 201–222. www.euppublishing.com/doi/pdfplus/10.3366/swc.2015.0124, accessed 2 June 2016.

Maguire, J. (2006). Sport and globalization: Key issues, phases, and trends. In A. A. Raney and J. Bryant (eds), *Handbook of Sports and Media.* 435–446. New York and London: Routledge.

Matheson, V. A. and Congdon-Hohman, J. (2011, August). International Women's Soccer and Gender Inequality: Revisited. College of the Holy Cross. http://college.holycross.edu/RePEc/hcx/Matheson-Congdon_WomensSoccer.pdf, accessed 25 May 2015.

Nadel, F. S. (1954). *Nupe Religion.* London: Routledge and Kegan Paul.

Olupona, J. K. (1991). Major issues in the study of African Traditional Religion. In J. K. Olupana (ed.). *African Traditional Religions in contemporary society.* 25–34. New York: International Religious Foundation.

Onyina, K. (2015, March). Football as a 'quasi' religion: A case study of the rituals and symbols of Accra Hearts of Oak fans. MPhil. Dissertation. University of Ghana, Legon.

Osaremen, E. J. (2016). Prophet Tb Joshua in fresh trouble with ex-Ghanaian footballer, Richard Kingston over alleged wife's witchcraft confession 'I Was Hypnotised'—Wife. Nigeriafilms .com. www.nigeriafilms.com/news/18850/48/prophet-tb-joshua-in-fresh-trouble-with-ex-ghanaia.html.

Pfister, G. and Hartmann-Tews, I. (2003). Women and sport in comparative and international perspectives: Issues, aims and theoretical approaches. In I. Hartmann-Tews and G. Pfister (eds). *Sport and Women: Social Issues in Inter-national Perspective.* 1–14. London and New York: Routledge.

Price, J. L. (2009). Playing and praying, sport and spirit: The forms and functions of prayer in sports. *International Journal of Religion and Sport,* 1, 55–80.

Roberts, J. (2016, 31 January). Gideon Baah talks about football and religion. (Inter-view with Gidean Baah). *Ghanaweb.* www.ghanaweb.com/GhanaHomePage/Sports Archive/Interview-Gideon-Baah-talks-about-football-and-religion-411861, accessed 11 February 2016.

Soccer News. (2016). Ghanaian footballers love spiritual help-Otabil. GhanaWeb. www.ghanaweb.com/GhanaHomePage/soccer/Ghanaian-footballers-are-ungrateful-Otabil-412645, accessed 11 February 2016.

Sports News. (2013). Nigerian pastor TB Joshua predicts draw in Ghana-Egypt clash. *Modern Ghana.* www.modernghana.com/sports/496650/2/nigerian-pastor-tb-joshua-predicts-draw-in-ghana-e.html, accessed 28 May 2015.

Thompson, S. M. (2007). Sport, gender, and feminism. In J. Maguire and K. Young (eds), *Theory, Sport and Society.* 105–127. Bingley, UK: Emerald.

Ter Haar, G. and Ellis, S. (2009). The occult does not exist: A response to Terence Ranger. *Africa,* 79(3), 399–412. DOI: 10.3366/E0001972009000874.

Wolcott, H. F. (2001). *Writing up – Qualitative research.* Thousand Oaks, London and New Delhi: Sage Publication.

Chapter 7

Religion and sport in multireligious Nigeria

The case of Kaduna City Interfaith Football Club

Corey L. Williams

Introduction

While religious conflict remains the most prominent story related to Nigeria's multireligious composition, the intersection of sport and religion offers opportunities for exploring and better understanding the complexity of Muslim–Christian encounters. Given the pervasiveness of religion in Nigeria and the importance placed on football for both entertainment and social unification, it is little wonder that religious organisations have become directly involved in utilising the sport for their own purposes. This chapter explores a number of Lagos-based football clubs owned by Christian organisations before transitioning to a case study of the Kaduna City Interfaith Football Club. The case offers a range of insights about how football has been used as a means to bring people together and act as a powerful bridge in the midst of violence and tension.

> Waiting for the bus to fill up and reach (beyond) maximum capacity was the hardest part of the journey, thanks to the lack of physical space, steaming humidity and the hawkers constantly swarming around the vehicles.... Just as I savoured a lull in the noise, an old blind beggar woman, guided on the shoulder by her young relative, sang Islamic prayers and shook a tambourine by my window. This noise, combined with the heat and cacophony of shouting and horn tooting, almost sent me over the edge ... [a short time later] A man boarded the minibus and stooped in front of the passengers to bellow the gospel at us. 'Brothers and sisters, before we complete this journey, let us pray!' Everyone lowered their heads and closed their eyes while the preacher called for the 'blood of Christ to cover this bus and protect us from thieves'. By the time the bus pulled out of the motor park and rattled along the expressway, we had received a full service of hymn, prayers, and a sermon steaming with ideological fervour ... I learnt from this point onward that there was no need to attend church in Nigeria – the church always found me no matter where I hid.[1]

This Lagos public transportation story from Noo Saro-Wiwa's, *Looking for Transwonderland* (2012), illustrates perfectly the pervasiveness of religiosity in contemporary Nigeria. Manifestations of religion are omnipresent across the country; from its sprawling urban centres to rural villages, coasts to deserts, physical and non-physical religious phenomena are bountiful and boundless. Whether part of the rising elite or the marginalised poor, there are unending opportunities to, as scholar Thomas Tweed puts it, 'intensify joy and confront suffering'.[2] Religious rituals, both private and public, are ubiquitous and reported belief in God is nearly universal.[3] As a recent Pew Research survey reveals, Nigeria is one of the most religious places on the planet with 87 per cent of Nigerians attending religious services at least once per week, 92 per cent praying daily, and 94 per cent absolutely certain of their belief in God.[4] But not only is Nigeria extremely religious, it is also truly multireligious, as one of the few countries in the world in which no single religious group or tradition commands a dominant majority.[5]

Religion and conflict

The most prominent story related to this multireligious composition in contemporary Nigeria is undoubtedly one of religious conflict. Indeed, almost 60 per cent of Nigerians claim that religious conflict is a very big problem in their country. This is the highest in Africa.[6] Events related to the Shari'a crises, the Danish cartoon and Miss World controversies, and violence and kidnappings at the hands of Islamist groups like Jamā'a Ahl al-sunnah li-da'wa wa al-jihād, better known as Boko Haram, and related splinter groups such as Jama'atu Ansarul Muslimina Fi Biladis-Sudan, better known as Ansaru, have solidified the popular perception that Nigeria is undergoing a clash of civilisations – depicted unequivocally in sensational headlines as religious warfare.[7] While each case of conflict is diverse and complex, conditions in Nigeria have created a powerful role for religious identity – an identity that bonds communities, as well as divides them in a myriad of competitions. As Afe Adogame notes about this process:

> The failure of successive governments to improve the general socio-economic conditions in Nigeria has led to the belief by some segments of the civil society that religion is the panacea to both individual and collective problems. Thus, religious communities have provided significant channels for the expressions of frustration as well as an avenue to legitimize alternative source of conflict resolution. Closely related are the politicization of religion and the religionization of politics by some religious entrepreneurs. The quest and scramble for political power has partly occurred within the framework of religion in ways that reinforced ethnic and regional antagonism ... the mixture of religion and partisan politics promotes mutual distrust and suspicion to

the extent that virtually every national issue is seen with religious lenses.[8]

While pundits speculate that a lethal combination of economic, political, and ethnic factors are also at play, there is very little completed research to verify these claims. In lieu of the situation that Adogame outlines, studies of multireligious Nigeria tend to be confined to examining violent flashpoints between Muslims and Christians in a few select regions of northern Nigeria, portraying it as a place of ruin, with widespread violence and rioting in the name of religion – further entrenching the depiction of a one-dimensional, facile discourse of brutal clash and intolerance. Yet, as Benjamin F. Soares has noted regarding Muslim-Christian encounters throughout all of Africa:

> their interactions in Africa are still not properly understood ... there is a vast array of possibilities between the idealised notion of the peaceful coexistence of Muslims and Christians and Bernard Lewis's notion of the 'clash of civilizations' that Samuel Huntington has popularised and made to seem inevitable.[9]

Religion and football in Nigeria

One such space where there are opportunities to explore the complexity of Muslim-Christian encounters is at the intersection of sport and religion. In Nigeria, this is especially apparent with football, which is generally considered Nigeria's national sport and is the most widely played. As a recent *Lonely Planet* travel guide claims, 'Football is the only game that matters in Nigeria'.[10] For those who know Nigeria well, this is hardly an exaggeration. In the relation between football and religion, one need look no further than the Super Eagles, which is Nigeria's male national football team. As Eruteyan Joseph Jeroh has commented:

> It seems apparent that few (if any) institutions have the ability of bringing people together the way sport does. This is primarily because the popularity of sports cuts across race, social class, gender and age barriers. Nigerians, irrespective of education, occupation, tribe or religion, unite to back the national football team (the Super Eagles) once there is any major competition.[11]

Daniel Agbiboa has noted a similar conclusion in relation to national identity in Nigeria: 'In fact, the only time when Nigerians share a sense of national identity is when the national football team – fondly known as the 'Super Eagles' – is having a match'.[12] Many share this idea that sport and football in particular has an ability to contribute some sense of unity in a country that has often been divided on the basis of factors such as ethnicity and religion. As Francisca Ordega, a player for Nigeria's female national football team, recently remarked about the ability of the sport to bond together members from different religious traditions: 'We are one, Muslim, Christian, nothing ... we serve the same God.'[13]

Given the pervasiveness of religion in Nigeria and the importance placed on football for both entertainment and social unification, it is little wonder that religious organisations have become directly involved in utilising the sport for their own purposes. This is especially true of Christian organisations and in recent years a number of football clubs have been initiated and funded by churches.[14] Two of the most well known groups are 'COD United FC', established by the City of David branch of the Redeemed Christian Church of God (RCCG), and 'MFM FC', established by Mountain of Fire and Miracles Ministries. Both Lagos-based clubs were founded in 2007 and now play in the same tier of the Nigerian National League (NNL). Given their links to Christian organisations and the close proximity of their respective prayer camps along the Lagos-Ibadan Expressway, a rivalry has developed and matches between the clubs are fittingly referred to as the 'Holy Ghost Derby'. On the website description, COD United FC says that it has the 'sole purpose of bringing the light of God to football'.[15] This religious aspect of the club is perhaps most visible in the club anthem[16] that is sung at the start of their home matches:

> We are COD United
> A Royal Priesthood
> Chosen Generation
> We Stand for Integrity
> and Excellence for all to Learn
> For Christ, Who is the Ruler
> He is the Lion of the Tribe of Judah
> He is the Alpha and Omega
> That's why we're Proud
> To lift His Name on Highest
> We lift His Name, Highest (4 Times)
> Halleluyah (4 Times)

Despite such an overt Christian display, both COD United FC and MFM FC have both Christians and Muslims on their squads. As MFM FC coach, Nduka Ugbade has remarked, 'There are Muslim players among them and nobody is forced to practice Christianity.'[17]

Another recent iteration of Christian organisations owning multireligious football clubs is 'My People FC', established by the Synagogue Church of All Nations in 2008. According to Prophet T. B. Joshua, the head of the Synagogue and also the founder of the club, football is an integral part of assisting youths and helping with nation building, but it also has an explicitly Christian dimension. As he stated in an interview shortly after the club was established:

> You know, as a [Christian] believer, you must use all proper means to help our youths in this country ... sports is a vital instrument in nation building, little wonder why so many of our youths are embracing it. My vision is to use sports to draw most of our youth out of satanic hands ... it is not for any monetary gain, it is all about soul winning through sports.[18]

Joshua's vision has also included direct involvement with the Super Eagles as a spiritual mentor and financier.[19] Yet, despite Joshua's overtly Christian mission, My People FC's coach, Attia Yusuf, recruits both Christians and Muslims. According to Yusuf, 'There is no discrimination within the team, everybody, no matter their tribe or religion is welcome, as long as you are disciplined and can play football.'[20]

Interestingly, this multireligious composition has created a downplaying of religious differences in each of these teams. All members of the teams pray together and unite around their shared belief in God. As Chairman of MFM FC, Godwin Enakhena, has stated: 'In MFM, prayer is one of our strong points. So it's compulsory that the team prays before a game, at half time and at the end of every game.'[21] Indeed, the team is well known for praying for close to an hour before each match. However, while the teams allow their players to practice their religion freely, there are requirements for attending certain church services. For instance, with COD United FC, all players are required to attend a church service at the RCCG headquarters during the last Sunday of the month. A similar convention can also be found within the stated core values of each team. For instance, the 'DIET Program' of COD United FC, includes both general core values of 'Discipline, Integrity, Excellence, and Teamwork', while also being underlined with verses from the Bible. As demonstrated from their website:

> Discipline: Training to act in accordance with rules. 'So then each one of us shall give account of himself to God' (Rom 14:7). Integrity: To be transparent, authentic, honest and trustworthy. We should be the same throughout even when no one is watching. 'Integrity should guide you, but a double life will destroy you' (Proverbs 11:3). Excellence: Do all things with all your heart and complete seriousness. 'Whatever you do, work at it with all your heart, as working for the Lord, not for men' (Colossians 3:23–24). Teamwork: Cooperative or coordinated effort on the part of a group of people acting together as a team with a common goal. 'We are encouraged to be one, united together in spirit and purpose' (Philippians 2:1–5).[22]

Thus, while religious differences are largely downplayed on the pitch, these Christian-owned clubs openly require even their Muslim players to attend their church services on occasion and their core values are directly linked with the Bible.

Kaduna City Interfaith Football Club

While these clubs are officially sponsored by Christian organisations, there are also many grassroots efforts, such as Kaduna City Interfaith FC. The following section offers a case study of this club and the diverse ways that sport and religion intersect and are viewed in this multi-religious group. The data is based on a combination of participant observation, informal conversations, six research interviews conducted with members of the group from January–February 2010, and email correspondence in November 2015.

Kaduna City Interfaith FC was established in 2000 by a small group of Christians in response to the conflict surrounding what has since become known as the Kaduna Riots. While there were undoubtedly many factors involved, most pundits agree that the conflict was directly linked with the decision by the Kaduna State Government to partially implement *Shari'a*. *Shari'a* is the main body of civil and criminal law for Muslims and is separate from the secular court system. However, unlike many other northern Nigerian states that had also recently adopted some form of *Shari'a*, Kaduna State was known to have a large portion of both Christians and Muslims and a majority of Christians opposed the implementation.[23] In fact, the Kaduna branch of the Christian Association of Nigeria (CAN) led a public protest against it. Counter protests led to rioting and violence that resulted in the deaths of an estimated 1,000–5,000 people, with many other thousands injured and displaced, and massive property damage.

It was in this midst that club founders, Thomas Jimiko and Osita Achike, began to think about starting a football club in the city of Kaduna that was aimed at uniting Christians and Muslims. I first met Thomas and Osita at a restaurant in Kaduna nearby the house I was staying in January 2010. Initially, I overheard them discussing that it had been ten years since the Kaduna Riots. We struck up a conversation and they began to tell me about an upcoming event they had planned with their football club to commemorate the Kaduna Riots. In subsequent interviews they told me about why they had started the club and how they viewed football as a powerful unifier in Nigeria. According to Thomas:

> There was madness everywhere in those days after *Shari'a*. People who had known each other their entire lives were killing each other … there was no trust between Christians and Muslims. Neighbours were burning neighbours' houses to the ground … in those days after Osita

and I talked about ways of getting around this madness. The only thing, the only thing we could imagine that would bring people together was football. It has power in Nigeria to do this. Religion was dividing us and killing us actually, but football unites people. It doesn't matter, you see, what religion you come from, what ethnicity you come from.

Osita offered a similar perspective:

The problem wasn't really *Shari'a*. That was just a spark. The problem was that people were not listening to each other. They were willing to kill, but not listen and dialogue ... religion was being used to divide Nigerians ... the same is true of ethnicity. It does not unite us.... Football is a sport that tears down any barriers. When football is being played, you see, Nigerians come together. This is why we thought of football when the city was being torn to pieces.

Whereas factors like religion and ethnicity were seen to be causing division, Thomas and Osita believed they could utilise football as a way to bring people together from different groups. At the same time, while the Kaduna Riots catalysed their interest, they also approached the possibility of starting a football club with their religious perspectives in mind. As Thomas recalled in an interview:

Osita and I are Pentecostal Christians ... the Bible tells us that we should be people of peace, not violence. The killings in Kaduna had nothing to do with Christianity. It is just people twisting the Bible to cause chaos ... in the Bible though we see Jesus using every means at hand to bring people together in peace ... if Jesus were alive today in Nigeria he would be using football to break down barriers and build peace. Jesus would be the ultimate football fan because of how much joy and unity it brings ... Jesus is all about reconciliation and that is what we hoped the club could achieve by using football to mediate the process.

Osita also added his own perspective:

This is nonsense this killing in the name of religion. No one who reads about Jesus should think it is allowable. Christians are told to promote peace, not war ... Christians and Muslims should be the best of friends. Yes, of course we can disagree and have conflict, but not with violence. This is never permitted ... the problem is that people use religion and *Shari'a* to divide, but Christianity and Islam can be also used to preach against the hate. This is what is normal and not the violence

... but sometimes we need other reasons like football to get us in the same place anymore because of the damage that has been done between communities. Football can be used as a bridge to reconcile people. At least that is what we are trying to accomplish.

Despite their view that religion had been used to divide Nigerians, Thomas and Osita were hopeful that their Christian beliefs could counter such division by focusing on aspects like peace building and reconciliation. Yet, as Osita remarked, given the situation in Kaduna a sport like football made it possible to bring people together in the first instance.

In terms of organisation, the Kaduna City Interfaith FC has remained at the grassroots level. It has no official connection with other leagues. The main activity involves a bi-weekly match among the club players at a public field. Each player must pay for their own kit as they have no sponsors and do not ask for donations. As the founders, Thomas and Osita, made very clear, this is intentional. They fear that asking churches or other organisations to get involved financially might spoil their non-hierarchical approach. This sets it apart from many of the other faith-based football clubs in Nigeria that have institutional support. As a result, however, the club has no assets and has remained relatively small. They have a devoted group of approximately 30 players and they now use WhatsApp Messenger to schedule matches and plan the roster. During my time with the club in 2010, this included about 20 players who identified as Christian and ten players who identified as Muslim.

I was invited to play with the group on several occasions and subsequently interviewed four additional players. This included two Muslims, Audu Babangida and Mohammed Ibrahim, and two Christians, Joseph Azuka, and Abraham Ugonna. In these interviews, I was most interested in why they joined the club, how they understand sport, and how this intersects with their religious beliefs. All four interviewees indicated that they joined the club in order to counteract what they see as a furthering divide within Kaduna. According to Joseph:

We used to live next to each other here in Kaduna ... Muslims and Christians shopping together and living in the same streets, but this is not the case today. The violence has meant that Christians and Muslims are moving away from each other. We do not know each other like before and we are divided more than ever ... this is why I joined the club. I am here to go against these forces. I am here to live and have fun with my Muslim and Christian brothers ... I think even being together and playing football is a spiritual experience. There have been times when Kaduna is falling apart around us and we still play together. This is really incredible, even miraculous, because we could be killing each other ... this speaks to the power of football to give us a reason to come together in a positive context to prevent conflict in the first place ... then the community building and reconciliation can begin.

Audu also affirmed this perspective:

I joined because being with these brothers is about unity. We are all Nigerians, we are all Africans, we all believe in God ... but Kaduna has had so many problems that the city is split apart. When I heard about this club, I thought, wow, this is how I can play a part in rebuilding trust. Instead of giving into the problem or ignoring all of our issues, I am here to work for unity and peace ... it is a way to actually fight against the violence in a peaceful and enjoyable way and to prevent conflict ... this means that anyone can have the power to change our city.

In terms of how the interviewees understand sport and how this intersects with their religious beliefs, I received a range of responses. For instance, according to Abraham:

God has given us sports like football. It is truly a gift because it is beautiful and it involves every part of our being – both bodies and spirits ... I feel most alive and connected to God when I am playing football. Our club, we play football in God's name. When we come together we are doing what God wants to happen in Kaduna and everywhere. God wants us to live with each other peacefully ... football necessitates being with others, so it is a communal activity. You cannot do it alone. The Bible tells us that being together in a group, like a church, is a spiritual endeavor. Sport is actually a spiritual endeavor as well if you think about it because it requires being with people.

Joseph offered similar ideas, but also focused on the physical and playful aspects of sport and how these interact with his understanding of Christianity:

There is no doubt that all sports are from God ... we are told in the Bible that we are created for community and sport can help us do this ... God also created us to be active and strong. To play football you must train and use your mind. It keeps you physically healthy and this is a godly practice ... it is of course a lot of fun as well, which is okay because God created us to enjoy his creation. Playing is not just for children. When we play a sport and enjoy it we are really enjoying God because he created our ability to play in the first place.

While the football club has managed to stay intact for 15 years, there have been many challenges that have at times caused conflicts. According to the founders, Thomas and Osita, one of the most persistent challenges is related to players in the club attempting to proselytise other players who identify with a different religion. While the club has openly debated having a rule that disallows proselytising, they have chosen not to put such a rule in place. According to Osita:

> Such a rule would take away from our purpose to bring people together and dialogue. We want conversations to be as open as possible ... who is to say what is dialogue and sharing and what becomes an evangelistic effort? Every one of us would be glad to see others come to our own faith, but we also do not wish to push others away because the point is to keep the dialogue going. While this is not perfect, we believe it is the best option.

While there is no rule, the club does speak about the following phrase often: 'God first, religion second'. The idea is that first and foremost all of the players believe and follow God. This is what unites them and brings commonality. When playing with the club, this element is expected to supersede any talk of religions and the differences between them. Interestingly, this commonality is also supposed to mean that regardless of whether they are Christian or Muslim, all of the players are expected to pray together before and after matches. Again, the prayers are expected to touch upon what the players have in common, rather than mentioning elements they do not share. For instance, I recorded one of the prayers by a self-identifying Christian at a club match in February 2010:

> We pray to you, God, and we are united in our efforts to praise and worship you. You are almighty and are in control of this team and this field. We come together because you have called each of us here to forget about our differences. God, you are the only power that is able to overcome the evil in this world. We submit our will to yours. It is not about us. It is about what you are doing in us. We come here as Christians, Muslims, and this does not matter. Our religion is only in second place. God, you are in first place and we ask that you protect us today from injury and any harm. Give us the strength to play well and enjoy your creation. We pray in your almighty name, Amen.

Beyond praying together, efforts to find commonality are also found in the club logo and anthem. The logo features simple symbols of a cross and a crescent contained within a circle. According to members of the club, this logo signifies that Christianity and Islam are within the same family and have common ground. As well, the club anthem, which is sung by the team before and after matches, contains a similar theme:

> We are Kaduna City Interfaith FC,
> With God as our witnesses,
> We praise and we strive,
> To bring our city together,
> To unite once again,
> Hooray, hooray!
> Football brings us together,
> God first, religion second,
> We fight together,
> We give it our best,
> Brothers, family, united
> Hooray, hooray!

Despite these efforts to focus on common ground, several players remarked that the club has not avoided conflict entirely. For instance, in 2013 a Christian member of the club converted to Islam with the direct influence by a Muslim member of the club. This caused many to be concerned that the purpose of the club was being undermined. According to Thomas, both players ended up leaving the club. As he recalled in our email correspondence in November 2015:

> This was a very difficult season for us because many disagreed and there were arguments about this. We founded this club with the intention to bring people together, right? But what happens when you bring very religious people together is that they talk and discuss their faith … how can we expect to come together and not talk about our faith? Football is a real bridge and it is hard to control what comes across that bridge … in this case both players left the club because they wanted to only talk about their religion. Most other players disagreed and they left. So there was conflict, but not too much. I was very happy about this because in Kaduna it can very quickly get out of control.

Apart from internal conflict related to proselytising, the club has also dealt with a range of external challenges. On occasion the relatives or friends of players have urged them to stop participating in the club. The reasons mainly revolve around a concern about the interfaith composition of the club and issues of safety. Regarding the composition, some are concerned that because it includes both Christians and Muslims that they hope to combine the religions in some way. As Osita informed me, 'They think we are part of the Chrislam group. This is not us, but they still think this and believe we are trying to not just reconcile and unite as brothers, but actually unite the religions'.[24] Regarding issues of safety, some think that given the persistence of the violence in Kaduna that continues to this day, the club is liable to be attacked. This is undoubtedly a key issue even for the members of the club who have expressed their own concerns about such a possibility. Indeed, the club has had to negotiate a number of safety issues in the past 15 years. There have been times due to dangerous circumstances in the area that they choose to cancel or postpone matches. The club has also been forced to negotiate where they play because certain areas of Kaduna are less safe for either Christians or Muslims. Nevertheless, 15 years on, the club remains and continues to withstand such challenges.

Conclusion

While this chapter has examined the intersection of sport and religion in Nigeria, there are undoubtedly other cases and contexts that deserve attention. In particular, other grassroots sporting organisations and those with female membership would offer interesting comparisons and/or contrasts. While religious conflict remains the most prominent story related to Nigeria's multireligious composition, the intersection of sport and religion offers opportunities for exploring and better understanding the complexity of Muslim-Christian encounters. Given the pervasiveness of religion in Nigeria and the importance placed on football for both entertainment and social unification, it is little wonder that religious organisations have become directly involved in utilising the sport for their own purposes. The case study on Kaduna City Interfaith FC offers a range of insights about how football has been used as a means to bring people together and act as a powerful bridge in the midst of violence and tension. As many of the players remarked, it has been football that has created circumstances for conflict prevention so that religious ideals of reconciliation and community building have a chance of being pursued. While this process has not been without its challenges, the case offers a more holistic and complex understanding of how Christians and Muslims respond to differences of opinion and conflict situations.

Notes

1 Noo Saro-Wiwa, *Looking for Transwonderland: Travels in Nigeria* (London: Granta, 2012), 21–22.
2 Thomas A. Tweed, *Crossing and Dwelling: A Theory of Religion* (Cambridge, MA: Harvard University Press, 2006), 54. Tweed offers the following definition of religion: 'Religions are confluences of organic-cultural flows that intensify joy and confront suffering by drawing on human and suprahuman forces to make homes and cross boundaries'.
3 While nearly universal, it is not. There are those whom are non-religious. For an example of this, see: Leo Igwe, 'Leaving Religion and Living Without

Religion in Nigeria', *Butterflies and Wheels*, 26 July 2011, www.butterfliesand-wheels.org/2011/ leaving-religion-and-living-without-religion-in-nigeria/ (accessed 16 May 2016).

4 'Tolerance and Tension: Islam and Christianity in Sub-Saharan Africa', *Pew Forum on Religion and Public Life*, http://pewforum.org/executive-summary-islam-and-christianity-in-sub-saharan-africa.aspx (accessed 16 May 2016).

5 Most countries are not religiously diverse, as most have a clear majority religion. Using the World Religion Database, the following countries join Nigeria in this unique composition: Bosnia and Herzegovina (55 per cent Muslim; 40 per cent Christian); Côte d'Ivoire (37 per cent IR; 34 per cent Christian; 28 per cent Muslim), Eritrea (49 per cent Muslim; 47 per cent Christian), Guinea-Bissau (45 per cent IR; 42 per cent Muslim), Liberia (42 per cent IR; 40 per cent Christian), Madagascar (51 per cent Christian; 47 per cent IR), Mozambique (50 per cent IR; 39 per cent Christian), Sierra Leone (46 per cent Muslim; 39 per cent IR), Togo (45 per cent Christian; 35 per cent IR; 19 per cent Muslim), Mongolia (32 per cent IR; 30 per cent NR; 22 per cent Buddhist), Israel and the Occupied Territories (50 per cent Jewish; 41 per cent Muslim). See: Todd M. Johnson and Brian J. Grim, 'World Religion Database: International Religious Demographic Statistics and Sources', *Brill Publications and Services*, www.worldreligiondatabase.org/wrd_default.asp (accessed 16 May 2016).

6 Pew Forum on Religion and Public Life, 'Tolerance and Tension', 9. Rwanda is tied with Nigeria.

7 Events outside of Nigeria have also contributed to this image. In particular, the killing of Lee Rigby in London by British Nigerian Muslims and the attempt by Nigerian Umar Farouk Abdulmuttallab to detonate an explosive aboard Northwest Airlines flight 253 en route from Amsterdam to Detroit. As Jacob K. Olupona remarks regarding Boko Haram,

> It's important to understand that Boko Haram did not emerge in a vacuum. It is almost a direct result of the failed state that is corrupt and unable to provide even a basic level of safety and services to the country's citizens, from education, to healthcare, roads, electricity, and even sanitation.
> See: Jacob K. Olupona, 'To Save the Girls, the World Must Help Nigeria', *The World Post*, 12 May 2014, www.huffingtonpost.com/jacob-k-olupona/to-save-the-girls-the-wor_b_5312078.html (accessed 14 May 2016).

8 Afe Adogame, 'Politicization of Religion and Religionization of Politics in Nigeria', in *Religion, History, and Politics in Nigeria: Essays in Honor of Ogbu U. Kalu*, edited by Chima J. Korieh and G. Ugo Nwokeji (Lanham, Maryland: University Press of America, 2005), 125.

9 Benjamin F. Soares, 'Introduction: Muslim-Christian Encounters in Africa', in *Muslim-Christian Encounters in Africa*, edited by Benjamin F. Soares (Leiden: Brill Academic Publishers, 2006), 2.

10 Tim Bewer, Jean-Bernard Carillet, Paul Clammer, Emilie Filou, Michael Grosberg, Anthony Ham, Katharina Kane, Adam Karlin, Tom Masters, and Kate Thomas, *West Africa* (Melbourne: Lonely Planet, 2009), 619.

11 Eruteyan Joseph Jeroh, 'The Multi-Dimensional Relationship Between Religion and Sport', in *Journal of Physical Education and Sports Management*, Vol. 3, No. 1 (January 2012), 2.

12 Daniel Agbiboa, 'Ethno-Religious Conflicts and the Elusive Quest for National Identity in Nigeria', in *Journal of Black Studies*, Vol. 44, No. 1 (2013), 4.

13 Dominic Bossi, 'Nigeria 'Has God on Their Team' as Super Eagles Show Religious Unity at 2015 Women's World Cup', *The Sydney Morning Herald* 12

June 2015, www.smh.com.au/sport/soccer/nigeria-has-god-on-their-team-as-super-eagles-show-religious-unity-at-2015-womens-world-cup-20150611-ghm48e.html (accessed 15 May 2016).

14 As far as I am aware, there are not currently any Muslim organisations in Nigeria that own professional football clubs. There are, however, prominent Muslims who own football clubs, such as Toyin Gafar, who owns Bolowotan FC. As well, Muslim organisations such as Nasrul-Lahi-Il-Fatih Society (NASFAT) run university level teams like those found at Fountain University.

15 'About C.O.D United FC', C.O.D United Football Club, www.codunitedfc.com/cu/about-c-o-d-united-fc/ (accessed 16 May 2016).

16 'Club Anthem', C.O.D United Football Club, www.codunitedfc.com/cu/club-anthem/ (accessed 15 May 2016).

17 Akrukaino Umukoro, 'Playing Football in God's Name', The Punch, 28 July 2013, www.punchng.com/feature/playing-football-in-gods-name/ (accessed 15 May 2016).

18 David Meshioye, 'Pastor TB Joshua—Why I Floated Soccer Team', in Complete Sports, Vol. 5, No. 4 (30 May 2009).

19 The former Super Eagles coach, Amodu Shuaib, was reported to have claimed that he owed 'the qualification of the Super Eagles for the world cup to Prophet T. B. Joshua'. See: Sola Bodunrin, 'Super Eagles' Onazi Attributes Success to T B Joshua' Naij.com 13 June 2015, www.naij.com/459667-super-eagles-onazi-attributes-success-to-tb-joshua.html (accessed 15 May 2016).

20 Umukoro, 'Playing Football in God's Name'.

21 Ibid.

22 'D.I.E.T. Curriculum', C.O.D United Football Club, www.codunitedfc.com/cu/club-anthem/ (accessed 15 May 2016).

23 Out of the 36 Nigerian states, the following 12 have instituted Shari'a: Zamfara, Kano, Sokoto, Katsina, Bauchi, Borno, Jigawa, Kebbi, Yobe, Kaduna, Niger, and Gombe. For more on Shari'a in Nigeria, see Johannes Harnischfeger, Democratization and Islamic Law: The Shari'a Conflict in Nigeria, (Frankfurt: Campus Verlag Press, 2008). See also: Frieder Ludwig, 'Christian-Muslim Relations in Northern Nigeria since the Introduction of Shari'a in 1999', in Journal of the American Academy of Religio, Vol. 76, No. 3 (September 2008), 602–637.

24 Chrislam is a new religious movement in Nigeria that intentionally fuses elements of Christianity, Islam, and African Indigenous Religions.

References

Adogame, Afe. 'Politicization of Religion and Religionization of Politics in Nigeria'. In Religion, History, and Politics in Nigeria: Essays in Honor of Ogbu U. Kalu, edited by Chima J. Korieh and G. Ugo Nwokeji, 125–139. Lanham, Maryland: University Press of America, 2005.

Agbiboa, Daniel. 'Ethno-Religious Conflicts and the Elusive Quest for National Identity in Nigeria'. Journal of Black Studies, 44.1 (2013): 3–30.

Bewer, Tim, Jean-Bernard Carillet, Paul Clammer, Emilie Filou, Michael Grosberg, Anthony Ham, Katharina Kane, Adam Karlin, Tom Masters and Kate Thomas, West Africa. Melbourne: Lonely Planet, 2009.

Bodunrin, Sola. ' "Super Eagles" Onazi Attributes Success to TB Joshua'. Naij.com, 13 June 2015. Accessed 15 May 2016. www.naij.com/459667-super-eagles-onazi-attributes-success-to-tb-joshua.html.

Bossi, Dominic. 'Nigeria "Has God on Their Team" as Super Eagles Show Religious Unity at 2015 Women's World Cup'. *The Sydney Morning Herald*, 12 June 2015. Accessed 15 May 2016. www.smh.com.au/sport/soccer/nigeria-has-god-on-their-team-as-super-eagles-show-religious-unity-at-2015-womens-world-cup-20150611-ghm48e.html.

COD United Football Club. 'About C.O.D United FC'. Accessed 16 May 2016. www.codunitedfc.com/cu/about-c-o-d-united-fc/.

COD United Football Club. 'Club Anthem'. Accessed 15 May 2016. www.codunitedfc.com/cu/club-anthem/.

COD United Football Club. 'D.I.E.T. Curriculum'. Accessed 15 May 2016. www.codunitedfc.com/cu/club-anthem/.

Harnischfeger, Johannes. *Democratization and Islamic Law: The Shari'a Conflict in Nigeria*. Frankfurt: Campus Verlag Press, 2008.

Igwe, Leo. 'Leaving Religion and Living Without Religion in Nigeria,' Accessed 16 May 2016. www.butterfliesandwheels.org/2011/leaving-religion-and-living-without-religion-in-nigeria/.

Jeroh, Eruteyan Joseph. 'The Multi-Dimensional Relationship Between Religion and Sport'. *Journal of Physical Education and Sports Management*, 3.1 (January 2012): 1–7.

Johnson, Todd M. and Brian J. Grim. 'World Religion Database: International Religious Demographic Statistics and Sources'. *Brill Publications and Services*. Accessed 16 May 2016. www.worldreligiondatabase.org/wrd_default.asp.

Ludwig, Frieder. 'Christian-Muslim Relations in Northern Nigeria since the Introduction of *Shari'a* in 1999'. *Journal of the American Academy of Religion*, 76.3 (September 2008): 602–637.

Meshioye, David. 'Pastor T B Joshua—Why I Floated Soccer Team'. *Complete Sports*, 30 May 2009.

Olupona, Jacob K. 'To Save the Girls, the World Must Help Nigeria'. *The World Post*, 12 May 2014. Accessed 14 May 2016. www.huffingtonpost.com/jacob-k-olupona/to-save-the-girls-the-wor_b_5312078.html.

Pew Forum on Religion and Public Life. 'Tolerance and Tension: Islam and Christianity in Sub-Saharan Africa'. Accessed 16 May 2016. http://pewforum.org/executive-summary-islam-and-christianity-in-sub- saharan-africa.aspx.

Saro-Wiwa, Noo. *Looking for Transwonderland: Travels in Nigeria*. London: Granta, 2012.

Soares, Benjamin F. 'Introduction: Muslim-Christian Encounters in Africa'. In *Muslim-Christian Encounters in Africa*, edited by Benjamin F. Soares, 1–16. Leiden: Brill Academic Publishers, 2006.

Tweed, Thomas A. *Crossing and Dwelling: A Theory of Religion*. Cambridge, MA: Harvard University Press, 2006.

Umukoro, Akrukaino. 'Playing Football in God's Name'. *The Punch*, 28 July 2013. Accessed 15 May 2016. www.punchng.com/feature/playing-football-in-gods-name/.

Chapter 8

Spirituality and martial arts

'Fitting' in the life-world

Jonathan Tuckett

Introduction

In this chapter I explore the martial arts of Kendo and Taekwondo as forms of naturalisation. Following philosophical phenomenology, naturalisation involves giving the person the means to 'fit' into their life-world – thereby easing basic existential worries such as the fear of death. I suggest that 'religion' and 'nationalism' are ways of categorising non-dominant and dominant modes of naturalisation. In turn, I look at how Kendo can be conceive as a 'nationalistic' mode of naturalisation and second at how Taekwondo can be conceived as a 'religious' mode of naturalisation. In conclusion I make some comments on how these modes of naturalisation interact with more traditionally conceived 'religious' modes like Christianity.

In speaking of the 'spirituality' of martial arts, I highlight a lacuna in which a collection of traditions have not been included in discussions of 'religions'. As observed by Maliszewski (1996: 20), 'the depth of association that many of these disciplines had with specific religious traditions has gone unrecognised' within academia. This association can be identified, I suggest, in debates on the 'sportification' of martial arts. I have chosen the specific cases of Kendo[1] (Japan) and Taekwondo (Korea) because they exemplify this debate on 'sportification' as a degeneration of the respective martial art. The issue, as it is presented in discourse, is that in promoting these disciplines as 'sports' as opposed to 'arts', a key aspect is thereby lost. Crucially, the term often deployed in this context is 'spirit' or 'spiritual'.

Modes of naturalisation

The terms 'spiritual' and 'religion' and the implicit suggestion that the 'spirituality' of martial arts is what makes them 'religious' are all deeply problematic. Of the term 'spiritual', Davidsen (2012) has commented that many of the scholars involved in the topic area of 'spirituality studies' are themselves practitioners and their works betrays normative, apologetic agendas.

The study of martial arts, and particularly those who draw connections to 'religion', is no exception in this respect.[2] As commented by Bennett (2015: 22), 'A growing number of English books about traditional Japanese swordsmanship are on the market. Most of them, however, are how-to manuals, biographies of master swordsmen, or translations and commentaries on classic texts – often historically naïve, mixing fact with fiction.' As practitioners themselves, these scholars have tended to underplay certain historical factors in the development of their martial arts that might portray them in a negative light. For instance, Michael Maliszewski's *Spiritual Dimensions of the Martial Arts* (1996), quoted above, not only highlights a scholarly lacuna, but adds the following: 'The *lack of serious attention by practitioners of these disciplines* as well as scholar's lack of attention to or participation in the martial arts is a central theme addressed in this book' (Maliszewski, 1996: 21, emphasis added). Blurring the lines between scholar and practitioner, such sentiments indicate an Eliadean style of study – i.e. one which presumes a transhistorical essence which martial arts contribute to manifesting.[3] Not only is Maliszewski looking to rectifying a scholarly lacuna, it becomes clear that he is evaluating the martial arts themselves for how well they have manifested this transhistorial spiritual essence.

In such a context, 'spiritual' has a metaphysical, ecumenical theological connotation. These scholars are subject to Fitzgerald's (1997, 2000) critique of the inherent Christian bias in the use of terms like 'religion' and 'spiritual' as analytic categories. The problem in the context of martial arts is this: it is not clear that practitioners who deploy the term 'spiritual' are making any 'metaphysical' associations when they do so. More specifically, the Christo-centric usage reinforces the secular/religious binary, one that sees 'secular' as public and 'religion' as private. But when the martial artists speak of the degeneration of the spiritual aspects of their disciplines, they mean exactly the opposite to this. In their usage a martial art is 'public' and a sport is 'private'. The 'public' nature of martial arts has been demonstrated by Bennett in the case of Kendo when demonstrating that the development of the martial art is bound up with Japanese notions of nationalism. Similarly, the emergence of Taekwondo is bound up in the emergence of Korean nationalism post-Japanese occupation. Indeed, Cook (2001) suggests that the creation of Taekwondo through the unification of several disparate disciplines represented a microcosmic version of the emerging macro unity of (South) Korea.

Framing this in the terminology of philosophical phenomenology what I suggest here is that 'nationalism' and 'religion' both serve the same purpose: to *naturalise* the person in their life-world. As Schutz understood it, Husserl's natural attitude is concerned with the problem of surviving and thriving.[4] Sheets-Johnstone (2016: 174) has connected this with 'religion' by suggesting that it stabilises feelings of ease with the world. In her Sartrean-inspired analytic, the emphasis is that systems like 'religion' (and 'nationalism') ease our sense of fear at the world – particularly the fear of death – by providing security, safety and the chance for well-being, and so enable us to carry on with our lives. That is, 'nationalism' and 'religion' establish the modes by which a person 'fits' into their social context – i.e. their relation and position to Others.[5] The difference between the two terms is *ideological*; a point which bears some similarity to Goldenberg's (2013: 40) definition of 'religion' as vestigial states: 'the cultural remnants of former sovereignties that persist within current states (current governmental jurisdictions)'. Religions, she suggests, present similar discursive and institutional practices to those in contemporary states (regarding 'nationalisms' in this context). Goldenberg (2013: 42) goes on to suggest that:

> vestigial states, now called religions, begin to evolve when self-governing groups, whether ancient or modern, cede sovereignty along with the capacity to commit violence to other groups. Most of the time, this happens when a group is conquered by invasion or colonization. If the vanquished group survives at all, it is denied independent control over most governmental functions and must accept limitations on its powers and jurisdiction.

'Religion' represents the way 'we' used to run our affairs and view the world. Divesting this of its Tylorian edge ('vestigial' = 'survival'), I suggest that 'religion' designates a *competing* mode of naturalisation to whatever our dominant mode is.

Discussions of 'spirituality' in this context are a means by which a person can express the 'fit' achieved by the mode of naturalisation. More formally, whatever else may be attached to the term 'spiritual' by the person using it, insofar as it is used here, I take it to mean something *serious*. Drawing on Sartrean phenomenology, I am following his distinction between the 'serious attitude' (related to the natural attitude) and 'play': 'The serious attitude involves starting from the world and attributing more reality to the world than to oneself; at the very least the serious man confers reality on himself to the degree to which he belongs to the world'; and

> The first principle of play is man himself; through it he escapes his natural nature; he himself sets the value and rules for his acts and consents to play only according to the rules which he himself has established and defined.
>
> (Sartre, 2003: 601)

'Spirituality' is *serious* to the extent that it affects our ability to survive and thrive.

In this context, I am therefore suggesting that 'martial art', like 'nationalism' or 'religion', is a term for designating a mode of naturalisation. Commonly understood, the term is a translation, stemming from the early 1900s, of the Japanese term *bujutsu*. However, while '*bu*' is translated as 'martial', '*jutsu*' can be translated as 'art', 'method', 'skill' and 'technique'. Kiyota (1995: 129) translates the full term as 'martial skill' and Bennett (2015: 1) uses 'martial technique'. *Bujutsu* refers to systems and techniques of fighting that were used by Samurai in real combat situations. *Bujutsu*, then, refers to *martial craft* where 'craft' refers to a set of functional skills. These *bujutsu* then developed into *budo*, a term that came into popular use *c.*1868–1912 and is also translated as 'martial art'.[6] Thus, for example, *kenjutsu* as referring to a specific set of sword skills became *kendo*.

It is the introduction of '*do*', more easily translated as 'way' or 'art' that is key to my point here. The change in terminology indicates a change in the way in which the skills of these various *bujutsu* were perceived and practiced. Primarily, this is a move away from battlefield application. But, the obvious question is, a move to what? Authors like Kiyota (1995: 131) and Mileszewski (1996: 64–65) see this as the 'spiritualisation' of these combat systems. Specifically, the introduction of the suffix '*do*' carries with it significant connotations, especially when translated as 'Way'. For Kiyota (1995: 15), the term signifies a 'way of life':

> Thus *kendo* (*ken* + *dô*) does not only mean the development of skill; it ultimately means the way of life shaped by the discipline cultivated in the process of leaning that art. *Dô*, in the Japanese context, is an experiential term, experiential in the sense that practice (the way of life) is the norm to verify the validity of the discipline cultivated through a given art form. In *kendo*, then, discipline refers to *kendô* practice which is designed to cultivate *mushin* (and revealed as *heijô-shin*). But since the term '*dô*' is an experiential term, *kendo* requires the implementation of *heijô-shin* in every walk of life.

It is this final comment that captures my point about naturalisation: Kendo is a means by which a person 'fits' in their life-world.

Martial art vs martial sport

The basic premise from which I am operating here is that 'martial art' is a name given to a mode of naturalisation. This becomes apparent in the debate on the 'sportification' of martial arts, the worry that what should be taken *seriously* is treated as a form of *play*. This point is also raised by Bennett (2015: 195):

The argument surrounding the difference between budo and sports has always been vibrant, but the main objections are that Kendo should never be reduced to a matter of victory or defeat and that it is not about fun or play. Kendo is supposed to be far more serious than that.

What I am suggesting here is that key to such debates is how this worry is often expressed as a concern for a loss of 'spirituality'. That is, to say that a practice is 'spiritual' is to indicate its *seriousness* and therefore relevance for 'fitting' with the life-world. In the next two sections we will see how – in debates of sportification – Kendo is bound up with Japanese 'nationalistic' naturalisation and Taekwondo closer approximates a 'religious' form of naturalisation.

Kendo

Kendo as it is practiced today generally involves sword-based combat using a *shinai* (bamboo stick) instead of real blades. The objective of Kendo is to strike an opponent's *bôgu* (armour) in prescribed target areas. What should be noted is that in its sole reliance on swords, Kendo differs from the majority of other martial arts, which tend to rely on hand-to-hand combat.

Literally translated, 'Kendo' means 'way of the sword' (Kiyota, 1995: ix). The term's earliest use, *c.*1967, seems to have been by Abe Munetô in a document outlining his *ryûha* (school) – the *Abe-ryû kendo denshi*. However, it would not find popular usage until the 1920s and what now takes the name previously went by such names as *gekitô*, *gekiken*, *tachi-uchi*, *kenpô* and *kenjutsu*. However, while modern Kendo represents a unified system, these names do not refer to earlier iterations. We must be clear that there were many different *kenjutsu ryûha*, each with their own distinctive style. Kendo then is an invented tradition, in that 'its teachings and training methodology, match rules, philosophical concepts, and so on were, for the most part developed or reformulated in the twentieth century' (Bennett, 2015: 21). Despite this, there is a modern perception that Kendo is 'the purest of the martial arts – being easily linked to the honourable sword-wielding samurai heroes of yesteryear' (Bennett, 2015: 20). As such, Kendo has become the dominant expression of *bushido* which was the mode of naturalisation developed by and for Samurai during the Sengoku period (1457–1603).[7]

Having closed its borders for nearly 200 years, Japan was forcibly reintroduced to the West by the arrival of Commodore Perry in 1853. The resulting Meiji Restoration in 1868 would see large-scale political and social changes, arguably, along Western models. This saw the dissolution of the Samurai as the dominant social class and the loss of their hegemonic control over the practice of *kenjutsu*. By consequence *kenjutsu* became more readily available to the wider populace amid rising nationalistic sentiments as Japan established itself among its Western competitors. Befu (1981: 52) has described this as the samuraization of Japan: 'characteristics such as loyalty, perseverance, and diligence said to be held by a small (but elite) segment of the population – the samurai – were gradually extended through propaganda, education, and regulation to cover the whole of the population'. We might say that rather than the group disappearing, it expanded to encompass the entire populace. In this regard, the Samurai sword became the symbol of Japanese spirit. This 'samuraization' fits with Smith's (1991: 16) suggestion that nations, in this modern context, 'provide individuals with "sacred centres," objects of spiritual and historical pilgrimage that reveal the uniqueness of their nation's "moral geography"'. That is, the nation naturalises its members in relation to the fundamental problem of surviving and thriving. *Kenjutsu* and the underlying *bushido* provided just these sacred centres. These were then enshrined in the Japanese educational system when *kenjutsu* was introduced to middle and normal schools in 1911. During the process that would lead to this, a report by the Ministry of Education adjudicating on the advantages and disadvantages of introducing *kenjutsu* in schools listed one of the advantages as 'rouses the spirit and boosts morale' (Bennett, 2015: 112). These changing social conditions would also see the transformation of the various *bujutsu* into *budo*, including *kenjutsu* into *kendo*. Bennett (2015: 3) observes that the various private organisations responsible for this succeeded in making these martial practices 'more germane to modern societal needs, with a focus on education and competition'.

The *budo* were then directed towards imperialistic and militaristic ends, heightening with the onset of the Second World War (with major consequences in Korea, below). This could be seen in the continuing transmission of *bushido* through the various *budo*. Even though *seppuku* (ritual suicide) was not enforced, indeed technically illegal in certain situations, its practice was nonetheless applauded by wider society. Shrines were often erected in dedication of those who had committed this ritual suicide. It was only after several officers notably committed *seppuku* before the Imperial Palace on the eve of surrender during the Second World War that the practice would begin to fade away. So significant were these *budo* for Japanese nationalistic (and imperialistic) identity, that occupation forces banned them, removing Kendo from school curricula after the Second World War.

Budo were then revived in the 1950s as 'democratic sports' that would lead to the entry of Judo into the Olympics in 1964. Significantly, much of the 'spiritual' aspects of Kendo had to be sheared away in order to convince occupation forces that they were not promoting militarism and/or ultra-nationalism. Again, to be spiritual in this context means to be natural in the Japanese life-world. It was only once Kendo was established as a sport that it was reintroduced to schools in 1953. The accompanying

Instructional Handbook for School Kendo explained that 'Kendo as a sport is not the same as kendo as a means of fighting ... The interaction represents an affirmation of each other's existence, and a recognition of the common thread of humanity' (quoted in Bennett, 2015: 176). Bennett, problematically, calls this rebranding of Kendo as a sport a 'civilising process', but I would suggest it is more accurate to describe it as a Westernising process – redeveloping Kendo into a form that would appease Western occupiers *and* their understanding of what it is to be natural. Perhaps most significant in all of this is the move away from 'nationalism' to 'religion'. Pre-war Kendo was for emperor, for country, for moral cultivation as a loyal subject, for imparting manners and discipline; postwar Kendo is for enjoyment. All spiritual and nationalistic rhetoric was exorcised and, at the school level, the term *budo* was replaced with *kakugi* (combative sport) in 1957.

Of course, such developments met a measure of resistance and Kendo associations responsible for disseminating Kendo in schools would highlight its link to Japanese cultural heritage. In the 1970s, Kendo was again promoted as a cultural pursuit and means of spiritual growth, the Japan Budo Association (JBA) releasing the 'Budo Charter' in 1977 which warned of the threat to the essence of *budo* by an over-emphasis on technical ability (JBA, 2004).[8] Actions such as these would lead to the reinstatement of the term *budo* within education curricula in 1989 (Bennett, 2015). However, due to practical restrictions, Kendo is only taught in 25 per cent of schools and other forms of *budo* are taught instead. At the same time, changing circumstances for students – where success at Kendo competitions can mean access to high-end careers – has resulted in an explosion of tournaments. In response, this has led to the emergence of several *budo*, including the Nihon Kendô Kyôkai (NKK), vehemently opposing 'the over 'sportification' and compromising of martial and cultural veracity' (2015: 4). The JBA, for instance, has argued that the emphasis on competition is caught up in the process of globalisation. Though not explicitly stated, there are wider concerns here about globalisation in line with a Western model, one which leads to erosion of the *budo*'s integrity. This resulted in 2008 in the JBA issuing the 'Philosophy of Budo' which made the following statement:

> *Budô* the martial ways of Japan, have their origins in the traditions of *bushidô* the way of the warrior. *Budô* is a time-honoured form of physical culture comprising of *jûdô, kendô, kyûdô, sumô, karatedô, aikidô, shôrinji kempô, naginata* and *jûkendô*. Practitioners study the skills while striving to unify mind, technique and body; develop his or her character; enhance their sense of morality; and to cultivate a respectful and courteous demeanour. Practised steadfastly, these admirable traits become intrinsic to the character of the practitioner.

The *Budô* arts serve as a path to self-perfection. This elevation of the human spirit will contribute to social prosperity and harmony, and ultimately, benefit the people of the world.

(JBA, 2009)

In a slightly different vein, Kiyota (1995: 2) discusses the concept of '*mushin*' (mind of no-mind), indicating where the seeming importance of Kendo lies. Here Kiyota notes how a Samurai, facing an opponent, will experience fear and asks the question of where this fear comes from? Drawing on Buddhism (though no more detail is given than this), Kiyota suggests that fear is created by one's own mind, particularly in the way it gives rise to the ego as the expression of self-preservation. When the practitioner finds him or herself dogged by fear, they are exhorted to perform a *sutemi* – literally, a 'body-abandoning' attack. Doing so cultivates the state of *mushin* described by the Zen master D. T. Suzuki in which an altered state of consciousness occurs that frees the mind from the ego. Kiyota goes on to explain 'whereas the foremost concern in Western sports is to respond to an external challenge and to defeat an opponent ... the foremost challenge in *kendo* is to tame the ego by internalising challenge' (1995: 3). This distinction between Western sport and Japanese martial art can be seen in the treatment of the *shinai* (Kendo's primary weapon) compared to a tennis racket. As the 'Mindset of Kendo Instruction' issued in 2006 by the NKK explains:

Kendo is a way where the individual cultivates one's mind (the self) by aiming for shin-ki-ryoku-itchi (unification of mind, spirit and technique) utilizing the shinai. The 'shinai-sword' should be not only directed at one's opponent but also at the self. Thus, the primary aim of instruction is to encourage the unification of mind, body and shinai through training in this discipline.

(NKK, 2007)[9]

The *shinai*, then, is not an implement like the tennis racket, it is a conduit for developing, or naturalising, the person.

Thus, the Western influence of globalisation that reconfigures the various *budo* as sports is seen to detract these aspects. In the case of Kendo, this expresses itself as a fear of loss of hegemony, particularly if it were to enter the Olympics. This concern is corroborated by the transformations in Judo, for which there is now no Japanese representative in the International Judo Federation. Guttmann (1993: 25) has observed that the transition of Japanese martial arts to the West often leads to 'transformation in accordance with Western assumptions about the nature of sports'. Again, this may be seen as a transition from a seriousness to playfulness. In many ways, Kendo has reacted to the 'cultural imperialism' alluded to by Guttman with a form of cultural imperialism of its own. As Kendo is progressively 'evangelised' (Bennett's phrase) around the world, there is still a strong emphasis that only the Japanese can fully understand the Way of Kendo (Bennett, 2015: 201). Conversely, for the Japanese outside of Japan, Kendo has been 'a cultural artefact that connected students, expatriate businessmen, immigrants, and their families to traditional Japanese culture and values' (Svinth and Green, 2003: 149). Both trends represent a keen focus within Kendo on its connection with *being* Japanese. A part of being Japanese is to do Kendo *and* only the Japanese can do Kendo properly.

Taekwondo

Taekwondo is ostensibly an offensive martial art in that it focuses on punching and kicking over grappling or using the opponent's attacks against them. Despite its name that translates as the Way of Hand and Feet, what makes Taekwondo distinctive from its counterparts, like Karate, is the emphasis on kicking – the adage goes that Taekwondo is 70 per cent kicking and 30 per cent punching. Particularly as a result of its entry into the Olympics, Taekwondo is now thought to be one of the world most popularly practiced martial arts (exact figures are hard to ascertain).

Taekwondo began in the 1950s as the culmination of a period of rapid change and upheaval in Korea that came to an end at the close of the Second World War with the termination of Japanese occupation. As part of the imperial expansion resulting from the Meiji Restoration, the Japanese had begun a successful colonising project in 1873 that fundamentally altered Korea's self-understanding as a state (Seth, 2011). In the build up to the Second World War, The Japanese attempted to naturalise the Koreans as 'Japanese'[10] by repressing down Korean organisations of every type and replacing them with Japanese equivalents. This would extend to a complete ban on all forms of native Korean martial arts, to be replaced with Japanese Kendo, Karate and Judo.

After the occupation and following the Korean War of 1950–1953, Taekwondo emerged due to a need to develop a strong (South) Korean identity. This involved the formalisation of several *kwans* (schools), supposedly preserved in secreted by Korean masters (Cook, 2001: 7). Initially these were united under Korean Taesoodo Association in 1955, which adopted the name 'Taekwondo' in 1961 under the influence of General Choi Hong Hi. Taekwondo was thus instigated as the Korean national martial art, and, consistent with a general sense of resentment against their former Japanese colonisers, was set in contradistinction to the predominant Japanese Karate. Since then the World Taekwondo Federation (WTF) has worked to standardise Taekwondo with a set curriculum and rules for competitions but has also seen global expansion of its own after gaining entry into the Olympics in 1988.[11] Nevertheless, rules and regulations are strictly determined by the Kukkiwon, the WTF headquarters in Seoul, and despite global proliferation there remains a Korean hegemony on the development of the martial art. Much like the case of Kendo and Judo, Taekwondo's inclusion in the Olympics raises the question of the difference between a martial art and a martial sport.

However, to move from what is ostensibly a 'nationalistic' form of naturalisation to a 'religious' one, I will shift focus onto Cook's (2001) account of Taekwondo in *Taekwondo: Ancient Wisdom for the Modern Warrior*. Cook, a 6th Dan in America, has twice received the Medal of Special Recognition from the Moo Duk Kwan in Seoul (2003 and 2011). In 2004 he received a Special Citation from the Korean government for 'forging a stronger relationship between Korea and the United States through the martial arts' (Chosun Taekwondo, 2014). He is considered one of the highest-ranking Taekwondo instructors in America.

Cook, I suggest, is typical of the trend identified by Donohue (2002) in the transmission of martial arts to the American context. The success of this transmission is due to the fact that these 'esoteric cultural imports fit so well the standard mythic elements of the American warrior hero' (Donohue, 2002: 67). This 'American warrior hero' fits with my understanding of naturalisation (in this case nationalistic): 'What is of ultimate significance is that he temporarily surrenders his independence and places his skill in the service of others' (Donohue, 2002: 67).[12] That is, he acts in the interests of the surviving and thriving of the group. Indeed, he is only a hero to the extent that his struggles are the struggles of others. In this respect the profusion of martial arts in America has been so successful because the pattern of naturalisation offered corresponds to an already existing pattern. The title of Cook's book, featuring the phrase 'modern warrior', thus fits this trend.

Donohue (2002: 70) also notes an American consumerist element in all of this. Americans, he argues, are brought up to understand the world in material and supernatural terms and the martial arts, due to their esoteric nature, are perceived to dip into the latter. Americans are thus fed on the notion of a stuff that will accelerate power and skill development. In the case of martial arts this is associated with *ki* – a property that features prominently in Cook's book – and the 'American understanding of this phenomenon is a simplistic one that ultimately relies on mystical and quasi-magical explanations' (Donohue, 2002: 70). 'Religion' becomes an applicable term in this context because Taekwondo is an option, among many, for providing this power. And although I will not touch upon the problematic material/supernatural distinction myself, the point of *ki* as a source of power is that it becomes a means by which the American notion of a promised land is attained (Donohue, 2002). As Donohue (2002: 74) concludes:

These arts then, are not only about human physical potential but about the human struggle to generate a coherent worldview, to invest life with meaning and develop mechanisms for relating to both their fellow human beings and the world they inhabit.

Cook's book, I suggest, is emblematic of this.

Important for both of Cook's disagreements with the 'sportification' of Taekwondo is its 'spiritual' heritage in the *hwarang*, a warrior elite who emerged during the Three Kingdoms period (57 BCE–668 CE). Significantly for Korean nationalist sentiment, the *hwarang* represent and predate the characteristics of the Samurai (Seth, 2011: 34–35). For Cook, the importance lies in the introduction of the *hwarang-do*, 'The way of the flowering manhood', by King Jinheung (526 CE–576 CE). This comprised the martial crafts of Kwonbop and Subahk with the Five Codes of Human Conduct (Cook, 2001: 3). The Five Codes were passed onto the *hwarang* by the Buddhist monk Wonkwang Popsa and would later become the basis of the Taekwondo Oath. Cook (2001: 3–4) explains that 'in an effort to satisfy their spiritual as well as their martial needs, the young warriors of the Hwarang also studied a mixture of music, dance, poetry, and philosophy'. This transition from *hwarang* to *hwarangdo* represents a clear move from martial craft to martial art: after Wonkwang 'a spiritual and ethical tradition began to flourish and permeate the underpinnings of martial philosophy establishing both a virtuous response to threat and a "way" or "path" towards superior living' (Cook, 2001: 4). Rutt (1961: 30) and others indicate that the *hwarang* were in a way representatives of the Sillan(-cum-Korean) national identity, heightened to both compete and undercut the Samurai and *bushido*.[13]

While this certainly locates Taekwondo as a nationalistic means of naturalisation for Koreans, can it thereby also be religious? Insofar as Cook, as an American writer, is keen to emphasise the spiritual aspects of Taekwondo, this suggests it can be so as he has no real investment in promoting Taekwondo as something only the Koreans can do. Compare, for instance, the claims among some Kendo practitioners that only the Japanese can fully understand Kendo. Were Cook to make a similar claim for Taekwondo this would be contradictory to his own aims. In this context, drawing a the parallel to *hwarangdo* and *bushido* is, for Cook, less about emphasising the 'Koreanness' of Taekwondo and more about highlighting the connection of the *hwarang* to Buddhism. Emphasising this connection highlights Taekwondo as a spiritual pursuit that determines his position in the question of 'sportification'.

In many respects, Cooks' reservations about the presence of Taekwondo in the Olympics mirror those of the JBA regarding Kendo. Of the issues that Cook highlights, the one that interests us – and him – the most is the worry that: 'that youngsters, too, may suffer from an overabundance of sport fighting by missing the spiritual and mental aspects so essential to the art of Taekwondo' (Cook, 2001: 145). This emphasis on young practitioners parallels an emphasis in Kiyota on the benefit of Kendo for education (Kiyota, 1995: 101–106). One of the issues that Cook is more conscious of in tackling this, however, is that Korean history provides numerous examples of martial arts being treated in a sportive fashion (Cook, 2001: 146). This awareness of Korean martial arts' history as 'play' leads Cook (2001: 148) to suggest competition 'as a means of self-evaluation. Ideally, the diligent practice of taekwondo pits one against one's self in the ultimate test of character'. He goes on to argue that the 'competition' against obesity may be of more value to the student than success in the sparring ring. He is further critical of the competitive 'win at all costs' attitude for undermining the defensive value of the martial art in that it threatens to undermine the teaching of Wonkwang and the directive to exercise good judgement before harming someone (Cook, 2001: 150).

This emphasis on 'defensive value' indicates the seriousness of the martial art for Cook. His book is particularly concerned with demonstrating the value of the martial art beyond the *dojang* (training hall). Again, this ties back to *hwarang*: 'While it is not required that a martial discipline be ancient to qualify as traditional, it can be helpful. Today, we find techniques that served the Hwarang in seventh century Silla being employed in modern day Taekwondo' (Cook, 2001: 155). The claim here being that Taekwondo's worth is validated by the continuing use (and success) of these ancient techniques. This is further developed to suggest these techniques are 'spiritually therapeutic' (p. 156). Taekwondo as a martial art, thus, is a holistic endeavour:

> Whereas the contemporary athlete may concentrate primarily on body-building and strategies specific to a given sport, the modern day warrior reverently trains not only in the physical aspect of taekwondo, but also seeks to bolster valuable mental and spiritual capabilities through studies in Asian history and ki development.
>
> (Cook, 2001: 156)

To be emphasised here is how Cook sees that the 'strategies' developed by the athlete are specific to their sport – i.e. they are only applicable within that sport – whereas, assumedly, the 'strategies' of the martial artists have applicability elsewhere. This view is corroborated by a quote from Grand Master San Kyu Shim: 'Commendable as the Olympics may be as a form of international competition, they are not a way of life, as the martial arts, in their true sense are' (quoted in Cook, 2001: 157). Again, this emphasis on a 'way of life' is a matter of naturalising the person within their life-world.

Speaking of *poomsae*,[14] for instance, Cook (2001: 69) concludes they provide 'an acute sense of one's place in the universe'. This is emphasised by the stories of Terry, Lee and Katy who are each faced with difficult, potentially dangerous circumstances. Each of whom then utilises Taekwondo to diffuse their situation. Lee is perhaps the most notable case for using the meditative practices of *poomsae* training to prepare him for a difficult business meeting, thereby highlighting the applicability of Taekwondo outside a combative arena. It is not clear if these anecdotes are created for emphasis or if they are real accounts. Regardless, they are fitted into part of an exposition on Taekwondo providing 'personal defence', different from self-defence in that rather than protecting against physical attack it is all encompassing. The development of *ki* through *poomsae* also validates Donohue's point above:

> Through the cultivation of ki, coupled with meditative visualisation and positive actions, the practitioner can conquer life's trials and tribulations, appearing both confident and self-assured in the process. Developing these qualities is vital to the overall health and welfare of the individual's mind, body, and spirit.
>
> (Cook, 2001: 116)

As such, particularly in the American context, it makes sense to speak of Taekwondo as a 'religious' form of naturalisation. It is not the dominant mode of naturalisation, but rather one that is *chosen*. Indeed, based on Donohue's comments about consumerism, one may note that the most nominally 'secular' state has potentially laid the best breeding ground for 'religions' as I have understood the term here.

Conclusions

What I have attempted to show throughout this chapter is that in focusing on the topic of 'spirituality' as the key aspect in the debate between 'martial art' and 'martial sport', practitioners wish to designate the former as *serious*. That is, martial arts are about naturalising the person, making them 'fit' in their life-world. As the cases of Kendo and Taekwondo demonstrate, this mode may be 'nationalistic' or 'religious' depending on whether it is the dominant mode of naturalisation for the group.

This, however, raises questions about the relation of Taekwondo, insofar as it is classifiable as a 'religion', i.e. a competing non-dominant mode of naturalisation, to other modes of naturalisation that may exist in the same milieu. That is, I am effectively suggesting that Taekwondo and Christianity perform the same function of enabling a person to 'fit' in their life-world. Here 'competition' becomes crucial. According to Goldenberg (2013: 41–43), 'religions' as vestigial states conceive of themselves as 'once and future states' who take what control they can as ceded them by the controlling state. Cook's (2001) argument that the principles of Taekwondo are consistent with Newtonian physics may be interpreted as a strategy in this vein of being consistent with the dominant mode of naturalisation (thereby underplaying the importance of *ki*). In my own terms this is to say that all modes of naturalisation are attempting to be the *dominant* mode while at the same time reconciling themselves with the presuppositions of that dominant mode. As such Taekwondo and Christianity would be competitors with one another, presumably vying for as much authority as the state will cede them.

To my knowledge there is little in the way of a Taekwondo response to Christianity. However, there is a growing response of Christians to Taekwondo and martial arts. While the negative responses, such as Vito Rallo's *Exposing the Dangers of Martial Arts* (2016), would fit the mould implied by my understanding of 'religion', more interesting are those cases where reconciliation occurs, e.g. Glyn Norman's *What the Martial Arts Taught Me About the Gospel of Jesus Christ* (2014). Christian concerns regarding martial arts seem to centre on two issues: (i) the permissibility of Christians to engage in violence, and (ii) the historical origins of martial arts. It is the latter issue that is more important in the present consideration as it is here that Christians identify the 'spiritual' aspects of martial arts. The views of Orlando (2016) are seemingly representative in this regard:

> The Christian martial artist must remove the religious overtones that are frequently taught as part of Eastern martial arts. Instead, he should concentrate on skills that enhance mental concentration, improve sensitivity to differing degrees of threat, and increase awareness of the interaction between attitude and performance. This is learning the fine art of strategic thinking.

The emphasis on skill would indicate the possibility of treating Taekwondo, say, as either martial craft or martial art, where the former presents no obvious issue for the Christian perspective. Dynamic Martial Arts,[15] for instance, also offer advice on how to set up a Christian-based martial arts club. And also in America, at least, there appear to be growing number of groups that utilise martial arts for evangelism.[16] In each case Taekwondo is represented as a craft, a tool to be utilised to achieve a separate goal.

However, it is perhaps too soon to tell how far such reconciliation may go and how influential or successful it might prove to be. Many of these Christian responses are found on blogs and websites (such as Orlando's) and it is not overtly clear what and whom their readership/audience comprises; Dynamic Martial Arts give no indication of how many other clubs have adopted their model for class structure. Nor are there any obvious indicators that the martial crafts utilising evangelicals are more successful than their traditional peers. Further, Taekwondo seems to be a popular tool in this regard, which is perhaps unsurprising considering its popularity, whereas Kendo is less so. This may have something to do with the fact that Kendo is still bound with Japanese-ness and does not fit with an American Christian model. This difference may yet prove to develop into a more complicated response and interaction between Christians and martial arts of differing disciplines.

Notes

1 See Tuckett (2016) for a more detail exploration of the case of Kendo.
2 Nor am I immune from this problem – I myself am a practitioner of Taekwondo. Worse still, I have recently become an instructor, placing myself in a position of authority that can (to a limited degree) shape the very tradition I am a part of. Much of what I have to say about Taekwondo must be treated as anecdotal rather than empirical. I have not yet been in the position to pursue formal, ethnographic research on this topic. The present considerations are primarily historical.
3 As an aside, Maliszewski's book happens to be dedicated to Eliade who helped in the composition.
4 It should be noted that the resolution of this problem is not necessarily about living as long as possible. In the case of the Samurai, for instance, it is about determining the proper way to die.
5 This understanding, which is consistent with Husserl's and Schutz's understandings of the 'natural attitude', can cause confusion in relation to the way 'natural' is used by naturalism (the prevailing methodology of Religious Studies). In the past I have preferred to employ the archeologism 'cyndelic' to curtail confusion. This Old English word can be translated as 'natural', 'proper', 'suitable', 'lawful' or 'rightful'. Thus, to be 'natural' in the sense of cyndelic is to effectively find one's 'place' within the life-world. The naturalistic understanding of 'natural' as a mathematical manifold is better approximated by the Old English 'gebyrde' which means 'natural', 'innate' or 'inborn'. However, considering the extensive Korean and Japanese terminology below I have found it more appropriate to retain the English word.
6 Admittedly, the English 'martial art' seems to be derived from the Latin ('Art of Mars') and was in use from the 1550s as a synonym for 'fencing', some 50 years before the arrival of the first Britain in Japan (Clements, 2006). There is thus a translation issue as a single English term is used for what, for the Japanese, are two separate things. Indeed, the introduction of various bujutsu to Europe seems to have coincided with the development of various budo from 1868 onward (Bennett, 2015).
7 For reasons of space I am unable to detail this development.
8 This was then redrafted in 2004.
9 Though he is not credited on the NKK website, this translation was in fact undertaken by Bennett (2015).
10 There was an inherent tension in this as Koreans would only ever be seen as second-class Japanese.
11 There is also a competing International Taekwondo Federation that is not permitted to compete in the Olympics.
12 Donohue also notes that it is part of this mythic image that the hero is 'he' (2002: 78n1).
13 There is not the space to explore Rutt's main argument that highlights the ambiguities surrounding the hwarang's true function.

14 A sequence of movements defending and attacking imaginary opponents.
15 See, for example, www.dynamicmartialarts.org.
16 See, for example, www.combatteam.com and www.kicksforchrist.com.

References

Befu, H. (1981), *Japan: An Anthropological Introduction*. Tokyo, Charles E. Tuttle Co.

Bennett, A. (2015), *Kendo: Culture of the Sword*. Oakland, University of California Press.

Berger, P. and Luckmann, T. (1966), *The Social Construction of Reality: A Treatise in the Sociology of Knowledge*. London, Penguin Books.

Chosun Taekwondo (2014), 'About Chosun' available from *Chosun Taekwondo*. Accessed 15/12/15. http://chosuntkd.com/about-chosun/.

Clements, J. (2006), 'A Short Introduction to Historical European Martial Arts', *Meibukan Magazine: House of the Pure Martial Arts*, 1: 2–3.

Cook, D. (2001), *Taekwondo: Ancient Wisdom for the Modern Warrior*. New Hampshire, YMCAA Publication Centre.

Davidsen, M. (2012), 'What is Wrong with Pagan Studies?', *Method and Theory in the Study of Religion*, 24 (2): 183–199.

Donohue, J. (2002), 'Wave People: The Martial Arts and the American Imagination', in D. Jones (ed.), *Combat, Ritual and Performance: Anthropology of the Martial Arts*. London, Praeger: 65–80.

Fitzgerald, T. (1997), 'A Critique of "Religion" as a Cross-cultural Category', *Method and Theory in the Study of Religion*, 9(2): 91–110.

Fitzgerald, T. (2000), *The Ideology of Religious Studies*. Oxford, Oxford University Press.

Goldenberg, N. (2013), 'Theorising Religions as Vestigial States in Relation to Gender and Law: Three Cases', *Journal of Feminist Studies of Religion*, 29(1): 39–52.

Guttmann, A. (1993), 'The Diffusion of Sports and the Problem of Cultural Imperialism', in E. Dunning *et al.* (eds), *The Sports Process: A Comparative and Developmental Approach*. Champaign: Human Kinetic Publishers: 125–137.

JBA (2004) 'The Budo Charter' available from *Nippon Budokan Official Website*. Accessed 15 December 2015. www.nipponbudokan.or.jp/shinkoujigyou/budo-chater.html.

JBA (2009), 'The Philosophy of Budo' available from *Nippon Budokan Official Website*. Accessed 15 December 2015. www.nipponbudokan.or.jp/shinkoujigyou/rinen_eng.html.

Kiyota, M. (1995), *Kendo: Its Philosophy, History and Means to Personal Growth*. London, Kegan Paul International.

Maliszewski, M. (1996), *Spiritual Dimensions of the Martial Arts*. Rutland, Charles E Tuttle Co.

NKK (2007), 'Concept of Kendo' available from *All Japan Kendo Federation*. Accessed 15 December 2015. www.kendo-fik.org/english-page/english-page2/concept-of-Kendo.htm.

Norman. G. (2014), *What Martial Arts Taught Me About the Gospel of Jesus Christ: Spiritual Lessons from the Dojo*. CreateSpace Independent Publishing Platform.

Orlando, B. (2016), 'Martial Arts and Christian Faith: Incompatible?' available from *www.Orlandokantao.com*. Accessed 7 June 2016. www.orlandokuntao. com/master_frameset.html.

Rallo. V. (2016), *Exposing the Dangers of Martial Arts: Mortal Enemies and Christianity*. Real Truth Publications.

Rutt, R. (1961), 'The Flower Boys of Silla (Hwarang): Notes on the Sources', *Transactions of the Korean Branch of the Royal Asiatic Society*, 38: 1–68.

Sartre, J.P. (2003), *Being and Nothingness*, trans. by H. Barnes. London, Routledge.

Seth, M. (2011), *A History of Korea: From Antiquity to the Present*. Plymouth, Rowman and Littlefield Publishers.

Sheets-Johnstone, M. (2016), 'Strangers, Trust, and Religion: On the Vulnerability of Being Alive', *Human Studies* 39 (2): 167–187.

Smith, A. (1991), *National Identity*. London, Penguin.

Svinth, J, and Green, T. (eds) (2003), *Martial Arts in the Modern World*. Westport, Praeger.

Tuckett, J. (2016), 'Kendo: Between "religion" and "nationalism"', *Journal for the Study of Religions and Ideologies* 15(4): 178–204.

Chapter 9

Playing and praying in the Premiership

Public display of beliefs in English football

Abel Ugba

Introduction

Religion uncharacteristically became the dominant issue in public and media discourse in much of England in early 2012. The discourse, also uncharacteristically, did not conform to the tone and focus of the usual media scrutiny of religion. There was none of the well-worn rhetoric about abortion, terrorism, same-sex marriage or euthanasia. The discourse was not initiated by the clergy or religious leaders but it emanated from an incident that happened during a football match between two English Premiership clubs – Bolton Wanderers and Tottenham Hotspur. During a televised Football Association (FA) Cup game on 17 March 2012, Fabrice Muamba collapsed while playing for Wanderers. Newspaper reports, quoting medical sources, later confirmed that he had suffered a cardiac arrest. The heart of the Bolton player stopped beating for 78 minutes, but he survived after many months in hospital. The incident led to the end of his footballing career, as he has since documented in *I'm Still Standing* (Muamba, 2012).

Much of the coverage of the incident in the mainstream media focused on Muamba's convalescence and the reaction of the football world and the medical community. Attention was also given to the plight of his family, particularly his fiancée, their son and Muamba's parents. However, the bulk of the coverage focused on beliefs and spirituality among athletes and the role of prayers in healing and sporting success. For a couple of months, religion was unusually alive in the pages of the British newspapers as it was subjected to legitimate and purposeful journalistic and intellectual scrutiny in much the same way as the economy or politics is reported in the media. This was a giant step, not least because journalists in Britain (unlike their counterparts in the US) have historically failed to prioritise the reporting of events concerning religion.

Various explanations have been canvassed for the attitude of British journalists towards religion. For example, an article published by the religious think-tank *Theos* blamed the decreasing volume of good reporting around religion on 'shrinking newspaper budgets and the transition to pay models favouring 'clickbait' over reportage' (Kesvani, 2016: 2). Lack of material resources neither justifies nor fully explains why British journalists have consistently treated religion as an inferior ideology. Much of the explanation rests with the preconception that many have of religion and their reluctance or inability to engage directly with it.

Religiosity is low in British society compared to the US and British journalists are far more secular than their US counterparts. As Hoover (1997: 291) puts it: 'no other Northern countries share the level of religiosity, either private or public, of North America'. In 2000, the BBC website reported that '48% of people in the UK claim to belong to a religion, compared with 86% of people in the US and 92% of Italians' (BBC, 2000). More recently the *Guardian* newspaper reported that the number of people without religion in England and Wales has outstripped the number of Christians (*Guardian*, 2016a). Citing a 2014 survey, the report stated that 48.5 per cent of the population affirmed that they had no religion compared to the 43.8 per cent who said they were Christians. Religiosity is even lower among journalists. This is significant because, as Mason (2008: 12) puts it, 'people's religious beliefs ... can affect their work as a journalist, too, regardless of their beat, medium or position'. A 2016 survey published by Oxford University's Reuters Institute for the Study of Journalism concluded that journalists in UK 'are less likely to be religious or spiritual in general terms and much less likely to affiliate with a particular religious group than the wider community' (Thurman *et al.*, 2016: 11). Against this backdrop of the British media's historical under-reporting of religion, the religion-laden coverage of the Muamba incident appears somewhat unusual and therefore deserving of further intellectual scrutiny.

Hence, it is my intention within this chapter to examine the content of selected media reports of the Muamba event, focusing on overt and implied religious tone and the diversity of views represented. I propose that the coverage raises new and interesting questions about the approach of secular media to the reporting of religion. In the first section of the chapter I briefly summarise some of the dominant views of religion and spirituality among athletes. Thereafter, I analyse newspaper articles concerning the medical emergency that nearly claimed Muamba's life. I have sourced these articles from selected mainstream newspapers in Britain.[1] In conclusion, I reflect upon the implications of this kind of media reportage, particularly in the UK, and suggest that it opens the way for fresh thinking around the relationship between religion and the media in general.

Connections and conflicts between sport and religion

It is not my aim within this section to provide an exhaustive review of extant research and scholarship on religion and sports.[2] Instead I highlight selected ideas that provide relevant theoretical context to my general arguments. Aside from being significant elements of many contemporary societies, religion and sport share many similarities and differences. One of the earliest interfaces between the two was in ancient Greece where athletes consulted the gods and goddesses, including Athena, before and after major competitions.

The early Olympic Games were suffused with references to the religions of the Greeks and Mount Olympus, from which the Olympics Games derived its name, was considered by the Greeks as the abode of their gods. Evidence of this ancient link between sports and religion is discernible even in contemporary times. For example Nike, the name of the multinational American sportswear manufacturer, was also one of the names of Athena, the Greek goddess that supposedly inspired success. Although sports and religion have intersected for many centuries, the nature of this relationship has varied across time and space. For example, a distinction must be drawn between sports participation that simultaneously fulfilled a religious obligation, as was the case with many ancient Greek sports, and many modern sporting activities whose primary goal is entirely non-religious. In the twenty-first century the motives and practices of spiritually-oriented sports men and women vary widely, a point to which I will return.

In addition to these historical links, sports and religion share many other connections. For example, researchers have highlighted similarities in the attitudes of sports fans and religious devotees (e.g. Burstyn, 2001; Young, 2012; Watson and Parker, 2013, 2014). Like many religions, most sports command armies of devotees who throng to hallowed spaces or stadia faithfully, week after week, to reaffirm their devotion. Burstyn (2001) states that the emotion and identification that sports fans display are closer to that of religious devotees than any other cultural practice. She describes sport as a 'secular sacrament' (p. 10) and concludes that the fanfare and ritual that are often the hallmarks of sporting spectacle have attained a level that is commensurate with the devotion and emotions that religious devotees have exhibited for thousands of years. The ceremonies and rituals associated with religion and sports both serve to establish or affirm the rules of belonging and participation and are often conduits for transmitting group values and ideas of success, heroism and failure.

Another explanation of the relationship between religion and sports is rooted Karl Marx's theorisation of capitalism, which emphasises the struggle for dominance by competing social groups (Trevor, 1980; Elster, 1986a, 1986b). This theoretical lens sees religion and sports as competing instruments of economic and cultural suppression and as contrasting societal forces that are vying for dominance in the socio-cultural sphere (Coakley, 2001: 29). Both elements are supposedly in the hands of power-seeking individuals and groups who utilise them in instrumental ways to control the 'masses' and make them acquiesce in their own suffering and subjugation. But this is a highly contested notion, not least because religion and sports in most countries are never entirely in the hands of the government or a single group. Rather, there are often layers and degrees of ownership and control. There is also international interference in the rules that govern their establishment and existence. For example, professional football clubs in the English Premiership are often owned by businesspersons and regulated by the FA, but they are in addition subject to relevant government regulations and international rules fashioned by the Union of European Football Associations (UEFA) and the Fédération Internationale de Football Association (FIFA). Their existence and function are also affected by the opinions of interest groups such as those of their supporters, the media, financial sponsors and match officials.[3]

Therefore, the 'control' that sports have over supporters is less direct and instead more connected to the values, ideas and sense of groupness that they nurture in them. For instance, some religions require adherents to renounce materialism and carnal pleasures in order to achieve the higher goals of morality and spiritual salvation (see Green, 2000). This is comparable to the self-denial and strict regime of physical and mental training that many professional athletes make their way of life in order to achieve sporting success and recognition. To the extent that sports and religion exert this form of control over the thoughts and actions of followers or participants, it could be argued that they serve as instruments of control. Granted, it is a 'control' that is not imposed, but one that is deemed vital by those affected by it because, among other things, it defines their essence as athletes, confirms their membership of an elite group, and restates their commitment to the sport they love.

Coakley (2001) has similarly argued that sporting occasions have a tendency to transport both participants and spectators away from the drudgeries of daily existence and provide them with a temporary 'high'. This idea is similar to Marx's contention that religion is an opiate and an ideology of oppression, or as Christiano et al. (2002: 127) puts it, 'a powerful conservative force that serves to perpetuate the domination of one social class at the expense of others'. In the opinion of such critics, and as an answer to, or explanation of, the human condition, religion produces illusions and diverts believers away from the true solution to their problems, distracting them from their real place in the world and making them acquiesce in their own exploitation and suffering. Clifford Geertz (1973), however, disputes the supposed opiate-like effect of sports, arguing that they are more likely to mirror the organisations and hierarchies in society than offer respite from them. In his study of Balinese cockfighting, Geertz concludes that although the glitz and drama of sporting events provide entertainment, they do not change conditions and statuses in society. His critics would, of course, point to the many athletes and sportspersons in the twenty-first century whose statuses have changed remarkably as a direct result of the material gains they have acquired through their involvement in sports.

A more easily discernible link of both religion and sports to conflict is the contention and contestations that have often characterised the relationship between 'competing' sides. I contend that the loyalty of most sports fans and many religious adherents is an emotionally laden type that, in most cases, unites as well as divides. In his conceptualisation of identity, Brubaker (2004: 46) states that emotionally laden identification involves 'both a felt solidarity or oneness with fellow group members and a felt difference from or even antipathy to specified outsiders'. Among sports fans and some religious adherents 'antipathy to specified outsiders' has sometimes translated into open conflict with the 'other' with disastrous consequences. Media reports of the 2016 European Football Championship games in France were dominated by clashes between fans of competing sides. A report in the *Guardian* of 12 June 2016 documented (supported with graphic photographs) a violent encounter between supporters of the England and Russian national teams (*Guardian*, 2016b). Although many religious groups would not consider the relationship they have with other religions as a competitive, it is clear even to the most casual observer that competition, whether for resources, members or societal recognition, has become a dominant feature of the operational strategy of many religious groups in the twenty-first century.

Apart from their similarities, the relationship between sports and religion is also characterised by a multitude of differences. For example, religion has often been thought of as a serious pursuit whose fundamental goal or purpose is far more than entertainment. Sport, on the other hand, has sometimes been seen mainly as a purely recreational and less serious pursuit. Eitzen (2014: 5) challenges this notion, stating: 'While seemingly a trivial pursuit, sport is important'. This is even more so in the twenty-first century when sports and big sporting occasions have increasingly incorporated the competitive, innovative and commercial traits of the creative industries. Financial investments into specific sports such as football, baseball, American football, golf and tennis seemingly increase year-on-year. Billions of people invest a great deal of their time and energies into supporting, following or participating in particular sports. The old saying, 'it's only a game' is less and less applicable to many sports, particularly those in the elite/professional category. Millions of people live for sport and because of it, while others have died for it. Many dimensions of sport today are probably as 'serious' as any other life pursuits. Sport is no longer just a game.[4]

The conflicts and coexistence of sport, religion, commercialism and politics are perhaps best epitomised in the public lives of faith-proclaiming professional sportsmen and women. Anecdotal evidence suggests that public display of beliefs by sportspersons has been more pronounced in the

US than in Britain mainly because religion has a more pronounced presence in American public life. More recently, however, there has been an increasing public display of religious symbolisms by footballers in the English Premiership and other sports. The dalliance between sportspersons and religion has been politicised and given wider recognition since the second half of the twentieth century, for example, by the conversion of former heavyweight boxing champion Cassius Clay (Mohammed Ali) to Islam and Mike Tyson's flirtations, also with Islam. Other boxing champions such as Evander Holyfield and Tyson Fury, the current British Heavyweight Champion, have also publicly confessed Christianity and ascribed their success to ecclesiastical interventions.

Critics have suggested that high-profile and widely-publicised attachment to particular religions, such as the ones I have identified above, is often not simply about religion or sport, but also about identity politics. In his analysis of the relationship between professional sports and conservative Christianity in the United States, Krattenmaker (2009) maintains that 'spontaneous' displays of faith by athletes in the American context are often intended to achieve aims other than simply showcasing beliefs. He states that such displays 'are not so spontaneous at all', but are, in fact, well-thought-out strategies by a 'network of evangelical chaplains and sports ministry organizations' to align religion – and in particular the Christian Right – with professional sports (p. 3). He further states that athletes in the United States have been encouraged and even cajoled into publicly professing their faith as a way to win public recognition or support for particular religious groups, movements or ideologies. Being a professional athlete in the US, Krattenmaker (2009) argues, can sometimes mean committing to becoming a poster child of Christianity and a supporter of the Christian Right's political agenda (see also Hoffman, 2010; Feezell, 2013; Parker and Watson, this volume).

Krattenmaker's argument is problematic on many levels, not least because it represents religion as an ideology that adherents imbibe and live by solely because they have been compelled to do so by other people or groups. Such a notion oversimplifies the complexities and dynamics of religious conversion and devotion. Moreover, his argument sits squarely within the functionalist theorisation of religion and in so doing fails to acknowledge that the substance or content of religion matters to those who subscribe to it. Religious conversion and devotion is not simply about the actions of converts, but about what or who individuals have been transformed (mentally and emotionally) into as a result of accepting a particular religious ideology. Max Weber (1930), for example, contended that Calvinists in seventeenth-century Europe relied on the contents of Protestantism to define self and social reality and to regulate their ethical, social and economic conduct (see also Green, 2000). However, what is not in doubt is that public display of belief by sportspersons is often a symbolic practice used by them to invest higher meaning in life and to convey the message that their existence and identity not is simply about sports. To the extent that these displays are meant to send a message to the 'other' – be they fellow sportspeople or the wider public – they can be termed a symbolic practice. In linking the personal with the social, Erving Goffman (1975) suggested that the actions of individuals are performances aimed at influencing the opinion of the 'other'. They are meant to make statements about 'self' and to elicit particular responses. In the next section I analyse media reports of Fabrice Muamba's near-death experience, highlighting the insights they reveal about the complex relationship between sport, religion and the media.

Muamba, religion and the media

On 17 March 2012 Fabrice Muamba nearly died. He collapsed as his team – Bolton Wanderers – engaged Tottenham Hotspur in a FA Cup match. The religion-laden tone of media coverage surrounding this incident is the focus of the present section, which is based on the following (selected) articles:

- Archbishop hails Muamba prayers (*Observer*, 8 April).
- Littlejohn's footballer prayers rant (*Folkstone Herald*, 29 March).
- Archbishop talks of prayer power (*Sunday Sun*, 8 April).
- Prayer gives hope but science saved Muamba (*Mail on Sunday*, 29 April).
- Catholic leader hails Muamba wishes (*Belfast Telegraph*, 7 April).
- He has asked that you keep him in his prayers (*Mailonline*, 23 March).
- Fabrice Muamba's collapse shows how prayer comes naturally to footballers (*Guardian*, 19 March).
- Exclusive praying for Muamba – Footie star's fiancée in plea to fans as he fights for life (*Sun*, 19 March).
- God is in control, please say prayers for Muamba (*Express*, 19 March).
- Littlejohn's footballer prayers rant (*Folkestone Herald*, 29 March 2012).
- Muamba lament runs amok in Kent (*Scottish Daily Mail*, 27 March).
- Prayer didn't save Muamba ... docs did (*Sun*, 23 March).

What follows is a qualitative content analysis of these articles aimed mainly at demonstrating that the intense and rigorous coverage of the incident constituted a major deviation from the British media's usual (somewhat lackadaisical) approach to the reporting of religion. Unlike conventional content analysis that aims primarily to generate replicable statistics and outcomes, qualitative content analysis encourages theory-directed textual analysis (Klenke, 2008). Therefore, my examination of the articles aims to identify and highlight textual evidence that qualifies them as serious and sophisticated journalism, the type that, until this particular incident, had been reserved for reporting on politics and the economy.

A report in the *Guardian* of 19 March 2012 depicted Muamba's collapse and the almost instantaneous introduction of religion as a major connected sub-theme:

> Fabrice Muamba dropped on the pitch as if dead. The next thing that happened, after the paramedics reached him, was a member of the opposing team dropped on his knees to pray. No one jeered. There has been an outpouring of prayer requests on his behalf since then. There is a hashtag on Twitter: even the front page of the Sun says 'God is in control', quoting Muamba's fiancée.
>
> (Brown, 2012)

This excerpt provides some indication of why Muamba's ordeal quickly caught the nation's imagination and why the discourse that followed was so heavily flavoured with religious ideas. Muamba collapsed during a 'live' game, which meant that millions of television viewers and social media users were instantaneously connected with the ordeal. In normal circumstances medical emergencies usually involve the patient, medical staff and perhaps a couple of relatives. In Muamba's case, the thousands of spectators in the stadium that day were eyewitnesses and participants in the initial efforts to revive him. The player who 'dropped on his knees' did so perhaps because it is the only way he has learnt to cope with unexpected tragic occurrences. But more likely he knew that that was the sort of reaction that Muamba, given his cultural and ethnic background,[5] would have expected or appreciated. Other newspaper accounts described Muamba as a devout Christian who was never discomforted if he had to discuss or showcase his beliefs. Whatever the motive of the player who went on his knees was, his actions set the stage for the trend of religiously infused responses that quickly became a national phenomenon. Andrew Brown, author of the *Guardian* report quoted above, described the mass evocation of prayers and other religious ideas that saturated the media and public reaction as 'hard to reconcile ... with our normal worldview' (Brown, 2012). Even harder to reconcile was how quickly and deeply journalists embraced the religious fervour that ensured. The *Sun* newspaper led the way on 19 March by publishing a front page article entitled 'God is in control'. The article stated:

> The fiancée of stricken footballer Fabrice Muamba begged fans to pray for him last night as his life hung in the balance. Devastated Shauna Muganda, 27, kept a bedside vigil and tweeted: 'God is in control'.
>
> (*Sun*, 2012a)

Shauna's request was also quoted by the *Sunday Express* in a report published also on the same day:

> Millions of TV viewers and fans in the stadium watched in horror as the Bolton Wanderers midfield player suffered a heart attack during his team's FA Cup clash with Tottenham Hotspur. His distraught family kept a bedside vigil during the crucial first 24 hours of his recovery with his manager Owen Coyle saying everyone was hoping for a 'happy outcome'. His devastated fiancée Shauna, 27, posted on the social networking site Twitter: 'God is in control. Please keep Fabrice Muamba in your prayers xx'.
>
> (Pilditch, 2012)

On 23 March, the *Sun* newspaper published another report that showed that football officials had begun to adopt the religious language that had started to dominate the media and public discourse:

> FABRICE Muamba's family last night thanked the millions of fans wishing for the footballer's recovery, saying: 'Our prayers have been answered ... Bobby Barnes, of the Professional Footballers' Association, said: 'I've spoken to his mother and father. They feel at the moment their prayers have been answered.' A family friend added: 'They believe the millions of prayers said for Fabrice have helped him pull through.'
>
> (*Sun*, 2012b)

Bolton Manager Owen Coyle, in the same report, stated that Muamba's family had given their blessings for the team's home match against Blackburn Rovers to go ahead the day after. Although 'God is in control' started to trend on social media after it was uttered by Muamba's fiancée Shauna, this was not the phrase that epitomised the national outpouring of prayers and 'get well' messages. Instead, it was 'Pray 4 Muamba', the three words that were publicised to millions of TV viewers by Gary Cahill, the Chelsea player, on 18 March during a match between Chelsea and Leicester City. Cahill had pulled up his jersey to reveal the slogan while celebrating scoring in that game. Although it is against FA rules for players and officials to wittingly display slogans during the course of a game, the referee made an exception on this occasion and did not penalise Cahill.

Following Cahill's the gesture, 'Pray 4 Muamba' dominated social media as well as the pages of many newspapers. Commenting on the media fervour, Home Editor Mark Easton stated in an article published on the BBC website:

> Have you prayed for Fabrice Muamba today? His family are exhorting the country to believe in the power of prayer, and I suspect many

millions of Britons, whether they have faith or not, will have felt moved to offer a silent appeal to an invisible power asking that the young footballer pull through.... The front page of today's Sun newspaper is devoted to the headline 'God is in Control' below the subheading 'Praying for Muamba'. 'In God's Hands' says the Daily Star. Chelsea defender Gary Cahill pulled off his shirt after scoring yesterday to reveal a vest encouraging supporters to 'Pray 4 Muamba', his former team-mate.

(Easton, 2012)

Individuals and groups responded to the invitation and offered prayers for the ailing player. Most controversially, Shepway Council in Folkstone (Kent) included prayers for Muamba among its prayer points just before a full meeting of its councillors, a decision that attracted the ire of Richard Littlejohn, a well-known journalist and contributor to a number of national newspapers. Littlejohn described the decision of the Council as 'the most absurd manifestation of this carnival of vicarious grief' (Littlejohn, 2012). But he was roundly condemned by the local newspaper and council chairperson, Ms Jennifer Hollingsbee, who retorted:

I do not feel we should isolate ourselves from what is happening throughout the rest of the country and the world. We like to demonstrate that we consider the wider community, as well as our own, through prayers. Fabrice Muamba, is a young talented footballer, a role model for many young people across the country, including Shepway. Our prayers were also for the six soldiers killed in Afghanistan and the victims and families of the Toulouse shooting, all three stories were widely reported and resonated within the hearts of many people both nationally and locally.

(Quoted in Kent Online 29 March 2012)

Another major dimension of the national media coverage was the clash between science and faith. Many commentators were critical of the religious ideas and the role of faith connected to Muamba's 'healing'. One headline in the *Sun* newspaper stated categorically that 'Prayers didn't save Fabrice Muamba ... doctors did' (*Sun*, 2012b). The article went on to express misgivings about how the contribution of the medical community to Muamba's recovery had been de-emphasised in favour of religious ideas. In stated that media coverage that emphasised beliefs to the detriment of medical intervention insulted the 'immense skills and dexterity' of doctors and paramedics who had worked hard to save Muamba.

Although 'Pray 4 Muamba' was the immediate trigger, there were contextual factors that accounted for the religious fervour that dominated the majority of media accounts. One of these factors was Muamba's ethnic or cultural background. Although a British citizen, Muamba is African, originally from Congo. As Brown (2012) remarked in his report in the *Guardian*, 'English footballers are not recruited from the churchgoing classes', but 'African ones such as Muamba are much more likely to be Christian or even Muslim'. Many African players in the English Premiership have discussed their religious beliefs publicly and made open and spontaneous displays of their faith on the pitch, especially after they have scored a goal. There is the well-known heavenward gaze, the beatific clasping of the hands, the raising of the index finger skyward, and the spreading out of the hands with the palms turned heavenward, although some of these gestures do not appear to be limited to those with an outward profession of faith. Some players have gone so far as to fall on their knees to offer thanks while others have assumed the Muslim prayer pose and touched the ground with their forehead. My point here is not that these gestures and other symbolic public displays of faith are unique to African players, but that African players have contributed to their popularity in English football. South American players too have made a significant contribution here. For example, Mexican international and former Manchester United forward, Javier Hernandez, has routinely been seen on his knees in the centre of pitch with his eyes closed and the palm of both hands spread heavenward in the run-up to kick-off. The devout Catholic has maintained this pre-match ritual in the Spanish and German leagues where he has played since his tenure at Manchester United ended. Hence, while clearly not unique, the connection between African players and spirituality was, I suggest, just one among a number of contextual factors that contributed to the spiritual/religious focus of the media coverage of Muamba's incident.

Conclusion

The aim of this chapter has not been to regurgitate the divergent views that dominated media reports of Muamba's near-death ordeal, or to critique those who spoke for or against religion. Nor has my analysis paid particular attention to the racialisation of the Muamba incident.[6] My main aim has been to demonstrate that media coverage of Muamba's near-death experience occasioned a major shift, albeit temporary, in the attitude of British journalists towards religion. For a short period of time, religion was alive amid the pages of British newspapers and on radio, television and social media. It was treated not as the poor relation of the economy, politics and international affairs, but as their equal. The evidence lies not just in the volume of materials produced, but in the depth and quality of their analysis. This was evidence of journalism embracing and dignifying religion, but one that was shortlived.

It would seem that the media interest in the immediate aftermath of the medical emergency comprised, in the initial stages at least, a mixture of reaction to Muamba's critical state and anticipation of a death that never happened. Later, as the threat of death subsided, 'Pray 4 Muamba' became a symbolic gesture indicating support for Muamba and his family in their ordeal. The journalists who in various ways embraced and embellished the religious fervour that surrounded these events did not set out to promote faith or the efficacy of prayer. However, their actions demonstrate that journalists possess the intellectual resources to report religion comprehensively and rigorously – if they so wish. Religion, it seems, is not dead within the echelons of British mainstream journalism. On the contrary, interest in, and engagement with, such matters appears nothing short of virulent when stirred by sudden or unexpected occurrences such as the Muamba's incident, the July 7/7 bombings in London or 9/11 terrorist attacks in New York. This sporadic approach to the reporting of religion, goes some way to suggesting that British journalists are still to acknowledge the fundamental role of religion in the everyday social realities of the UK public. That said, only time will tell whether this brief but significant engagement with religion has had a longer-term impact on the attitude of journalists in this and other 'secular' contexts.

Notes

1 In total I have selected 12 articles of various lengths published in ten different newspapers between 19 March and 29 April of 2012. Except for the *Scottish Daily Mail*, *Folkstone Herald* and the *Belfast Telegraph*, the selected newspapers have a national outlook and reach.
2 For such discussion see Watson and Parker (2014).
3 Arsenal Football Club, one of England's longest-established professional clubs, is now mainly owned by American sports tycoon Stan Kroenke with other domestic and overseas investors holding various quantities of shares (www.arsenal.com/the-club/). However, Arsenal's on-field affairs and competitive engagements are regulated by national, European and World governing bodies, while organised fan groups have input into decision-making through their participation at the Club's Annual General Meeting.
4 For further discussion on the seriousness and significance of sport, see Harvey (2014).
5 Born to Congolese parents in Kinshasha in 1988, Fabrice Muamba spent his early childhood in the Democratic Republic Congo. He came to England at the age of 11 with his mother to reunite with his father, who had fled the country to escape politically motivated violence and civil war. Many media accounts describe him as a 'devout Christian' (see 23 April 2012 report on Christian Today website), a trait that is often linked to his African heritage and upbringing.
6 One evidence of the racialisation of this incident was the abusive tweet sent by Liam Stacey, an undergraduate student at Swansea University, for which he was subsequently jailed for 58 days by District judge John Charles in Swansea. Liam's action was roundly condemned by several Twitter contributors and he faced disciplinary hearing at the University (www.theguardian.com/uk/2012/mar/27/student-jailed-fabrice-muamba-tweets).

References

BBC. 2000. UK is 'losing' its religion, 28 November (accessed 18 May 2016).

Brown, Andrew. 2012. Fabrice Muamba's collapse shows how prayer comes naturally to footballers. (*Guardian*, 19 March).

Brubaker, Rogers. 2004. *Ethnicity without Groups*. London and Cambridge, MA: Harvard University Press.

Burstyn, Varda. 2001. 'Sport as a Secular Sacrament'. In D. Stanley Eitzen (ed.) *Sport in Contemporary Society. An Anthology*. New York: Worth.

Christiano J. Kevin, Swatos, William H Jr. and Kivisto, Peter. 2002. *Sociology of Religion: Contemporary Developments*. Walnut Creek, Lanham, MD, New York and Oxford: Altamira Press.

Coakley, Jay J. 2001. 'Sport in Society: An Inspiration or an Opiate?' In D. Stanley Eitzen (ed.) *Sport in Contemporary Society. An Anthology*. New York: Worth.

Easton, Mark. 2012. Prayers for Muamba. www.bbc.co.uk/news/uk-17429779 (accessed 7 October 2016).

Eitzen, Stanley D. 2014. *Sports in Contemporary Society: An Anthology*. Oxford: Oxford University Press.

Elster, Jon. 1986a. *Karl Marx: A Reader Karl Marx 1818–1883*. Cambridge: Cambridge University Press.

Elster, Jon. 1986b. *An Introduction to Karl Marx*. Cambridge: Cambridge University Press.

Feezell, Randloph 2013. 'Sport, Religious Belief, and Religious Diversity', *Journal of the Philosophy of Sport*, 40:1, 135–162.

Geertz, Clifford. 1973. 'Deep Play: Notes on a Balinese Cockfight'. In *The Interpretation of Cultures,* New York: Basic Books.

Goffman, Erving. 1975. *The Presentation of Self in Everyday Life*. Harmondsworth: Penguin.

Green, Vivan Hubert Howard. 2000. *A New History of Christianity*. New York: Continuum.

Guardian 2016a. People of no religion outnumber Christians in England and Wales – study. www.theguardian.com/ (accessed 23 May 2016).

Guardian 2016b. Euro 2016: England and Russia fans clash before and after match. www.theguardian.com/ (accessed 7 October 2016).

Harvey, Lincoln. 2014. *A Brief Theology of Sport*. London: SCM.

Heidegger, Martin. 1977. *The Question Concerning Technology and other Essays*. (Translated by William Lovitt). New York: Harper and Row.

Hoffman, Shirl James. 2010. *Good Game: Christianity and the Culture of Sports*, Baylor, TX: Baylor University Press.

Hoover, Steward M. 1997. 'Media and the Construction of the Religious Public Sphere'. In Stewart M Hoover and Knut Lundby (eds) *Rethinking Media, Religion and Culture*. London and New Delhi: Sage Publications.

Kesvani, Hussein. 2016. Journalists are less religious, but faith reportage is vital. www.theosthinktank.co.uk/comment/2016/05/16/british-journalists-are-getting-less-religious-but-faith-is-still-a-vital-part-of-the-new#sthash.RLhZIwVf.dpuf (accessed May 2016).

Klenke, Karin. 2008. *Qualitative Research in the Study of Leadership*. Bingley: Emerald Group Publishing.

Krattenmaker, Tom. 2009. *Onward Christian Athletes: Turning Ballparks into Pulpits and Players into Preachers*. Lanham, MD: Rowman & Littlefield Publishers.

Littlejohn, Richard. 2012. Muamba lament runs amok in Kent, *Scottish Daily*, 27 March (accessed through Pressreader on 7 October 2016).

Mason, Debra L. 2008. The life of a journalist – keeping the faith, *Quill*. May, pp. 10–13.

Muamba, Fabrice. 2012. *I'm Still Standing*. London: Trinity Mirror Sport Media.

Pilditch, David. 2012. God is in control, please say prayers for Fabrice Muamba, *Sunday Express*, 19 March (accessed on 7 October 2016).

Sun. 2012a. God is in control, 19 March, Front page (accessed 7 October 2016).

Sun. 2012b. Prayer didn't save Fabrice Muamba … doctors did, 23 March (accessed 7 October 2016).

Thurman, Neil, Cornia, Alessio, and Kunert, Jessica. 2016. *Journalists in the UK*. Oxford: Reuters Institute for the Study of Journalism, University of Oxford.

Trevor, Ling. 1980. *Karl Marx and Religion: In Europe and India*. London: Macmillan.

Watson, Nick J. and Parker, Andrew. 2013. *Sports and Christianity: Historical and contemporary perspectives*. London: Routledge.

Watson, Nick J. and Parker, Andrew. 2014. *Sport and the Christian Religion: A Systematic Review of Literature*. Cambridge: Cambridge Scholars Publishing

Weber, Max. 1930. *The Protestant Ethic and the Spirit of Capitalism*. London: Allen and Unwin.

Young, Kevin. 2012. *Sport, Violence and Society*. London: Routledge.

Western perspectives on sport and Christianity

Western perspectives on
sport and Christianity

Chapter 10

Sport, society, religion and the Church of Scotland

Grant Jarvie

Introduction

From curtailing sporting pastimes in parish life, to promoting organized church sport, to tensions over Sunday sport, to sport being involved in the trafficking of children, to famous icons such as Eric Liddell, the University of Edinburgh Olympic gold medal winner at the Paris Olympics of 1924 whose commitment was to God first and athletics second, the Church of Scotland (COS) has had a long and sometimes troublesome relationship with sport. This chapter explores the relationship between sport, society, religion and the COS, and in so doing it expunges the myth that this relationship is new, for it is not.

In order to explore COS views on a wide range of issues from competitiveness to money, relationships, the family and much more, this chapter draws upon newspaper articles, minutes of meetings, church papers, the old and new statistical accounts of Scotland and two significant reports to the Church and Nation Committee of the Church of Scotland, the first of which was in 1964 and the second in 2014.

The chapter, while not exhaustive, asks what is the relationship between the COS and sport and how does this contribute to what we know about religion and sport. In order to address this question the chapter is organized around the following themes: (i) an overview of the relationship between sport, religion and Scottish society; (ii) an overview of the historic relationship between sport and religion in Scotland; (iii) a substantive account of the views of the church, nation and society committees of the COS in 1964 and 2014; and (iv) a return to the relationship between sport and religion with a plea for better ethics, better faith and better sport.

Sport, religion and Scottish society

Religion has had a significant historical presence in Scottish sport and society. In 1618 James VI issued a manifesto authorizing the practice of Sunday Games. In the *Book of Sports* (and much to the alarm of Puritans),

James VI endorsed the widespread participation of sports after church on Sundays but also placed an emphasis on sports participation for exercise and health reasons (Sportscotland, 2014). Religion and sport have rarely been indifferent to one another and this is perhaps not surprising given some of the similarities and differences between Scottish sport and religions, both: have rituals before during and after major events; have heroes and heroines; can evoke excitement and emotional commitment; have places and buildings for communal events; are controlled through structured systems and authority; can be linked to quests for control over body, mind and spirit. In general, some or all of the following themes have been associated with aspects of Scottish sport:

- the relationship between sport, religion and capitalism;
- the relationship between sport, religion, health and well-being;
- the relationship between religion, gender and sport;
- muscular Christianity, amateurism and social class;
- the relationship between sport, religion and parish life;
- the extent to which folk games and the origins of sport contributed to religious rituals, festivals and folk-lore;
- changing trends and social attitudes towards sport and the Sabbath;
- sport and religion as faith and identity.

Some of these themes are worth developing and exploring in a little more detail.

Muscular Christianity, amateurism and social class

The orthodox history of the relationship between Scottish sport and religion has been reproduced in numerous accounts of the connection between amateurism, class, gender and religion through the advent of the muscular Christian. Perhaps too much has been made of the moral power of this ideology, exercised through the connections of a networked society and closely associated with the public school system. Too many have uncritically accepted the orthodox story of the development of muscular Christianity emanating from the athletic missionaries of the British, including Scottish, public schools. What is often overlooked in these accounts is not only its *contemporaneous* meaning for some athletes but also that, like all forms of religion, amateurism itself was/is a social system: a social system that reproduced both power relations and sexism. Like all 'isms', amateurism as a social practice consisted of sets of beliefs and rituals that were supported by social institutions. For the muscular Christian who adhered to amateurism, the attitude towards money and economic reward was viewed as being secondary to other, more important, aspects of human life. The poor across a range of countries were invariably left to live on forms of metaphysical income rather than materially sustainable livelihoods.

Sport and religion as identity

A further theme worthy of consideration is the way in which sport and religion often get closely associated with matters of identity. The increasingly common use of sport being caught up with forms of religious identity fails to fully understand the social complexity of the relationship between, faith, religion and liberal humanism. The overly simplistic affiliation between a sports team, the identity of sports fans and religion often fails to distinguish whether the claimed identity or the relationship between different aspects of identity is a person's main affiliation or loyalty, or just one point of an identity among a group of various reference points. If being a follower of Christianity, Islam, Judaism, Shintu or Hinduism is the only form of primary or personal faith a person has then such religious identification would carry a burden of having to resolve the many choices a person faces in other parts of their lives.

Individuals can take up different positions on matters involving social, political, moral or other judgments without ceasing to be a Christian or Muslim. The US, Turkey and India all have secular constitutions but these have the common aim of protecting religion. By not permitting the establishment of any particular faith, secularism seeks to ensure that the state cannot be used as an instrument to persecute minority religions and that no religion can be imposed by law on an unwilling populace. At the same time, too fundamental a view of the relationship between sport and religion fails to recognize that varying attitudes to religious tolerance have been socially important in the history of the world. The basic recognition of a multiplicity of identities would militate against seeing certain sports teams or fans in exclusively religious or sectarian terms.

Fundamentalism, faith and liberal humanism

Certain fundamental beliefs have come to form part of the juridical religious dogma that sustains several institutional structures and sport has not been immune from the effects of these. Scottish sport is far from secular but the issue is, in part, whether doctrinal systems are impenetrable and therefore reduced to either condemning each other or in the case of fundamentalism, potentially doing battle with one another. The catalogue of atrocities committed in the name of religion shows how dangerous all forms of dogma may be and the initial point to be made here is that the relationship between Scottish sport and religion is far from innocent.

Many fundamentalist Christian groups have embraced sport as a mechanism for reducing their separation and exclusion from society while increasing their legitimacy and power within it. Fundamentalists in all religions tend to emphasize a need to return to basic, moral religious roots and develop a personal relationship with God, Allah, Christ, Mohammad, or the Other, whoever that may be. The fundamentalist view is the absolute view that allegedly offers clear-cut answers to personal and social problems. The key point, however, is to recognize that, in the quest for seeking legitimacy and exclusivity, all forms of fundamentalism promote forms of reification and separatism. By shielding internal tensions, a fundamentalist approach to sport would repress forms of communitarianism, and promote conformism, intolerance and patriarchy.

A qualifying comment needs to be made in relation to the liberal humanist claim that religion can be eradicated from human life. This remains an article of faith for many secular humanist groups, and yet it should not be forgotten that (i) at best, liberal humanism may have been rooted in nineteenth-century Christian denominations such as the Quakers or the Unitarians and (ii) at worst, in its extreme form liberal humanism itself is often viewed as religion-like in terms of its adherence to particular views about humanity, politics and religion. According to Gray (2002: 69), liberal humanism is an absolute form of religious doctrine. Gray argues that the secular view that we live in a post-religious era is a Christian, if not Western, invention. Liberal humanism, in other words, is framed as a form of religious humanity forged in a period before the work of John Stuart Mill (1806–1873) and whose intervention, lest we forget, upheld the abolition of slavery. Today's liberal humanism could be viewed as a contemporary version of an eccentric nineteenth-century cult that is clearly modelled on Christianity, despite the secular claims that are made. Yet, the Christian principle of individual liberty contrasts with and is often at conflict with other faiths.

Sport, religion and capitalism

At its most extreme, the relationship between sport, religion and capitalism is ever present in Smith and Westerbeek's (2004) account of the new sporting cathedrals of the Western world. These writers point out that sport is a kind of religion that satisfies religious needs for participants and spectators and that at the heart of the optimal sporting and religious experience is spiritual enlightenment. The sports business, they warn, could destroy everything that makes sport suitable as a religious substitute. In other words, Smith and Westerbeek (2004) believe that the specialness of sport can be destroyed by business if it fails to comprehend the spiritual components of the product by diminishing the power of the rituals, the stories, the gods and the temples that can be promoted through sport as religion. In short, these authors uncritically buy into the idea that sport, like religion, mobilizes communities, forges identity, provides meaning, infuses passion and enlivens the soul. Many of the problems that limit this sort of analysis are closely tied to a frame of reference that is presented as universal but, in reality, rarely unpacks or delineates within or between matters of faith. Perhaps more importantly, development is based upon spiritual rather than social possibilities. The political implications of this lack of social thinking can often be disturbing. By framing development purely in spiritual and capitalistic terms, Smith and Westerbeek (2004), while acknowledging the potential of the sports business, tend to reproduce certain social arrangements that are idealist and far from liberating for some people.

Sport, spirituality and well-being

Spiritual gifts, argue Walters and Byl (2008), are special abilities or capacities given by God for the edification of other people. Yet, the issue that these writers seek to address is a quest for a Christian and/or spiritual approach to health and well-being. While this contribution to an understanding of physical well-being is as much about the women who seek spirituality through mountain biking as it is about the religious experience of the man who loves to run, it is essentially a Christian guide to healthy body, mind and spirit. It presents a biblical view of the human body, approaching and expressing well-being through notions of creationism, evolution, redemption, God's care for one's body; the opposite of sinning causing healing and fulfillment. It presents a view of spirituality as directly expressed through a Western Christian narrative and it might be viewed as part of a new age movement, or other religious social movements that strive, in this case, to place spirituality at the heart of well-being, health and personal development.

Robinson's (2007) series of essays provides one of the most comprehensive overviews of the *promise and possibilities* brought about by the need to explain the relationship between sport and spirituality. It is complex because there is no single definition of what spirituality is or might be, and rather than provide a single definition, Robinson provides a model of spirituality that draws upon practice, experience and belief. Spirituality in relation to sport is multi-disciplined, drawing upon history, sociology, psychology, physiology and much more. The notions of hope, faith, acceptance and sense of purpose are practicalities for Robinson and yet, as is illustrated, the spiritual journey can be both individual and corporate. At both of these levels, the quest for spiritual meaning demands a process of, according to Robinson (2007), articulation, reflection, meaning development and a response.

Yet the decisive words in the passages above are promises and possibilities, and, although Robinson strives hard to avoid the abstract, the metaphysical and the symbolic, there is little discussion of whether, having travelled along the journey of spirituality, the athlete finds spiritual freedom or something else equally vague. More often than not, the vague suggestions of possibility or promises of something better fail to take account of political and/or economic conditions or whether spiritual freedom is, in fact, something different from human freedom. There can be substantive debates about well-being, freedom and capability and whether the spirituality and the end of the spiritual journey adds real capability that helps the individual or the group achieve, for instance, a better lifestyle or better range of choices, or does the quest for spirituality help constrain the search for human freedoms either through sport or otherwise? If the spiritual journey through sport helps improve social choices and freedoms, then it may be seen as a valuable tool that may or may not increase or decrease the capability gap between nations or groups or individuals.

Scottish sport, the Sabbath and church, nation and society

In Scotland, as elsewhere, the Christian attitude to sport and competition has long been ambivalent. Although there are allusions in the Old Testament to sports (e.g. swimming in Isaiah 25:11, archery in I Sam 20), these are not usually in the context of competition. The reference to racing in Jeremiah 12:5 is one of the few in the Old Testament to what might be seen as competitive sport.

While Paul in his letters makes reference to a number of sporting events, apparently without disapproval, in the first centuries of Christendom the Christian response to sports was often one of strong suspicion. Many of the earliest Christian preachers and theologians considered participation in 'games' antithetical to the Christian way of life. This was not only because of the reputation of the competitors' lifestyles, but also because public games were seen as being deeply intertwined with pagan and nationalist cultic worship.

The German Reformation leader Martin Luther encouraged his followers to participate in forms of exercise that were considered honourable and useful, such as dancing, archery, fencing and wrestling. For a period of a little more than a century from about 1540 onwards, those in power in Scotland alternately restrained and encouraged sport. Religious reformers wanted to control behaviour on the Sabbath. The Stewart monarchs supported archery practice after Mass; James VI approved of sport but after the Reformation the Kirk sought to place restraints on sport.

In the early church, the response to sports was often one of suspicion, but movements such as muscular Christianity in the nineteenth century embraced sport more fully (Church of Scotland, 2014). It was argued that sport produced discipline and virtue in its participants. This view was closely associated with religion, with similar sentiments taking expression in Scotland in the Boys' Brigade movement.

Of course, post-colonial revisionism and other schools of thought have thoroughly re-examined the practices of athleticism and muscular Christianity in so far that they were not politically neutral and often sought to challenge indigenous sporting practices (Jarvie and Thornton, 2012). In turn, some have argued that, while competition can elevate the character of those who are involved, there can be unhelpful pressures on athletes, such as enhancing their performance through all possible means (Jarvie and Thornton, 2012).

Writers, academics and critics have not been slow to comment on the relationship between the Church in Scotland and sport. Walker and Gallagher (1990) examined the place of football in protestant popular culture in Scotland; Bradley (2004) has critically considered the relationship between religion, politics, society, identity and football in Scotland; Holt (1992) talks of football and men's devotion to it in 1960s, 1970s and 1980s Scotland as not being too dissimilar to what Durkheim referred to as an elementary form of religious life; Woods (2010), reporting on the preparations of a Scottish athlete to run in the London Marathon, recalled that this included getting baptized with the athlete going on to explain that there were other reasons for becoming a Catholic, the new faith had acted as a performance enhancer; and Jarvie and Thornton (2012) have repeatedly called for a questioning of what is meant by better faith, better ethics and better sport while acknowledging that sport and religion in Scotland if far from neutral.

Few however have considered the attitudes of the COS to sport and physical recreation and how these have changed over time. The publication of two Church Nation reports in 1964 and 2014 affords such an opportunity. In 1964 a *Report of the Committee on Church and Nation* thought it necessary to re-examine and pronounce the issue of how Christians should use Sunday, including statements on sport, exercise and physical recreation (Committee on Church and Nation, 1964). An examination of the use of the Sabbath was not new since previous assemblies of the COS issued statements in 1933, 1946, 1947, 1959, 1960, 1962, 1963 and 1964 (Committee on Church and Nation, 1964). The use of religious scriptures to rationalize outcomes in the 1964 report was evident and it drew upon; the Sabbath in the Old Testament, the Sabbath in the New Testament, the Sabbath in the early church, the Lord's Day in the New Testament, the Lord's Day in the early church, the merging of the Sabbath and the Lord's Day, the reformation and what Luther and Calvin had to say on the matter and the Scots Confession of 1560 which makes no mention of Sunday at all (Committee on Church and Nation, 1964: 360–362). The question of how one puts one's Sunday to best use in the eyes of the 1964 Church had considerable religious sanction and Christian authority that could be brought into play if needed but at its heart the church was wrestling with how to balance worship, serious reading, family life, works of mercy, physical recreation and the rest of the day's activities (Committee on Church and Nation, 1964).

The hierarchy of the COS seemed to be in no doubt about the hierarchy of activities but on the specific question of physical recreation the report was more accepting of the daily needs of the people in 1960s Scotland (Committee on Church and Nation, 1964: 367). Physical recreation was viewed as having a natural place in the day and was deemed as being necessary and desirable. The report commented upon the differential access to fresh air and exercise arguing that such access was 'more difficult to come by for those who live in a tenement[1] house or city slums' (Committee on Church and Nation, 1964: 367). Modern methods of production, the report goes on, 'leave men and women far less physically tired than in days gone by and therefore there is a need for more bodily exercise' (Committee on Church and Nation, 1964: 367). The overall rationale was that physical recreation was deemed to be part of reasonable Sunday if taken in moderation. While the Committee on Church and Nation were clear that the decision on such matters must be left to the conscience of the individual, it did not stop short on its advice on youth and physical recreation strongly suggesting that:

> It is surely preferable that the young especially should have healthy opportunities healthy recreation than that they should be left to compulsory idleness, which so often breeds not only boredom but mischief and delinquency.
>
> (Committee on Church and Nation, 1964: 367)

The attitude to the Sabbath and sport in Scotland has long been contested and while the 1964 report might have attempted to provide a way forward it was still being discussed in the daily newspapers some 50 years later. Not to mention the fact that a version of the story was also popularized in David Putnam's cinematic classic *Chariots of Fire*. By July 1982, the film had amassed £49.4 million, making it, at the time, the biggest foreign production in US box office history. The narrative in the film was built around Eric Liddell, the Scottish athlete, later to become a missionary in China, who was picked to run in the 100 yards at the 1924 Paris Olympic Games but refused to compete because the final was scheduled to take place on a Sunday. Liddell is introduced in the film as an established Scottish rugby international who turns to running as a form of secular preaching. The conflicts in the film between amateurism, idealism, realism, god and nation, sport and social class are crucial to the narrative, with Liddell's metaphysical, evangelical running qualities representing a central theme throughout. Liddell's faith was deep-rooted within a Scottish evangelical fundamentalist tradition. The core of this faith was a burning conviction in personal salvation through the merits of Jesus. To bring men and women to this spiritual climax was one of the ultimate aims of the Scottish evangelicals who shared many similarities with the Scottish covenanters; both were fervent, both were puritanical, and both, in their heyday, were anxious to see their ideals adopted by the rest of society. The story presented in *Chariots of Fire* transforms Liddell's evangelical ideology into a metaphorical statement about the ultimate possibilities that could be achieved through sport. The framing of this story tended to depoliticize the role of the evangelicals within Scottish society but also situated the notion of freedom within a religious frame of reference.

Fast-forward to August 2004, where on the beaches around the northwestern tip of the small Scottish Island of Lewis, could be found Nicola Breciani and Francesco Palatella, professional surfers from Italy, who dedicated their lives to finding the perfect wave; a quest that had taken them from California, to Costa Rica, Australia, Bali, South Africa, Burma and Scotland. Both were unaware of the controversy that surrounded them about surfing on a Sunday (Martin, 2004). In an article that was headed 'Lewis hands surfers a never on Sunday warning', Martin (2004) explained the tension between the quest to increase tourism and income generation and the longstanding tradition of Sunday being a day of worship, rest and reflection. The Rev. Iver Martin of the Stornoway Free[2] Church of Scotland, commenting upon the issue of surfing on Sunday pointed out 'that the Sabbath is very special here and we have to fight to keep it sacred' (Martin, 2004: 13). The Rev. Martin was referring to plans by a local businessman to host an international surfing competition and festival on the Island of Lewis. The local Western Isles Council had earlier voted unanimously against opening a multi-million pound sports hall on the Sabbath, while a paintball company twice had its application for a Sunday Licence refused. Some seven years later in 2011, the same Rev. Martin, attacked the way in which human rights law was being used to undermine the Sabbath (Wade, 2011). Wade contends that the legislation was designed to stop discrimination against minority faiths and yet, on the Island of Lewis, where the religious community has long held sway, the human rights law could rob an indigenous population of its distinctiveness (Wade, 2011). Logic and the law suggest that, in time, the question may be resolved in favour of 7-day golf or surfing, but the sabbatarian answer as it currently stands is that golf clubs and leisure centres are not unique to island life and that Sunday on the Island of Lewis remains special.

The notion of the sacred Sabbath, as illustrated above, has impacted upon sport in other ways, most notably when sportsmen or sportswomen have been asked to put sport before the Sabbath and have refused to do so. In February 2010, the devoutly Christian Scottish forward, Euan Murray, returned to play for Scotland in a rugby international against Wales. It was the strength of his faith rather than his body that had ruled him out of the opening international match against France because it was due to be played on a Sunday. This example will not be the last but it would be misleading to suggest that such issues dominate COS debates on sport, for they do not. The content of the 2014 *Church and Society Report*, published some 50 years after the 1964 report affords a much broader discussion of COS attitudes towards aspects of sport in the twenty-first century. Delivered as blue paper report to the General Assembly of the COS this was timed to coincide with the 2014 Glasgow Commonwealth Games thus affording a more popular coverage of the contents.

On the question of Sunday sport the 2014 Church and Society Report simply noted that in the modern world much sport takes place on Sunday and that for some this posed an intrinsic problem while for others there was only a problem if it clashed with church service times (Church and Society Committee, 2014: 7: 10). Yet unlike the 1964 report the 2014 document offers comment on a wider range of issues thus enabling a COS view to be expressed on aspects of sport and Christianity in the early twenty-first century and it is to this that I wish to briefly turn.

Christianity, competition, 2014 and all that

The 2014 report to the Church and Society Committee set out to consider a specific set of questions. The report was not exhaustive but selective in its treatment of sport in Scotland and was aimed at taking advantage of 2014 being the year of the Glasgow 2014 Commonwealth Games to highlight COS views on a number of sporting matters that while not strong enough to lead to the production of a white paper (COS policies) they none the less formed the basis of a blue paper (COS discussion paper). This was endorsed by the General Assembly of the COS that sat in session during April of 2014 and therefore can be seen to form a COS view on a number of matters (Church of Scotland, 2014). The questions and issues that the report sought to address were as follows:

- Is competitiveness in sport a good thing or not?
- Which sports men and women might be identified as good and bad role models and why?
- What issues can arise for families when a child shows a particular sporting talent?
- What does the phrase 'winning at all costs' mean?
- What lessons can be learned from losing?
- In a sporting context how might Jesus' command to do to others what we would have them do to us be interpreted (Luke 6: 31)?
- In what ways does money influences sport?

- In what ways has technology impacted on ethical dimensions of sport and competitiveness?
- In what innovative ways might churches resolve the dilemma of sport coinciding with Sunday worship?

In providing guidance on such a wide range of questions the answers might best presented around a number of themes, including those of competition, family relationships, Sunday sport, coaches, equalities, opponents, Christianity and the role of sports chaplains.

The response starts by asserting that sport in its many forms is enjoyed at many levels by many people in Scotland (Church of Scotland, 2014: 3: 23: 7.1). Competitiveness in sport can draw out the best in people, but can also give rise to unworthy behaviour. So how can we enjoy sport, loving our neighbours and treating others as we would want to be treated, and still give expression to the competitive spirit? As indicated earlier, on the question of Christianity and sport the report acknowledges that in the early church, sports were often regarded with suspicion, and that in the nineteenth century movements such as 'muscular Christianity' embraced sport more fully. More recently, some argue that, while competition can elevate the character of those involved, there can be unhelpful pressures on athletes that may encourage them to enhance their performance through any means (Church of Scotland, 2014: 3: 23: 7.2).

On the question of competitiveness and winning and losing it was asserted that the word competition could mean both '*striving together*' and '*striving against*'. In 1 Corinthians 12, Paul invokes an image of *striving, together and against*, to highlight both our interconnectedness and interdependence (Church of Scotland, 2014: 3: 23: 7.3). The report stresses that both elements of striving are important and the report qualifies this by saying that in remembering the command to love God with all our heart, soul, strength and mind, competitors *strive together*, with God and others, pushing themselves to perform to the best of their abilities (Church of Scotland, 2014: 3: 23: 7.3). Competitiveness between individuals or teams, where there is mutual respect, exemplifies '*striving together*'. Whether winning or losing, sport can encourage a sense of belonging, co-operation and teamwork, fostering self-control, persistence and self-discipline. COS believe that all involved in competitive sport can be guided by Jesus' words: 'So in everything, do to others what you would have them do to you' (Church of Scotland, 2014: 3: 23: 7.3).

On winning or losing the thrill of achieving one's goal is viewed by COS as a major part of the reward for a game well played. However, it may also be that despite playing well, the opponent's performance is superior and one does not win. In competitive sport, COS suggest that we are responsible for pleasing God first, before everyone else (Church of Scotland, 2014: 3: 23: 7.4). Those who are defeated may feel they have lost face, or have let others down. It may take time to come to terms with losing, but defeat can also provide valuable lessons. On the question of relationships the COS is unequivocal on the importance of the family, coaches, opponents, the struggle for equality and the role that specialist sports chaplains might play in the twenty-first century world of sport.

On the question of families being able to see a family member excel it is suggested that this provides great joy (Church of Scotland, 2014: 3/23: 7.5.1). However, the families of sports people may need patience and compassion during difficult training schedules or disappointing results. Sport teaches vital life lessons, including discipline and working as part of a team, working hard to achieve success and accepting defeat graciously (Church of Scotland, 2014: 3: 23: 7.5.1). Those supporting young people in sport should uphold high standards of behaviour. However, in our enthusiasm it is easy to push boundaries, shouting abuse at officials or opponents, for example.

Coaches should also seek to encourage and inspire, challenging athletes to push their limits, to perform to the best of their abilities and help athletes deal with success and disappointment (Church of Scotland, 2014: 3: 23: 7.5.4). While it is important that coaches address the ethical dimension of competition, this is an area where sports chaplains could complement their role. Sports chaplains are concerned with the holistic well-being of people in sport, helping players to recognize that there is more to life than winning, adulation and money (Church of Scotland, 2014: 3: 23: 7.5.5). Whether one has a religious faith or not, chaplains can help people to recognize the importance of esteem, love and hope.

Opponents should be treated in the way that we want to be treated with respect, playing hard but not seeking an unfair advantage. COS point out that in Hebrews 10 we are encouraged to 'consider how we may spur one another on toward love and good deeds' (Church of Scotland, 2014: 3: 23: 7.5.6). This idea of encouragement to excel translates well to the context of competition in that opponents motivate each other to rise to the challenge of the contest while playing fairly and respecting each other.

On issues of equality, while women's sport in Britain has never been stronger, inequalities in earnings between the genders remain (Church of Scotland, 2014: 3: 23: 7.7.1). Those from minority ethnic groups are significantly less likely to participate in sport, particularly at club level, than their white counterparts. The 2012 London Paralympics showcased disability sport in an unprecedented way, but more needs to be done. For people with a disability, participation can help rehabilitation both physically and socially, reducing stigma and discrimination. In many countries there is little access for disabled people to appropriate sports facilities or technological aids. Opportunities to compete are compromised by insufficient funding to train or to travel. People who live in remote areas in Scotland, too, may have limited access to the kind of facilities that are available to city-dwellers. This it is important to remember that sport in Scotland is dived as much by class and geography as it is by gender (Research Scotland, 2016).

Better faith, better ethics, better sport

In the contemporary world, is it necessary to have a strong relationship between sport, religion and faith or does an adherence to religious faith make things worse in terms of tolerance, recognition and reconciliation? Faith carries a premium in the contemporary world and yet from faith schools, faith-based welfare through to religious justifications for debt relief and even warfare it is hard to escape it. Faith-based sports movements continue to exist despite the increasing secularization of certain societies. Those who support the notion of better faith, better ethics and better sport tend to view forms of faith as an ethical underpinning for debates about religion, spirituality, politics and sport. Those who do not support the notion of better faith, better ethics and better sport tend to argue from a humanist perspective that being in the possession of a divinely prescribed rulebook does not put one on the moral high ground in which there is a hierarchy of moral ideologies. It is worthwhile briefly considering the arguments for and against such propositions.

The arguments for better faith, better ethics and better sport tend to rely on a number of assumptions. The assumed demise of old political ideologies has left all areas of public life, including sport, with a sense of uncertainty about what is right and wrong. Developments in genetic science continue to present ethical dilemmas for sport, not least the possible cloning of athletes. Broader bio-ethical issues such as abortion and euthanasia are rarely out of the headlines. For those who support faith-based answers to difficult problems, it is argued that faith can make an important contribution in the prioritizing of policies. Faith groups are frequently sought out by government and related agencies because they contain highly motivated and committed volunteers. A major English study into sport volunteering confirmed the need for more informal patterns of sports volunteering given the chaotic lifestyles of young people in general (Sport England, 2003). Faith-informed volunteers often run local schemes and, while the faith element may be strong, it often remains in the background. The question being whether faith-based volunteering is better or worse than other forms of volunteering and if so in what ways is the case or can be evidenced. The problematic assumption is that better faith, better ethics, better volunteering in sport is part of an answer to the broader crisis of volunteering. Faith-based welfare provision has become so popular in the US and, to a lesser extent, Britain, that governments want to remain neutral on matters of faith but all parties, whether it be in politics, religion or sport, seem to want dedicated adherents.

The arguments against better faith, better ethics and better sport also tend to rely upon a number of assumptions primarily associated with humanists or atheists. Humanists tend to deny the possibility of moral rulebooks but believe that certain actions are right and wrong in areas such as freedom, tolerance, equality and justice. Emotive arguments about sport need to be informed by relevant comparative evidence as the possible antidote to making uninformed choices. Humanists view too strong an adherence to religion and sport as divisive and serving self-interests. Humanists would seek to provide forms of intervention that promoted tolerance in areas such as ethnicity and racism in sport and be naturally suspicious of sporting organizations that promoted single-faith sport as a model for better faith, better ethics and better sport. Humanist sport would promote pluralist sport based upon the assumption that cultural and religious-based sporting groups will only come to tolerate each other if they are educated together through sport and other areas. For humanists, seeking to promote or privilege forms of sporting experience at the expense of others is immoral but also dangerous because it promotes a sort of tribalism that capitalism, globalization and the contemporary world needs to outgrow. Yet, the problem, for anyone seeking faith-based forms of sporting involvement as the antidote to the contradictions of the modern sporting world, or even a faith-based model of global sport of realism and hierarchies remains with sport as in other facets of life – namely, which faiths and why?

Conclusions

The sense of allegiance that many hardcore Scottish sports fans have for a particular team is almost religious-like, in the sense that fans share a common history and share in a particular relationship and identity with other sports fans and groups. Hardcore sports fans and strong believers of faiths share a common distinguishing aspect of ascriptive identity. Those who belong to such groups identify deeply with them and typically experience membership of such groups as morally significant. For example, the sectarian animosity that has historically attached itself to Scotland's Celtic versus Rangers football matches is often characterized as groups of football fans partaking in a common history and standing in a particular relationship to another group of fans. It has promoted government intervention aimed at eradicating sectarian bigotry in football in Scotland by introducing specific but in effective legislation. In other senses, it might also be asked whether to be a Muslim or a Jew or a Christian or Catholic in Scotland is also to suggest that one's identity is intimately bound up with membership of a group, or at least the value that such a belief has is fundamentally important to the believer in a similar but also different way that a hardcore of Old Firm sports fans value the allegiance to a team?

This chapter has recognized that religions exist in all known societies; religious beliefs and practices vary from culture to culture and to the extent that sport involves a set of symbols and rituals, some of which may be religious, it is not difficult to see why some are quick to point out that sport continues to invoke religion in social life. Today, we find both religious organizations using sport and sports participants turning to religion in different ways. It is far from clear whether sport inhibits or promotes religious beliefs, and whether, in certain instances, such beliefs help to develop social cohesion, networking, or even psychological advantage in sport today.

History has taught us that proclaiming the principle of tolerance and justice in a multi-faith society is not sufficient to make a reality of it. There is some truth in the observation that the cultural war between the religious and the secular is an important social division locally, nationally and internationally and yet it is not openly acknowledged in the way that other social divisions such as 'race', gender and forms of social inequality are. The influence of religion on sport may have declined but it has not disappeared and we have seen in this chapter that in an examination of a church-based organization the potential influence of religious faiths does not necessarily mean better sport or a more acceptable world. However, there are many points of entry and exit into and from the struggle to make the world a better place and both sport and religion and sport, religion and Scottish society provide points of entry and consequently should not be overlooked.

Notes

1 A run-down and often overcrowded apartment house, especially in a poor section of a large city.
2 Stornoway is the main town on the Isle of Lewis, part of the Scottish outer Hebrides and is also the home of the Western Isles Council. Just over 6,000 people live in the town, which represents about a third of the Islands total population.

References

Bradley, J. (ed.) (2004). *Celtic Minded: Essays on Religion, Politics, Society, Identity and Football*. Glendaruel: Argyll Publishing.

Church of Scotland (2014). General Assembly Church and Society Council Report. Edinburgh: Church of Scotland (May).

Committee on Church and Nation (1964). 'The Christian Use of Sunday'. Edinburgh: Church of Scotland (May).

Gray, J. (2002). 'The Myth of Secularism?'. *New Statesman*, 20 December: 69–70.

Holt, R. (1992). *Sport and the British*. Oxford: Oxford University Press.

Jarvie, G. and Thornton, J. (2012). *Sport, Culture and Society*. London: Routledge.

Martin, L. (2004). 'Lewis Hands Surfers A Never on Sunday Warning'. *Observer*, 8 August: 13.

Research Scotland (2016). *Equality and Sport Research*. Glasgow: Research Scotland.

Robinson, S. (2007) 'Sport and Spirituality'. In Parry, J., Robinson, S., Watson, N. and Nesti, M. (eds). *Sport and Spirituality: An Introduction*. London: Routledge, 1–38.

Smith, A. and Westerbeek, H. (2004). *The SportsBusiness Future*. Basingstoke: Palgrave Macmillan, 90–117.

Sport England (2003). *Sports Volunteering in England 2002*. Sheffield: Leisure Industries Research Centre for Sport England.

Sportscotland (2014). A chronology of Scottish Sport. Edinburgh, www.sport scotland.org.uk/trophies/chronology-of-scottish-sport/ (accessed 10 May 2015)

Wade, M. (2011). 'Putting the Fear of Golf in Them'. *The Times*, 7 March: 4–6.

Walker, G. and Gallagher, T. (1990). *Sermons and Battle Hymns: Protestant Popular Culture in Scotland*. Edinburgh: Edinburgh University Press.

Walters, P. and Byl, J. (2008). *Christian Paths to Health and Wellness*. Champaign, IL: Human Kinetics.

Woods, D. (2010) 'Baptised Lemoncello has Faith in Himself to Deliver'. *Scotland on Sunday*, 12 February: 25.

Chapter 11

Protestantism and sport in the 'Bible Belt' of Norway in the first half of the twentieth century

Nils Martinius Justvik

Introduction

During the years around 1900, the leaders of the Norwegian Sports Association (NSA) – 'Centralforeningen for Idræt' – travelled all over the country to promote sport. In 1906, one of these leaders, Captain Henrik Angell, travelled to the southernmost area of Norway – the region called Agder or Sørlandet. After these sport-promoting journeys, Angell and the other leaders published their observations in the Annual issued by the national sports association. Angel's visits to about 16 different communities in Agder had made a great impression on him. Despite a good turnout at these gatherings, Angell found the level of interest in sport to be low. One of the reasons for this was emigration, with a high number of physically fit, ambitious young people trying their luck in the US. In addition, and even more detrimental to sporting activity in some communities was, 'the raging religious piety which does not accept sport or any display of human joy of life' (Angell, 1906). The leaders of the NSA did not experience anything like this in any other place that they visited. Their travel reports covered most of the country and also the areas neighbouring Agder. This is noteworthy because the southernmost parts of Norway and the coastal areas of western Norway are often labelled as the country's 'Bible Belt' (Repstad, 2009).[1]

In this chapter, I explain why sport was so harshly rejected by many of the communities in this particular region of Norway. What kind of religiosity developed in this area in the decades around 1900, and what challenges did these communities and the various popular movements face with respect to religion? In order to address these (and other) questions, the history of the regional branch of the Young Men's Christian Association (YMCA) is a topic that I explore. My focus is on the changing attitudes to sport in the regional YMCA in the first half of the twentieth century.[2]

The region of Agder and its religious development

Agder (or Sørlandet) is situated in the southernmost part of Norway. Agder comprises the two counties of Aust-Agder and Vest-Agder, and has close to 300,000 inhabitants. Historically, the area has not always been seen as a distinct region. Agder was originally regarded as a part of southwestern Norway, and the name *Sørlandet* (meaning the southernmost part of the country) came into being in 1902, through an article written by a poet from Agder, Vilhelm Krag, in the newspaper *Morgenbladet.*

In the wake of the Napoleonic wars, Norway established its own constitution under a common king with Sweden. For centuries Norway had been in a union with Denmark in a subordinate position. At the beginning of the sixteenth century, the Danish-Norwegian union was influenced by the Lutheran Reformation and the double monarchy went from having a Catholic church to introducing Lutheranism. Church and monarchy were closely linked, with the king as the head of the Lutheran church. The second paragraph of the Norwegian Constitution of 1814 states that 'the Evangelical-Lutheran religion remains the public religion of the State'. After establishing a parental obligation to raise children according to the basic principles of the religion, the paragraph reveals a contemporary lack of tolerance: 'Jesuits and monastic orders are not permitted. Jews are still prohibited from entry to the Realm.'[3] The dominant position of the Lutheran state church had been established. In 1845, a legal act granting the freedom of religion was passed in the Norwegian Parliament. In the following decades, this made it much easier for all kinds of Christian denominations to flourish, both within the state church and outside of its boundaries where different lay movements developed.

In Agder, and elsewhere in Norway, historians and sociologists have searched for turning points in religious development (Aagedal, 2003; Seland, 2006; Slettan, 1992). They report a dissolution of the monoculture constituted by the state church from about 1800 until 1870. During this period, the lay movement both inside and outside of the state church was strengthened. The subsequent period (1870–1970) is considered 'the golden age of the conversionist Christian laymen's movement in the various communities in Agder' (Repstad, 2002). One of the basic features of this era was that of recurring revivals. Historian Bjørg Seland, who has studied the lay movement of Agder during these 100 years, discerned a certain pattern: three consecutive waves of revivals occurring at intervals of about 30 years. The first wave took place around 1870, the second around 1900, and the third during the years between the two world wars (Seland and Aagedal, 2008).

The basic characteristics of these revivals were examined by Ole Hallesby, Professor of Theology and Chairman of Norway's largest inner mission organisation during the first half of the twentieth century (Justvik,

2007). Hallesby focused on the 'one needful thing' – being a saved sinner; his message had four important elements: (i) the centrality of the Cross, (ii) the Bible above all other sources, (iii) the need to experience conversion, and (iv) faith sharing in intense activism (Erdozain, 2010; Justvik, 2014). An oft-cited biblical phrase, 'for I decided to know nothing among you, except Jesus Christ and him crucified' (1. Corinthians 2.2.), led to Hallesby's eschatological ethics, which is presented in his book on Christian ethics – *Den kristelige sedelære*. What kind of lives should converts lead?

> Christ focused his powerful and talented personality on one task only: to save sinners. He wished that all his friends would do the same, and they understood his ambition. Like their master, they saw both mind and life as having a common focal point: 'the one needful thing'. And they knew, like him, that only by such single-mindedness would it be possible to rescue their fellow human beings (Luke 12:14). Focused like sportsmen who exercise (1 Corinthians 12:24–27), they lead their lives avoiding all other tasks delaying their pilgrimage (Matthew 18:8), or preventing them from fulfilling their mission: Allowing as many people as possible to experience heaven (1 Corinthians 8:13).
>
> (Hallesby, 1928 cited in Justvik 2007)

The revivals affected most of the communities in Agder. In several locations tensions arose between those who were part of the revivalist movement and those who were not. Captain Angell, representing the NSA, together with other leaders, visited a large number of local associations affiliated with the national organisation called Norway's Youth Organisation (NYO) (Noregs Ungdomslag). My next task is to examine these two organisations.

Two popular movements in cooperation – the Norwegian Sports Association (NSA) and Norway's Youth Organisation (NYO)

The NSA was founded in 1861 after a disagreement between the union partners Norway and Sweden. As a result of this disagreement, the military defence of the country became topical and a number of shooting associations sprang up nationally. Many of these became the backbone of the national sports association, together with gymnastics groups. The leaders of the NSA were future military officers who, by the vehicle of sport, aimed to develop physical fitness in the generations to come to enable them to defend the country (Olstad, 1987). In 1893, in the aftermath of the constitutional crisis of 1884, which paved the way for an increase in the birth of shooting associations, the NSA split into two. The shooting associations left the NSA and formed their own national association. The NSA – renamed 'Centralforeningen for Idræt' – continued as the organisation for sport in general (Olstad, 1987).

Prior to Norway's peaceful secession from its union with Sweden in 1905, the focus on the military had been strong. Thus, the leaders of the NSA revitalised the ideals of bringing up a generation fit for the challenges to come and began travelling widely throughout the country, often funded by the government. Post-1905 a new nation, independent of others, was to be created and an initiative called the 'New Working Day' was embarked upon. The idea of good public health and physical fitness was an integral part of the message from the leaders of the NSA, a message that was intensified in this period.

As we have seen, most of the leaders of the NSA were officers, but around the turn of the century, another group of leaders was recruited – the teachers. One important representative of this new group was Bertel Andreas Grimeland, both headmaster and lieutenant. He took extended trips all over the country and at the annual meeting of one of the regional branches of NYO in Agder in 1905, he lectured on the importance and the position of sport in the country (Olstad, 1987). In 1904, Grimeland had presented on sport in the associations of the local branches of NYO, first emphasising the significance of sport for its own sake, and then 'for the sake of the fatherland (...)':

> We need young people who are patriotic to the extent that they sacrifice everything to serve and defend their country. However, the young people will not be able to build or to protect their country if they lack the physical strength and toughness, determination and tenacious endurance that sport alone can induce. If the [NYO] associations want to attain the goal – the defence of the fatherland – they have to accept the means, i.e., sport. There are no other means by which a people can maintain its strength and defence ability – in times of peace in particular.
>
> (Grimeland, 1904)

Founded as a national organisation in 1896, NYO was, from the beginning and well into the next century, occupied with strengthening nationalistic or patriotic ideas among its members. As part of its educational work, NYO published papers on a wide range of topics such as language, history, traditions, public health, sport, Christianity etc. Lecturers with knowledge on these various topics, including the leaders of the NSA, were recommended by NYO. From the turn of the century onwards, the organisation received funding from the Norwegian government to encourage and strengthen the idea and the necessity of a strong military. Captain Henrik Angell's visits to the different NYO associations in Agder in 1906 were part of this encouragement. Entitled 'Norwegian Sport', his speech aimed to encourage young people in the communities to start exercising.

In Agder, NYO was divided into two county organisations – the Vest-Agder and the Aust-Agder regional branches. The larger Vest-Agder branch had between 25–30 associations in the first decade of the twentieth century. Article one of the basic regulations of this branch from 1893 states that the main objective of the organisation is to work in favour of a wholesome way of life for young people. After a brief description of what should be addressed at branch meetings, the article ends by specifying the need to arouse interest in sport among young people (Lande, 1968).

It is important to note that NYO was not hostile to Christianity. However, in many communities in Agder there were episodes of great tension between the conversionist Christian laymen's movement and NYO associations. NYO supported and worked in favour of a more culturally liberal and open-minded Christianity. In some communities the local vicar or priest was a member of the NYO association. Indeed, in the community of Søgne, just outside Kristiansand, the vicar was one of the founders (Flatelid, 1984).

What was the consequence of such a specific focus on sport at the beginning of the twentieth century? As we have seen, the organisation invited leaders from the national sports association to lecture about sport and its importance in the local associations and at annual gatherings or festivals. One consequence of this was an increased awareness of the significance of sport among NYO members. Another consequence was a decision at the annual festival of the Vest-Agder regional branch in 1905 to have sports competitions during the festival in the coming years. In 1910, at the annual festival of the Aust-Agder branch of NYO, a sports competition was held. The winner was Helge Løvland, who went on to win the decathlon in the 1920 Olympics in Antwerp (Nilsen, Refsnes and Larsen, 1967).

A final effect of the focus on sport locally was the process of enrolling all of the local associations and the two regional branches of NYO into the NSA. Both local regional branches of the NSA had 19 ordinary sports clubs and 39 NYO associations. In the neighbouring regions of Agder – Telemark and Rogaland – only ordinary sports clubs were members of the NSA and there were no associations from NYO. It is important to acknowledge that most of Rogaland and especially the southern parts of Telemark are part of the so-called Norwegian 'Bible Belt'. In the county north of Rogaland, 22 ordinary sports clubs and 45 NYO associations were members of the NSA. How might we interpret this mutual attraction between the local associations of NYO and the NSA in Agder?

The initial story about Captain Angell having discovered the raging piety that did not accept any kind of human joy of life is key to this question. The recurring revivals paved the way for the eschatological ethics – having a close focus on 'the one needful thing' – being a saved sinner on his way to heaven.[4] In the various communities, there was also a liberal group of people – members of the local associations of NYO – who were not part of the revivals. Despite the fact that the revivalists constituted only a minority in the community, tensions between revivalists and the NYO members were severe in places. Historian Bjørn Slettan indicates that between 10–20 per cent of the population in general belonged to the revivalist groups, but their influence exceeded by far the sheer percentage (Slettan, 1992).

Why did those who were interested in sports activity not form separate sports clubs? During the first decades of the twentieth century, organised sport was mainly an urban or a city phenomenon. When describing his childhood and adolescence in a rural community in Agder at the beginning of the twentieth century, Helge Løvland explained that any form of organised sports instruction was non-existent. He said that work on the farm served as training. While ploughing, he did weight-training by wearing a large rucksack heavy with stones (Løvland, 1971). In 1919, Norwegian sport was reorganised into 'Norges landsforbund for idrett', and during the next 20 years, sports clubs were established all over Agder. Prior to 1919, those interested in sport had to rely on the NYO for training and competition. In one of the largest rural communities outside the cities in Agder – Vennesla – we find an NYO association from 1889 and a sports club from 1896. In this context, it is important to note that the same group of people who founded the NYO association founded a sports association seven years later (Tønnessen, 1946).

One activity which, from the very beginning of the NYO, was linked to sport and which intensified tensions with revivalist groups, was folk or circle dancing. In 1906, Captain Angell commented on the lack of organised sport in the mountains – the upper parts of Setesdalen – the most important valley in Agder. However, he excused the mountain people because they had to use skis in their daily lives and for transportation during the winter. During the summer they had no other needs apart from their daily work and wandering in the mountains where they had summer mountain pastures:

> In these villages, they have a physical activity which is so good and beautiful; Norwegian folk dances – 'gangaren' and 'hallingen' – excellent substitutes for almost any physical exercise – the physical activity of excellency. From ancient times the young people have gathered at a clearing in the forests – 'leikarvollen' – and those places do not seem to have been destroyed the same way as in many other places in the country. In the national dance, we find splendid physical fitness.
>
> (Angell, 1906)

In the Lutheran tradition, dancing used to belong to a group of activities referred to as adiaphoria, e.g. going to the theatre, playing cards, etc. This word implied that the activities which fell within the definition of adiaphoria were neither sinful nor reputable – they belonged somewhere in between. In the pietist tradition from the eighteenth century, dancing and several other activities were indeed looked upon as sin. The revivalist groups adhered to such pietist thinking, reacting strongly to the dancing traditions in the villages and in NYO. For this group of converts, it was crucial to refuse worldly pleasures such as dancing.

The Young Men's Christian Association of Norway and Agder

At the annual conference of the national YMCA in 1928, 27 local groups from Agder seceded from the organisation and founded a youth organisation based upon the principle that Paul communicated in the New Testament: 'For I decided to know nothing among you, except Jesus Christ and him crucified' (1. Cor. 2.2). For a couple of decades, there had been a discussion about the focal point of the work carried out in the national YMCA. The new organisation – the Southern Country Christian Youth Associations (SCCYA) (Sørlandets Kristelige Ungdomsforening) – had one paramount objective: to bring the Christian message to young people. Displays of human joy were not to be part of the work carried out by the organisation. Sport was one of these distractions yet at the annual conference of the YMCA in 1928, sport was widespread in the conference programme for the first time – too widespread for the 27 local groups of the YMCA in Agder. The backdrop for the creation of this new local youth organisation, the SCCYA, is of significance when it comes to why the organisation took such a firm stand on sport and it is to an examination of the founding of the hegemonic arm of the SCCYA – the Kristiansand Youth Association (KYA) – that we now turn.

The Norwegian YMCA was founded in 1880 by 23 representatives from 11 youth associations. The influence from the flourishing German Youth Associations (Jünglingsverein), first and foremost in Rhein-Westfalen, was the strongest, but there were also other sources of influence, such as the British YMCA (Voksø and Kullerud, 1980). The KYA was founded two years after the national organisation, but did not become a member until 1890 – when it did so on one condition – unchanged article one in the KYA's basic regulations: 'The objective is partly the formation of a meeting place for young Christians, but also the conversion of those who have lost their faith in Christ' (Jensen Oftenæss, 1932). The national YMCA accepted this and over the next few decades the article was a guiding star for the work carried out in the KYA. Only working methods leading young people to Christ were endorsed. Doing sport was not an accepted method, but music was. From the start, the KYA had been well known for its choirs and smaller or bigger bands and orchestras (Jensen Oftenæss, 1932). The national YMCA had a much wider objective: the promotion of sound Christian and popular education, preaching the gospel, but also speaking about general educational topics (Voksø and Kullerud, 1980).

The national YMCA developed in accordance with its wider objective and around 1910 the organisation was criticised for marginalising religious topics. The Vest-Agder branch of the YMCA was a leading critic mostly because its work was characterised by a solely Christian ethos (Staalesen, 1907). The national YMCA was also criticised for its wider scope by the retiring chairman of the Vest-Agder branch, Reidar Kobro, in his final speech in 1913. During the previous year Kobro had reflected on the lack of Christian leadership and embodied values within the organisation. Young Christians had reacted to the secular profile of several associations (Voksø and Kullerud, 1980).

On retirement Reidar Kobro did not leave the organisation. He was elected to the Board of the national YMCA in 1916, and in 1918 became the vice-chair. In 1923, he resigned from the Board. The reason for this was the lukewarm engagement of the YMCA in the topical theological struggle of the 1920s: Conservative versus liberal theology. In 1920, the Conservatives, headed by Professor Ole Hallesby, had proclaimed no cooperation with the liberals. Reidar Kobro belonged to the Conservatives and wanted the YMCA to take a firmer stand against the liberals. In 1928 – the same year the 27 associations seceded from the national YMCA – Kobro was appointed Dean in Kristiansand in the diocese of Agder coming home to his Christian conservative brethren in his congregation and in the diocese, but perhaps first and foremost in the Christian Youth Association. Kobro's struggle before his withdrawal from the national Board in 1923 was significant in the formation of the SCCYA (Justvik, 2007).

Sport in the Southern Country Christian Youth Associations (SCCYA) of 1928

Between 1920 and 1940, a focus on young people was a joint feature of all the Christian groups and churches in Kristiansand. One of the most successful groups was the KYA, which was the hegemonic association in Agder (Tønnessen, 1974). What were the methods or strategies behind their success? Testimony from my own empirical research on this topic provides some explanation. Here one of my informants articulates his experiences of the two groups he attended in Kristiansand during this period – a Sunday Bible Class in the Inner Mission Association and a Wednesday evening youth club at the KYA:

> In 1925, I became a member of the Bible Class; soon after I joined the Youth Club for boys aged 14 and up. Both were decisive for me becoming a convinced Christian. First of all I have to mention the

preaching, but the Christian friendships contributed greatly. Mutual consideration was widespread in this milieu, and especially noteworthy was the great care a 20-year old man showed for the younger boys in a Bible study group I attended.

(Justvik 2007)

One incident made a particular impression on this individual. At a summer camp in 1926 arranged by the KYA in the beautiful islands outside the picturesque town of Lillesand, he was asked to open a meeting in the prayer house on the island of Ågerøya. He quoted from Psalms 73:23–24: 'Nevertheless I am continually with you. You have held my right hand. You will guide me with your counsel, and afterward receive me to glory.' This incident never left his memory, close to 80 years after it happened.

In summary, despite this dogmatic focus, it is clear that young boys needed physical activity and to be active in a diverse range of activities. This was equally true for those who turned up every week for the various Christian meetings in the KYA. However, this need for activity was not facilitated by the Association. Hence, the boys themselves had to do something about this.

The 'Christian' football club Orion and the secular football clubs

In the western parts of Kristiansand around 1930, a group of boys of the same age met regularly several days a week at the KYA premises downtown. In the spring, summer and autumn they also gathered during the evenings in one of the local parks – Oak Grove (Egelunden) – to play football for as long as they could still see the ball. Neither then or now is Oak Grove a suitable place for football, but the boys loved to play and gradually improved to such a level that they wanted to test their skills against football clubs in the Kristiansand region.

All of the clubs in the area had been founded in this way – by boys playing recreational football. The established teams started out as clubs representing different parts of the town. The football club Start, which is currently playing in the second tier of elite football in Norway and which is the football club of Agder, was founded by a group of boys in their teens in 1905 (Øverland and Jakbsen, 2005). The name of the club emanating from the football players in Oak Grove was Orion, for unknown reasons. Formal organisation of such activities was not common and no related written materials are available. All we know is that a small number of these boys had leadership abilities. There are no applications for membership in the files of the Vest-Agder branch of the NSA.

Despite this lack of formal organisation, Orion played against many of the local football clubs, but only against their second teams. To play against the first teams, they would have to play on Sundays, which was prohibited as long as 90 per cent of the Orion players were members of the KYA. This was one of two unwritten laws of Orion: no football on Sundays. Such a law caused serious problems for players who wanted to achieve their potential as football players and for them this necessitated a change of club. The other law of Orion related to cursing, which was not allowed.

During the 1930s, talented Orion players developed their skills to a high level, leading to increased interest from the more established football clubs. Some of the boys were tempted by this and left Orion. One of the Orion players who did not leave put it like this: 'If some of the Christian young boys left Orion for Start, it was perceived as though he had lost his faith in Christ.' The one needful thing – being a saved sinner was not good enough. Another Orion player put this view of sport in perspective:

> I remember that some boys, myself included, all members of the KYA, travelled to Oslo for the international match at which a famous natio-nal team player would be awarded Gullklokka (the Golden Wrist Watch) after having played 25 international matches. There were five of us boys who were afraid we might meet a certain Bible school student, studying in Oslo. He thought it dubious to put so much effort into sport.
>
> (Justvik, 2007)

'If your right eye causes you to sin, tear it out and throw it away!' (Math. 5.29)

During the 1930s, the leaders in the various churches and Christian groups must have been aware of the growing interest in sport among their young members. In Mandal, a town 50 miles west of Kristiansand, in a newspa-per called *Samleren*, published by the local Inner Mission Association, we find a questionnaire from 1937 about attitudes to sports competitions. All 12 of the people who responded to the questionnaire accepted the wholesome effect of sport, but all agreed that Christians could not compete on Sundays. Eric Liddell, gold medallist in the Paris Olympics, who refused to compete on Sundays, was an icon to many of the 12. The editor conclu-ded: 'If you foresee any hindrances to your life as a Christian ... tear your eye out or cut your hand off' (Samleren, 1937).

The editor of the local newspaper reacted severely to this in an editorial under the heading 'The Devil's Invention'. The editor characterised some of the negative statements as 'conceited words to young people they do not understand – music out of tune from people mentally out of balance' (Mandals Avis, 1937). He might have been influenced by what happened in Mandal when an SCCYA secretary revealed his personal experience of sport in *Det kristelige ungdomsbladet*, a Christian magazine for youth: 'gliding through the air on a pair of skis ... the wonderful shivering during the jump, or the intense suspense eventually released in the landing'. The secretary must have experienced an existential crisis because:

> Football, ski jumping and other activities were the essential elements in our lives, and we admit that, for some of us, the fight of our lives was sport or Christ. It cost us dearly to resign from membership in the sports club, but Christ became the most important, and sports competitions had to give way to life as Christians.

The secretary stated firmly that the word sin was not associated with football matches or competitions of any kind, but that there were three reasons for the believer to refrain from such events:

> (1) The contemporary chase for breaking records takes both time and resources. Be aware that 'physical exercise does have value'. (2) Sundays and holidays, days of rest mentally and physically, are always the preferred days for competitions. (3) The atmosphere of the competition area and the accompanying parties in particular are alien to us.

The editor of *Samleren* recommended that if your right eye causes you to sin, tear it out and throw it away. The secretary of the SCCYA uses a particular metaphor to explain his attitude to the temptation of sport: both of his legs have been cut off (*Det kristelige ungdomsbladet*, 1937).

One month later, in April 1937, the KYA invited the scouts, the sports clubs and the Christian Youth groups in the Kristiansand region to a meeting on the topic of: 'A proper Sunday – competitions and conventions on Sundays' (*Fædrelandsvennen*, 1937a). The speaker for the day was the chaplain of the cathedral in Kristiansand, Chaplain Gundersen who had close connections to the KYA, and high standing among the general public. The turnout was overwhelming – 500 to 600 men and women. Gundersen stated the joint problem for both religious and secular groups: too many activities were fixed to Sundays and holidays and this caused problems for both groups. According to the exchange of views after the address, a further meeting was scheduled for the week after – this time only the leaders of the religious and secular groups were to attend (*Fædrelandsvennen*, 1937c; *Christianssands Tidende*, 1937b).[5] A leader of one of the sports clubs appealed positively to the leaders of all of the clubs to turn up. The Vest-Agder branch of the NSA was explicitly mentioned. The purpose of the meeting was to solve the challenge: too many events and competitions on Sundays. This was a problem for all the groups present and they were to discuss it in a friendly way (*Christianssands Tidende*, 1937a).

The turnout of leaders from the sports clubs was impressive and at this second meeting the leaders were given more time to speak. Towards the end of the meeting they agreed upon a resolution:

> The mass meeting of youth urgently appeals to the Kristiansand municipal council to decide that all businesses in town will close at 13:00 on Saturdays and to enforce development of the projected athletic grounds in order to facilitate as many sports competitions as possible on Saturdays.
>
> (*Fædrelandsvennen*, 1937c)

The two mass meetings were of vital importance for the development of the relationship between sport and Christianity. Some of the barriers between the two movements were lowered, resulting in greater mutual understanding. The resolution put forward at the Norwegian bishops' annual meeting in the autumn of 1937 was hardly distinguishable from that of the Kristiansand meeting (Hodne, 1993). It is difficult to tell whether the resolution had any impact on the Kristiansand municipal council. The projected athletic grounds were built ten years later – after the Second World War (Tønnessen, 1974).

Of course, there were other effects of these mass meetings. Just after the Second World War, a meeting was held in the parish hall of the Kristiansand cathedral on the topic of building a 'sports chapel' 50 miles from Kristiansand in the area where people went cross country skiing in the winter. In the report from the meeting, there is mention of services being held before the war at a cottage owned by one of the sports clubs and built in the hiking area north of Kristiansand. We cannot tell for sure, but the mass meetings in the spring of 1937 may have paved the way for Sunday services at this cottage owned by Oddersjaa – the world's oldest (and still operative) ski club. The idea of a sports chapel was nothing new. It had been discussed at the mass meetings, and the Reverend Strømme had been eager to promote it. He had studied theology in Oslo at the beginning of the 1930 and been involved in the building of the first 'sports chapel' in Norway – Nordmarkskapellet – in the hiking area close to Holmenkollen ski stadium in Oslo. In 1946, an abandoned farm in the hiking area west of Kristiansand was transformed into a sports chapel by the KYA and this rapidly became a success and had to be expanded.

How do we interpret this new trend – the mutual understanding between Christianity, or more specifically the KYA, and sport – towards the end of the 1930s? In my research into attitudes to sport in churches and Christian groups in Agder from 2007, I did not find anyone from the churches and the Christian groups who participated in sport at a high level during the 1920s and 1930s. As we have seen above, if a football player left Orion for Start, he was no longer a Christian (Justvik, 2007). Despite this, the leaders of the hegemonic Christian association, the KYA, must have discovered the growing interest in sport among young people, in addition to an increased interest in hiking on Sundays. The hiking interest was also widespread among people in general. The two mass meetings were an initial attempt at lowering the barriers between church and sport, and connections made between the two resulted in some services being held at the cottage owned by Oddersjaa.

On the one hand, the KYA leaders must have thought that hiking on Sundays was an inevitable development among both Christians and non-Christians. Thus, the church had to follow the people; if people did not come to church, the church would have to go to the people. Furthermore, people did not commit a sin when they were hiking. Quite the contrary, people used their God-created bodies by being physically active in the nature created by God. By taking this stance, the leaders of the KYA introduced a message about a God who had created the earth including mankind. The First Article of the Apostles' Creed had been introduced. In the revivalist tradition, 'the one needful thing' – to be a saved sinner – was the core message and the Second Article of the Apostles' Creed about Jesus was central. This was also true for the KYA, but there was a slight change. At the beginning this did not affect their view on sport, but later on – during the first decades after the Second World War – it did. The mid-twentieth century was too early for this change (Justvik, 2007).

Conclusion

In this chapter I have explored why sport was historically rejected in many of the communities in the Agder region of Norway. Referred to as the conversionist Christian laymen period, the 100 years between 1870 and 1970 is of special relevance in this respect for the southernmost area of the country. Religious revivals were typical of the era and historian Bjørg Seland has discovered three consecutive 30-year waves of such activity between 1870 and the 1930s. These revivals (and the culture associated with them) influenced Agder to such an extent that the area has become the core of what has been labelled the Norwegian 'Bible Belt'. As I have outlined, two other movements – the NSA (1861) and NYO (1896) – tried to establish themselves in Agder, both intending to promote physical activity among young people to develop healthy and sound generations capable of defending their country.

The conversionist Christian laymen's movement had a negative view of all cultural expressions outside of their own. For them Christians had to be occupied with 'the one needful thing' – being a saved sinner trying to save others. Hallesby's 'eschatological ethics' referred to above is important to understanding the attitude and not least the tense relationship with the other organisations.

The YMCA in Norway had a wider scope of interest than the 'eschatological ethics' of the conversionist movement, thus activities differed. Physical activities and topics related to wider society were adopted by the YMCA. This was not true for the Vest-Agder branch of the YMCA. From inclusion into the YMCA in 1890 until the secession of the 27 associations in 1928 and the foundation of a new organisation (SCCYA), the hegemonic association in the Vest-Agder branch had tenaciously claimed the right to focus on 'the one needful thing', and nothing else, least of all sport.

During the 1930s, the SCCYA leaders gradually discovered the difficulty in restraining the great interest in sport among the young people. The young boys in the SCCYA founded the football club Orion with certain rules to get acceptance from their organisation – no cursing and no matches on Sundays and holidays. Even hiking in areas around Kristiansand during church service hours on Sundays was a challenge to the leadership of the SCCYA. However, the extensive use of Sundays for matches and competitions was a corresponding challenge for the young people occupied with sport. There may have been strategic thinking behind the two mass meetings on the topic for Christian youth clubs and sports clubs along the line of: if you cannot beat them, join them. The outcome of the meetings must have exceeded all expectations and paved the way for constructive cooperation in the future: services in the cottage owned by the oldest, still operative ski club Oddersjaa – the precursor to the popular sports chapel after the war – and a resolution calling for fewer activities on Sundays by appealing to the municipal authorities to speed up the building of new athletic grounds.

Last, but not least, there was an underlying, conscious element of theology in what the leadership of the SCCYA had done. The biblical phrase 'for I decided to know nothing among you, except Jesus Christ and him crucified' corresponds to the Second Article of the Apostles' Creed, which in the future too would constitute the basic element in the SCCYA's work among young people. Through their actions, the leaders highlighted a new element – the First Article of the Apostles' Creed: God is the creator of both heaven and earth, both body and nature. Therefore, man must be physically active, both in sport and in the hiking areas, even on Sundays.

Notes

1 See also Øidne (1957) for an account of different cultural regions in Norway.
2 Two pieces of my own empirical work serve as the basis for this chapter (see Justvik, 2007, 2017). Most of the material related to the regional branch of the YMCA is taken from my doctoral thesis and is drawn from interviews with informants, related newspaper searches and other written materials (Justvik, 2007). For more on religious change in the Agder region see: Repstad (2002, 2008, 2009) and Repstad and Henriksen (2005), Seland (2006), Seland and Aagedal (2008) and Slettan (1992).

3 (My translation). www.stortinget.no/no/Stortinget-og-demokratiet/Lover-og-instrukser/Grunnloven-fra-1814/ (accessed 11 October 2015)
4 We find this dogmatic or monochromatic perspective in other fields, not only with respect to sport (see Justvik, 1998 and 2007).
5 The two newspapers, *Fædrelandsvennen* and *Christianssands Tidende*, belonged to the left-wing and right-wing political parties respectively. The Labour party had its own local newspaper, but did not report from the meeting.

References

Aagedal, O. (2003). *Bedehusfolket: Ein studie av bedehuskultur i tre bygder på 1980- og 1990-talet*. Doctoral Thesis, Sociology, University of Oslo. Trondheim: KIFOPerspektiv, no. 12.

Angell, H. (1906). Rapport fra kaptein H. Angell. *Centralforeningens Årbok*, 45, pp. 113–116.

Baker, W. J. (2007). *Playing with God: Religion and Modern Sport*. Cambridge: Harvard University Press.

Christianssands Tidende (1937a, 8 April). Alle sportsstevner bør henlegges til lørdag eftermiddag. La oss sørlendinger gå I spissen her.

Christianssands Tidende (1937b, 17 April). Stevner om Søndagen.

Det kristelige ungdomsbladet (1937, March). Ynglingeforeningens blader.

Erdozain, D. (2010). *The Problem of Pleasure: Sport, Recreation and the Crisis of Victorian Religion*. Woodbridge: Boydell.

Flatelid, L. (1984). Søgne Ungdomslag. In O. Eikestøl (ed.), *Søgne før og nå, volume 4 Lokalhistoriske glimt fra kultur- og næringsliv* (pp. 262–308). Flekkefjord: S. B. Hegland.

Fædrelandsvennen. (1937a, 7 April). Søndagen og idretten.

Fædrelandsvennen. (1937b, 8 April). De mange sportsstevner – og kristelige stevner med – må bort fra søndagen.

Fædrelandsvennen. (1937, 17 April). Idrettsfolkene er trette av søndagsstevnene og ønsker disse overført til lørdag. Men da må kristenfolket støtte kravet om en ny idrettsplass, og lørdagen må bli en utvidet fridag.

Grimeland, B. A. (1904). Idrætsarbeidet og ungdomslagene. *Centralforeningens Årbok*, 43, pp. 83–86.

Hallesby, O. (1928). *Den kristelige sedelære*. Oslo: Lutherstiftelsens Forlag.

Hodne, Ø. (1993). *Kirke og fritid. En studie i norsk mellomkrigskultur*. Oslo: Novus Forlag.

Jensen Oftenæs, O. (1932). *Kristiansand Ynglingeforening (KFUM) I 50 aar 1882–1932*. Kristiansand: Christiansands Tidende Trykkeri.

Justvik, N. M. (1998). *Frikirkelige og lavkirkelige miljøers forhold til arbeiderbevegelsen i Stokken 1912–1945*. Oslo: Master Thesis, Faculty of Humanities, University of Oslo.

Justvik, N. M. (2007). *Kristenfolkets forhold til idrett: Endringer på Sørlandet i etterkrigstida*. Oslo: Doctoral Thesis, Faculty of Theology, University of Oslo.

Justvik, N. M. (2014). Aspects of Muscular Christianity in Norway and the United States: A Historiographical Comparison. *Journal of Religion and Society*, 16, 1–17. http://moses.creighton.edu/JRS/toc/2014.html (accessed 5 April 2014).

Justvik, N. M. (2017). *Idrett i Sør: Vest-Agder Idrettskrets 100 år: 1917–2017.* Kristiansand: Portal Forlag.

Ladd, T. and Mathisen, J. A. (1999). *Muscular Christianity: Evangelical Protestants and the Development of American Sport.* Grand Rapids Michigan: Baker Books.

Lande, G. (1968). *Vest-Agder Ungdomslag 75 år 1893–1968.* Kristiansand: Vest-Agder Ungdomslag.

Løvland, H. (1971). Det endte godt i Antwerpen. In A. Møst (ed.), *Høydepunkter i norsk friidrett 1896–1971* (pp. 20–22). Oslo: Norges Fri-idrettsforbund.

Mandals Avis (1937, 9 March). 'Djevelens Oppfinnelse'.

Nilsen, R., Refsnes, H. E. and Larsen, K. (1967). *Vest-Agder Idrettskrets 50 år 1917–1967.* Kristiansand: Fædrelandsvennens Trykkeri.

Olstad, F. (1987). *Norsk idretts historie: Forsvar, sport, klassekamp 1861–1939.* Oslo: Aschehoug.

Putney, C. (2001). *Muscular Christianity: Manhood and Sports in Protestant America 1880–1920.* Cambridge: Harvard University Press.

Repstad, P. (2002). Mellom inderlighet og spissborgerskap. En samfunnsforsker ser på sørlandspietismen. In Hilde Inntjore (ed.), *Agderkirken: Artikler fra høgskolens sommerseminar i historie, Lillesand 2000* (pp. 95–109). Kristiansand: Skriftserien no. 83, Høgskolen i Agder.

Repstad, P. and Henriksen, Jan-Olav (eds) (2005). *Mykere Kristendom? Sørlandsreligion i endring.* Bergen: Fagbokforlaget.

Repstad, P. (2008). From Sin to a Gift from God: Constructions of Change in Conservative Christian Organizations. *Journal of Contemporary Religion*, 23 (39), 17–31.

Repstad, P. (2009). A Softer God and More Positive Anthropolgy: Cahnges in a Religiously Strict Religion in Norway. *Religion*, 1–6.

Samleren (1937, 6 March). En kristen og sportskonkurransen. Tidens kanskje mest aktuelle spørsmål besvares av noen av våre erfarne kristne.

Seland, B. (2006). *Religion på det frie marked: Folkelig pietisme og bedehuskultur.* Kristiansand: Høgskoleforlaget.

Seland, B. and Aagedal O. (2008). *Vekkelsesvind: Den norske vekkingskristendommen.* Oslo: Det Norske Samlaget.

Slettan, B. (1992). *'O, at jeg kunde min Jesum prise ...': Folkelig religiøsitet og vekkelsesliv på Agder på 1800-tallet.* Oslo: Universitetsforlaget.

Staalesen, J. (1907). *Festskrift I anledning af unge mænds kristelige forenings 25 aars jubilæum: 17de mai 1882–17de mai 1907.* Kristiansand S: Johanssen & Tangens Bogtrykkeri.

Tønnessen, J. N. (1974). *Kristiansands historie 1914–1945: I krigens århundre.* Kristiansand: Christiansands Sparebank.

Tønnessen, T. (1946). *Vennesla Idrettslag 50 år – 1896–1946.* Stavanger: Dreyers grafiske anstalt.

Voksø, P. and Kullerud E. (1980). *I trekantens tegn: Norges Kristelige Ungdomsforbund gjennom hundre år.* Oslo: Triangelforlaget

Øidne, G. (1957). Litt om motsetninga mellom Austlandet og Vestlandet. *Syn og Segn*, 63, 97–114.

Øverland, F. and Jakobsen, A. (2005). *Start i hundre: fra gutteklubb til eliteserielag 1905–2005.* Kristiansand: I. K. Start & Fædrelandsvennen.

Chapter 12

Sport, celebrity and religion

Christianity, morality and the Tebow phenomenon

Andrew Parker and Nick J. Watson

Introduction

In recent years, academic discussion surrounding the lives and lifestyles of celebrity sports stars has provided fruitful ground for critiquing the role of sport in modern-day society. Rarely, however, has celebrity been discussed in relation to the sport-media-religion nexus. Drawing upon literature concerning the historical development of celebrity and sociological analyses of celebrity as a concept, this chapter argues that celebrity status is situated at the heart of an individualised and ideologically grounded late capitalist culture in which visual media is central to the production of social identities. In turn, the chapter seeks to uncover ways in which celebrity status and 'stardom' might be viewed as powerful signifiers in terms of popular cultural perceptions of sports performers. In so doing, the chapter considers one of the sports stars of more recent years, American Football player Tim Tebow, and analyses how his image has been used in order to depict specific messages relating to notions of faith, religion and spirituality.[1]

Sport, celebrity and popular culture

The theme of sporting celebrity is something that has attracted a significant amount of attention in recent years. Evident here has been a sense that the autobiographical details of contemporary sports figures represent key sites through which cultural change can be observed, interpreted and analysed. In this chapter we consider one particular sporting celebrity, American Football star Tim Tebow, and assess his image in terms of its contribution to debates surrounding sport, spirituality and celebrity culture. The central argument is that while Tebow affords many of the traditional hallmarks of celebrity status, his identity remains rooted within the context of certain moral, ethical and religious values, all of which shape the contours of his public profile.

Celebrity figures do not emerge in a cultural and political vacuum. On the contrary, they are products of the social circumstances upon which their very existence depends. Technological advancements in recent years have spawned both a growth and intensification of media resources that, in turn, has led to the wider popularisation of sport as a cultural spectacle (Bernstein and Blain, 2003; Boyle and Haynes, 1999; Rowe, 2003; Whannel, 1992). Today sports coverage features large amid the offerings of numerous television and communication networks as the sport-media relationship becomes ever more intimate and lucrative. Such interest necessarily brings with it fame and popular cultural exposure for a number of star performers. Golfer Tiger Woods, tennis player Serena Williams and motor racing star Lewis Hamilton are modern-day examples whose level and depth of recognition reflect and in many ways surpass that of previous 'sporting greats': George Best, Muhammad Ali, Michael Jordan – all of whom sampled fame and notoriety to one degree or another (Whannel, 2002, 2005). Thus, as sports-media coverage has developed and intensified, so too has the popular cultural appeal of performers themselves. Under such circumstances, sporting profile and prowess can seamlessly transmute into celebrity status (Cashmore and Parker, 2003; Chung, 2003).

Against this backdrop, it is perhaps not surprising that the identity and influence of sports celebrities has emerged as a contemporary theme of enquiry within a range of academic disciplines (Andrews and Jackson, 2001; Smart, 2005). Of specific interest for writers in this genre is how and why professional sports stars transcend their occupational locales to become wider public figures, national ambassadors, global commodities and/or popular cultural icons (Haynes, 2004, 2005; Harris and Clayton, 2007).[2] Such discussion has tended to focus on sports performers from Western industrialised nations, a trend which is significant for its absences as well as impositions. It would be fair to say, for example, that in the US and the UK at least, a sense of popular cultural saturation has developed during recent years in relation to images and narratives of particular sporting figures, of which Michael Jordan, Tiger Woods and David Beckham are familiar examples. Part of this monopolisation has as much to do with the sports that these stars represent as it does, their individual ability and potential. The intensification of the modern-day sport-media relationship has not been entirely uniform in terms of the amount of attention some sports have come to attract in comparison to others. To this end, there is a related tendency to ignore, or at least overlook, a broader range of sporting heroes/heroines; individuals that, to all intents and purposes, mean just as much (if not more) to millions of people as national and international celebrities and yet who, for some reason are not considered in quite the same way.

Sport, celebrity and social thought

At the collective level, social scientists have put forward a number of explanations as to why and how the cult of celebrity has emerged, the majority of which focus on the shifting social and cultural terrain of modern-day life. One of the most prominent of these explanations is that of Rojek (2001) who identifies three main reasons for these shifts: (i) the democratisation of society, (ii) the technological advancements of the mass media age, and (iii) the demise of formalised religion. Taken together what these three factors appear to characterise is a change in the overall complexion of advanced industrial society in what some have called the postmodern age. For Rojek (2001), the demise of monarchical and religious influence coupled with a ubiquitous saturation of media personalities has led to a new fluidity and re-distribution of power in social life, broadly resulting in celebrities taking the place of previously prominent figures (see also Smart, 2005; Ward, 2011).

Like a host of other high-profile occupations, professional sport generates an institutional climate conducive to the construction of celebrity status. Sports performers become famous as a consequence of their physical and cognitive abilities; by way of their charismatic demeanour, or sometimes both. As we have seen, for a small number, fame transmutes into an altogether more intense form of recognition around which celebrities are born and who, according to Boorstin's (1961: 58) oft quoted (and perhaps somewhat over-used) phrase, might simply be 'well-known for their well-known-ness'. A plethora of writers have attempted to plot the logic of this transformative process, but the fact remains that celebrity is a highly contested concept that has eluded any real sense of academic definition to date.[3] Inherent in the melee of explanatory and analytical offerings on the subject is a conflation of terms and descriptors that are commonly rendered synonymous – 'stars', 'superstars', 'heroines', 'heroes', 'icons' – and yet which in many ways present their own specific differences and idiosyncrasies (Andrews and Jackson, 2001; Rojek, 2001; Turner, 2004). Characterised by notions of fame, charisma and exception, celebrityhood is a commodification of the human form; the epitome of economic fetishism, the process and product of representations and images promoted and exchanged via the complex interplay of modern-day media networks. Permeating every thread of the social fabric, celebrity sports stars represent the epitome of vicarious achievement and conspicuous consumption (Cashmore and Parker, 2003).

The speculative nature of debate surrounding celebrityhood has been evident in analyses concerning taxonomies of celebrity status. Devoid of any real sense of empirical assessment, such discussions demonstrate how notions of 'stardom/fame', 'celebrity' and 'iconicity' have been contested.[4] That said, some writers have commented productively on how various 'levels' of celebrity might exist and how this can affect the extent to which sports personalities impact or transcend their local, regional and national contexts. For example, Kear and Steinberg (1999) argue that icons comprise quintessential (often religious) representations of culture; their status determined not by their iconicity alone but by the levels of 'subjective identification' to which they are open and the degree to which their depiction transcends and outgrows its origins. Yet as Ward (2011: 32) has pointed out, while celebrities may, at times, serve as 'sources for personal transformation and aspiration', rarely, it seems, do 'fans' regard their popular cultural idols as 'divine beings' or benchmarks of ethical and/or moral stability (see also Laderman, 2009). In this sense, though the notion of 'celebrity worship' has become an accepted part of everyday parlance, the reality is that the relationship between celebrity culture and religion is, at best, partial and limited (Ward, 2011).

Of course, as far as modern-day capitalism is concerned commodification is all-inclusive, nothing and no one escapes its grasp (Featherstone, 1991; Shilling, 2003). The culture of which celebrity status is such an integral part is one in which images of sporting celebrities circulate, on billboards, in magazines and in television commercials. We consume their image, their looks, their fame, their talent, their wealth, their popularity. As Ward (2011: 3) argues, '[C]elebrities matter not because of who they are but what they represent'. Unlike the majority of celebrity sports stars, Tim Tebow is neither the epitome of vicarious achievement nor a model of conspicuous consumption. His celebrity status emanates not simply from his sporting prowess but from the moral, ethical and religious values which he embodies and which the spectacle of his sporting achievements demonstrates. Indeed, in many respects it would be naïve to compare Tebow with other sports stars on a number of counts. For one thing, while he may have made the initial transition from sporting fame to national celebrity, he falls well short of the iconic status afforded certain others. Likewise, while his high school and college sporting achievements were significant, his career as a professional in the National Football League (NFL) was relatively modest and short lived.

It is here that we can observe vestiges of Debord's (1968) influential thesis in relation to *Society of the Spectacle*. For Debord, the celebrity plays a specific role amid the banal surroundings of modern society where the influence of consumption and commodification dictate the fragmentation of everyday life:

> The celebrity, the spectacular representation of a living human being, embodies this banality by embodying the image of a possible role. Being a star means specializing in the *seemingly lived*; the star is the object of identification with the shallow seeming life that has to compensate for the fragmented productive specializations which are

actually lived. Celebrities exist to act out various styles of living and viewing society – unfettered, free to express themselves *globally*. They embody the inaccessible result of social *labor* by dramatizing its by-products magically projected above it as its goal: *power and vacations*, decision and consumption.

(Debord, 1968, para. 60, original emphasis)

The concept of consumption is necessarily pertinent to the present discussion. There is an entire industry dedicated to producing images of sporting celebrities. However, what Debord (1968) reminds us of is that consumption is only one part of a broader social relation in capitalism, a key feature of which is production. Without production there is no consumption. A common characteristic of contemporary sociological debate is the de-centring of the labour process in favour of a leaning towards the importance of consumption as a point of reference. Such discussion has had a tendency to focus perhaps too readily on particular schools of thought at the expense of certain others. In fact, to deny the importance of production is to deny the very logic of our existence within the context of capitalism. As the defining principle of capitalist society, labour underpins all that is produced and, therefore, all that is consumed. In this sense, consumption is just one 'moment' in the social relations of production when (and where) labour has particular (exchange) value. That 'moment' is the manifestation of the labour process.

For athletes like Tim Tebow, production is not simply about the manufacture of a personalised image. Rather it also concerns the sporting *labour* that he fulfils. In this sense, production and consumption combine; the former grounded in the labour process surrounding his athletic prowess and lifestyle (his embodied sporting practice and habitual disposition), the latter representing the mainstay of his celebrity existence. Thus, Tebow's identity is more complex than Debord's (1968) analysis infers. His commodified persona represents a range of diverse elements collectively promoting specific conceptions of gender, religion and identification. In turn, Tebow is revered not simply as a consequence of his manufactured image but also as a result of his work, his labour, his productivity. Without hard physical work Tebow would not have perfected his sporting talents and would not have emerged as a star performer. Indeed, a certain kind of work has played a central role in his emergence; work which resonates well with the critiques put forward by Brohm (1978) and Rigaeur (1981) in their analyses of the relationship between sporting performance, Taylorism, mass production and nationalism. Notwithstanding his natural sporting talent, Tebow is a product of the repetitious process of becoming a successful athlete whereby a relentless pursuit of one's dream comes only via a series of predictable and heavily prescribed workplace behaviours. That said, while production is important in terms of his popular cultural identity, consumption is tantamount to the maintenance of this position. Without work, Tebow has no value. Without value, he ceases to exist as a consumable item (Smart, 2005).

Sport, celebrity and Tim Tebow

As academic commentary around the sport-celebrity relationship has increased, so too has that concerning the sport-celebrity-Christianity nexus (see Feezell, 2013; Newman, 2010; Rial, 2012). Common here are criticisms surrounding the extent to which sport is used as a ready-made billboard for the promotion of Christian values and as a platform for proselytising sports stars (see Epstein, 2011; Krattenmaker, 2010).

Enter Tebow: chosen-one, sporting messiah, moral and ethical guardian, corporate and commercial standard bearer, modern-day muscular Christian; calm, compassionate, 'down-to-earth'; quintessential all-American (Moore, Keller and Zemanek, 2011). What shapes this identity? Tebow, it seems, is a cultural phenomenon as much for his religious beliefs as he is for his sporting prowess. Born in the Philippines in 1987, the fifth (and youngest) child of Baptist missionaries, Tebow's childhood was steeped in the morals and values of evangelical Christianity. Home-schooled alongside his siblings, he later attended Trinity Christian Academy in his hometown of Jacksonville moving to Allen D. Nease High School in Ponte Vedra, Florida, thus taking advantage of a 1996 change to Florida state law, which allowed home-schooled students to participate in public high school athletic programmes (now more commonly known as the 'Tebow Law'). As his sporting profile developed, awards and accolades followed. Next up was an athletic scholarship at the University of Florida (2006–2009) during which time Tebow's capital increased further. Despite initially being named as the University's second-string quarterback in 2006, Tebow took over as starter in 2007 winning the Heisman Trophy that same year, the first college sophomore to do so (placing third and fifth in the same competition in 2008 and 2009 respectively). In 2007 he also won the Davey O'Brien Award, in recognition of his status as the nation's best quarterback. Tebow's success also impacted the fortunes of his team – the Florida Gators twice winning the Bowl Champion Series (BCS) during his tenure (2006 and 2008) – and those of his coach Urban Myer, whose cultural capital flourished during the same period (Fish, 2009). By the end of his college career, Tebow held a plethora of National Collegiate Athletic Association (NCAA), Southeastern Conference (SEC) and University of Florida records and had been voted most valuable player (MVP) by his teammates for three consecutive seasons (2007, 2008, 2009) (Tebow, 2011).

Perhaps not surprisingly, Tebow was heavily touted for the glitz and glamour of the professional game and after seeing out his senior season at

Florida (2009), he was selected by the Denver Broncos in the first round of the 2010 NFL Draft signing a five-year contract said to be worth in the region of $11 million. It would be fair to say that Tebow's transition from the collegiate to the professional ranks was not without its ups and downs. Certainly, concerns around his potential to make the grade in the NFL circulated from the very beginning – his passing ability being a point in question. He started the last three games of his first season with the Broncos and became full-time starting quarterback six games into the 2011 programme, taking over from Kyle Orton. After displaying poor form early on, things improved for the Broncos as the season progressed with Tebow inspiring them to a number of 'come from behind' wins. But during the latter stages of the 2011 season the Bronco's form stuttered and in the wake of the arrival of newly recruited quarterback Peyton Manning, Tebow was eventually traded to the New York Jets in March 2012. Finding himself in relatively unchartered territory as a peripheral team member and out-of-favour newcomer, Tebow received little game time with the Jets and was released in April 2013, signing with the New England Patriots later that year (June 2013). With footballing obscurity beckoning, Tebow again failed to make any significant impression and having competed in just two pre-season games, he was subsequently released by the Patriots in August 2013. His professional footballing career seemingly over, he took up the role of college football analyst with the broadcaster ESPN in December that same year.

Has US sport ever seen an athlete quite like Tim Tebow? As we have noted, in terms of his level of impact as a high-profile football player, Tebow's career has been modest to say the least. As for his influence as a religious role model, the impact could be said to have been slightly greater. In by-gone days, there were those whose religious beliefs singled them out as influential sporting figures: Billy Sunday, Gil Dodds, George Foreman, Joe Gibbs, all played a role in fore-fronting the Christian message in and through North American sport (see Ladd and Mathisen, 1999). Accompanying these stalwarts of US culture are sporting contemporises from further afield, one of the most famous of which, Eric Liddell, posthumously gained Hollywood acclaim (see Cashmore, 2008). While we might reflect on these sporting notables as stars of a previous age, what we must also acknowledge is that they operated largely before the advent of the mass media and, in this sense, their stardom should be viewed as both partial and limited in modern-day terms. These individuals were certainly famous and may well have been star performers, but they were not celebrities in the contemporary sense of the word.

Tim Tebow is a hybrid, at once a sportsman and moral custodian, who allows his religious beliefs to be framed as a public spectacle. Indeed, further fuelling the 'Tebow phenomenon' is the controversy that his Christian values have courted. In this sense, Feezell (2013) argues, Tebow has become something of a polarising figure in US popular culture generating criticisms and plaudits in equal measure along the way. At one level, the key characteristics of his spiritual profile are in no way unique – explicit expressions of thanks to God in relation to his sporting talents and successes, kneeling in prayer during games (commonly referred to as 'Tebowing'), the acknowledgement of sport as a 'platform' for ministry, the framing of himself as moral and ethical role model, off-field good works and impeccable track record, bestselling (autobiographical) author – all of which are commonplace among celebrity Christian athletes. During his college days, Tebow was known for displaying references to Bible verses on his eye black, a practice that lead the NCAA to amend its regulations to prevent such occurrences. Though other athletes had undertaken similar courses of action, the amendment, perhaps somewhat unsurprisingly, came to be referred to as the 'Tebow Rule' (Epstein, 2011). Equally controversial was Tebow's participation in a television advertisement screened in February 2010 during the first quarter of Super Bowl XLIV, when an organisation advocating a particular set of moral values, *Focus on the Family*, aired its presentation 'Celebrate family, celebrate life', in which Tebow's mother Pam delivered an explicit 'pro-life' message directly relating to the circumstances surrounding his own birth.

What should we make of all of this? In his in-depth examination of Tebow's popular cultural profile, Feezell (2013: 137) explores the nature and extent of the controversy surrounding the Tebow phenomenon and attempts to unpack the 'critical reaction to his public religiosity'. Drawing on Krattenmaker's (2010) highly disparaging (some might say polemical) account of the sport and Christianity relationship in the US, Feezell (2013) explores the key tenets of the Tebow narrative in order to present a broader analysis of how the sport-celebrity-religion nexus plays out in contemporary society. For Krattenmaker (2010), the sport-Christianity dyad raises a number of concerns, not least: the intentional infiltration of evangelical Christianity into commercialised sport, the inappropriate framing of the faith-sport relationship, and the proselytisation of religious views by high-profile ('platform') sports personnel. Utilising these assertions as a kind of conceptual canvass, Feezell (2013) considers a number of issues in relation to Tebow's alleged 'conspicuous piety' and the appropriateness (or not) of his behaviour. He does this by addressing a series of broader questions: is it appropriate to bring faith into sports? To what extent (if at all), is it acceptable for high-profile athletes to impose their religious worldview (and associated moral and ethical opinions and beliefs) onto others? How and to what extent might such practices be insensitive, divisive and contrary to a balanced awareness and appreciation of religious diversity? Does such an approach have the potential to raise questions as to the depth and level of the theological ideas in play? In terms of the kind of public reaction Tebow and other Christian athletes often generate, Feezell's (2013: 142) conclusions are as follows:

Tebow's behavior is polarizing because he appears to ignore or at least not acknowledge that the world of religious belief is complicated and diverse. Given the highly public nature of Tebow's conspicuous piety, no wonder that thoughtful people are troubled by either his ignorance or his unconcern with how belief, both private and public, should come to grips with facts about religious diversity.

Having established a number of reasons as to why one might consider Tebow's conspicuous piety as problematic, Feezell (2013) goes on to consider how such opinions and beliefs might be framed differently in a world characterised by religious diversity. In so doing, he makes the case for an alternative framing of the sport-celebrity-religion relationship. For Feezell (2013), the issue is not that sports and faith should be kept apart, rather that high-profile Christian athletes have a series of moral and epistemic responsibilities in relation to their expressions of faith precisely because they are who they are.

Feezell (2013) begins his analysis by making a series of assumptions. These are as follows: (i) that people have a variety of religious beliefs; (ii) that religions make truth claims (i.e. about what is true and what is correct); and (iii) given the myriad regional, national, and international events that nowadays speak to notions of 'religious disagreement', it is increasingly difficult for a well-informed person to ignore religious diversity within the context of contemporary society. Feezell (2013) follows up these assumptions with two key questions: in light of such diversity how should one view other religions, and second, how should one's own religious beliefs be held? Utilising the work of McKim (2001), Feezell (2013) then constructs a series of propositions around the concepts of 'confident exclusivism' (the demonstration of exclusivist beliefs) and 'fallibilism' (the notion that one's own views may be wrong and that the views of someone else may be right) in relation to the ways in which Tebow and other celebrity athletes often express their own religious beliefs. For Feezell (2013), and on the basis of the assumptions and propositions raised, such expressions are fundamentally flawed on three levels. First, that as a well-informed, privileged and educated person, Tebow has a responsibility to exhibit a greater sense of awareness to notions of 'impartial reflection' when it comes to his religious beliefs. Second, that Tebow has a responsibility to move from a position of 'confident exclusivism' with regards to his faith, to one which demonstrates a sense of fallibilism which, by its very nature, would facilitate a broader sense of reflection, humility and modesty in relation to the articulation of his own beliefs and the existence of other 'religious possibilities'. Third, Feezell (2013) argues that because of his life-long saturation in evangelical Christianity, Tebow demonstrates a spiritual blind-spot with respect to his status as a role model insofar as this appears to go beyond the 'modelling' of moral and ethical standards and into the epistemic realm where there is an intentionality around 'doxastic matters' (p. 156).[5] That is, the approach taken by Tebow is one which appears keen to proffer not simply how people should behave but what they should believe – all of which, for Feezell (2013: 157), amounts to a lack of responsibility on the part of the celebrity Christian athlete:

> Privileged persons, including Tebow, have a strong reason to hold religious beliefs fallibly. Fallibilist religious believers will be disposed, both practically and attitudinally, to express certain praiseworthy intellectual traits of cognizers. Moreover, celebrated athletes who believe themselves to be role models will have special responsibilities to be epistemic role models, characterized by intellectual impartiality, openness, humility and modesty, and tolerance. To the extent that Tebow and others do not develop and express these traits with respect to their religious beliefs and in their expressions of religiosity, we have reasoned reservations about their conspicuous religiosity and they have good reasons to change their attitudes and behavior.

Whether or not Tim Tebow's departure from the sporting limelight will serve to temper the way in which he articulates his religious beliefs, only time will tell. This is, of course, a decision for him. A career in sports broadcasting may inadvertently facilitate – or even necessitate – such change. Whatever happens, because of the popular cultural capital that he still commands, Tebow will need to tread carefully the tightrope of religious advocacy, if he is to avoid accusations of conspicuous piety and if he is to become (and remain) the spiritual role model that he aspires to be. At the same time, he will need to maintain some level of popular cultural exposure to bolster his personal appeal. Modern-day muscular Christian or not, in the commodified world of sports-media, visibility is everything.

Conclusions

Scrutiny and conjecture surrounding the public and private lives of celebrity sports stars are part of everyday media discourse. Whether sporting celebrities are famous because of their athletic prowess and talent or simply 'known for their well-knowness' both we and they have come to accept (and expect) the intrusive strategies of the world's media and the inquisitive gaze which this affords. Since exploding onto the high school and collegiate football scene, Tim Tebow has never been far from the centre of popular cultural life in the US. Yet on entering retirement from the sport, he now faces the prospect of being eased out of the media gaze. Where, we might ask, does this leave Tebow as a sporting celebrity and/or as a spokesperson on wider social issues?

There are a number of things to consider here. First, we must acknowledge that Tebow's celebrity profile did not emerge in a social, cultural and political vacuum. On the contrary, part of the reason for his appeal is the synchronicity with which his own sporting potential developed alongside the sport-media-business expansion of the 1990s and the religious undertones of US society. Second, we must recognise that Tebow's celebrity status is primarily a national rather than an international/global issue. His is a celebrity born out of cultural acceptance as a quintessentially all-American figure steeped in the values of evangelical Christianity. Third, and as is often the case for celebrity figures, time ultimately changes the nature and level of their influence and, in this sense, while Tebow's impact in and through sport may alter or diminish, that is not to say that he will disappear completely from public view. As we have argued, one of the hallmarks of celebrity status is that it allows individuals to transcend their occupational locales, conferring upon them an on-going popularity that often manifests itself within a range of alternative social settings. Latterly, Tebow has taken up a position in the sports-media which will go some way to maintaining his profile as a public figure. Fourth, despite the amount of media coverage afforded to him, we must guard against assuming that we actually *know* anything about Tim Tebow as a person. All we can say with any degree of certainty is that we know something of him in terms of his popular cultural image; his mass media representations and his celebrity identifications – of which Christianity is a key characteristic. Finally, we must accept that these representations are, more often than not, strategically managed and finely crafted portraits of the person whom marketing and advertising executives wish (and need) to depict. The celebrity-media relationship is symbiotic. Sports celebrities simply cannot maintain their popular cultural position without a marketised media presence.

For Tim Tebow himself, recent years have witnessed continued influence in the marrying of his popular cultural image and his religious identity. In light of the critical analysis put forward here with regard to the formulation and expression of that identity, what remains to be seen is how long this level of status and influence will prevail.

Notes

1 Sections of this chapter have previously appeared elsewhere (see: Bolsmann and Parker, 2007; Cashmore and Parker, 2003; Howe and Parker, 2012; Nalapat and Parker, 2005 and Parker, 2009). For a slightly lengthier version of the entire chapter see: Parker and Watson (2015).

2 The term 'stars' is used here to denote those who have become well-known publicly as celebrity figures. For more on the construction (and consumption) of 'stars' see Dyer (1988). For more general insight into sporting celebrity and notoriety see Cashmore (2004, 2005, 2006) and Milligan (2004).

3 Academic offerings on the broader concept of celebrity are nothing new. For more on this subject see the work of Boyle and Haynes (1999), Debord (1968), Evans and Wilson (1999), Gamson (1994), Giles (2000), Marshall (1997), Monaco (1978), Smart (2005) and Turner, Bonner and Marshall (2000). For specific discussion on taxonomies of celebrity see Rojek (2001) and Turner (2004).

4 For specific discussion on taxonomies of celebrity see Rojek (2001) and Turner (2004). For more on the icon/iconicity dyad, see Kear and Steinberg (1999).

5 For more on sports celebrities as role models see Rojek (2006).

References

Andrews, D. and Jackson, S. (2001), (eds) *Sports Stars: The Cultural Politics of Sporting Celebrity*. London, Routledge.

Bernstein, A. and Blain, N. (eds). (2003), *Sport, Media, Culture: Global and Local Dimensions*. London: Frank Cass.

Bolsmann, C. and Parker, A. (2007), 'Soccer, South Africa and Celebrity Status: Mark Fish, Popular Culture and the Post-Apartheid State', *Soccer and Society*, 8 (1): 109–124.

Boorstin, D. (1961), *The Image: A Guide to Pseudo-events in America*. New York, Atheneum.

Boyle, R. and Haynes, R. (1999), *Power Play: Sport, the Media and Popular Culture*. London, Longman.

Brohm, J-M. (1978), *Sport: A Prison of Measured Time*. London, Pluto.

Cashmore, E. (2004), *Beckham* (2nd edn). Cambridge, Polity Press.

Cashmore, E. (2005) *Tyson. Nurture of the Beast*. Cambridge, Polity Press.

Cashmore, E. (2006), *Celebrity/Culture*. London, Routledge.

Cashmore, E. (2008), 'Chariots of Fire: Bigotry, Manhood and Moral Certitude in an Age of Individualism', *Sport in Society*, 11 (2):159–173.

Cashmore, E. and Parker, A. (2003), ' "One David Beckham …?" Celebrity, Masculinity and the Socceratti', *Sociology of Sport Journal*, 20 (3): 214–232.

Chung, H. (2003), 'Sport Star *vs* Rock Star in Globalizing Popular Culture', *International Review for the Sociology of Sport*, 38 (1): 99–108.

Debord, G. (1968), *Society of the Spectacle*. Detroit, Black and Red.

Dyer, R. (1988), *Stars*. London, British Film Institute Publishing.

Epstein, A. (2011), 'Religion and Sports in the Undergraduate Classroom: A Surefire Way to Spark Student Interest', *Southern Law Journal*, 21 (1): 133–147.

Evans, A. and Wilson, G. (1999), *Fame: The Psychology of Stardom*. London, Vision.

Evans, J. (2005), 'Celebrity, Media and History', in J. Evans and D. Hesmondhalgh (eds) *Understanding Media: Inside Celebrity*. Buckingham, Open University Press.

Featherstone, M. (1991). 'The Body in Consumer Culture', in M. Featherstone, M. Hepworth and B. S. Turner (eds), *The Body: Social Processes and Cultural Theory*. London: Sage, pp. 171–197.

Feezell, R. (2013), 'Sport, Religious Belief, and Religious Diversity', *Journal of the Philosophy of Sport*, 40 (1): 135–162.

Fish, M. (2009), 'What Price Glory? The Star's Value'. ESPN.com. 11 December. Available at: www.espn.com/espn/otl/news/story?page=fish/09121, accessed 28 July 2017.

Gamson, J. (1994), *Claims to Fame: Celebrity in Contemporary America*. Berkeley, CA, University of California Press.

Giles, D. (2000), *Illusions of Immortality: A Psychology of Fame and Celebrity*. London, Macmillan.

Harris, J. and Clayton, B. (2007), 'The First Metrosexual Rugby Star: Rugby Union, Masculinity and Celebrity in Contemporary Wales', *Sociology of Sport Journal*, 24 (2): 145–164.

Harvey, D. (1989), *The Condition of Postmodernity*. Oxford, Blackwell.

Haynes, R. (2004), 'The Fame Game: The Peculiarities of Sports Image Rights in the United Kingdom', *Trends In Communication* 12 (2): 101–116.

Haynes, R. (2005), *Media Rights and Intellectual Property*. Edinburgh, Edinburgh University Press.

Hoffman, S.J. (2010), *Good Game: Christianity and the Culture of Sports*. Baylor, TX, Baylor University Press.

Howe, P.D. and Parker, A. (2012), 'Celebrating Imperfection: Sport, Disability and Celebrity Culture', *Celebrity Studies*, 3 (3): 270–282.

Kear, A. and Steinberg, D. L. (eds) (1999), *Mourning Diana: Nation, Culture and the Performance of Grief*. London, Routledge.

Krattenmaker, T. (2010), *Onward Christian Athletes: Turning Ballparks into Pulpit and Players into Preachers*. New York, Roman and Littlefield.

Ladd, T. and Mathisen, J. A. (1999), *Muscular Christianity: Evangelical Protestants and the Development of American Sports*. Grand Rapids, MI, Baker Books.

Laderman, G. (2009), *Sacred Matters: Celebrity Worship, Sexual Ecstasies, the Living and Other Signs of Religious Life in the United States*. New York, New Press.

Marshall, P. (1997), *Celebrity and Power: Fame in Contemporary Culture*. Minneapolis, MN, University of Minnesota Press.

McKim, R. (2001), *Religious Ambiguity and Religious Diversity*. New York, Oxford University Press.

Milligan, A. (2004), *Brand it Like Beckham: The Story of How Brand Beckham was Built*. London, Cyan Books.

Monaco, J. (1978) *Celebrity: The Media as Image Makers*. New York, Delta.

Moore, M. E., Keller, C. and Zemanek, J. E. (2011), 'The Marketing Revolution of Tim Tebow: A Celebrity Endorsement Case Study', *Innovative Marketing*, 7 (1): 17–25.

Nalapat, A. and Parker, A. (2005) 'Sport, Celebrity and Popular Culture: Sachin Tendulkar, Cricket and Indian Nationalisms', *International Review for the Sociology of Sport*, 40 (4): 433–446.

Newman, J. I. (2010), 'Full-Throttle Jesus: Toward a Critical Pedagogy of Stockcar Racing in Theocratic America', *Review of Education, Pedagogy, and Cultural Studies*, 32 (3): 263–294.

Parker, A. (2009), 'Sport, Celebrity and Identity: A Socio-legal analysis', in J. Harris and A. Parker (eds) *Sport and Social Identities*, London, Palgrave Macmillan, pp. 150–167.

Parker, A. and Watson, N. J. (2015), 'Sport, Celebrity and Religion: Christianity, Morality and the Tebow Phenomenon', *Studies in World Christianity*, 21 (3): 223–238.

Rial, C. (2012), 'Banal Religiosity. Brazilian Athletes as New Missionaries of the Neo-Pentecostal Diaspora', *Vibrant: Virtual Brazilian Anthropology*, 9 (2): 128–159.

Rigaeur, B. (1981), *Sport and Work*. New York, Columbia University Press.

Rojek, C. (2001), *Celebrity*. London, Reaktion.

Rojek, C. (2006), 'Sports Celebrity and the Civilising Process'. *Sport in Society* 9 (4): 674–690.

Rowe, D. (2003), *Sport, Culture and the Media*. Buckingham, Open University Press.

Shilling, C. (2003), *The Body and Social Theory* (2nd edn). London, Sage.

Smart, B. (2005) *The Sport Star: Modern Sport and the Cultural Economy of Sporting Celebrity*. London, Sage.

Tebow, T. (2011), *Through My Eyes*. New York, Harper Collins.

Turner, G. (2004), *Understanding Celebrity*. London, Sage.

Turner, G., Bonner, F. and Marshall, P. (2000), *Fame Games: The Production of Celebrity in Australia*. Melbourne, Cambridge University Press.

Ward, P. (2011), *Gods Behaving Badly. Media, Religion and Celebrity Culture*. London, SCM Press.

Whannel, G. (1992), *Fields in Vision: Television, Sport and Cultural Transformation*. London, Routledge.

Whannel, G. (2002), *Media Sports Stars: Masculinities and Moralities*. London, Routledge.

Whannel, G. (2005), 'Pregnant with Anticipation: The Pre-history of Television Sport and the Politics of Recycling and Preservation', *International Journal of Cultural Studies*, 8 (4): 405–426.

Chapter 13

Church, sports, and tragedy

Religion and rituals of public mourning in the Ibrox disasters of 1902 and 1971

James C. Deming

Introduction

On 2 January 2001, club dignitaries, former players, and fans of Glasgow Rangers Football (soccer) Club gathered at Ibrox Stadium, the club's home, for the unveiling of a larger-than-life statue of the team's much beloved former captain, John Greig. Although Greig was present and participated in the ceremony he was not its focus. Instead, in a brief service, led by Church of Scotland minister Stuart McQuarrie, the gathering marked the anniversary of a disaster at Ibrox 30 years before and to remember the fans that had died there. In commemoration of the tragedy, the names of the 66 victims were inscribed on the statue's plinth, along with those from two earlier disasters in 1961 and 1902 (*Daily Record*, 2001; *Telegraph*, 2001, p. 1).

The immediate cause of the 1971 Ibrox catastrophe remains something of a mystery. It took place immediately after a Glasgow Rangers–Glasgow Celtic rivalry match that ended in a 1–1 draw. As fans made their way out of the stadium it is thought that someone tripped on the treacherous Stairway 13, setting off a cascade down the steps crushing or asphyxiating the victims under the weight of bodies. The 1961 accident, in which two supporters were killed, was something of a precursor to that of 1971 as it also occurred on Stairway 13 and in much the same circumstances. Two more incidents took place on the same stairway in the late 1960s, but on these occasions there was no loss of life. In 1902 Rangers had won the right to host the annual England–Scotland match. The club hurriedly added extra capacity to accommodate the expected large crowd. It was in this area that the stands gave way plunging hundreds to the ground below. Twenty-five were killed and more than 500 others were injured (Shiels, 1998; *Telegraph*, 2001; Walker, 2004).

The magnitude of the 1902 and 1971 disasters struck particularly deep. The dead represented the epitome of 'bad deaths'. They were sudden, violent, and the victims were primarily boys and young men, cut down early in life while enjoying a moment of recreation. As the Rev. William

Morris, Church of Scotland minister at Glasgow Cathedral said after the 1971 disaster, 'Tragedy is doubly poignant when it falls at a time of holiday and happiness' (*Glasgow Herald*, 1971a). In some ways the grief that followed these accidents was similar to that after private loss. Routine is shattered. Time is disjointed. The everyday feels out of place or inappropriate. Reality seems to dissolve away. In response, a variety of rituals and conventions are employed to re-insert the bereaved back into the community of the living. The scale of the disasters, however, spread the trauma beyond the world of family and friends. It was a moment that seems to fit John Morley's (1971, p. 79) observation about World War I. 'Mourning,' he wrote, 'succumbed before the vast numbers of the dead; faced with this, family mourning and its conventions were an insufficient comment.' It was up to the community, and especially its political and religious leaders, to perform the rites of mourning to restore social solidarity. For clergy, however, this meant negotiating the intersection of their roles as arbiters of the passage from life to death, their responsibilities as guardians of social morality, and popular expectations. Failure to do so, or to be perceived to do so inappropriately, could compromise their legitimacy. As Emile Durkheim (1915, p. 397) noted, 'society does not leave it to religious forces to punish the negligent; it intervenes itself, and reprimands the ritual faults'.

Consequently, this tension at a moment of social distress offers a valuable opportunity to observe the dynamics of popular expectations with established authority and priorities. The disasters at Ibrox Stadium present a particularly unique occasion in that they occurred in the same location, within the same city, with victims from similar social and religious milieux, and who were engaged in a similar activity, watching football. Even the games were of similar import. For 1902 it was a rivalry contest with Scotland's 'auld enemy'. In 1971 it was one of the most intense rivalries in the world of sport, Scottish football's 'Old Firm', Celtic versus Rangers. Yet the tragedies took place nearly 70 years apart allowing a perspective of remarkably similar events across two-thirds of the twentieth century.

Scotland versus England, Ibrox Park, 2 January 1902

Death was never far from the lives of Victorians. Even though overall life expectancy was gradually increasing by the end of the nineteenth century, for the lower classes insufficient nutrition and poor living conditions still prevailed. Added to this were risky working conditions and a rather laissez-faire approach to regulation. Consequently, accidents, large and small, resulting in death were frequent. As a major manufacturing and ship-building centre, Glasgow had its share of catastrophes. For example, the newly launched steamship *Daphne*, capsized on its launch in 1883, trapping 124 men working in the hold (*Glasgow Herald*, 1883). A year later, 14 were killed in a stampede at the Star Theatre when a disgruntled employee literally yelled 'fire' in a crowded theatre (*Glasgow Herald*, 1884). Twenty-seven young women were killed in 1887 when the walls of the factory in which they were working collapsed. Finally, four firemen died in 1898 in the Renfield Street fire (*Glasgow Herald*, 1898).

In the wake of the *Daphne*, Templeton factory and Renfield Street disasters, a pattern of public practices developed. Expressions of dismay and sympathy arrived from home and abroad, many reported in the local press. City officials promised a thorough investigation and assured that those at fault would be held accountable. The Lord Provost of Glasgow would convene a public meeting at which leading citizens would put forward and approve various proposals relating to the disaster. The most important were a formal declaration from the city of its grief, sympathy, and hope for comfort for the victims, and the establishment of a relief fund in their behalf.

An exception was the stampede at the Star Theatre after which the only offer of aid came from the theatre's owner who promised to see that the dead received a proper burial (*Glasgow Herald*, 1884). Other than an investigation by the city engineer, nothing else was said or done. The difference would seem to be that in the former disasters the victims were engaged in honest labour or public service. Those who died at the Star Theatre, known as the Gaiety Theatre by the popular classes, had been participants in the less reputable activity of bawdy popular entertainment. In the case of the 1902 Ibrox disaster, the Lord Provost of Glasgow, Samuel Chisholm, at first seemed to hesitate, but five days after the accident finally convened a public meeting in the banquet hall at City Chambers to address the suffering. In this way the city's leadership assumed direction of the processes of public mourning.

Glasgow's religious leaders played a relatively minor role in these actions. The public assembly was essentially a city council meeting writ large. While some clergy from a variety of denominations were among the list of dignitaries, it was dominated by politicians, social elites and officials from a number of football clubs and organizations like the Scottish Football Association. Most of the motions and accompanying speeches were made by public figures of some stature, such as the Provost, the Sherriff of Glasgow, the Lord Dean of Guild and a local Member-of-Parliament. A motion to thank the medical personnel who tended the victims was seconded by Dr Walter Ross-Taylor of the United Free Church of Scotland, and the Roman Catholic bishop of Glasgow proposed that the assembly thank Chisholm for taking the initiative. At no time was there an effort to include religious content in the proceedings (*Glasgow Herald*, 1902b).

The restrained role of the church in the proceedings at City Chambers was not necessarily remarkable. According to Scottish Presbyterian practice clerical involvement with the dead occurred largely away from both church and public space. The convention was for a pastor to go to the home of the deceased where the body lay. He would lead the mourners in Psalms and prayers and maybe say few words of comfort. From there the deceased would be taken to a cemetery for burial. If a minster joined the procession it was principally as a fellow mourner (Gorer, 1965).

More was said from the pulpit, in religious organizations, and in the pages of magazines and newspapers. Many of the ministers who addressed the catastrophe shared the general tenor of remorse, sympathy and comfort. Father O'Brien, of Holy Cross Church in Govan, described to his congregation the suffering he had witnessed at the Western Infirmary and asked that they remember the victims in prayer. The United Free Church of Scotland's Synod of Glasgow formally expressed its sympathy and prayed that God would comfort and heal the bereaved and injured. It went on to urge parishioners to let their sympathy 'take form in a practical and substantial manner', a reference to the relief fund. For his part, the Sunday following the accident the United Free Church minister, Peter Smith, preached from Job 13:15, 'Though He slay me yet will I trust in Him' (Smith, 1902, p. 1). In a time when 47 per cent of the children of the lower orders died before age 15 (Clark, 2007) pastors were well accustomed to addressing heart-wrenching deaths. Smith's choice of Job is interesting in the way his story mirrored that of Glasgow. Similar to Ibrox, Job's despair derived from the loss of all his children in a building collapse (Job 1:18–19). Thus, Smith noted that in the light of the catastrophe of a few days earlier, 'the experience of Job is not an uncommon one need not be pressed on those gathered here today'. He closed the sermon urging the congregation, 'Through the clouds of the present let us press on to the cloudless land' (Smith, 1902, p. 5).

While comfort and consolation was one pastoral objective, ministers also sought to give meaning to the catastrophe. Thus, Smith proclaimed both hope and admonition. 'Once more,' he said, 'the community and the nation, especially its youth, are urged in Divine providence to prepare to meet God.' By means of the disaster,

> We are forced by sorrow back upon God, and experience the sweet-ness and all sufficiency of His grace. Under its pressure men cry to God, who had never done so before, or had ceased doing it, thus faith is quickened and the principles of righteousness wrought out.
>
> (Smith, 1902, p. 3)

This type of admonition was common in clerical responses to the 1902 disaster. However, where ministers like Smith saw a call all for spiritual vigilance, other members of the clergy approached the catastrophe from the perspective of broader anxiety about the corruption of the working class culture (Hargreaves, 1986; Hay, 1982; Holt, 1989). For these ministers the accident was a divine warning of sudden death and final reckoning before the Almighty, but was accompanied by passage of judgement on the moral value of football spectatorship and the game itself. Thus, Andrew Laidlaw, moderator of the Glasgow Synod of Church of Scotland, declared, 'Very startlingly, the pleasure-seeking crowd was awakened to know that in the midst of life they were in death.' Ministers, he said, had frequently warned about the 'pleasure-seeking of the younger generation, and detestation of the rudeness and very often the blasphemous language which was to be frequently heard in the crowds who attended football matches' (*Glasgow Herald*, 1902c, p. 11) His colleague, Andrew Douglass, railed against the generation's excessive 'mania for sport' by which tens of thousands could be so engrossed as to 'forget their duty to God and His Church' (*Glasgow Herald*, 1902c) . Most strident was the Rev. Dr Paterson of the University of Aberdeen. In the midst of a graduation sermon he savaged both fans and football. Reflecting a wider sentiment about sports and recreation in general (Erdozain, 2010; Holt, 1989), Paterson charged that sports were 'of little use' as by nature they are mere 'frivolous amusements and enervating luxuries to the crowd of lounging and smoking spectators'. The popularity of football, he claimed, 'was a sign of degeneracy' comparable to the games of ancient Rome (*Glasgow Herald*, 1902c, p. 6).

This divide among church leaders was evidence of a degree of ambivalence in respectable society in general regarding the breadth and depth of football's popularity. The modern game had originated in the exclusive schools and universities of England, with the avowed purpose to inculcate ideals of manliness, cooperation and fair play. As the working classes adopted its practices, however, football was slipping from the control of elites who knew better. Commercialization of the game, represented by professionalism and spectatorship, seemed antithetical to the proper spirit of sport by which participation, not winning, was an end to itself (Holt, 1989; McLeod, 2013; Walvin, 1994). Instead, football had moved from a pastime played for personal enrichment, to one in which hundreds of thousands willingly surrendered a share of their slim resources to watch with fanatical attention as a few skilled players did their work. Perhaps even more disturbing was the passion with which fans followed their chosen team. For ministers like Douglass, their enthusiasm was misplaced and overwhelmed Christian devotion (Parker and Weir, 2012). To some ministers football was more vice than virtue. Consequently, the tragedy at Ibrox could be seen to have more in common with the Star Theatre stampede than the loss of life in honest labour as in the Templeton and *Daphne* disasters.

Such a view exposed some contradictions. One was the overwhelming popularity of football among working class men and boys. Refusing to mourn with the bereaved risked offending a segment of society that church leaders feared they were losing (Brown, 2009; Currie *et al.*, 1977; McLeod,

1974). Second, the church and church-related organizations were complicit in the game's popularity. Many of today's professional UK teams in began in churches. For example, Aston Villa formed from Villa Cross Wesleyan Chapel; Fulham FC grew out of St. Andrew's Sunday school; Everton from St. Domingo's Sunday School; Burnley from a chapter of the YMCA, and Glasgow Celtic was first organised as charity project to raise money to assist the city's Irish poor (Bradley, 2004; Lupson, 2006). Beyond these connections, by forming youth teams and running leagues many religious organizations were at least partially responsible for football's democrat-ization. For example, in Birmingham in 1880, 84 of its 218 teams were church related. A similar make-up could be found in cities across England. In Scotland, it was above all the Boy's Brigade, a church-related organiza-tion somewhat akin to the Boy Scouts, which dominated. So ubiquitous was this organization that many boys who later became professional players, and thousands more who became devoted fans, had their first experience of organized soccer within its leagues (Harvie, 1994).

Thus, at the time of the Ibrox tragedy, football existed as something of a cultural borderline. Was it an activity that eroded society's moral fibre, or was it something respectable people might condone if not necessarily embrace? Glasgow's Lord Provost decided to join the mourning thereby bringing the government in line with public sentiment. This was a tacit legitimation of football's place in national culture. Church leaders, however, were not politicians. Politicians may compromise principle in the cause of governing, but ministers were entrusted with society's spiritual and moral integrity. As with gambling and alcohol, activities that might be publically accepted were not necessarily up-lifting and could be degrading. In 1902, clergy were divided over football's relation to these ideals. Some pastors were willing to accept the game as demonstrated by acknowledging and sharing in the grief of the people. Others were unable to look past the taint of a professional football match that had led to the disaster. While perhaps not overtly crossing the line, their pronouncements about the tragedy could be seen to flirt with the declaration that the catastrophe represented some kind of divine judgement upon an immoral people.

Glasgow Rangers versus Glasgow Celtic, Ibrox Park, 2 January 1971

In the wake of the tragedy on Ibrox's Stairway 13 in 1971, officials fol-lowed a template for the city's mourning similar to that of 69 years before. In each the Provost called for a public relief fund. Numerous expressions of grief, remorse and sympathy from dignitaries, politicians and organiza-tions were received and publicized. Many of these, such as that from the Queen, included pledges of donations for the bereaved. The government promised a thorough investigation into the cause of the accident and a formal occasion for public mourning was arranged. At the same time, there were significant differences between 1971 and 1902 in how the city sought to address the grief of its citizens. In 1971 Rangers took a direct role in the bereavement process. Almost immediately it postponed forthcoming matches. This gave team manager, Willie Waddell, time to organize players and officials into groups to ensure that the club would be represented at every funeral. Church leaders were also more visible in the early days of mourning than was the case in 1902. For example, James Currie, Church of Scotland pastor and avid Rangers fan, was called on by club officials to come to the stadium and minister to the injured and comfort the families of those killed. On the same evening, Currie's colleague, Arthur Gray, appeared on Scottish Television to conduct a service of readings, prayers, and words of consolation (Coffey, 1988; Gray, 1971). And, of course, ministers conducted funerals and visited hospitals.

At the same time Rangers players and officials were doing much the same. It was their activities that were most frequently in the public eye. Photographs and news stories repeatedly documented the way in which players served as public mourners (*Glasgow Herald*, 1971b). Rev. Robert Bone commended them from the pulpit of Glasgow Cathedral for sharing in the grief of the bereaved: 'They have seen in a week as much sorrow as many do in a lifetime' (Ralston, 2001, p. 1). Sandy Jardine, a Rangers defender on the field that day, recalled, 'Effectively, we stopped being a football club.' As Daily Record reporter Gary Ralston, summarized, Rangers had become 'a high-profile counselling unit' (Ralston, 2001, p. 1).

The Provost of Glasgow, Sir Donald Liddle, quickly assumed an active and prominent role as the lead of the city's rites of mourning. He went to the site of the accident, promised a thorough public safety investigation, attended a requiem mass for the victims, and openly expressed on several occasions his dismay over the accident and sympathy with the injured and bereaved. At one news conference he tearfully confessed, 'It is beyond my grasp to comprehend it – I am broken-hearted at this tragedy' (*Glasgow Herald*, 1971c). As for the relief fund, he established this purely by administrative action as quickly as possible. Finally, Liddle arranged for a memorial service at the Church of Scotland's Glasgow Cathedral (*Glasgow Herald*, 1971d).

The memorial service in the city cathedral may have provided more of a sacred gloss to the proceedings of 69 years earlier, there were still elements of civic service. Of the more than 3,000 that attended, the *Glasgow Herald* noted, 'The congregation was made up mainly of civic dignitaries, relatives of those who died or were injured, and directors, players and supporters of Rangers and Celtic football clubs' (*Glasgow Herald*, 1971a). The service itself was a civic-religious rite, with the balance favouring the church. The ceremony was conducted by the minister of the cathedral, the Rev. Dr William Morris, who led the congregation in hymns, prayers, and delivered the memorial address. He was assisted by Rev. Bone, pastor of Ibrox Parish Church, who offered a few comments and the commemorative prayer. There were also links to the civic aspects of the moment. As minster of the established church's city cathedral, Morris was both clergyman and city minister, while Rev. Bone was called upon because it was in his parish that the accident had occurred. In the memorial address Morris made a point to stress the unifying effect of the catastrophe. They came together, he proclaimed, 'as a city with our civic leaders, representatives of all aspects of our city's life' to offer sympathy to the bereaved (*Glasgow Herald*, 1971d, p. 18). Meanwhile, he read the lessons and led the procession of the congregation from the building. Similar scenes took place in towns and parishes throughout the region. Perhaps the most gripping was that of the small town of Markinch from which five teenage boys were killed on Stairway 13. An estimated 1,000 mourners, including the chairman of Rangers and five players, as well as the town Provost and members of the town council, descended on the parish church for their funeral. As the Rev. William Hastie Miller said, 'Saturday was a black day for Scotland. It was a black, black day for Markinch' (*Glasgow Herald*, 1971e, p. 20).

Absent from the service and others like it, was any hint of a question as to football's moral worth. In 1902 there was uncertainty, especially among Protestant clergy, about how to respond to the disaster. There were questions as to whether the victims had been engaged in dubious activity along the lines of drinking, gambling or the music and dance hall, and thereby more worthy of censure than commiseration. By 1971, however, it was not unusual for a Church of Scotland minister to attend a football game. Rev. Currie, for example, was first introduced to his new congregation as 'a Rangers' supporter'. Glasgow minister, Arthur Gray, used his first paycheck as an assistant minister to buy a Rangers season ticket. As chaplain to the supporters' federation and informally for the club, Currie was spared such an expense as he was accorded free entry to the stadium (Coffey, 1988; Gray, 1971).

Similarly, rather than question the propriety of spectatorship, Rev. Bone, praised 'the ordinary man in the crowd who, despite danger, turned back to help the man he did not know'. Writing on behalf of The Moderator of the General Assembly of the Church of Scotland, the Right Rev. Dr Hugh O. Douglass sent the denomination's condolences and prayers for comfort and healing. In the course of memorial address at the cathedral, Dr Morris noted that

> too often in the last three years, we have gathered here in our city's ancient church for this sad duty: workers dying in a factory fire, policemen killed in the course of duty, and now the shouts of a holiday crowd suddenly transformed into cries of pain and the shocked hush of tragedy.
>
> (Glasgow Herald, 1971a)

He was referring to 22 workers who died in a fire at a carpet warehouse in 1968, as well as two policemen who were killed in the line of duty in December 1969. Morris' statement was simple, but its very casualness indicates how much attitudes had changed since the first Ibrox disaster. It seemed obvious to preacher and people alike that a tragedy at a football match should inhabit the same space in public life as workplace disasters or even sacrifice in public service.

What these rituals did not necessarily provide was a sense of meaning in the tragedy. What significance was there to the shock, pain, suffering and anguish? Owen Chadwick observed of the aftermath of the sinking of the *Titanic* in 1912, that largely missing from reactions to its loss were references to providence. Commenters seemed more concerned to separate God from the disaster than see in it a revelation of divine purpose (Chadwick, 1975, pp. 261–263). This would seem to have been the case following the catastrophe on Stairway 13 as well. No one, publically at least, seems to have associated the dead and injured with God's judgement, or discerned in the tragedy a warning to the living to diligently prepare their souls for death. In fact, explicitly religious content was nearly absent from public discourse surrounding the tragedy. Presumably, in the weeks following sermons would have touched on the disaster, and the spiritual would have been part of private funerals. Unlike in 1902, however, media coverage largely ignored these events. Even with the requiem mass and memorial service at Glasgow Cathedral little was said about religious content. Instead they ascribed greater significance to more secularized references to the anguish of the moment and the consoling efforts of players and management.

Even so, a note of the providential could still be detected. This narrative was closely associated with the virulent religious-ethnic bigotry that often characterized relations between Glasgow's Protestant and Irish Catholic communities. To a disturbing degree, these hatreds had coalesced around Glasgow Rangers and Glasgow Celtic. Being a Rangers supporter could well be a declaration of the uncompromising unionism of the Orange Order at its most bellicose. With Celtic the situation was a bit more complex as its fans base was more diverse, but the club's general identity was Irish-Catholic (Bradley, 2004; Murray, 2004; Giulianotti and Gerrard, 2001; Walker, 1990). By the 1960s, however, a degree of embarrassment had developed among clergy and public figures, regarding the association of the Old Firm with confessional bigotry. Rev. Bone went so far as to denounce Rangers from the pulpit in 1969 for its sectarian policies. In response Rangers' management noted that Bone was more than happy to accept complementary tickets despite the club's infractions (Murray, 1984). Consequently, in the wake of the disaster the sight of personnel from the two clubs sitting side-by-side raised hopes that public loss would be a catalyst for the healing of sectarian enmity. The desire was that the

estranged communities would be brought together in the common experience of mourning the dead. At the time this did not seem an entirely unre-
alistic possibility. Players and fans from both teams were deeply affected
by scale of the tragedy. For example, Celtic's manager, Jock Stein,
expressed, what many were thinking. 'Surely this terrible tragedy,' he said,
'must help to curb the bigotry and bitterness of Old Firm matches. When
human life is at stake this kind of hatred seems sordid and little' (McPhail,
1971, p. 1). The editor of *The Celtic View*, official newspaper of Celtic FC,
was more blunt. Using the common names identifying the loyalties of the
opposing fans, the paper said, 'There were no Billys or Dans, lying still
under these shrouds at Ibrox on Saturday. Only dead people, with families
and friends' (*The Celtic View*, 1971, p. 1).

Given that at least nominally the problem was bound to confessional
identities, religious leaders felt a special responsibility for its solution.
Thus, even though all the victims were Protestant, on the Wednesday following the tragedy, a congregation of 1,200 attended the Roman Catholic
cathedral for a requiem mass celebrated by the Archbishop James Scanlon.
The Glasgow Herald's coverage of the event made a point of noting that
officials, managers and players of both Rangers and Celtic sat side-by-side
through the rite. The moment of reconciliation seemed to extend to the
fans as officers of supporters' clubs for both teams, were present together
at the various proceedings, as were a number of ministers from several
denominations. Respect for the dead and bereaved seemed particularly
powerful. At the requiem mass Bishop Scanlon explained, 'In offering this
Mass today we of the Catholic community are paying the highest tribute in
our power to the victims of Saturday's appalling disaster' (*Glasgow
Herald*, 1971c, p. 1). Finally, the single largest gift to the disaster fund
came from a Roman Catholic priest, Father John Curtin, who donated
£25,000 of the more than £100,000 he had won in the football pools,
which included the Rangers–Celtic match (*Glasgow Herald*, 1971f, p. 10).

A few days later the 'official' memorial service was held in the Church
of Scotland, Glasgow Cathedral. Approximately 3,000 attended, either in
the building itself or watching on closed-circuit television outside in a west
Scotland January. The service was also broadcast by BBC television,
thereby providing a national audience as well. Within the sanctuary, civic
dignitaries and families of the victims were provided prominent placing. As
with the mass at St. Andrew's Cathedral, Rangers and Celtic management,
players and representatives of supporters' clubs were present and provided
preferred seating. And like 1902, a cross-section of the city's denominations attended, this time including a rabbi and Greek Orthodox priest. The
focus of much of the attention, however, was on the bishop representing
the Catholic Church. According to the Glasgow Herald, at one point in the
service Dr Morris looked to the assembled clergy directly, saying, 'At Ibrox
a week ago, as in a war, suffering taught men of different faiths and rival

prejudices that they were brothers.' He went on to urge that this be the beginning of a lasting movement. On the other hand, it is worth noting that despite a broadening ecumenism at neither the Catholic mass, nor the Protestant memorial service did a member of the different denominations actively participate in the ceremonies (*Glasgow Herald*, 1971a).

The theme of reconciliation was taken up in greater detail in the Church of Scotland magazine, *Life & Work*. In an article entitled 'Let There Be No Wasted Sorrow', Church of Scotland minister, Rev. Arthur Gray explicitly addressed the violence and hatred that marred the Old Firm rivalry. The piece was prefaced by three photographs filling the facing page. One was of both a Celtic and Rangers player in close conversation on the field. The middle picture was of Celtic and Rangers players sitting side-by-side during a memorial service. The last featured Celtic and Rangers captains shaking hands before a game. The caption read, 'Respect and healthy rivalry between captains Gemmell and Greig' (Gray, 1971). This could be reading too much into a century-old ritual, but Gray's message was clear. In the rituals of football, as in the rites of mourning, the players demonstrated the potential for mutual respect despite differences. The problem, then, was not the players but club administrators who saw ethnic-religious tensions as good for business, as well as fans who let bigotry seep into club loyalties.

Thus, Gray addressed the article as an open letter to Rangers management. First explaining that he was a life-long fan, Gray tried to come to grips with the tragedy of Stairway 13 and give it purpose. 'The worst disaster of all,' he said, 'would be our failure or refusal to learn from the pain and suffering that have shadowed your Club and so many hearts and homes.' He singled out the fact that, while Celtic had had employed a number of Protestants, including its manager, Jock Stein, Rangers had never signed a Roman Catholic in management or on the field. 'Hasn't the time come,' he asked, 'for young Rangers players to be sought entirely for their ability and character without enquiring into which Communion of the Church they were baptized?' (Gray, 1971, p. 13) He went on to ask that the directors of the clubs sit down with police and agree on a way to weed out 'those whose interjections about the Pope or the Queen become so tiresome'. The unity in sympathy evident at St. Andrew's and Glasgow Cathedral, Gray observed, was a good start, and that 'No one even on the extremist Protestant wing has dared to raise his voice in protest'. Now it was up to Rangers management to 'continue to show the dignity in the burdens laid upon them, and expressed at both the requiem mass and memorial service'. In conclusion he declared, 'Sorrow that does not bring some expression of reconciliation is the permanent disaster in human life' (Gray, 1971, p. 13).

Despite the many hopes for mutual understanding, encapsulated in Gray's appeal, it was not long before fans slipped back into old patterns of behaviour. Perhaps most disgraceful was the Old Firm Scottish FA Cup final in 1980 which deteriorated into a riot after the final whistle, as fans from both sides invaded the field and police charged into the melee on horseback in order to restore order. For their part, Rangers management continued to insist that it did not have a confessional test for new signings, yet it was not until 1989, with considerable public and church pressure, that the club signed its first Catholic player. As the Rangers' webpage commented about the Ibrox disaster, 'Sadly, but perhaps inevitably, ... the 'healing' process proved little more than a nine-day wonder' (Rangers Football Club, 2010, para. 10).

Church, sports, and tragedy

In his book, *Death, Grief and Mourning*, Geoffrey Gorer (1965) argued that in twentieth-century western society death, dying and grief has been increasingly 'stigmatized as morbid, unhealthy, demoralizing'. Mourning, therefore, is treated as if it were 'a weakness, a self-indulgence, a reprehensible bad habit accompanied by feelings of guilt and unworthiness' (p. 113). It should be have 'no public expression, and indulged, if at all, in private' (p. 111).[1] This may have been the case with personal grief which increasingly has been confined to the private sphere, but it did not seem to fully apply to the aftermath of the Ibrox disasters. Morely's (1971) comment about the insufficiency of private mourning in the face of mass death seems more fully relevant. In fact, it would appear that if anything, between 1902 and 1971 public rituals of grief became more intricate and involved. In Protestant Scotland this included greater participation by church and clergy that, in turn, provided a degree of solemnity to the process that would seem to be missing from the public business meeting in 1902.

The process by which these changes developed over time involved a complex interplay of church doctrine and practice, civil authority and public sentiment. For example, the translation of rituals of mourning from a civic action in the city chambers into a memorial service conducted by members of the clergy in the city cathedral could be seen as a factor of civil religion. It also reflected a change in Scottish Protestant practices regarding the church and mourning. Prior ecclesiastical restrictions about clerical involvement in funerals had given way to a more open approach to rites for the dead and comfort for the grieving. This could involve a reciprocal interaction between church practice and public sentiment regarding a more intimate relation of religion and death. In 1902 there had not been an expectation that the church should be directly involved in public rituals of grief. In 1971, by contrast, such involvement was deemed entirely appropriate and it is likely that the church's failure to commit to such a role would have violated a public sense of religious propriety. Paradoxically, it is difficult to escape a sense, at least from related press coverage, that, in the words of Gorer's (1965) conclusion that in modern funerals, 'the clergyman who conducted the funeral was a technician hired to do his job' (p. 40).

Similarly, in 1902 the church was divided in its response to the destruction of lives in the stadium collapse. Some ministers saw providential lessons in the tragedy, rooted in the need for faith and proper piety, couching this message in a general tone of consolation. For others, the disaster's connection to professional football was an opportunity to challenge the moral worth of the game and its fans. In late-Victorian Scotland, football was morally disputed ground. The concern of religious leaders in 1971 was not the legitimacy of football, the merits of fandom, or divine judgement. Though still largely working class, football was thoroughly integrated into the broader culture such that there was no hint of a discussion of its morality, nor of that of its spectatorship. Clergyman and labourer alike could attend a game and share a word about the results after Sunday service. An issue of social morality, however, remained. Providence and judgement in a spiritual sense may have faded, but the catastrophe was now seen as an opportunity to heal century-old religious-ethnic hatred.

The hope that the victims of Ibrox Stadium's Stairway 13 would be memorialized in an end to the sectarianism was not to be. In the stands and on the streets the invective and violence appeared to continue unabated. In 2005 the problem was still such that the public broadcaster the British Broadcasting Corporation (BBC), televised an exposé on the subject (Robinson, 2005). As late as 2011, the Scottish Parliament felt it necessary to implement the *Offensive Behaviour at Football and Threatening Communications (Scotland) Act 2012*, which criminalized some spectator conduct, such a sectarian chants or songs, common at Old Firm matches. Given this history, officials worried that when Rangers and Celtic played at Ibrox, 2 January 1996 – the 25th anniversary of the tragedy on Stairway 13 – a minute's silence honouring the victims would be marred by rival fans. Their fears proved unwarranted as, to the relief of all, the propriety of the ritual was preserved. Concerns were renewed for the 30th anniversary in 2001. Rangers did not play that day. Instead it was when the memorial to those killed at Ibrox would be unveiled. As it turned out, fans form both sides laid flowers, scarves and team jerseys at the fence near where the tragedy had occurred (Harrington, 2001). Such, it would seem, was the power of commemoration.

Conclusion

The experience of death and grief has the capacity to unite, but also to divide, especially in a time of fluid social and cultural forms. Both are evident in the place and priorities of Glasgow's clergy in the mourning process that followed the disasters of 1902 and 1971. At the turn of the twentieth century professional football occupied an ambiguous social space. It was extremely popular among working class men and boys, but it also operated outside of the respectable ideals of amateurism and propriety. In convening a public meeting to comfort and assist the bereaved, civic leaders tacitly indicated an acceptance of football as a legitimate part of popular culture. A significant number of ministers did not agree. For them the problem with football was one of social and moral proportion. Fans' obsession with the game was a threat to proper attention to spiritual things. That so many spectators had packed into Ibrox that the stands gave way seemed a timely warning about the dangers which football posed to the health and soul. In 1971 the legitimacy of professional football was no longer disputed. Instead, religious leaders sought to use the common experience of grief to heal the ethnic-religious hatred and violence that coalesced around the Rangers–Celtic rivalry. The effort was embodied in public acts of mourning when rivals joined together to honour the dead. In time, however, the hostility resumed save for moments of commemoration on anniversaries of the tragedy, when all came together in respect for the dead. The rituals of public mourning had the capacity to unite, but football and ethnic and religious identities continued to divide.

Note

1 For further discussion of the manifestations of mourning within sporting contexts see Brennan (2008).

References

Bradley, J. M. (2004). Celtic Football Club and the Irish in Scotland. In J. M. Bradley (ed.), *Celtic Minded, Essays on Religion, Politics, Society, Identity ... and Football* (pp. 19–83). Argyll, Scotland: Argyll Publishing.

Brennan, M. (2008). *Mourning and Disaster: Finding meaning in the mourning for Hillsborough and Diana.* Newcastle upon Tyne, Cambridge Scholars Press.

Brown, C. (2009). *The Death of Christian Britain: Understanding Secularisation, 1800–1902* (second edn). New York: Routledge.

Chadwick, O. (1975). *Secularization of the European Mind in the Nineteenth Century. The Gifford Lectures in the University of Edinburgh for 1973–4.* Cambridge: University of Cambridge Press.

Clark, G. (2007). *A Farewell to Alms: A Brief Economic History of the World.* Princeton and Oxford: Princeton University Press.

Coffey, W. (1988). *God's Conman: The Life and Work of the Reverend James Currie.* Moffat, Scotland: Lochar Publishing.

Currie, R., Gilbert, A. and Horsley, L. (1977). *Churches and Churchgoers: Patterns of church growth in the British Isles since 1700.* Oxford: Clarendon Press.

Daily Record. (2001). Fans Deliver Tribute to Ibrox Victims.

Durkheim, E. (1915). *The Elementary Forms of the Religious Life*. Swain, J. W. trans. London: Allen and Unwin Limited.

Erdozain, D. (2010). *The Problem of Pleasure* (Vol. 22). Woodbridge, Suffolk: Boydell Press.

Giulianotti, R. and Gerrard, M. (2001). Cruel Britannia? Glasgow Rangers and 'Hot' Football Rivalries. In G. Armstrong (ed.), *Fear and Loathing in World Football* (pp. 23–42). Oxford, New York: Berg.

Glasgow Herald. (1883). The Clyde Disaster. 5 July, p. 7.

Glasgow Herald. (1884). Letter to the Editor. 4 November, p. 4.

Glasgow Herald. (1898). Fatal Fire in Renfield Street. 10 January, p. 9.

Glasgow Herald (1902a). Public Meeting in Glasgow. 12 April, p. 10.

Glasgow Herald. (1902b). 12 April, p. 1.

Glasgow Herald. (1902c). References to the Disaster – The Established Synod. 8 April.

Glasgow Herald. (1971a). Rangers Players at Disaster Funerals. 7 January, p. 10.

Glasgow Herald. (1971b). Poignant moments at memorial service, date, p. 18.

Glasgow Herald. (1971c). Players and Fans Attend Requiem Mass. 6 January, p. 1.

Glasgow Herald. (1971d). Disaster Fund Reaches £150,000. 7 January, p. 5.

Glasgow Herald. (1971e). 1000 mourn Markinch boys who died in Ibrox disaster. 8 January, p. 20.

Glasgow Herald. (1971f), Pool-Winning Priest's £25,000 to Ibrox Fund. 7 January, p. 10.

Gorer, G. (1965). *Death, Grief and Mourning in Contemporary Britain*. London: The Cresset Press.

Gray, A. (1971). Let There Be No Wasted Sorrow Arthur Gray Sends an Open Letter to Rangers F.C. (February), 13.

Hargreaves, J. (1986). *Sport, Power and Culture: A social and historical analysis of popular sports in Britain*. Cambridge: Polity.

Harrington, A. (2001). Thousands Join in Silent Homage. Fans and Former Players Share Memories of the Day that Disaster Struck on Stairway 13, *Herald Scotland*. 3 January, p. 1.

Harvie, C. (1994). Sport and the Scottish State. In G. Jarvie (ed.), *Scottish Sport in the Making of the Nation. Ninet-minute Patriots?* (pp. 43–57). Leicester: Leicester University Press.

Hay, J. R. (1982). Soccer and Social Control in Scotland, 1873–1978. In M. M. R. Cashman (ed.), *Money, Morality and the Media* (pp. 223–243). New South Wales, Australia: University of New South Wales Press.

Holt, R. (1989). *Sport and the British: A Modern History*. Oxford: Oxford University Press.

Lupson, P. (2006). *Thank God for Football*. London: Azure (SPCK).

McLeod, H. (1974). *Class and Religion in the Late Victorian City*. Hamden, CT: Archon.

McLeod, H. (2013). Sport and Religion in England. In N. J. Watson and A. Parker (ed.), *Sports and Christianity: Historical and Contemporary Perspectives* (pp. 112–130). New York, London: Routledge.

McPhail, J. (1971). 'The Old Firm Match that Didn't Matter', *Celtic View*. 7 January, p. 1.

Morley, J. (1971). *Death, Heaven and the Victorians*, Pittsburgh, PA: University of Pittsburg Press.

Murray, B. (1984). Opportunity Lost after Ibrox Disaster, *Glasgow Herald*. 25 October, p. 11.

Murray, B. (2004). *The Old Firm: Sectarianism, Sport, and Society in Scotland*. Edinburgh: John Donald Publishers.

Parker, A. and Weir., J. S. (2012). Sport, Spirituality and Protestantism: A Historical Overview. *Theology, 115*(4), 253–265.

Ralston, G. (2001). Fans from Both Sides Wept for the Dead; Old Firm rivals United in Grief for the 66 Who Lost Their Lives on Stairway 13, *Scottish Daily Record*. 1 January, p. 1.

Rangers Football Club. (2010). The Ibrox Disaster: Stairway 13. Retrieved 2 February 2010.

Robinson, M. (2005). *Scotland's Secret Shame*. London: BBC.

Shiels, R. (1998). The Fatalities at the Ibrox Disaster of 1902. *Sports Historian*, 18 (November), p. 148.

Smith, P. (1902). Pastor's Address. 'Now Men See Not the Bright Light Which is in the Clouds – Job 37:21'. *Tidings. Cambridge Street United Presbyterian Church, 149* (April), pp. 1–5.

Telegraph. (2001). Thousands Pay Tribute to Victims of Ibrox Disaster. 3 January, p. 1.

The Celtic View (1971). View Point. A Glimmer of Hope for a Better Future. 7 January, p. 1.

Walker, G. (1990). 'There's Not a Team Like the Glasgow Rangers': Football and Religious Identity in Scotland. In T. G. Walker (ed.), *Sermons and Battle Hymns: Protestant Popular Culture in Modern Scotland* (pp. 157–159). Edinburgh: Edinburgh University Press.

Walker, G. (2004). The Ibrox Stadium Disaster of 1971. *Soccer and Society*, 5 (Summer), 170–175.

Walvin, J. (1994). *A History of the People's Game: The History of Football Revisited*. Edinburgh, London: Mainstream Publishing.

Chapter 14

Sport and Christianity in American cinema

'The beloved grew fat and kicked' (Deuteronomy 32:15)

Seán Crosson

Introduction

> Lord, we know our lives are not about football, but we do thank you for allowing us to play tonight.
>
> *(Facing the Giants*, Alex Kendrick, 2006)

Christianity has been an enduring feature of films featuring sports or sporting figures since the early twentieth century, such that religious icons, references and rituals have now become naturalised as familiar and recurring presences in the cinema. Recent Christian drama films such as the American football-themed *Facing the Giants* (2006) and the surfing biopic *Soul Surfer* (2011), have employed the emotive and seductive qualities of the mainstream sports film to affirm Christian themes. They each remind us that sport is a powerful vehicle for the promotion of faith-based narratives; while offering the considerable challenges of sporting competition, the drive to success and its realisation by characters who foreground their Christian belief, may appear to provide convincing evidence to some of the importance of Christian faith.

Film, as a form that is characterised by its ability to convincingly capture aspects of the world around us, also responds to societal developments, including the manner through which sport and Christianity have interconnected historically. For administrators and promoters of particular sports, conscious that they were engaged with a cultural form viewed at times with considerable suspicion, Christianity provided an important means of legitimising sport and its importance in society, a feature reflected in particular in American films featuring sport from the early twentieth century. This process took a number of forms including the trope of the boxer-and-the-priest and the manner through which athletes themselves appeared to incorporate aspects of Christian figures. Both sport and Christianity are also central supporting elements for a core ideology in American life, the American Dream, and this is apparent in one of the most popular and recurring trajectories found within the American sports film.

Through a close reading of relevant film texts, this chapter will map the developing relationship between sport and Christianity as revealed in American cinema.

Cinema and religion

As has occurred with sport (to which we will return shortly), cinema has come to hold a crucial role in people's lives, a role that has at times been compared with religion. Indeed, Andrew Sarris (1998: 15) has described most Hollywood films by the 1930s as 'semi-religious light shows built around the rituals of family and courtship'. This focus on the ritual function of film has preoccupied one major strand of critical discourse concerning the emergence of genres in cinema with Rick Altman (1984: 9) contending that:

> By choosing the films it would patronize, the audience revealed its preferences and its beliefs, thus inducing Hollywood studios to produce films reflecting its desires. Participation in the genre film experience thus reinforces spectator expectations and desires. Far from being limited to mere entertainment, filmgoing offers a satisfaction more akin to that associated with established religion.

This view of cinema as offering an experience comparable to that provided by religion has also been expressed by screenwriter Paul Schrader (1972: 8) (screenwriter of *The Last Temptation of Christ* (1988)) who described both the cinema – particularly via what he calls a 'transcendental style' – and religion as capable of bringing 'man as close to the ineffable, invisible and unknowable as words, images, and ideas can take him'. Equally, for S. Brent Plate (2008: 2–3) in his important study of the relationship between film and religion:

> Religion and film are akin. They both function by recreating the known world and then presenting that alternative version of the world to their viewers/worshippers. Religions and films each create alternate worlds utilising the raw materials of space and time and elements, bending them in new ways and forcing them to fit particular standards and desires. Film does this through camera angles and movements, framing devices, lighting, costume, acting, editing and other aspects of production. Religions achieve this through setting apart particular objects and periods of time and deeming them 'sacred', through attention to specially charged objects (symbols), through the telling of stories (myths) and by gathering people together to focus on some particular event (ritual). The result of both religion and film is a re-created world: a world of recreation, a world of fantasy, a world of ideology,

a world we may long to live in or avoid at all costs. As an alternative world is presented at the altar and on the screen, that projected world is connected to the world of the everyday, and boundaries, to a degree, become crossable.

Partly due to the parallels Plate identifies, religion and religious figures have featured prominently throughout cinema's history, including within films featuring sport and sporting figures. Indeed, as Melanie J. Wright (2006: 2) notes in a further study of the relationship between these two major forces in modern life, despite concerns expressed by religious figures regarding the cinema particularly in the first half of the twentieth century, 'Religion has not been displaced by a new medium: it has colonised it, and has found itself challenged and altered in the course of the encounter'. Religious icons, references and rituals have become such a recurring part of popular cinema that their presence is arguably overlooked by many film-goers. This also applies to films featuring sport which regularly feature athletes seeking inspiration or support in prayers before events or through the various religious icons they wear.

Christianity and sport in American life

The prominence of Christianity, particularly in Hollywood depictions of sport (by far the most numerous and influential)[1] is not surprising given the association of Christianity with sport in American life. This relation-ship is by no means coincidental and reflects distinct aspects of the history of sport and its development in the Western world. While sport has come to occupy a place in American life – and in many other societies across the world – comparable to that taken by religion in the past (Forbes and Mahan, 2000: 163),[2] this development was by no means straightforward or uncomplicated and the rise in popularity of sport faced considerable challenges. Indeed, the codification and institutionalisation of sport, includ-ing the formalisation of rules, and the establishment of national and regional sporting associations and authorities that took place in the nine-teenth century, was part of an attempt to control and ameliorate concerns and suspicions regarding sporting activities themselves. Sport was viewed with considerable suspicion in this period and well into the twentieth century, particularly among the establishment of Europe and the United States who often regarded it as a valueless distraction associated with a range of vices including drinking, gambling and violence and 'at worst a manifestation of cultural decline and barbarism' (Gruneau, 1993: 86). However, sport would nonetheless become increasingly important for this same establishment, its cultivation and continuity. The development of modernity and capitalism, and the attendant problems they gave rise to, including the fragmentation and attenuation of traditional communities and beliefs, contributed to a reevaluation of sport and the role that it might play in society. In this context, issues of personal and social advancement became increasingly important and sport was deemed to have an important role to play in their development. Sport's role in these respects has been traced through the influence of British public schools and imperialism, and French romanticism in the nineteenth century (Holt, 1990: 74–85).

However, in order to 'cleanse' sport of its decadent associations, Christianity was employed as a crucial legitimiser of its importance. This development is most evident in the nineteenth century in the 'muscular Christianity' tradition that emerged in the public schools of Victorian Britain and spread across the world and saw in sport a means of instilling Christian principles allied to a vigorous masculinity in young men (Watson *et al.*, 2005). The influence of these developments would eventually (following initial resistance) become evident in the United States where the growing realisation of the importance of sport, particularly in often religious-run educational institutions, was linked to fears around national weakness and a belief in the ability of sport to produce men of action (Putney, 2003; Streible, 2008). Particularly from the 1880s onwards, with the popularisation of intercollegiate competitions in boat racing and subsequently baseball, athletics and American football, sport came to play an increasingly prominent role in American society and culture. For those in positions of authority, sports became much more than diversions from study; as in the development of sport in the British public school system, they were promoted as a means of instilling discipline, proper Christian values, and imparting leadership skills and an appreciation of the value of teamwork in students while affirming the social barriers that distinguished these students from working-class men (Corn and Goldstein, 1993; Putney, 2001).

Sport and Christianity in American film

This nineteenth-century background to the emergence of sport, and the role of Christianity in legitimising and affirming its significance, is important to consider when we reflect on the depiction of sport and Christianity in film. Its relevance is evident in a series of films concerned with saving street children from a seemingly inevitable life of crime that emerged in the mid-1930s. These films owed much to the 'muscular Christianity' tradition referred to already and a relevant example is the classic gangster film *Angels with Dirty Faces* (1938) in which Father Connelly (Pat O'Brien) employs basketball to take children in his parish off the streets and help them 'straighten out', enlisting the assistance of local gangster Rocky Sullivan (James Cagney) to teach them to play 'according to the rules'. The following year, Spencer Tracy was awarded an Academy Award as Best Actor for his role as Father Flanagan in *Boys Town* (1938), a film concerning a real-life rural reform school in which boxing was employed to produce 'sturdy young bodies and stout young hearts' (Boddy, 2008: 104). In *Boys Town*, when arguments break out between boys, they are settled according to the rules of boxing; as Father Flanagan remarks, 'all fights here are according to Hoyle, and they're in the ring'. An Irish-American priest featured again in Leo McCarey's *Bells of St Mary's* (1945), where Father Charles 'Chuck' O'Malley (Bing Crosby) and Mother Superior, Mary Benedict (Ingrid Bergman) also employ boxing to cultivate discipline among the children in their care. In these films, Christianity and Christian figures play a similar role to that in the nineteenth century; they provide authority and legitimation for the increasing popularisation of sport in American life through its employment towards apparently Christian ends.

Indeed, occasionally Christian figures find words of inspiration in the Bible for their sporting actions. In *Trouble Along the Way* (1953), Father Burke (Charles Coburn), rector of small Catholic St. Anthony's college, which is in debt to the tune of over $170,000, decides the only way out of debt is to establish a successful football programme. He justifies his belief with reference to lines from the Bible (Deuteronomy 32:15): 'the beloved grew fat and kicked', and enlists former disgraced football coach 'of some of the country's leading universities' Steven Williams (John Wayne) to realise his ambition. Williams does not believe, however, that the team can be successful and illegally enlists pro-footballers. The rector is appalled when he finds out but the school is saved nonetheless when the church decides to continue funding it despite the debt.

As in many other films of the era that feature Christian figures, a heavy emphasis is apparent within *Trouble Along the Way* on Christian faith as the means to address whatever challenges are faced: As Father Burke remarks at one point (quoting Jesus (Mathew 8:26)): 'Why are ye fearful, oh ye of little faith?' Later still he reassures Williams, despite his considerable doubts concerning the feasibility of a successful football programme at St. Anthony's, 'Now, I'm sure with a little faith, all of our other difficulties will disappear'. And so, it would seem to pass, even if it is the generous intervention of the church rather than sport that ensures the college remains open.

In this emphasis, *Trouble Along the Way* may appear to depart somewhat from the more familiar trajectory of the American sport film by which sport often appears to provide utopian possibilities that can transcend the sometimes tarnished and challenging present, and past, circumstances of those who engage in sporting activities or follow those who are (Crosson, 2013: 157–171).[3] We will return to this trajectory shortly but for now I would like to consider this departure as not atypical of the time in which *Trouble Along the Way* was made and released and indeed reflecting a transitional phase in the representation of sport in American film. Furthermore, despite the corrupt actions of Williams, the football programme at St. Anthony's is not discontinued. By the film's close, while Father Burke retires, his final act is to ensure that a reformed Williams continues for at least another year as football coach – thanks to the Latin fine print on his contract.

A further film from the 1950s that also employs a Christian figure while acknowledging negative aspects to sporting life is *Angels in the Outfield* (1951), a film remade under the same title in 1994. While both films stress the importance of Christian faith, the original has as a central focus a foul-mouthed baseball coach, Guffy McGovern (Paul Douglas) who is visited by an angel – sent on behalf of archangel Gabriel – to complain of the coach's use of foul language; as the angel remarks to McGovern, 'You've been busting snoots ... polluting the air with your foul talk long enough.... Lay off swearing and fighting, and I'll win you some ball games. I might even win you a pennant'. In return for refraining from foul language and bad behaviour the angel, along with his 'boys' (angelic former players), assists the coach's team on an unlikely winning run.[4]

What we are witnessing in films such as *Trouble Along the Way* and *Angels in the Outfield* is the negotiation in film of the movement of sport to the centre of American life, a movement often assisted by the imprimatur of Christianity and Christian figures. A further example of this negotiation is evident in *The Jackie Robinson Story* (1950), featuring the legendary and ground-breaking African American baseball player himself in the lead role. Robinson, as well as being one of the greatest baseball players of his generation, was also the first African American in the modern era to play Major League baseball in the United States, successfully crossing the baseball 'colour line' when he lined out for the first time for the Brooklyn Dodgers in 1947. Robinson's decision to join the Dodgers is informed significantly by religious considerations, at least according to its representation in Alfred E. Green's 1950 film. When he asks his mother for advice, she encourages him to seek guidance from his local Minister, which Robinson duly does. For the Minister, Robinson's decision is a big thing not just for the player himself but 'for the whole coloured people', and his role as a representative of the African American community is a further prominent focus of the film. However, the role here of this religious figure in ultimately encouraging Robinson to cross the colour line assists again in the legitimation of his decision to pursue a career in sport.

A sport particularly in need of religion's imprimatur was boxing, banned in much of the United States until the early twentieth century and yet one of the most popular sports featured particularly in American cinema, with the sub-genre's roots lying in the very earliest years of film production (Streible, 2008). However, boxing in film has provided an ambiguous, yet revelatory, picture of sport in society, often focusing on the dark and corrupt aspects of this sport, but also (particularly in more recent decades) seeing in it an opportunity for those marginalised and less fortunate to realise the American Dream (Grindon, 1996). In the early to mid-twentieth century however, it was the darker aspects that were often emphasised in film, though a process is apparent whereby religion (as in the nineteenth century) assisted in its legitimisation.

Kasia Boddy has identified a recurring trope in American cinema of the 'Boxer-and-the-Priest' (Boddy, 2008: 268), which came to prominence from the 1930s onwards. Vladimir Nabokov's *Lolita* features a parodic reference, told to central protagonist Humbert by Charlotte Haze, to this trope: 'The boxer had fallen extremely low when he met the good old priest (who had been a boxer himself in his robust youth and could still slug a sinner)' (Quoted in Boddy, 2008: 268). The theme of the-boxer-and-the-priest is evident in one of the most influential American films of the 1950s, *On the Waterfront* (1954) where the local priest, Father Barry (Karl Malden), provides the moral centre and conscience for a film concerning ex-boxer Terry Malloy (Marlon Brando) who is seduced into a life of crime working for the mob on the docks. In a central sequence Malloy attempts to confess to his involvement in the death of a dockworker, which Father Barry refuses to hear in the confessional. In a direct challenge to Malloy, the world of sport and the necessity to do the right thing are contrasted as Malloy is challenged by Father Barry to identify the man responsible for the killing:

MALLOY: But, you know, if I spill, my life ain't worth a nickel.
FATHER BARRY: And how much is your soul worth if you don't?
MALLOY: They're askin' me to put the finger on my own brother. Johnny Friendly used to take me to ball games when I was a kid.
FATHER BARRY: 'Ball games'. Don't break my heart. I wouldn't care if he gave you a life pass to the Polo Grounds. So you've got a brother, eh? Let me tell you something: You've got some other brothers. And they're getting' the short end ... while your Johnny's getting mustard on his face at the Polo Grounds. Ball games! Listen. If I were you, I would walk right.... Never mind. I'm not asking you to do anything. It's your own conscience that's got to do the asking.
MALLOY: 'Conscience'. That stuff.... That stuff can drive you nuts.

Nevertheless, as in *Trouble Along the Way* it is ultimately not sport that is condemned but rather its corruption by those who won't play by the rules. While Father Barry has himself a sporting background as 'a pretty good ball player and something of an amateur boxer in his college days' (Schulberg, 1988: 43), in what has become one of the most quoted sequences in cinema history, it is the lost potential for success that sport might have offered him that is most regretted by Malloy. His boxing career ended prematurely after he was convinced by his brother Charley to take a dive for the mob:

You remember that night in the Garden, you came down to my dressin' room … and said, 'Kid, this ain't your night. We're goin' for the price on Wilson?' You remember that? … I coulda taken Wilson apart. So what happens? He gets the title shot outdoors in a ballpark … and what do I get? A one-way ticket to Palookaville. You was my brother, Charley. You shoulda looked out for me a little bit … I coulda had class. I coulda been a contender. I coulda been somebody … instead of a bum.…

A further film from the 1950s that also exhibits the boxer-and-the-priest trope is seminal director John Ford's most commercially successful film, *The Quiet Man* (1952).[5] Indeed, *The Quiet Man* actually includes two 'priests', one Protestant, one Catholic, in a work which features John Wayne in the central role of Irish-American boxer Sean Thornton who returns to Ireland in search of his ancestral home. Local Protestant Minister Reverend Playfair (Arthur Shields) had boxed in his youth, and both he and the Parish Priest, Father Lonergan (Ward Bond), play crucial roles in facilitating the recovery (and eventual integration into a new community) of the traumatised Thornton after his accidental killing of an opponent in the ring in the United States.

Significantly, fighting has a crucial role to play in this process. A core theme of *The Quiet Man* is the rehabilitation of the boxer, and arguably boxing itself, facilitated by the religious figures in this community. Thornton is reluctant to fight again after his final traumatic fight in the ring, despite being provoked repeatedly by a local farmer, Squire 'Red' Will Danaher (played by former professional boxer Victor McLaglen), his wife's brother, who refuses to part with her dowry. However, with the assistance and implicit encouragement of former boxer Reverend Playfair (the only local person who is aware of Thornton's boxing past), he eventually confronts Danaher to demand the return of the dowry leading to one of the longest fight sequences in cinema. While fought over several miles of Irish countryside rather than in the ring, there are clear attempts to regulate the contest within the rules of boxing, with local bookmaker and matchmaker, Michaleen Oge Flynn (Barry Fitzgerald), declaring at one point (when others try to get involved), 'This is a private fight. The Marquis of Queensbury rules will be observed on all occasions'. By the end of the fight, Thornton gains Danaher's respect ('You know, Yank. I've taken quite a likin' to you' he remarks) and the two are pictured arm in arm on their way to Thornton's house for dinner. It would seem that the boxer and boxing, with the assistance of the local Catholic priest and Protestant Minister, have been rehabilitated.

The boxer-and-the-priest trope (if somewhat reworked as the boxing-trainer and the priest) received its most memorable recent appearance in Clint Eastwood's Oscar winning film *Million Dollar Baby* (2004). The film was, however, one of the most controversial Oscar winners of recent years. The most controversial aspect of *Million Dollar Baby* was the unsettling and highly emotionally charged final part of the film. Though initially reluctant, trainer Frankie Dunn (played by Eastwood) eventually agrees to manage female boxer, Maggie Fitzgerald (Hilary Swank), convinced in particular by the persistence and belief in her of his assistant, Eddie Scrap-Iron Dupris (Morgan Freeman), in the run-down gym he owns. Fitzgerald enjoys considerable success at first in the ring under Dunn's management and finally gets a chance to fight for the World Welterweight Championship. However in the fight itself against the reigning champion Billie 'The Blue Bear' (Lucia Rijker) she is seriously injured by an illegal blow from her opponent that leaves her with an acute spinal cord injury and little hope of full recovery. Unable to live with the severely restricted mobility she is likely to endure for the remainder of her life, Fitzgerald begs Dunn to end her life, which he eventually, if reluctantly, does.

Prior to assisting Fitzgerald to end her life, Dunn seeks advice from his local priest, Father Horvak (Brían O'Byrne), a figure with whom Dunn discusses questions of faith and seeks advice from on a number of occasions during the film. Significantly the scene concerned is shot inside Father Horvak's church, beginning with the camera tracking up the central aisle to where Dunn and Father Horvak sit, capturing the altar, crucifix, religious iconography and various religious signifiers as we approach the two already in conversation. The placing of this scene inside the church and the rendering of religious icons in this manner was a significant change from the original screenplay; in Paul Haggis' *Million Dollar Baby: Rope Burns*, this is an exterior scene which takes place on the steps of the church rather than indoors (Haggis, [n.d.]: 113). The choice of an interior location emphasises the religious context that Frankie has placed himself within in an attempt to come to terms with Fitzgerald's request to die. It is also the context he will clearly have to step outside to agree to her request. As the conversation develops between the two, it is clear in the anguished responses of Frankie that he is contemplating a step beyond his religious faith:

FATHER HORVAK: You can't do it, you know that.
FRANKIE: I do, Father. You don't know how thick she is, how hard it was to train her. Other fighters would do exactly what you say to them and she'd ask, 'why this' and 'why that' and do it her own way, anyway. How she fought for the title.... Wasn't by anything, it wasn't by listening to me. But now she wants to die and I just want to keep her with me. And I swear to God, Father, it's committing a sin by doing it. By keeping her alive, I'm killing her. Do you know what I mean? How do I get around that?
FATHER HORVAK: You don't. You step aside, Frankie. You leave it with God.

FRANKIE: She's not asking for God's help. She's asking for mine.

FATHER HORVAK: Frankie, I've seen you at mass almost every day for 23 years. The only person who comes to church that much is the kind who can't forgive himself for something. Whatever sins you're carrying, they're nothing compared to this. Forget about God or Heaven and Hell. If you do this thing, you'll be lost, somewhere so deep, you'll never find yourself again.

While Frankie's decision to assist Fitzgerald with ending her life is clearly at odds with Christian doctrine (and was the subject of considerable criticism on the film's release) (Davis, 2005), this controversial aspect of *Million Dollar Baby* is arguably counterbalanced by a Christian message at the heart of the film. Sharon Roubach has contended that while the film represents euthanasia as an act of mercy and love, it is nonetheless a work with a central Christian message based on the image of the Holy Trinity, an aspect of Catholic faith which is foregrounded within the film in an earlier discussion between Frankie and his priest:

FATHER HORVAK: What's confusing you this week?

FRANKIE: Same old one God, three gods.

FATHER HORVAK: Frankie, most people figure out in kindergarten, it's all about faith.

FRANKIE: Is it sort of like snap, crackle and pop all rolled up in one big box?

FATHER HORVAK: You're standing outside my church comparing God to Rice Crispies? The only reason you come to mass everyday is to wind me up. It's not going to happen this morning.

FRANKIE: Well, I'm confused.

FATHER HORVAK: No you're not,

FRANKIE: Yes I am.

FATHER HORVAK: Then here is your answer: there is one God. Anything else? 'Cause I'm busy.

FRANKIE: What about the Holy Ghost?

FATHER HORVAK: He's the expression of God's love.

FRANKIE: And Jesus?

FATHER HORVAK: Son of God. Don't play stupid.

FRANKIE: What is he then; does that make him a demi-God?

FATHER HORVAK: There are no demi-gods, you fucking pagan.

This unusual, and in its closing somewhat irreverent consideration of a central article of faith within Christianity, may point to a larger message within the film as a whole in which the three main characters themselves personify aspects of the Holy Trinity. For Roubach (2007):

Million Dollar Baby is a boxing movie that uses imagery associated with the Holy Trinity – personified by the film's three protagonists [Frank Dunn (Clint Eastwood) as God the Father; Maggie Fitzgerald (Hilary Swank) as 'Like Jesus', and Eddie Scrap-Iron Dupris (Morgan Freeman) as 'the Holy Ghost'] – to put forth a view that the essence of Christianity relates to belief and love. The Trinity also lends itself as a medium for Eastwood's reflections of notions of home and family, through a comparison between biological dysfunctional families and human bonds based on love and compassion.

Roubach's reading of *Million Dollar Baby* identifies a further recurring aspect of the relationship between sport and Christianity as depicted in American film. The extent to which sporting figures may themselves personify or are paralleled with Christian figures. Indeed, occasionally Christian figures have 'crossed the ropes' to participate in sporting events themselves. John Derek played Episcopalian Minister Gil Allen in *The Leather Saint* (1956) who fights professionally (unknown to his superiors), under the fight name 'Kid Sunday', to earn money to buy rehabilitation equipment for a children's hospital in his parish. *The Leather Saint* anticipated in some respects the more recent film, *Nacho Libre* (2006), a work based on the true story of a Mexican priest, Rev. Sergio Gutiérrez Benítez or Fray Tormenta ('Friar Storm'), who competed as a masked luchador, or Lucha libre (free wrestling) wrestler for 23 years in order to raise money for the orphanage he directed. Rev. Sergio Gutiérrez Benítez is transformed into a friar-cook at a Mexican orphanage, Ignacio 'Nacho Libre' (Jack Black). The Hollywood requirement to have a romantic interest attached leads to the rather unconvincing suggestion of a possible romance between Nacho and the strikingly beautiful Sister Encarnación (Ana de la Reguera). In line with many other films within the sports film genre, Nacho unsurprisingly wins the climatic bout that provides the film's climax thereby earning the money necessary to buy a bus and improve the facilities for the orphans.

 With the exception of films such as *The Leather Saint* and *Nacho Libre*, it is rare that we find such Christian figures in sporting roles in film. Indeed, the choice of director Jared Hess to take a comedic approach to such a possibility in *Nacho Libre* reflects the presumed absurdity of such an occurrence (certainly from the perspective of expected audiences), and this absurdity is emphasised within the film itself. More typical is the incorporation of religious tropes into athletes or the creation of parallels between the lives of athletes and those of figures associated with Christianity. A relevant early example is *The Babe Ruth Story* (1948), a biopic of the legendary baseball player.

 As several commentators have noted, the depiction of Babe Ruth in this much criticised film owes much to Christian exemplars. For Gerald Mote (quoted in Ardolino, 2003: 112), 'the movie is played as though ... Babe Ruth were Moses ... as gospel'. For Frank Ardolino (2003: 116), the film presents Ruth as 'the sacred bambino, born to save baseball and to heal children with the miraculous power of his home run', while Deborah Tudor (1997: 56) contends that the film 'creates a legendary hero akin to Christ in the sense that Ruth becomes a sacrificed (sports) god, whose exploits brought only good to the world'. Indeed, a Christian figure – Brother Matthias (Charles Bickford) at St. Mary's Industrial School for Boys – introduces baseball to Ruth and encourages his developing talent, and baseball is itself associated with religion within the film. When a younger player encourages Babe to sue baseball after he is fired (unfairly the film suggests) by the Boston Braves, Babe responds 'sue baseball? That would be like suing the church'.

Ruth, as depicted in *The Babe Ruth Story*, is transformed into an almost Christ-like figure, surrounding himself with children and capable, it would appear, of inspiring those children when necessary to recover from paralysis or life-threatening illnesses. In one incident while visiting Chicago for a World Series game between the Chicago Cubs and Ruth's New York Yankees, he visits a dying boy named Johnny (Gregory Marshall) and promises to hit him a home run. As we watch Johnny listening to the game over the radio, Babe calls his shot, hits the home run, and the boy would appear to recover from his illness.

Babe eventually succumbs to a serious unnamed illness himself, but even here while dying in a hospital bed the film suggests he was willing to risk his own life – in a further Christ-like gesture – to save others by testing an experimental serum for his illness. In these later scenes, Babe also receives a Miraculous Medal from a young boy concerned about his illness and he proceeds to pin the medal to his shirt; we are then given a close up shot of the medal to affirm again Babe's saintliness. If we were still in any doubt, the narrator reminds us over the final moments of the film, that to all the many fans who followed Babe during his life, Babe ended up 'offering his life to help them and theirs'.

The Babe Ruth Story is not unique in its approach to its subject as sport films have often provided mythologised depictions of the athletes represented, frequently drawing on Christian exemplars to do so. One of the most successful sport film franchises, *Rocky*, is a significant example in this respect. Indeed, the first Oscar winning film of the series, *Rocky* (1976) opens (after the screen filling letters of Rocky) not with a shot of the fighter but of Jesus Christ, holding the Eucharist. The camera eventually zooms out from a shot of Christ's face to reveal it as part of a mural on the wall of a gym – appropriately called the 'Resurrection AC' – where Rocky is fighting. The tilting of the camera down from Jesus to Rocky makes a clear, and perhaps overly obvious, connection between the two figures. *Rocky*'s director John G. Avildsen (2005) has acknowledged that he wanted to make this connection noting that 'I'll go from him to Rocky and I've already got a lot of the people on my side'. In this admission, Avildsen not only reveals his motivation but also his expectation of audience recognition and sympathy with the image of Jesus Christ, affirming the dominant Christian values of the film as a whole as well as the audience he was hoping to attract to watch it. The Christianity of *Rocky*'s eponymous central protagonist, Rocky Balboa (played by the film's writer Sylvester Stallone), is also affirmed at several points in the film, particularly in moments in which we see him praying before big fights. As with *The Babe Ruth Story*, Rocky too is depicted as a saviour and as the film progresses and his identity is revealed, it becomes apparent that what he is redeeming is marginalised and underprivileged White working-class masculinity (Crosson, 2013).

It is clear from the opening of the film, including through the depiction of his apartment and the area in which he lives, that Rocky comes from an underprivileged working-class Italian-American background and the challenging circumstances he faces economically as well as physically are apparent. Despite his humble beginnings, and limited boxing ability, Rocky nonetheless succeeds in getting a fight with the African American world heavyweight champion, Apollo Creed (Carl Weathers). Even though he is written off in advance as having no chance, Rocky succeeds in taking the champion to 15 rounds in a closely fought contest. In the film's emotionally charged and uplifting ending, we witness a battered but still standing Rocky call for his partner Adrian (Talia Shire) while the crowd chant his name; he has had his opportunity, gone the distance and in the process redeemed White working-class masculinity.

What *Rocky* successfully charts – and arguably is the most influential example of – is what I have called the 'American Dream trajectory' (Crosson, 2013). A crucial role of sport (and the sports film) has been its engagement with, and often affirmation of, this central ideology in American life, the American Dream of opportunity, upward social mobility and material success so central to that society. This ideology continues to be a powerful force, an ideology repeatedly affirmed by leading figures in American society, including in two major addresses in 2011, by President Barack Obama.[6] The persistence of this 'meritocracy myth' (McNamee and Miller, 2009), in the face of all the evidence that points to its fallacy, owes much to two of the most influential cultural forces in American life, sport and film. Individually, both have contributed greatly to the affirmation of this ideology, a fact underscored when we encounter them together within film.

Sport provides one of the most popular and influential cultural practices for the affirmation and potential achievement of the American Dream. As noted by Howard Nixon (1984: 25), 'Sport is an appropriate vehicle for testing the ideology of the American Dream because the legitimizing beliefs of the sports institution mirror basic tenets of the American Dream'. These beliefs were summarised by Harry Edwards in his influential study *The Sociology of Sport* (1973). Though first published in 1973, the study still remains relevant to the depiction of sport – and religion – within the American sports film. Through a survey of references to sport in American magazines, newspapers and a major athletic journal, Edwards identified a 'dominant American Sports creed'. Similar to those beliefs that underscore the American Dream, Edwards saw this creed as encompassing a series of beliefs concerned with affirming the advantages and benefits of participating in organised sports. Edwards summarised this creed under seven headings, incorporating 12 principal statements, which reflected the ideological goals of sport, including centrally 'Religiosity' and 'expressions relating sports achievement to traditional American Christianity' (1973: 69). As we have already considered, this concern has been a recurring feature of the sports film from its emergence in the United States in the early twentieth century (Crosson, 2013).

Much as with sport in the earlier part of the twentieth century, the American Dream trajectory has equally benefited from the imprimatur of religious association. This trajectory has been one of the most popular and commercially successful of the past 40 years and is a recurring feature of the American sports film genre, often allied with and supported by references to Christianity. A relevant recent example from the early twenty-first century is the Walt Disney Pictures baseball themed production *The Rookie* (2002). *The Rookie* makes explicit a feature evident across baseball themed films as a whole (including such seminal films as *The Natural* (1984) and *Field of Dreams* (1989)): the indebtedness to Christianity for the authority of baseball in American life.[7] *The Rookie* begins with a narrator describing the origins of the town of Big Lake, Texas, connecting this origin myth of a man who believed oil existed in the barren location of the town, with religion (through the two nuns that supported him financially and the priest whose advice also appears to have helped him realise his dream), the playing of baseball, and legendary figures in the game:

> when the nuns told their parish priest about the man's dream and their investment in it, now, he counseled them to try and get their money back. Sheepishly, they admitted that it was too late, that the money was already spent. Well, the priest, he sighed, shook his head, and offered just one small bit of advice – bless the site with rose petals, and invoke the help of Saint Rita, patron saint of impossible dreams. And while the workers waited for the oil that would eventually come, they played baseball. Played baseball so well that some were able to give up the dirt and the despair and went on to play major-league ball in the glory days of Ruth and Gehrig.

This sequence also begins suggestively with a crane shot that provides a God-like and mythologising perspective on the man stamping the ground beneath his feet in a barren and windswept landscape. With the discovery of oil, following the blessing with rose petals and the apparent intercession of Saint Rita, oil workers arrive to the area that would become Big Lake, and baseball (which we witness workers play) provides, the narrator tells us, a further avenue for success for townspeople. As a worker strikes the ball into the air, the narrator continues that Saint Rita 'decided to bless our little town just one more time', and the ball appears to land in the near-present, caught by a young boy (who is revealed to be the film's main protagonist, baseball player Jimmy Morris) in Groton, Connecticut.

The repeated reference to Saint Rita (evident later in Morris' good luck charm, a St. Rita prayer medal) reflects the recurring presence of religion in the film, also apparent in the moments of prayer of the high school baseball team (which Morris coaches) before each game. Furthermore, the opening crane shot is repeated towards the end of the film, when Morris (Dennis Quaid) enters a Major League baseball stadium for the first time as a player, despite been 35 years old. On entering the gates of Rangers Ballpark in Arlington, Texas, a similar crane shot accentuates the stadium's size and impressiveness, looking down on Morris again (as with Big Lake's founder in the opening shot of the film) from a God-like perspective and emphasising the church like architecture of the stadium. In each of these moments, baseball and the dreams associated with it are given the significant imprimatur of religious association, a central tenet of the both the dominant American sports creed and the mainstream sports film (Crosson, 2013).[8]

Conclusion

Much as it has done in American society as a whole, Christianity and Christian figures have provided an important imprimatur for the depiction of sport in American film. While mainstream films may acknowledge the more decadent aspects of sport, Christianity is frequently employed to counterbalance such elements and ultimately suggest the importance of sport in American life. The recurring presence of Christian figures, particularly priests, in the American sport film has facilitated the acceptance and popularisation of sport – including formerly banned sports such as boxing – via its depiction in film. Filmmakers have also looked for inspiration to Christian figures and motifs in their sympathetic rendering of athletes. A fundamental and recurring concern in many of these depictions is the affirmation of a central ideology in American life, the American Dream. Sport, with the support and imprimatur of Christianity, has functioned throughout the twentieth century as one of the most popular cultural vehicles for the apparent affirmation of the American Dream trajectory, a trajectory repeatedly employed within Hollywood cinema.

Notes

1 As noted by Scott Robert Olson, 'Worldwide, audiences are 100 times more likely to see a Hollywood film than see a European film ... Hollywood satisfies 70% of international demand for television narrative and 80% of demand for feature films' (1999: 23).
2 For Ellis Cashmore, sport, in a manner comparable to religion historically, has become 'loaded with symbolism, imagery, myths, rituals; in short, the meaning-making apparatus that we associate with any other area of cultural life' (Cashmore, 2000: ix).
3 As David Rowe has summarised (1998: 355), in Hollywood sports films customarily 'all manner of social, structural, and cultural conflicts and divisions are resolved through the fantastic agency of sports'.
4 Significantly, bad language is less a focus of the 1994 remake; here angels respond to a young boy's prayers and Christian faith is foregrounded centrally. As the foster-mother of the home in which the young boy lives remarks at one point in the film, 'you've got to have faith, you've got to believe, you've got to look inside yourself – the footprints of an angel are love, and where there is love, miraculous things can happen. I've seen it'.
5 Indeed, the popularity of *The Quiet Man* is evident in the trailer of *Trouble Along the Way*, which describes Wayne as 'The Quiet Man in love with trouble'. Trailer available on YouTube at www.youtube.com/watch?v=moExVXryj0A (accessed 10 September 2014)
6 The first speech, 'The Country We Believe In' was delivered on 13 April 2011 to The George Washington University, Washington, DC while the second was given in an address in Dublin during an official visit to Ireland on 23 May 2011.
7 For further on this see Erickson (2001: 40–58).
8 For a discussion of a further relevant film – *The Blind Side* (2009) – with respect to sport, Christianity and the American Dream, see Crosson (2013: 78–85).

References

Altman, R. (1984), 'A Semantic/Syntactic Approach to Film Genre', *Cinema Journal*, 23 (3): 6–18

Ardolino, F. (2003), 'From Christ-like Folk Hero to Bumbling Bacchus: Filmic Images of Babe Ruth, 1920–1992', in S. C. Wood and J. D. Pincus (eds) *Reel Baseball: Essays and Interviews on the National Pastime, Hollywood and American Culture*. Jefferson, NC: McFarland, pp. 107–119.

Avildsen, J. G. (2005), 'DVD Commentary', *Rocky* (1976), *Sylvester Stallone Rocky Anthology (Ultimate Edition 6 Disc Box Set)*, Sony Pictures Home Entertainment.

Boddy, K. (2008), *Boxing: A Cultural History*. London: Reaktion Books, 2008.

Cashmore, E. (2000), *Sports Culture: An A–Z Guide*. London; New York: Routledge.

Corn, E. J. and W. Goldstein (1993), *A Brief History of American Sports*. New York: Hill and Wang.

Crosson, S. (2013) *Sport and Film*. London; New York: Routledge.

Davis, L. J. (2005), 'Why "Million Dollar Baby" Infuriates the Disabled', *Chicago Tribune*, 2 February, available at: http://articles.chicagotribune.com/2005-02-02/features/0502020017_1_mission-ranch-inn-disability-film, accessed 15 June 2016.

Edwards, H. (1973), *The Sociology of Sport*. Homewood, IL: The Dorsey Press.

Erickson, G. (2001), ' "Jesus Is Standing at the Home Plate": Baseball and American Christianity', in W. M. Simons (ed.) *The Cooperstown Symposium on Baseball and American Culture, 2000*. Jefferson, NC: McFarland, pp. 40–58.

Forbes, B. D. and J .H. Mahan (eds) (2000), *Religion and Popular Culture in America*. Berkeley, CA: University of California Press.

Grindon, L. (Summer 1996), 'Body and Soul: The Structure of Meaning in the Boxing Film Genre', *Cinema Journal*, 35 (4): 54–69.

Gruneau, R. S. (1993), 'The Critique of Sport in Modernity: Theorizing Power, Culture, and the Politics of the Body', in E. Dunning and J. A. Maguire (eds) *The Sports Process: A Comparative and Developmental Approach*. Champaign, IL: Human Kinetics Publishers, pp. 85–109.

Haggis, P. [n.d.] *Million Dollar Baby: Rope Burns*. p. 113. Available at www. ateliers-scenario.com/_media/million-dollar-baby.pdf, accessed 10 May 2016.

Holt, R. (1990), *Sport and the British: A Modern History*. London: Oxford University Press.

Kleinhans, C. (1985), 'Working Class Film Heroes: Junior Johnson, Evel Knievel and the Film Audience', in P. Steven (ed.) *Jump Cut: Hollywood, Politics and Counter Cinema*. New York: Praeger Publishers, pp. 64–82.

McNamee, S. J. and R. K. Miller, Jr. (2009), *The Meritocracy Myth*. Lanham, MD: Rowman & Littlefield.

Nixon II, H. L. (1984), *Sport and the American Dream*. Champaign, IL: Leisure Press/Human Kinetics.

Olson, S. R. (1999), *Hollywood Planet: Global Media and the Competitive Advantage of Narrative Transparency*. London: Routledge.

Plate, S. B. (2008), *Religion and Film: Cinema and the Re-creation of the World*. London: Wallflower.

Putney, C. (2001), *Muscular Christianity: Manhood and Sports in Protestant America, 1880–1920*. Cambridge, MA: Harvard University Press.

Putney, C. (2003), 'Muscular Christianity', *The Encyclopedia of Informal Education*, available at: www.infed.org/christianeducation/muscular_christianity.htm, accessed 15 April 2016.

Robson, T. (2010), 'Field of American Dreams: Individualist Ideology in the U.S. Baseball Movie', *Jump Cut: A Review of Contemporary Media* 52, available at: www.ejumpcut.org/currentissue/RobsonBaseball/text.html, accessed 27 March 2016.

Roubach, S. (2007), 'In the Name of the Father, the Daughter and Eddie Scrap: Trinitarian Theology in *Million Dollar Baby*', *Journal of Religion and Film*, 11 (1). Available at: www.unomaha.edu/jrf/vol.11no1/RoubachMillionBaby.htm, accessed 10 February 2016.

Rowe, D. (1998), 'If You Film It, Will They Come? Sports on Film', *Journal of Sport & Social Issues*, 22 (4): 350–359.

Sarris, A. (1998), *'You Ain't Heard Nothin' Yet': The American Talking Film – History and Memory, 1927–1949*. New York: Oxford University Press.

Schrader, P. (1972), *Transcendental Style in Film: Ozu, Bresson, Dreyer*. New York: Da Capo.

Schulberg, B. (1988), *On the Waterfront: The Final Shooting Script* [l955], Hollywood: Samuel French Trade.

Streible, D. (2008), *Fight Pictures: A History of Boxing and Early Cinema*, Berkeley, CA: University of California Press.

Tudor, D. V. (1997) *Hollywood's Vision of Team Sports: Heroes, Race, and Gender*. New York and London: Garland Publishing.

Umphlett, W. L. (1984), *The Movies Go to College: Hollywood and the World of the College-life Film*. Rutherford, NJ: Fairleigh Dickinson University Press.

Watson, N. J., S. Weir, and S. Friend (2005), 'The Development of Muscular Christianity in Victorian Britain and Beyond', *Journal of Religion and Society*, 7. Available at: www.veritesport.org/downloads/The_Development_of_Muscular_Christianity_in_Victorian_Britain_and_Beyond.pdf, accessed 14 May 2016.

Wright, M. J. (2006), *Religion and Film: An Introduction*. London and New York: I. B. Tauris.

Filmography

Angels in the Outfield (1951), Clarence Brown. Beverly Hills, California: Metro-Goldwyn-Mayer.

Angels in the Outfield (1994), William Dear. Walt Disney Studios, Burbank, California, US: Buena Vista Pictures.

Angels with Dirty Faces (1938), Michael Curtiz. Burbank, California: Warner Bros.

Babe Ruth Story, The (1948), Roy Del Ruth. Los Angeles, California and New York City, New York: Allied Artists.

Bells of St Mary's, The (1945), Leo McCarey. Los Angeles, California: RKO Pictures.

Boys Town (1938), Norman Taurog. Beverly Hills, California: Metro-Goldwyn-Mayer.

Blind Side, The, (2009), John Lee Hancock. Burbank, California: Warner Bros.

Facing the Giants (2006), Alex Kendrick. New York,: Samuel Goldwyn Films.

Field of Dreams (1989), Phil Alden Robinson. Los Angeles, California: Universal Pictures.

Jackie Robinson Story, The (1950), Alfred E. Green. Santa Monica Blvd, Los Angeles, California: Eagle-Lion Films.

Last Temptation of Christ, The (1988), Martin Scorsese. Universal City, California: Universal Studios.

Leather Saint, The (1956), Alvin Ganzer. Hollywood, California: Paramount Pictures.

Million Dollar Baby (2004), Clint Eastwood. Burbank, California: Warner Bros.

Nacho Libre (2006), Jared Hess. Hollywood, California: Paramount Pictures.

Natural, The (1984), Barry Levinson. Culver City, California: TriStar Pictures.

On the Waterfront (1954), Elia Kazan. Culver City, California: Columbia Pictures.

Quiet Man, The (1952), John Ford. Los Angeles: Republic Pictures.

Rocky (1976), John G. Avildsen. MGM Tower, Century City, Los Angeles: United Artists.

Rookie, The (2002), John Lee Hancock. Burbank, California: Walt Disney Pictures.

Soul Surfer (2011), Sean McNamara. Culver City, California: TriStar Pictures.

Trouble Along the Way (1953), Michael Curtiz. Burbank, California: Warner Bros.

Chapter 15

Christianity, boxing and Mixed Martial Arts

Reflections on morality, vocation and well-being

Nick J. Watson and Brian Brock

Introduction[1]

> The boxer's job is to injure, maim, and render his opponent uncon-
> scious. Indeed, if the opponent dies from his injuries, it simply means
> that the fighter who hit him was very good at landing punches where
> they most likely to do the most damage.
>
> (Patmore, 1979, cited in Kerr, 2005: 42)

> I pray for my opponents before fights ... God gives us talents and I'm
> using mine to the best of my ability.... It gives me strength to know
> that God is in my corner then no one can beat me ... I use religion as a
> strength not a weakness, and it helps me. I do my training and then he
> does his bit ... I've a wife and two kids to provide for and if that
> means killing you in the ring, that's what I will have to do.
>
> (Heavyweight boxer, Tyson Fury, cited in Gore, 2011: 7)

The provocative titles of the biographies of a number of well-known
professional Christian boxers, such as *God in My Corner* (Foreman, 2007),
Knocking out the Devil (Svab, 2011), and *Holyfield the Humble Warrior*
(Holyfield, 1996), raise a host of ethical quandaries and for the social scientist and theologian. However, a recent review of literature on sports and
Christianity (Watson and Parker, 2014) found that aside from Phil
Shirley's insightful popular book, *The Soul of Boxing* (1999), that is based
on fascinating interview data with some of the world's most well-known
boxers who hold religious beliefs (e.g. Tyson, Holyfield, Watson), academic literature on this topic is sparse.

Hillman's (1951) essay on the morality of boxing published in the
journal *Theological Studies* and a short chapter on the pastoral dilemmas
of the sport (Leone and Leone, 1992) appear to be the only academic offerings to date. That said, an essay by the distinguished Catholic moral theologian, Richard McCormick (1962) in the periodical *Sports Illustrated*,
and more recent reflections by Gordon Marino (e.g. 2003, 2010a, 2010b,

2014), a professional boxing trainer and professor of philosophy, are essential reading. These writings are complemented by a range of brief yet thoughtful examinations of theological issues in boxing (e.g. Galli, 2005; Gore, 2011; Watson and Brock, 2014), and more recently, Mixed Martial Arts (MMA) (e.g. Blakely, 2014; Carter, Kluck and Morin, 2012; Schneirderman, 2010; Waller, 2017; Watson and Bolt, 2015), published in periodicals, news media and blogs. In sum, theological ethicists have yet to seriously address the apparent oxymoron of the 'Christian boxer/Mixed Martial Artist'.

Accordingly, Schwarze (2010: 1) recently noted that he had been unable to 'track down a good essay presenting a Christian case against MMA ... but it may be worth spending some time to work through this issue properly'. Considering that approximately 700 churches in America have begun to integrate MMA into their ministry-streams (Blakely, 2014), our intention here is to begin to address Schwarze's proposal.

While acknowledging that there are a number of significant differences in the historical development, governance and physical and structural characteristics of boxing and MMA, given this is an 'exploratory' analysis, they will be examined together. This examination is based on the premise that both sports can be differentiated from other violent/dangerous sports (e.g. ice hockey, rugby, horse racing, snow sports, sky-diving, etc.) by the fact that within their rules, inflicting physical violence upon one's opponent is the primary (but not exclusive)[2] *goal* rather than the *means* by which another end is reached – winning the game. For example, while a rugby player may be seriously injured while being tackled by (or when tackling) an opponent, within the rules of play the task is to stop the opponent advancing into the territory of one's own team. This is the reason why the notion of 'foul play' exists in relation to acts which display intent to injure beyond what would be deemed necessary in terms of the normal levels of physical contact involved in game play. Though such penalties are evident in both boxing and MMA (outlawing biting, for instance), they seem to exist more to protect the reputation of the sport than the health of the athletes concerned.

The 'instrumental' nature of violence in boxing and MMA compared to sports such as rugby, and the well-documented risks of traumatic brain injury, concussion, irreversible neurologic dysfunction, eye injuries, psychiatric conditions and death, has led to the British Medical Association (and other medical bodies) repeatedly calling for a ban on these activities (BMA, 2008; McCrory, 2007; White, 2007). Reflecting on the mounting evidence of National Football League (NFL) players who have suffered brain damage as a result of their sporting careers, social commentator Krattenmaker (2013) suggests that this area is a clear 'moral thorn' for Christians. Our task then is to wrestle with this, and related ethical questions, in three themed sections: (i) boxing: a brief history, (ii) MMA: a brief history, and

(iii) a theological ethical critique and assessment. The first two sections provide a historical, social and theoretical framework and context via which to understand the application of theological ethics to the following three theses: (a) Boxing and MMA are immoral and are thus not appropriate or helpful for humans (with Christian belief) to participate in, and/or watch; (b) Boxing and MMA are immoral and are thus not appropriate or helpful for humans (with Christian belief) to participate in, and/or watch; however, within 'God's economy'[3] these activities may engender *some* moral goods (e.g. positive character development and healthy civil engagement = social harmony etc.), (c) Boxing and MMA are valid and appropriate activities as a means of character and gender development (in the spirit of 'muscular Christianity') as well as the development of positive values and healthy civil engagement, which may lead to crime reduction and social cohesion and harmony. We also provide a relatively extensive bibliography from across the disciplines to equip scholars for further exploration of these issues. The need to provide historical, social and theoretical background information prior to our ethical analysis is clear: 'sport related violence' is described by Young (2012: 4) as 'potentially harmful acts that cannot be easily separated from the sports process and that only begin to make sense when the socially, culturally and historically embedded character of sport is closely scrutinized'.

Boxing: a brief history

Archaeological artefacts in the form of stone representations found in the Middle East dated around the fifth century BC portray pugilist activities, that is, men in fighting with hand wrappings (Brasch, 1970). Hand-to-hand combat in the form of boxing was also a popular sport for the Ancient Greeks and Romans often being arranged around public holidays and festivals and for funeral services. In addition to Olympic boxing (688 BC–369 BC), the Ancient Olympic sport of the Pankration (trans. 'the all-power thing' or 'total force') is arguably the best-known sporting activity of the ancient world. This was an event in which participants could use a mixture of boxing and wrestling skills to 'beat one's opponent into submission or death' (Spivey, 2005: 10). Considering that virtually any form of violence was permitted in these competitive bouts, aside from biting and eye-gouging, the resemblance to modern MMA is clear and this point will be further explored in due course. Needless to say, boxing (and the Pankration) for the ancients was a brutal and savage affair with virtually no rules, regulations, weight classifications or consideration of the sacredness and dignity of the human person – the opponent and victim of physical violence.

The Ancient Olympic events of boxing and the Pankration were eventually banned due to their denigration into 'murderous gladiatorial combats'

(Brasch, 1970: 5). This decision emanated principally from the Christian Emperor, Theodosius, something that was strongly supported by early Christian and Jewish writers, including the Church fathers, Tertullian, Philo of Alexandria and Chrysostom (Poliakoff, 1987), who argued against the barbaric violence perpetrated through these so-called sports. Aside from the medieval schools of 'duelling' and 'swordsmanship' that some-times included elements of pugilistic training, boxing as a sport – and a form of public entertainment – did not again emerge until the seventeenth century in England, and was generally referred to as 'prize-fighting' (often bare-knuckle).

Most historical accounts of the birth of modern boxing identify James Figg (1684–1734) as its founder. A renowned prize-fighter, Figg also had an entrepreneurial streak in that he recognised the need for a less lethal means to settle disputes than sword and pistol and one which, at the same time, would entertain the aristocracy (Murphy and Sheard, 2008). Another boxing pioneer was Jack Broughton who in 1747 drafted the first written rules of the sport and again capitalised on the vicarious entertainment that it pro-vided for the upper classes. As Murphy and Sheard note 'by present stand-ards boxing was an extremely violent and bloody activity in this period' (p. 42). While a whole host of socio-cultural determinants impacted the development of modern boxing in the subsequent 200 years (See Boddy, 2008; Johnes and Taylor, 2011; Sugden, 1996; Sheard, 2004), it was not until 1880 that the Amateur Boxing Association (ABA) was formed in England. The professionalisation and institutionalisation of boxing (one of the first sports to have professional athletes) was then cemented by the administration of the Queensbury Rules in 1865. Essentially, these regula-tions paved the way for boxing as we know it both in the UK and in Europe and North America: the use of gloves and timed rounds; weight classifica-tions; a points system that included penalties for low blows, head-butting and holding; and eventually the provision of groin-protectors, gum-shields and head-guards (Murphy and Sheard, 2008). The increasing popularity of boxing in the late nineteenth century and early twentieth centuries quickly attracted the attention of religious groups, who were the first of many to forcefully appeal for the abolition of the sport.

Advances in medical knowledge during the 1920s increased the empiri-cal evidence by which the devastating effects of boxing on the human body could be demonstrated, including serious injury/disablement and death (Mainwaring and Trenerry, 2012; McCrory, 2007; Shurley and Todd, 2012). This evidence appears to have served merely to intensify the debate between lobbyists for and against the sport, not least following the death or disablement of a number of well-known professional fighters (e.g. Michael Watson, Nick Blackwell and Johnny Owen). Interestingly, many within the Catholic and Jewish faith have historically been explicitly sup-portive of boxing, primarily as a form of inculcating a series of moral values and as a mechanism for servicing elements of social control and character development (i.e. discipline, self-respect, work ethic etc.) (Berkowitz, 2011; Dee, 2012; Gems, 2004, 1993). This idea has been the focus of a range of recent studies (and political initiatives) that have explored if and how combat sports, such as boxing and MMA, are linked to criminality and anti-social and pro-social behaviour (e.g. Endersen and Olweus, 2005; Jenkins and Ellis, 2011; Rutten *et al.*, 2011; Salter and Tomsen, 2012). The most illustrative example of how Catholic and Jewish leaders championed boxing is in late nineteenth and early twentieth-century America.

At the lower end of the socio-economic spectrum a melting-pot of immigrant groups – European Jews, Italians, Irish, African-Americans and Hispanics – began to live together from the late nineteenth century onwards mainly on the eastern seaboard of the US in cities such as New York and Boston. Urban squalor, overcrowding, ethnic rivalry, labour competition and gang warfare often characterised male immigrant life, and the Catholic clergy and Jewish Rabbis actively developed boxing clubs and ran competitions to help to counter these social ills (see Gems, 2004, 1993; Koehlinger, 2012). In the twenty-first century these ideas are still deeply embedded in the boxing-religion discourse. For example, George Foreman, the former heavyweight world champion boxer, Christian Minister and founder of the George Foreman Youth Centre (2014), has argued that boxing, 'makes young people less violent' (cited in Marino, 2014: 57).

Social scientists from across the disciplines have examined many issues such as class, 'race', gender, conceptions of the heroic, embodiment and media representations within the sport of boxing,[4] much of which has its roots (to some degree or another) in the historical period of the late nineteenth and early twentieth century. The fact that the appeal of the 'Great White Hope' in boxing (a 'race' and class issue) in North America and the UK is closely linked to the popularity (and media coverage) of the sport, is then interesting, as the attraction (and popularity) of boxing in the US is on the decline. This has been attributed to the exponential increase in popularity of MMA and the 'success and prescience of White champions' in this sport (Rhodes, 2011: 354), that only became professional in 1993.

Mixed Martial Arts: a brief history

Prior to the development of MMA in the early 1990s, boxing had long been regarded by many as the most violent and controversial of sports. Challenging this notion, Spencer (2011) (MMA fighter and sociologist), provides a concise explanation of the emergence and growth of MMA:

> A new and equally violent and taxing sport has emerged …. MMA competitions feature competitors in a ring or caged-in area, inflicting

pain on their opponents, by punching, kicking, elbowing, and kneeing [them] ... into submission. While only men participated in MMA competitions, women now enter into these contests. Countries within Europe, North and South America, and Asia regularly host MMA competitions. Ultimate fighting championship (UFC) in the United States and Canada, and Great Britain draws crowds of 20,000 or more, in addition to millions of televised viewers worldwide.

Globally, MMA seems to have 'arrived', and Spencer states that it has now eclipsed boxing in popularity. MMA incorporates a plethora of techniques from different traditional Asian martial arts that have permeated western culture (e.g. judo, wrestling, Ju Jitsu) and boxing. The etymology of 'martial arts' (from the Latin) is 'arts of Mars', the Roman God of War (Carter, Kluck and Morin, 2012). Preparation for war has historically been the remit of martial arts pursuits, although recently in more westernised forms they have been adapted as recreational and competitive activities.

As the popularity of MMA in its raw form (no-holds-barred) mushroomed in the US, a number of political figures called for a nationwide banning of the sport. Labelling Ultimate Fighting Championship (UFC)[5] events as 'human cockfighting', a 'blood sport' and 'bloodbath' in 1996, US Republican senator John McCain was the most vociferous in his moral condemnation, and this led the administrators of the sport to introduce some new regulations. Somewhat ironically, this led to the further legitimisation and growth of the sport. That said, 'the basic nature of the fights has not changed. The purpose of cage fighting is still to punch, kick, and pound a man or woman into submission' (Carter, in Carter, Kluck and Morin, 2012:1). This infliction of intentional physical violence has led to a growing body of medical literature (alongside that relating to boxing) that demonstrates the ever-present risk of serious injury and disablement (Ngai, Levy and Hsu, 2008; Seidenberg, 2011). This evidence has also led medical authorities (e.g. British Medical Association) to lobby for an outright ban on MMA, as with boxing (White 2007).

As to the many socio-cultural variables surrounding MMA, it is Spencer's (2009, 2011, 2012) ethnographic work that is arguably the most notable, addressing notions of gender (especially hegemonic masculinity), narratives of pain, loss and injury, embodiment, (homo) eroticism, racism, morality and violence. In turn, other academic analyses of this sporting phenomenon have begun to emerge. Figurational sociologists, Garcia and Malcolm (2010) and Van Bottenburg and Heilbron (2006) have examined the historical origins of MMA (and violence) in light of Elias' 'civilizing process' and theory of 'sportization' (i.e. codification and rule development). To the best of our knowledge, however, the only academic research into the relationship between Christianity, violence and MMA is Borer and Schafer's (2011) study that explored the internal conflict that Christian

MMA spectators (fans) experience in watching such violent activity. Borer and Schafer contextualise this research within the American 'culture wars' and analyse Internet data from the confessional accounts of open discussions on 'blog entries', using key search phrases as 'Christian UFC', 'Christian MMA' and 'Violence Christianity'. Their key aim was to identify how self-defined Christians and MMA enthusiasts sought out 'nuanced ways to address the internal conflict between their religious beliefs and their leisure practices' (Borer and Schafer, 2011: 165). One blogger's comments (cited in Borer and Schafer, 2011: 177), identify a range of ethical problems for the theologian:

> While beating another's face may not be the 'Christian thing to do', what we have to realize is that Christians are a minority in a secular world. We are called to preach the Gospel everywhere. Be it pro wrestling, MMA fighting ... it's up to you to bring Christ to the one next to you.

The findings of Borer and Schafer's research provoke us to ask why violent entertainment is so appealing to many observers (Guttmann, 1998), including Christians. Having provided brief insight into the historical and social development of boxing and MMA, including an identification of some of the multiple ethical quandaries that exist around the enactment of these pursuits, our next task is to put forward a theological ethical critique and assessment.

A theological ethical critique and assessment

Past analyses of the morality of boxing (and other violent sports) by sports ethicists have been dominated theoretically and philosophically by traditional arguments surrounding issues of paternalism and autonomy (Dixon, 2007; Parry, 1998; Schneider and Butcher, 2001; Simon, 2007). The conclusions and recommendations offered in this small corpus of work predictably span the paternalism-autonomy spectrum while typical practical suggestions surround: (i) restricting or banning, blows to the head; (ii) stipulating the compulsory use of head-guards (which, perhaps somewhat ironically, has been shown to be generally ineffective in protecting from brain damage, (BMA, 2008)); and (iii) better educating boxers and coaches as to the health risks involved in the sport.

Sociologists and psychologists have also presented a wide-range of theories and conceptual ideas to explain the multiple dimensions of violence in sport (and in particular boxing and MMA) (see, for example, Burstyn, 2004; Guttmann, 1998; Kerr, 2005; Messner, 1990; Young, 2012). These writings explore the complexities between definitions and explanations of assertion, aggression and violence and the diverse sociological, psychological, cultural, economic, political and historical variables that have moderated the acceptance, ritualisation, institutionalisation and celebration of violence in sports. A hegemonic, hyper-masculine ideology, for example, has been a pervasive characteristic of sports, such as, boxing and MMA (Burstyn, 2004). Eller (2006: 31) helpfully summarises the significant literature on violence in the social sciences into two schools of thought, which also reflects the sports literature on this topic:

> The two most general perspectives are the 'internal' and the 'external' – that is, whether the cause or source of violence is 'inside' the violent individual (in his head or her 'mind' or personality or genes) or 'outside' the violent individual (in the social situations, values structures in which he or she acts). These two overarching perspectives correspond roughly to biology and psychology on the one hand and sociology and anthropology on the other....

The social science literature that has examined violence in sport is extremely helpful in contextualising our discussion. But we now turn to the discipline of theological ethics for further insight into the apparent paradox of the 'Christian boxer/Mixed Martial Artist'. The following narrative provides a provocative start point:

> The boxer Manny Pacquiao is a devout born-again Christian. He has earned world titles in eight weight divisions and was anointed 'Fighter of the Decade' by the Boxing Writers Association of America. Before a recent bout, I pressed Pacquiao about the apparent conflict between his devotion to the God-man who insisted that we turn the other cheek and his concussive craft. There was a silence. I was worried that I stepped over the line and said, 'I'm sorry if I offended you with that question.' The Pac Man responded, 'No it is a good question. I think it is wrong that we try to hurt one another, but I also think that God will forgive us (him and his opponent) because it is our calling.' I could have pushed, 'But why would God give you a calling that was sinful?' but instead I back-peddled and left it at that – that is, at ambivalence.
>
> (Marino, 2014: 57)

Pacquiao's comments express a familiar vague awareness of the resistance to a straightforward embrace of violence that has characterised the Christian tradition, mixed with outright misunderstandings of that tradition, and thus offer an opportunity to revisit Christian thinking about many of the issues involved, in order to develop a more nuanced theological account of the contemporary activities of boxing and MMA. It is a sign of Pacquiao's worldview – having been shaped by the narratives and practices of the Christian community – that he not only openly presents himself as a

Christian, but also confesses that, 'it is wrong that we try to hurt one another'. Such a belief has traditionally emerged from the Christian sense of the value of human bodily integrity growing from the confession of God as the Creator of all things good. Christians confess that their bodies and lives are therefore not their own but are to be used to God's glory, to be lived with (and suffered with) when they give us problems, or, when we even wish to be rid of them. Our own bodies are divine gifts to us, to be received with gratitude and solicitude (Barth, 1961: 324–364; Hauerwas, 2001). Recognising the profound ways in which gratefully attending to one's body shapes one's own life, teaches Christians what it means to respect the bodies that God has given to others. It is this recognition that has traditionally grounded the inviolable prohibitions elaborated in civil and criminal laws (such as in the assessment of penalties for maiming others), as well as many other realms of human life. Such prohibitive measures were evident in the middle ages, for example, where concrete limits were set around how vigorously one could pursue the corporeal punishment of prisoners, slaves or children (Aquinas, 1929: 2a2ae 65 art2).

Since one of the premier designations of the coming messiah is the 'Prince of Peace', (Isaiah 9:6), readers of the New Testament have been puzzled by Jesus' using a whip to clear the Temple (John 2:15) and his comment that 'the one who has no sword must sell his cloak and buy one' (Luke 22:36, cf. Matthew 10:34). Passages like these, along with Old Testament depictions of godly warriors in Israel have provoked long-running debates around the question of the appropriate Christian stance towards violence. Is Jesus' statement that 'those who live by the sword will die by the sword' (Matthew 26:52) a prohibition of Christian involvement in violence, or a description of what will happen if they do? This is not the forum in which to recount the various arguments on this matter (cf. Yoder 2009a); our aim here having been only to explain why, theologically speaking, we cannot discuss boxing and MMA without entering lengthy debate about the problems of legitimate violence, which are often gathered under the heading 'the just war tradition'. It was within the constraints of this tradition that the long-running discussion among Christians took place, as they sought to explain how those who confess allegiance to the Prince of Peace, whose reign is not otherworldly but supervenes on all worldly rulers, could ever be involved in killing or violence towards other humans.

Though he was by no means the first to think about these issues, Augustine is considered the founder of this tradition because his answer remains the basis of mainstream Christian understandings of just war: because *every* Christian is in *every action* called to love the neighbour, no violence against, or killing of other humans can ever be justified, a prohibition prominently enshrined in the ten commandments (Exodus 20:13; Augustine, 1998: I: 20–21, XIX.5–6). Because human societies can never be just, if violence and vengeance are pursued by private parties, the fact that some will commit violence against others needs to be dealt with by the rightful political authorities who, the New Testament informs us, are divinely sanctioned to deploy violence (Romans 13:1–7). That St. Paul links this authority with the sword seems to imply that political authorities have the theologically sanctioned right even to use lethal violence (O'Donovan, 2005: 101–124). Augustine's conclusion was that there is no basis for Christians to engage in violence, or killing, unless they are part of the government of a society that can deploy violence and is committed to doing so only in order to safeguard against the vulnerability of the weak. That is, such a government deploys violence only out of love for the victimised other. Based on his theological reading of the whole of the Christian scriptures, Augustine thus concluded with the demand that any Christian engagement in violence be defended as an act of love for one's neighbour.

This brings us back to Pacquiao's assertion that boxing is his calling and so his sin of wishing to hurt his neighbour will be forgiven. This sentiment again betrays significant Christian formation because this may indeed be an answer that Christian soldiers throughout the ages of Christendom may have given when asked about the theological status of their desire to kill and maim. At best the Christian soldier could hope to engage in battle in the course of prosecuting a war that was genuinely to protect the innocent from avaricious aggression and to do violence to his enemies that was commensurate with Christian love – that is, which did not fall into bloodlust, rape, pillage and wanton pleasure in destruction. To the extent that the Christian soldier undertook violence in this way, they were entitled to pray for forgiveness, not for murder (because killing by an authorised authority would not constitute murder) but for having not done so in ways that embody a spirit of Christian love. Whatever we make of this position, and it is certainly hard for most of us to imagine, it has been the default theological framework within which Christian soldiers through the centuries have assessed the moral defensibility of their actions, and who could at least understand their moral dilemmas about deploying violence as legitimate, if difficult, part of embracing the vocation of the soldier – a vocation that was ultimately justified by scripture, and a long theological tradition.

The same cannot be said of Pacquiao who seems (at least implicitly) to claim this tradition for himself as a boxer. This raises the question of whether or not he is warranted in calling his participation in such pursuits a vocation. The term vocation has a long and complex history that is, again, too nuanced to recount here (see Ramsey, 1953). Suffice to say that a sphere of human activity may be called one's vocation, as Augustine insisted, only if the Christian can defend it as a legitimate contribution to the life of our neighbours (and to the furtherance of God's kingdom), and to do so on the basis of the Christian creeds, in which the core emphases of scripture have been encapsulated. Prophets, priests, kings, mothers and fathers, farmers, cooks, craftspeople, pastors and teachers – these are all social roles which have almost universally been understood by Christians through the centuries as legitimate vocations, the term 'vocation' being verbally derived from 'calling'. Given their seemingly inextricable involvement in immoral activities actors, gladiators, magicians, mediums, soothsayers, thieves, abortionists and prostitutes have, throughout the ages, been denied any claim to calling their activity a vocation in Christian terms. Such activities were never understood to have a legitimate claim to be recognised as activities to which God might ever call a believer. The claim that a given pursuit might earn one a pay check, or even serve a social function in some sense were never considered sufficient reasons to justify forms of life that seemed ultimately degrading and destructive of the humanity of those involved. Such human activities might be recognised as 'jobs' or legitimate pursuits in any given society, and might in perverse ways even point to the one who can save us from such degradations. But they can only be considered parodies of true Christian vocations, into which God calls human beings so that they can serve the up-building of one another and His kingdom?

That there have been long-running debates about whether or not soldiers (and police officers) can claim to be pursuing a legitimate Christian vocation is relevant to our discussion here. The earliest Christians thought it impossible for Christians to be soldiers, not least because Roman soldiers swore allegiance to Mars, the god of War (Tertullian, 1978: XII). The immediate effect of this confession was to ensure that the first wave of Christian martyrs were Roman soldiers executed for sedition in refusing their military oath. With the conversion of Constantine this equation decisively changed because the oath was removed or attenuated by attaching it to the Emperor, now a Christian and pledged to serve the God of peace. At this point it must again suffice to say that the debate about whether or not a Christian can be a soldier, has never been fully resolved among Christians and the early Christian sensibility that there is a fundamental contradiction between the routine deployment of violence and the Christian confession, has been reinvigorated in recent decades (cf. Hauerwas, 2004; Yoder, 2009b). Though some youth programmes in MMA have been linked to police training (Marino, 2014), no serious argument has yet been offered to defend it as an outgrowth of a military vocation.

Given the foregoing arguments, what we can say at least is that the claim that boxing and MMA are legitimate Christian vocations would have to receive far more robust theological justification than they have to date. Until that justification is offered, the infinitely elastic appeal to Christian engagement in these sports being a form of missional evangelism (which at least expresses an awareness that it can only be justified by explicating it as an act of love for one's neighbour) is insufficient to establish it as a legitimate Christian vocation. Such an appeal no more validates boxing and MMA than a whole range of other illicit activities in the absence of a richer account of how the activity should be understood, as an act of love and service. To this end, its protagonists must explain why, as followers of the Prince of Peace, we should consider it one of the many forms of life configured as a form of life, which aims to receive with gratitude the gifts of the Creator given to us and to others.

There is one final aspect of the tradition of just war thinking that continues to shape this arena of human activity as it has re-emerged in the modern period. The underlying aim of the whole just war tradition in all its permutations was not to justify, but to *limit* and even *eliminate* violence if and where possible (Bonhoeffer, 2005). The language of just war is most often used today in reduced form which assumes that just war names a set of rules that can tell political decision makers when it is justifiable to enter a war, as well as what it is permissible to do in the course of a war. The important point to note, however, is that the condition of the emergence of this tradition was an agreement at a deeper level among Christians over the centuries; that Christians are always on the side of de-escalation, precisely because they recognise the God-given value of the neighbour's bodily integrity and because they are fundamentally peacemakers. It is on the basis of this fundamental moral and theological commitment, for instance, that modern laws about gun control have emerged in certain countries, such as those in the UK, and alongside them detailed policies about police not carrying guns on their person (Schlabach, 2007). In this light the militarisation of police forces currently underway in the United States (Appuzo, 2014) should not be seen as unrelated to the rising popularity of violent sports and the role they play as entertainment for the masses (Marino, 2014; Morin, 2011). Together, they can be read as indications of the decay of the presumption for de-escalation that characterised the Christian tradition of thinking about violence.

One of the other places where we can see the impact of this waning moral sensibility in the developed west is in the endurance of rules in sport that limit certain forms of violence – biting, eye-gouging, stopping competitive fights after a certain number of blows have struck the head, or when an opponent is in an arm or leg lock that will inevitably lead to the breaking of a limb or suffocation. Given the logic of these sports, why not allow such tactics? A common answer to this question by practitioners today might be that it is 'not good for the image of the sport' to appear wantonly bloody or violent, though some might also worry about the permanent disablement of opponents. What we are suggesting is that these attempts to rein in certain types of violence are, in the modern world, the tail end of the moral agreement that just war thinking encapsulated, within which long-running and morally serious attempts in Christendom to flesh out the meaning of Jesus' command to love one's neighbour were honed. On these grounds Christians involved in sports like boxing and MMA should at the very least be outspoken promoters of continual adjustments of rules and the practices of refereeing fights in order to continually ratchet down the harms inflicted on opponents – a moral and spiritual imperative that impinges equally on Christian practitioners, coaches and spectators and is applicable to every sport which contains elements of violence.

If Christians are to argue (as we are inclined) that today it is illegitimate to call boxing and MMA Christian vocations, this raises the question of why so many contemporary Christians experience these activities as a realm of freedom and liberation. Here the Christian theologian faces the pastoral imperative to ask: What does the rising popularity of MMA, at the expense of boxing, tell us about the state of our current societies? Here closer attention to specific cultural configurations is crucial. As one documentary filmmaker has well captured, in some southern US states cage fighters often narrate their participation in the sport as part of a search for an authentic life, a life others will remember (Fightville, 2011). For them MMA offers an answer to the vacuous-ness and banality of life for young people today, especially young White men in an area with some significant economic and social deprivation. Other themes that often emerge are the quest for personal honour and dignity, which goes hand-in-hand with a desire for self-determination. Though consumer capitalist economies do not seem to offer much life satisfaction to young aggressive and ambitious males (especially from the working classes), it trains us to feel that things are more 'real' if money is riding on it: when one's livelihood is on the line, training and fighting have not only become one's job, but this job has been recognised as significant by society.

Most of these themes are struck in the Hollywood feature film that did more to popularise MMA among North American Christians than anything else: *Fight Club*. The release of this film in 1999 arguably tapped into the precise crisis of American masculinity that middle-class evangelical pastors in the US had been trying to access, first with ventures designed to shore up the tradition of marriage, such as the Promise Keepers, but quickly turning to more aggressive recoveries of masculine virtues (Eldredge, 2010), of which Christian MMA movements are arguably the most extreme (Borer and Schafer, 2011; Morin, 2011). Mark Driscoll and Ryan Dobson were some of the more prominent Christian advocates of MMA to emerge after *Fight Club*, but they are by no means the only ones, as documented in the recent documentary *Fight Church* (2014). In a society in which males in the formerly dominant social class have suffered a loss of opportunity due to the processes of economic rationalisation and globalisation, often experience themselves as losing authority in the home (as the dominance of patriarchal presumptions crumble in the wake of the sexual revolution and the women's rights movement), and feel embattled as they try to protect the pulpits of their churches from the rising tide of female ministers, it is perhaps unsurprising that a hyper-masculine, martial domain has been seen as a promising development. The gains in self-respect and self-discipline exhibited by participants are not in any way denied when we nevertheless assert that it is not MMA which has redeemed and repurposed rudderless lives (Marino, 2003, Rutler 2013). MMA has only managed to capture a legitimate protest against a vacuous and denuding society that offers so little to so many because such gory forms of entertainment have come to be seen as not only attractive but pleasurable (Morin, 2011).

Conclusion

The aim of this chapter has been to critically examine the seemingly para-doxical existence of the Christian boxer or MMA exponent. Of the three potential theses that were presented at the outset, our reflections have led us to believe that:

> Boxing and MMA are immoral and, are thus, not appropriate or helpful for humans (with Christian belief) to participate in, and/or watch; however, within 'God's economy' these activities may engender *some* moral goods (e.g. positive character development and healthy civil engagement = social harmony, etc.)

So, while we are sympathetic with the sentiments of the fight legend George Foreman, who suggests that boxing 'makes young people less violent', as Christian theologians, we are uncomfortable with the *intentional* (sinful?) interpersonal violence directed at an opponent, who is fashioned in the image of God. Boxing and MMA may indeed develop some positive character attributes and perhaps allow some individuals to divert deeply felt pathologies of anger and violence away from the general public – the local gang member, a wife, a child. But Christian scholars and ministers (including those ministering in *Fight Church*) need to begin to explore the underlying reasons *why* fellow Christians participate in such activities and why other physical sports that do not involve intentional violence could not be used to the same effect? Half a century ago, the Catholic moral theologian, Richard McCormick, proffered similar thoughts:

> regardless of what answer we come up with, it is both a sign and guarantee of abiding spiritual health to face issues at their moral root. It is never easy to question the moral character of our own pleasure and entertainment.
>
> (McCormick, 1962, p. 1)

Since the 1960s, the thirst for violent sports has arguably increased exponentially in western industrialised societies amid a globalised and mediatised age, and it is therefore incumbent on theologians representing the Church to continue to think hard about such 'pastimes'. A wide range of questions remain. For example, inquiring into the necessity of such athletes distancing themselves from their own bodies (Morin, 2011), investigating the profile and culpability of contemporary spectators on such sports (Borer and Schafer, 2011; Marino, 2014) and considering the question of female participation in such sports (Fields, 2008), to name but a few.

Notes

1 This work was first published in the *Journal of Religion and Society* (2015).
2 We acknowledge that the 'purpose' of boxing and MMA may not be *solely* be physical violence. For example, there may also be a 'mutual quest for excellence' (the Latin root meaning of competition in sport; see, Watson and Parker, 2014), in which, opponents honour and respect one another by trying to bring the best out of each other. This is often demonstrated in a post-fight embraces and, *at times*, honourable words spoken of one's opponent in pre and post-fight media interviews.
3 Where we use the term 'God's economy' in this chapter, we are referring generally to God's expression of Himself in history, through the values and moral goods of humanity (and thus, the Holy Spirit). This rendering of the term, then means that in the complexity and messiness of human life, certain activities, such as boxing and MMA may, at the same time, involve questionable motivations on behalf of the participants/spectators, result in harmful/sinful/immoral outcomes and manifest Christian moral goods (see Vines, 1996).
4 For example, see: Cashmore, 2004; Heiskanen, 2012; Jefferson, 1980; Marqusee, 1995; Oates, 2006/1987; Radford, 2005; Rhodes, 2011; Wacquant, 2007; Woodward, 2007.
5 Ultimate Fighting Championship (UFC) is a MMA promotion company and a subsidiary of the parent company William Morris Endeavor, based in Las Vegas, Nevada, US. It is the world's largest MMA promoter featuring the majority of the sport's top-ranked fighters. UFC produces and manages a series of worldwide events covering ten weight divisions and which are governed by the Unified Rules of Mixed Martial Arts.

References

Appuzo, M. (2014) War Gear Flows to Police Departments, *New York Times*, 8 June, A1. Available online: www.nytimes.com/2014/06/09/us/war-gear-flows-to-police-departments.html?_r=0 (accessed 1 January 2015).

Aquinas, T. (1929) *Summa Theologica*, vol. 10, Fathers of the English Dominican Province trans., London: Burns Oates and Washbourne.

Augustine (1998) *The City of God Against the Pagans*, R. Dyson ed., Cambridge: Cambridge University Press.

Barth, K. (1961) *Church Dogmatics, Vol. III, The Doctrine of Creation Part 4*, G. W Bromiley and T. F. Torrance eds., Edinburgh: T&T Clark.

Berkowitz, M. (2011) Jewish Fighters in Britain in Historical Context: Repugnance, Requiem, Reconsideration, *Sport in History* (Special Edition: Boxing, History and Culture), 31, 4: 423–443.

Blakely, R. (2014) Choke They Neighbour: Cage-Fighting Preachers who Grapple for God, *The Times* (London), 1. Available online: www.thetimes.co.uk/tto/news/world/americas/article4053673.ece (accessed 1 September 2014).

Boddy, K. (2008) *Boxing: A Cultural History*, London: Reaktion Books.

Bonhoeffer, D. (2005) *Ethics*, C. Green ed., Minneapolis: Fortress.

Borer. M. I. and Schafer, T. S. (2011) Culture War Confessionals: Conflicting Accounts of Christianity, Violence, and Mixed Martial Arts, *Journal of Media and Religion*, 10, 4: 165–184.

Brasch, R. (1970) *How Did Sports Begin?* New York: David McKay.

British Medical Association (2008) *Boxing: An Update from the Board of Science*. A Source from the BMA Science and Education Department and the Board of Science. Full Text Available online: http://bmaopac.hosted.exlibrisgroup.com/exlibris/aleph/a21_1/apache_media/15BMGJ6PDYJ3HVSYNKPHV81SYB8ATR.pdf (accessed 18 September 2013).

Burstyn, V. (2004) 'Hit, Crunch, and Burn': Organized Violence and Men's Sport, in V. Burstyn, *The Rites of Men: Manhood, Politics and the Culture of Sport*, London: University of Toronto Press: 163–191.

Carter, J., Kluck, T. and Morin, M. (2012) Is Cage Fighting Ethical for Christians? *Christianity Today*, 29 May, 1–2. Available online: www.christianitytoday.com/ct/2012/january/cage-fighting.html (accessed 6 June 2012).

Cashmore, E. (2004) *Tyson: Nurture the Beast*, Cambridge, UK: Polity.

Dee, D. (2012) 'The Hefty Hebrew': Boxing and British-Jewish Identity, 1890–1960, *Sport in History*, 32, 3: 361–381.

Dixon, N. (2007) Boxing, Paternalism, and Legal Moralism, in W. J. Morgan (ed.), *Ethics in Sport* (2nd edn), Champaign, IL: Human Kinetics: 389–406.

Eldredge, J. (2010) *Wild at Heart: Discovering the Secret of a Man's Soul* second edn, first edn 2001, Nashville: Thomas Nelson.

Eller, J. D. (2006) *Violence and Culture: A Cross Cultural and Interdisciplinary Perspective*, Toronto, Canada: Thomson Wadsworth.

Endersen, I. and Olweus, D. (2005) Participation in Power Sports and Antisocial Involvement in Preadolescent and Adolescent Boys, *Journal of Child Psychology and Psychiatry*, 46, 5: 468–478.

Fields, S. (2008) *Female Gladiators: Gender Law and Contact Sport in America*, Urbana, IL: University of Illinois Press.

Fight Church (2014) Junge, D. and Storkel, B. directors, Kostbar, E. and McKel-heer, J. producers, release date 16 September, Film Harvest.

Fight Club (1999) Fincher, D. directed, Bell, R. and Lindson, A. produced, release date 6 October, Fox 2000 Pictures.

Fightville (2011) Epperlein, P. and Tucker, M. produced and directed, release date 12 March, Heros Film.

Foreman, G. (with Abraham, K.) (2007) *God in My Corner: A Spiritual Memoir*, Nashville, TN: W Publishing.

Galli, M. (2005) Should We Ban Boxing? The Unusual Arguments against the 'Sweet Science' Cut Many Ways, *Christianity Today* (Web only), Available online: www.christianitytoday.com/ct/2005/octoberweb-only/52.0c.html?tab=shared&start=2 (accessed 1 September 2014).

Garcia, R. S. and Malcolm, D. (2010) Decivilizing, Civilizing or Informalizing? The International Development of Mixed Martial Arts, *International Review of the Sociology of Sport*, 45, 1: 39–58.

Gems, G. R. (1993) Sport, Religion, and Americanization: Bishop Sheil and the Catholic Youth Organization, *International Journal of the History of Sport*, August: 233–241.

Gems, G. R. (2004) The Politics of Boxing: Resistance, Religion, and the Working Class Assimilation, *International Sports Journal*, 8, 1: 89–103.

George Foreman Youth Centre (2014) Youth Centre. Available online: www.georgeforeman.com/youth_center (accessed 2 September 2014).

Gore, W. (2011) I Pray for my Opponents before Fights, *The Catholic Herald*, September 16, 7.

Guttmann, A. (1998) The Appeal of Violent Sports, in J. Goldstein (ed.), *Why We Watch: The Attractions of Violent Entertainment*. New York and Oxford: Oxford University Press: 7–26.

Hauerwas, S. (2001, original pub. 1976), with Richard Bondi, Memory, Community and the Reasons for Living: Reflections on Suicide and Euthanasia. Published in Berkman, J. and Cartwright, M. *The Hauerwas Reader*, Durham, NC: Duke University Press, 577–595.

Hauerwas, S. (2004) *Performing the Faith: Bonhoeffer and the Practice of Nonviolence*, Grand Rapids, MN: Brazos.

Heiskanen, B. (2012) *The Urban Geography of Boxing: Race, Class, and Gender in the Ring*, London: Routledge.

Hillman, E. (1951) The Morality of Boxing, *Theological Studies*, 301–319. Available online: www.ts.mu.edu/readers/content/pdf/12/12.3/12.3.1.pdf (accessed 31 May 2013).

Holyfield, V. (with Holyfield, B.) (1996) *Holyfield the Humble Warrior: The Amazing Story of the Three-Time Heavyweight Champion of the World*, Carlisle, UK: Trust Media Distribution.

Jefferson, T. (1998) Muscle, 'Hard' Men and 'Iron' Mike Tyson: Reflections on Desire, Anxiety, and the Embodiment of Masculinity, *Body and Society*, 4, 1: 77–98.

Jenkins, C. and Ellis, T. (2011) The Highway to Hooliganism? An Evaluation of the Impact of Combat Sport Participation on Individual Criminality, *International Journal of Police Science and Management*, 13, 2, 117–131.

Johnes, M. and Taylor, M. (Guest eds) (2011) Special Edition: Boxing, History and Culture, *Sport in History*, 31, 4: 357–520.

Kerr, J. H. (2005) New Beginnings: A Reversal Theory View of Violence, in J. H. Kerr, *Rethinking Aggression and Violence in Sport*, London: Routledge: 38–45.

Krattenmaker, T. (2013) NFL Violence a Moral Thorn for Christians: Faith takes a Hit as Evidence Mounts of Players who Suffer Brain Damage, *USA Today* (online column). Available online: www.usatoday.com/story/opinion/2013/10/09/nfl-concussions-football-christians-column/2955997/ (accessed 1 September 2014).

Koehlinger, A. (2012) *Rosaries and Rope Burns: Boxing and Manhood in American Catholicism, 1890–1970*, Princeton, NJ: Princeton University Press.

Leone, C. and Leone, D. (1992) Death in the Ring: A Pastoral Dilemma, in S. J. Hoffman (ed.), *Sport and Religion*, Champaign, IL: Human Kinetics, 265–270.

Mainwaring, L. M. and Trenerry, M. (Guest eds) (2012) Special Issue: Sports Concussion, *Journal of Clinical Sport Psychology*, 6, 2: 203–301.

Marino, G. (2003) Apologia Pro Pugilatione, *Philosophy Now*. Available online: https://philosophynow.org/issues/41/Apologia_Pro_Pugilatione (accessed 1 September 2014).

Marino, G. (2010a) Fighting Violence with Boxing in Chicago, *Huffington Post* (Blog). Available online: www.huffingtonpost.com/gordon-marino/fighting-violence-with-bo_b_2516790.html (accessed 1 September 2014).

Marino, G. (2010b) Boxing with Humility, *In Character: A Journal of Everyday Virtues*, Posted 13 May. Available online: http://incharacter.org/observation/boxing-with-humility/ (accessed 1 September 2014).

Marino, G. (2014) The Hurting Game: A Boxing Coach Ponders the Morality of Watching Combat Sports, *Christianity Today*, April, 54–58.

Marqusee, M. (1995) Sport and Stereotype: From Role Model to Muhammad Ali, *Race and Class*, 36, 4: 1–29.

McCormick, R. A. (1962) Is Professional Boxing Immoral? *Sports Illustrated*, 5 November. Available online: www.si.com/vault/1962/11/05/670209/is-professional-boxing- immoral (accessed 1 September 2014).

McCrory, P. (2007) Boxing and the Risk of Chronic Brain Injury, *British Medical Journal*, 335: 781–782.

Messner, M. A. (1990) When Bodies are Weapons: Masculinity and Violence in Sports, *International Review for the Sociology of Sport*, 25, 3: 203–218.

Morin, M. (2011) Confessions of a Cage Fighter: Masculinity, Misogyny, and the Fear of Losing Control, *theOtherJournal.com*, 28 June, http://theotherjournal.com/2011/06/28/the-confessions-of-a-cage-fighter-masculinity-misogyny-and-the-fear-of-losing-control/ downloaded 17 January 2015.

Murphy, P. and Sheard, K. (2008) Boxing Blind: Unplanned Processes in the Development of Modern Boxing, in D. Malcolm and I. Waddington (eds), *Matters of Sport: Essays in Honour of Eric Dunning*, London: Routledge: 40–56.

Ngai, K. M., Levy, F. and Hsu, E. B. (2008) Injury Trends in Sanctioned Mixed Martial Arts Competition: A 5-Year Review from 2002 to 2007, *British Journal of Sports Medicine*, 42: 686–689.

Oates, J. C. (2006/1987) *On Boxing*, New York: HarperCollins.

O'Donovan, O. (2005) *The Ways of Judgement*, Grand Rapids, MI: Eerdmans.

Parry, S. J. (1998) Violence and Aggression in Contemporary Sport, in M. J. McNamee and S. J. Parry (eds), *Ethics and Sport*, London: Routledge: 205–224.

Poliakoff, M. (1987) *Combat Sports in the Ancient World: Competition, Violence, and Culture*, New Haven, CT: Yale University Press.

Radford, P. (2005) Lifting the Spirit of the Nation: British Boxers and the Emergence of the National Sporting Hero at the Time of the Napoleonic Wars, *Identities: Global Studies in Culture and Power*, 12: 249–270.

Ramsey, P. (1953) *Basic Christian Ethics*, London: SCM

Rhodes, J. (2011) Fighting for 'Respectability': Media Representations of the White, 'Working-Class' Male Boxing 'Hero', *Journal of Sport and Social Issues*, 35, 4: 350–376.

Rutten, E. A., Schuengel, C., Dirks, E., Geert, J., Stams, M., Gert, J., Biesta, J. and Hoeksma, J. B. (2011) Predictors of Antisocial and Prosocial Behaviour in an Adolescent Sports Context, *Social Development*, 20, 2: 294–315.

Rutler, G. W. (2013) The Christian Boxer, *Crisis Magazine*, April, 1–5.

Salter, M. and Tomsen, S. (2012) Violence and Carceral Masculinities in Felony Fights, *British Journal of Criminology*, 52: 309–323.

Schlabach, G. ed., (2007) *Just Policing, Not War: An Alternative Response to World Violence*, Collegeville, PN: Liturgical Press.

Schneider, A. and Butcher, R. (2001) Ethics, Sport and Boxing, in W. J. Morgan, K. V. Meier and A. Schneider (eds), *Ethics in Sport*, Champaign, IL: Human Kinetics: 357–369.

Schneiderman, R. M. (2010) Flock is Now a Fight Team in Some Ministries: More Churches Promote Martial Arts to Reach Young Men, *New York Times*, P. A1. Available online: www.nytimes.com/2010/02/02/us/02fight.html?_r=1&pagewanted=print (accessed 7 June 2012).

Schwarze, C. (2010) The Christian and the Cage Fighter, *Sydney Anglican Network*, 27 January. Available online from: www.sydneyanglicans.net/life/day-today/the_christian_and_the_cage_fighter/ (accessed 24 August 2011).

Seidenberg, P. H. (2011) Mixed Martial Arts: Injury Patters and Issues for the Ringside Physician, *Current Sports Medicine Reports*, 10, 3: 147–150.

Sheard, K. (2004) Boxing in the Western Civilizing Process, in E. Dunning, D. Malcolm and I. Waddington (eds), *Sport Histories: Figurational Studies of the Development of Modern Sports*, London: Routledge: 15–30.

Shirley, P. (1999) *The Soul of Boxing: What Motivates the World's Greatest Fighters*, London: Harper Collins.

Shurley, J. P. and Todd, J. S. (2012) Boxing Lessons: A Historical Review of Chronic Head Trauma in Boxing and Football, *Kinesiology Review*, 1, 3: 170–184.

Simon, R. L. (2007) Violence in Sport, in W. J. Morgan (ed.), *Ethics in Sport* (2nd edn), Champaign, IL: Human Kinetics: 379–388.

Spencer, D. C. (2009) Habit(us), Body Techniques and Body Callusing: An Ethnography of Mixed Martial Arts, *Body and Society*, 15: 119–143.

Spencer, D. C. (2011) *Ultimate Fighting and Embodiment: Violence, Gender and Mixed Martial Arts*, London: Routledge.

Spencer, D. C. (2012) Narratives of Despair and Loss: Pain, Injury and Masculinity in the Sport of Mixed Martial Arts, *Qualitative Research in Sport, Exercise and Health*, 4, 1: 117–137.

Spivey, N. (2005) *The Ancient Olympics: A History*, Oxford, UK: Oxford University Press.

Sugden, J. (1996) *Boxing and Society: An International Analysis*, Manchester, UK: Manchester University Press.

Svab, D. (2011) *Knocking out the Devil* (Kindle Edition only), Amazon Media EU.

Tertullian, (1978) The Chaplet, or De Corona, in A. Roberts and J. Donaldson, *The Ante-Nicene Fathers*, Grand Rapids, MI: Eerdmans: 93–104.

Van Bottenburg, M. and Heilbron, J. (2006) De-Sportization of Fighting Contests: The Origins and Dynamics of No Holds Barred Events and the Theory of Sportization, *International Review for the Sociology of Sport*, 41: 259–282.

Vines, W. E. (1996). *Vine's Complete Expository Dictionary of Old and New Testament Words*, Nashville, TN: Thomas Nelson.

Wacquant, L. (2007) Bodily Capital among Professional Boxers, in A. Tomlinson (ed.), *The Sport Studies Reader*, London: Routledge: 261–266.

Waller, S. (2017), 'Fist, Feet and Faith': An 'Elite' Interview with 'Fight Church' Pastor Jude Roberts. *Sport in Society*. Online only, DOI: 10.1080/17430437.2016.1269087.

Watson, N. J. and Bolt, B. (2015) Mixed-Martial Arts and Christianity: 'Where Feet, Fist and Faith Collide', *The Conversation*, 5 January. Available online: http://theconversation.com/mixed-martial-arts-and-christianity-where-feet-fist-and-faith-collide-34836, accessed 17 January 2017.

Watson, N. J. and Brock, B. (2014) Religion in the Ring: Death, Concussion and Brain Bleeds. *Theos, Public Theology Think-Tank*, London, Invited Essay, 15 December. Available online: www.theosthinktank.co.uk/comment/2014/12/15/ religion-in-the-ring-death-concussion-and-brain-bleeds, accessed 17 January 2017.

Watson, N. J., and Parker, A. (2014) *Sport and the Christian Religion: A Systematic Review of Literature* (Foreword, Scott Kretchmar; Preface, Brian Brock), Newcastle upon Tyne, UK: Cambridge Scholars Publishing.

Woodward, K. (2007) *Boxing, Masculinity and Identity: The 'I' of the Tiger*, London: Routledge.

White, C. (2007) Mixed Martial Arts and Boxing Should be Banned, *British Medical Journal*, 335: 469.

Yoder, J. (2009a) *Christian Attitudes to War, Peace, and Revolution*, J. Koontz and A. Alexis-Baker eds., Grand Rapids, MI: Baker.

Yoder, J. (2009b) *The War of the Lamb: The Ethics of Nonviolence and Peacemaking*, G. Stassen, M. Nation and M. Hamsher eds, Grand Rapids, MI: Brazos.

Young, K. (2012) *Sport, Violence and Society*, London: Routledge.

Chapter 16

Hillsborough and the Church of England

The Right Reverend Bishop James Jones KBE

Introduction

In Professor Elaine Graham's book *Between a Rock and a Hard Place: Public Theology in a Post-Secular Age* (2003) she writes about the role of the Church of England in the work of the Hillsborough Independent Panel, which she describes as 'a vivid example of speaking truth to power'. The Panel was set up in 2010, 21 years after the Hillsborough disaster in which 96 Liverpool football fans were killed. Throughout these two decades the families of the 96 were the ones that had tried to speak truth to power but felt that their appeals and their questions had fallen on deaf ears. Their one consolation was a drama-documentary called 'Hillsborough' by Jimmy McGovern and a book written by Professor Phil Scraton called *Hillsborough: the Truth* (1999). Meticulously researched, they both challenged the prevailing view that the fans were responsible for their own death and catalogued a series of alleged failures that showed that this was a disaster waiting to happen. Professor Scraton, whose book was itself a cogent speaking of truth to power, was appointed to the Hillsborough Independent Panel where his knowledge and expertise contributed significantly to the delivery of the Panel's Terms of Reference. Also appointed to the Panel was Katie Jones who had led the research for the Jimmy McGovern drama-documentary. She brought the same energetic intelligence to the Panel's research. She died at a tragically young age in 2015.

The purpose of this chapter is to highlight the role of the Church of England in the Hillsborough Independent Panel. There is a danger in doing so as by concentrating on one element it can distort the narrative and obscure the significant parts played by others. Nothing should ever detract from the role of the families and the survivors without whose anger, determination, patience and endurance there would never have been any redress for their 96 loved ones. These virtues (yes, anger is a virtue when it is deployed against injustice) were anointed by a dignity that graced their grief. It is rare for anything to be achieved by a single person performing as a soloist. Even when the dynamics of a culture push an individual to the forefront that narrative is always woven out of the many stories of others who have played their own part. Thus, the work of the Hillsborough Independent Panel was the summation of the efforts of expert colleagues and of a dedicated secretariat who worked together to deliver the Terms of Reference, that had been shaped through consultation with the families. In so doing it led to the quashing of the verdicts of the original inquests and to the appointment of a new Coroner, Lord Justice Goldring, to oversee new inquests in 2013. After the longest inquest in British Legal history on 26 April 2016 the Jury overturned a verdict of accidental death and unanimously exonerated the fans of any responsibility and by a majority of 7:2 returned a determination of 'unlawful killing'.

What follows in these pages is a reflective narrative about my own roles as Bishop of Liverpool (1998–2013) and as Chair of the Hillsborough Independent Panel (2010–2012). I offer it as raw material[1] for those who wish to explore and research the role of the Church of England and one of its pastors in contemporary society, while acknowledging that there has been a small handful of social-scientific publications surrounding Hillsborough (e.g. Brennan, 2008a, 2008b, 2009; Boyle, 2001; Darby, Johnes and Mellor, 2005; Walter, 1991). It is necessarily selective and descriptive but seasoned with observations where appropriate. Any student of this subject will need and want to supplement it with other accounts. I offer it chronologically.

I became Bishop of Liverpool in 1998. Part of my preparation for coming to the Diocese was reading Blake Morrison's, *As If* (Granta, 1997) a moving and disturbing account of the trial of the juveniles Robert Thompson and Jon Venables who had murdered a local two-year-old, James Bulger, in 1993. This and other tragedies such as the Heysel Stadium and Hillsborough made me think that here were a people 'of sorrows and acquainted with grief'. A Bishop is a pastor and either through natural disposition or through their training as a priest reaches out to people in their grief. The following year, 1999, would see the 10th anniversary of Hillsborough. I was visited by Trevor Hicks and his former wife, Jenni Hicks, (of the Hillsborough Family Support Group, HFSG) whose two daughters Sarah and Victoria had died at Hillsborough. They asked if I would preside at the Annual Service of Remembrance in the Stadium at Anfield. They shared with me the path they had travelled over the previous ten years and made me aware of the unresolved questions about the disaster, the unrequited grief of the families, the continuing pursuit of truth and justice and the open wound in the City that had yet to heal.

I readily agreed for several reasons. As a pastor I was affected by their grief. My predecessor the Rt Rev David Sheppard and his Catholic colleague the Most Rev Derek Worlock had presided at memorial services in both the Church of England and Catholic Cathedrals and accepting their invitation seemed a proper continuity. My reason for doing so was built on how the Church of England understands its own role as the Church for

England. The Kingdom of God is not just the Church but the World. Nothing, not even human indifference, diminishes the sovereignty of God and His rule over the earth. God came for the whole world whether we believe in him or not. Or go to Church, or not. When a person calls on a Vicar or a Bishop they are not asked whether they are a member of the Church or even whether they come to Church. The only question is 'where do you live'. If you are in the parish or the Diocese the Vicar and the Bishop are there to serve you in that corner of God's earth for which they are pastorally responsible. It is rather quaintly known as 'the cure of souls'.

Not everybody understands this, and not everybody in the Church either understands or appreciates this dimension of mission. Church members can sometimes complain that they do not see enough of their Vicar or their Bishop and feel that they have a prior claim on their ministry. But a Church that is established and integrated into the fabric of the nation both locally and nationally has a particular responsibility to serve the whole community and not just the congregation.

I attended and took part in the 10th, 15th and 20th anniversaries of Hillsborough at Anfield. The anniversary falls into two parts. The first is a Service of Remembrance with the reading of the names of the 96, prayers and the singing of 'Abide with Me'; the second part has the shape of a Rally when the leaders of the HFSG and other invited guests address the gathering on the struggle for truth, justice and accountability for the 96.

The 20th anniversary was greatly anticipated. Over 30,000 people came to Anfield. There had been anniversaries for other major disasters such as the Bradford Stadium, Lockerbie, Kings Cross, Piper Alpha, 7/7 and the Marchioness. Yet none has attracted such vast numbers. It says something about the density of the solidarity on Merseyside and the fact that no family in the region was left unaffected by the 96 deaths. It says something too about how football binds people together in passionate loyalties and in the hero-worshipping of both players and managers. Raymond Boyle in his chapter on religion in his thesis *Football and Cultural Identity in Glasgow and Liverpool* (1995: 51) shows how 'the continued interest and popularity of football in these cities is.... An indicator of the importance of ritual and spectacle in urban life'. With its power to bind people together football has a religious dimension. At the Hillsborough Anniversaries the religion of prayer and hymns blends with the religion of player and chants. The song 'You'll never Walk Alone' is both a spiritual and a sporting anthem. But if sport has the religious effect of binding people together it also has the religious force of dividing people and appealing to different tribal loyalties.

I presided at the 20th anniversary jointly with the Catholic Auxiliary Bishop of Liverpool, Tom Williams. His ministry had been as a parish priest in Liverpool whose population is predominantly Catholic. He knew and was known by the people. As we came out on to the pitch I said to him that I hoped that during the 'Rally' nobody would mention the name of the Prime Minister. Gordon Brown had said recently that there would never be another inquiry into Hillsborough and this had gone down badly with both the families and the fans. I said that he would be boo-ed. Tom was not so sure. I deferred to his knowledge of the people. In the event, Andy Burnham, the Secretary of State for the Department of Culture Media and Sport, was invited to the podium. He started to read a speech and mentioned the Prime Minister. A lone voice from the stands interrupted him with a shout 'Justice'. Then the whole crowd got to their feet and joined the chant, 'Justice for the 96!' If you had rehearsed the crowd they could not have chanted in greater unison. I was sat at the front facing the stands and vividly remember feeling the force of the protest. The crowd was emotional and angry. Andy Burnham was deeply affected by the reaction of the people and on his return to London persuaded the Prime Minister to respond positively to the call that there should be a fresh examination into the issues surrounding the Hillsborough disaster. Local MPs, such as, Maria Eagle and Derek Twigg together with Andy Burnham and others such as Lord Wills who was also a Minister, would be able to testify to the difficult discussions that went on within Government and to the political dynamics that eventually led to the decision by the Home Secretary, Alan Johnson, to announce the setting up of the Hillsborough Independent Panel.

Senior Civil Servants such as Ken Sutton who headed up the Panel's Secretariat were intimately involved in devising a unique instrument of investigation called 'The Hillsborough Independent Panel'. I was initially approached by Ken Sutton and along with other City leaders was consulted about suitable names, including Senior Church figures that the Home Secretary might approach to serve on the Panel. Liverpool had a religious heritage which with its two Cathedrals dominating the skyline is more pronounced than in most English cities. Ken visited me three times and on the second he asked if I would be prepared to serve on the Panel myself, on the third he asked what my response would be if the Home Secretary were minded to invite me to Chair the Panel. I said that I would need to consult my colleagues as I would have to shed some responsibilities that would have an impact on them. And that I would want to consult the Archbishops. I assessed the opportunity pastorally and personally. I knew that for the City, for the families, the survivors and the fans the setting up of a Panel would bring a degree of hope in their struggle to hold people accountable for the tragic events of Hillsborough. As a pastor the invitation appealed to my sense of calling to help those who for two decades had felt that they were victims of an injustice. Further down the line I came to realise more fully that this was a significant opportunity for the Church and an expression of the need for public theology in a post-secular age.

In the Hillsborough narrative the families of the 96 felt let down by the police, the press, politicians, Parliament and even the judiciary. So where does a community turn when it has lost trust in its primary institutions? It could be said that the Church should be included among those who let down the families of the 96. In the days immediately following the disaster the vast majority of Liverpudlians turned, as they always have at times of crisis, to the Church to provide a focus for their grief and despair. And the Church and its leaders responded sensitively and magnificently. Chaplains worked ceaselessly at the hospitals in Sheffield, local clergy sought to bring comfort at each of the funerals, ecumenical Church leaders made themselves available to families and the memorial services in the two Cathedrals provided solace for Liverpool and across the nation. The Ecumenical Church Leaders led the service at Anfield on the first anniversary on Easter Day 1990. However, many in the Church in the following years came to accept the stories that were told in newspaper, inquest and inquiry and it should not be a surprise that the HFSG did not see in the Church and its leaders a natural ally in their campaign for truth and justice.

The repeated requests of the families were for truth and justice. These are pillars of the Christian faith. But the Church like all institutions has been blighted by individuals within it who have betrayed those values of its founder. Nevertheless in Liverpool in spite of its own share in these betrayals the Church has a reputation for championing the dispossessed. When it was mooted to the families that my name was in the frame as Chair the reaction was nevertheless mixed. There were other candidates who were more familiar with the Hillsborough narrative whom some of the families favoured. The decision to appoint me as 'Chair' of the Panel was, I am told, a recognition that I was uniquely well placed to combine forensic and objective skills with a pastoral sensitivity. Both would be needed if the Panel process was to escape from the previous patronising approach of those in authority, including some of the earlier attempts to review what had happened.

When it was announced on 16 December 2009 that I was to Chair the Hillsborough Independent Panel there were questions about why it was not to be a judge-led inquiry. The Terms of Reference were set out:

> The Hillsborough disaster was a personal tragedy for hundreds of people and an event of major national and international significance in the subsequent minimisation of safety risks at football matches and similar sporting events.

As such, government and local agencies in South Yorkshire are committed to maximum possible public disclosure of governmental and other agency documentation on events surrounding the disaster.

The Hillsborough Independent Panel has been appointed to oversee this disclosure process, consulting with the Hillsborough families and statutory agencies where necessary, and to carry out the associated activities outlined in the panel remit below.

Exceptionally, the independent panel will be provided with access to Hillsborough documentation held by Government and local agencies relevant to events surrounding the tragedy in advance of the normal 30-year point for public disclosure.

The fundamental principles will be full disclosure of documentation and no redaction of content, except in the limited legal and other circumstances outlined in a disclosure protocol.

The remit of the independent panel will be to:

oversee full public disclosure of relevant government and local information within the limited constraints set out in the accompanying protocol;

consult with the Hillsborough families to ensure that the views of those most affected by the tragedy are taken into account;

manage the process of public disclosure, ensuring that it takes place initially to the Hillsborough families and other involved parties, in an agreed manner and within a reasonable timescale, before information is made more widely available;

in line with established practice, work with the Keeper of Public Records in preparing options for establishing an archive of Hillsborough documentation, including a catalogue of all central Governmental and local public agency information and a commentary on any information withheld for the benefit of the families or on legal or other grounds;

produce a report explaining the work of the panel. The panel's report will also illustrate how the information disclosed adds to public understanding of the tragedy and its aftermath.

Although there was never any explicit specification that the Chair should have pastoral skills, I found that from the start I was drawing upon my pastoral experience. Ken and I debated how the Panel would engage first with the families. He and his team had worked extensively with them in the consultation process leading up to the announcement. We decided that the Panel would meet each other for the first time on the very day that we met with the families for the first time. We had barely seen the colour of each other's eyes before we met the three family groups. The distrust of those in authority was endemic. We had to demonstrate to them that the Panel had not begun to form a view about anything or anyone before meeting them and listening to their concerns. We began each of the three meetings by keeping a time of silence and at the outset of the meeting with the HFSG, naming the 96 loved ones:

Jon-Paul Gilhooley
Philip Hammond
Thomas Anthony Howard
Paul Brian Murray
Lee Nicol
Adam Edward Spearritt
Peter Andrew Harrison
Victoria Jane Hicks
Philip John Steele
Kevin Tyrrell
Kevin Daniel Williams
Kester Roger Marcus Ball
Nicholas Michael Hewitt
Martin Kevin Traynor
Simon Bell
Carl Darren Hewitt
Keith McGrath
Stephen Francis O'Neill
Steven Joseph Robinson
Henry Charles Rogers
Stuart Paul William Thompson
Graham John Wright
James Gary Aspinall
Carl Brown
Paul Clark
Christopher Barry Devonside
Gary Philip Jones
Carl David Lewis
John McBrien
Jonathon Owens
Colin Mark Ashcroft
Paul William Carlile
Gary Christopher Church
James Philip Delaney
Sarah Louise Hicks
David William Mather
Colin Wafer
Ian David Whelan
Stephen Paul Copoc
Ian Thomas Glover
Gordon Rodney Horn

Paul David Brady
Thomas Steven Fox
Marian Hazel McCabe
Joseph Daniel McCarthy
Peter McDonnell
Carl William Rimmer
Peter Francis Tootle
David John Benson
David William Birtle
Tony Bland
Gary Collins
Tracey Elizabeth Cox
William Roy Pemberton
Colin Andrew Hugh William Sefton
David Leonard Thomas
Peter Andrew Burkett
Derrick George Godwin
Graham John Roberts
David Steven Brown
Richard Jones
Barry Sidney Bennett
Andrew Mark Brookes
Paul Anthony Hewitson
Paula Ann Smith
Christopher James Traynor
Barry Glover
Gary Harrison
Christine Anne Jones
Nicholas Peter Joynes
Francis Joseph McAllister
Alan McGlone
Joseph Clark
Christopher Edwards
James Robert Hennessy
Alan Johnston
Anthony Peter Kelly
Martin Kenneth Wild
Peter Reuben Thompson
Stephen Francis Harrison
Eric Hankin
Vincent Michael Fitzsimmons
Roy Harry Hamilton
Patrick John Thompson
Michael David Kelly

Brian Christopher Mathews
David George Rimmer
Inger Shah
David Hawley
Thomas Howard
Arthur Horrocks
Eric George Hughes
Henry Thomas Burke
Raymond Thomas Chapman
John Alfred Anderson
Gerard Bernard Patrick Baron

It was a pastoral acknowledgement of the families' grief individually and collectively and a signal to them that the Panel would exercise its forensic responsibilities sensitively.

It surprised some Panel members and those unfamiliar with the history of the struggle for accountability that we had to engage with three separate groups. HFSG, Hillsborough Justice Campaign and Hope for Hillsborough. Whenever that point was expressed and whenever tensions emerged between the three I would often offer a pastoral observation: 'many marriages do not survive grief so why should friendships, especially those forged through grief'. It is a feature of other disasters that different groups emerge after the tragedy with similar tensions. Anger is one of the symptoms of grief. Flashes of misplaced anger can be dumped on relatively minor disagreements that escalate out of all proportion and aggravate division. Whenever tensions between the family groups impacted on the Panel our response was informed by this pastoral understanding. Our Terms of Reference required us to keep all the families and their concerns at the centre of our work. We had regular meetings with them throughout. I chaired a sub group of the Panel that had particular responsibility for family liaison. I sensed something of a break-through in our relationship when family members began to volunteer 'this is the first time we've really been listened to', 'this is the first time that anyone has ever taken us seriously'.

The skill of listening was implicit in the Terms of Reference. After over 20 years of trying to speak truth to power the families had developed a sixth sense about who was really listening to them. Attentive listening is a pastoral attribute and in retrospect I see that it was my responsibility as the Chair to encourage the Panel to engage in such attentive listening first to the questions that the families raised and second to the answers that came out of the newly accessed documents.

Often those aggrieved who have suffered a miscarriage of justice call for a judge-led inquiry. Understandably in a judicial system that has been guilty of failure you want that same system to undo the injustice. But judicial inquiries necessarily involve interviewing people under oath, which has implications on cost and time as suspects and witnesses engage lawyers. Some inquiries have taken over ten years and cost in the region of £200 million. From the point of view of the aggrieved justice is further delayed and denied. And although set up to satisfy their longing for justice the families often feel alienated by the process. A Panel operates differently and herein lies its uniqueness. The two that I have chaired (Hillsborough Independent Panel and Gosport Memorial Hospital Independent Panel) include in their Terms of Reference the requirement to consult with the aggrieved from the outset. Indeed, early consultation shapes the Terms of Reference. Once the Terms have been agreed the Panel members are recruited on the grounds of appointing experts with the appropriate expertise to deliver the Terms of Reference. The Panel's task is to listen to the families and interrogate the documents in the light of their questions. The information forthcoming from the disclosed documents is then scrutinised, analysed and interpreted by the Panel's experts who produce a Report. The centrality of the families' interests is further assured by the Families First principle where the Report is shown first to them before being laid before Parliament. The fact that the families have little trust in authority makes them fearful that those with power, especially those who might be indicted, might try to alter the Report before publication.

Shortly after the Hillsborough Independent Report was published I did an interview for the BBC on Radio 4's Sunday Programme (a weekly religious news and magazine programme) and sought to explain the process. I received a letter from the Oxford theologian Professor Chris Rowlands, Canon Theologian of Liverpool Cathedral, who commented on and commended the principle of putting the families at the centre of the search for truth and justice. He saw it as an example of liberation theology whereby putting the victims of injustice at the heart of the process of investigation was in itself the beginning of their liberation.

Part way through our work when we had accessed some 400,000 documents and had begun to analyse them we were scratching our heads wondering how these things could have come about. We coined the phrase that never appeared in the final Report and that has been on our lips ever since: 'this is the patronising disposition of unaccountable power'. When people in authority exercise power with little or no accountability they do so often benignly. But sometimes less so. It is the lack of accountability that can make their actions patronising, making decisions about other people and not listening attentively to their needs and concerns. Justice requires us to elevate the object of the verb to parity with the subject of the verb.

In the opening of the Preface to the Hillsborough Report I quoted from Lactantius and his Institutes – a fourth-century Christian apologist from North Africa (Bowen and Garnsey, 2003) – to which Professor Rowlands had drawn my attention. 'The whole point of justice consists precisely in providing for others through humanity what we provide for our family through affection' (Book 6.12.3).

A good parent elevates the needs of their offspring to at least the level of their own or higher. Therein lies justice within the family or household. Thus, a just society is one in which those who have power are at pains to elevate the needs of the powerless to the same level as their own. For the three months leading up to the publication of the Report I read every day Luke Chapter 18, 1–8 and the Parable of the Widow and the Unjust Judge:

> Then Jesus told them a parable about their need to pray always and not to lose heart. He said, 'In a certain city there was a judge who neither feared God nor had respect for people. In that city there was a widow who kept coming to him and saying, "Grant me justice against my opponent." For a while he refused; but later he said to himself, "Though I have no fear of God and no respect for anyone, yet because this widow keeps bothering me, I will grant her justice, so that she may not wear me out by continually coming." And the Lord said, "Listen to what the unjust judge says. And will not God grant justice to his chosen ones who cry to him day and night? Will he delay long in helping them? I tell you, he will quickly grant justice to them. And yet, when the Son of Man comes, will he find faith on earth?"'

Hitherto I had always thought that this was a parable about prayer. But there are several more points to this parable. One of them is about justice denied. Justice is mentioned five times. Jesus told it into a world where there was so much injustice that he knew people would be sorely tempted to give up believing in a God of justice and throw in the towel. Like the widow pleading with the judge who did not give a damn about God or other people to grant her justice, the women left bereft by the death of the 96 for two decades had begged for people to listen to their pleas and grant them justice for their loved ones.

As we finalised the Panel's Report we debated long and hard about the most appropriate place to publish it in the presence of the families. We wanted a building in which we could protect the privacy of the families and allow them to absorb the Report's conclusions with dignity. It needed also to be a place where the families could remember their loved ones with reverence. We anticipated a massive media interest and knew that the building would need to be versatile enough to allow us to corral the media away from the families until they were ready to meet them. Various buildings in Liverpool were considered – the new museum, the Town Hall, St George's Hall.

After consultation with the families and detailed discussion the Panel unanimously settled on the Church of England Cathedral. It fulfilled all the criteria. There was also a consonance with my own position both as Chair of the Panel and Bishop of Liverpool. For the Cathedral is the seat of the Bishop and the public symbol of his ministry. Furthermore, given the Book of Remembrance for the 96 held in the Cathedral and its history in hosting a memorial service for those killed and affected by the tragedy there was a strong sense of continuity within the Hillsborough narrative. In my opinion the museum would have given out the message that the Report was about history, whereas the Panel already knew that its message would also be about the present and the future. In the event, St George's Hall became the venue for the Vigil organised by the City Council for the families, survivors and fans immediately at the end of the day after the Panel had reported.

Many people commented on the media pictures of the Cathedral as the families entered and left and at the press conference held in the Lady Chapel. The scale of the building seemed commensurate with the weight of expectation. The building is also known around the world and given the international renown of Liverpool Football Club seemed a fitting icon for its global reach.

The sacredness of the space seemed appropriate to the sanctity of the 96 lives lost in tragedy. It seemed to me that the religious character of the building gave the day a dimension that transcended the mundane in which the police, the press, politicians, Parliament, the judiciary and even the world of football had been found wanting, and elevated the proceedings to the eternal values of truth and justice for which the families had longed for decades. The newly appointed Dean of Liverpool, Pete Wilcox, observing the families listening to the Panel members summarising the Report felt it was like 'looking through a window on to heaven'. Here in the House of God, I felt, truth was calling out to justice.

The day began with the Panel addressing the families and summarising their Report. When the Panel's medical expert, Dr Bill Kirkup, reported that the postmortem documents indicated that many of the 96 might have lived had there been an emergency response appropriate to the disaster, three people fainted.

After the briefing we gave each of the families' representatives a copy of the Report. We were fulfilling the promise that they would be the first to read it in its entirety. Because of the history of distrust we had assured the families that the final Report would not be altered by those in authority. Not even the Prime Minister, whom I had met the day before, had seen it beforehand. At my meeting with David Cameron where I had outlined the work of the Panel I was impressed by his grasp of the detail and by his coining of the phrase that the families had suffered 'a double injustice' – the injustice of the tragedy and the injustice of the subsequent failures to address their concerns down the decades. It was a phrase that the Prime Minister went on to use in the House of Commons on 12 September, which we were able to relay live to the families in the Cathedral. I sat with them as they listened both to the Prime Minister and to the House of

Commons debate that followed. Both exceeded the families' expectations. After the two press conferences – first by the Panel and second by the families – and an opportunity for the families to question the Panel about the Report, I thanked them all for their remarkable forbearance during a grueling and harrowing day. I then added that I would now go to the Chapter House at the other end of the Cathedral that had been turned into a Chapel for the families to use throughout the day, and remember with reverence the 96 and pray that truth and justice would prevail in God's world. At the conclusion of the Panel's work this was the first time I mentioned God publicly. Over the years some families had shared with me privately their difficulty in believing in God given the tragedy they had suffered. Yet on this day I found that during the hour I spent in the Chapter House nearly all the families followed voluntarily to kneel or to stand or to look upon the Book of Remembrance. There was a solace in the silence. Kneeling in the Bishop's Stall I found my heart both heavy and light. Heavy with a renewed sense of the families' reawakened grief; light with the hope that at last truth, unshackled, was calling out to justice in the House of God, the Cathedral.

On a personal note, when people asked me how I felt during it all I compared it with taking the funeral of a member of your own family when you tighten the valve on your own emotion. Some days later when the pressure had lowered I found myself unexpectedly in tears. It was a moment of catharsis for me yet incomparable with the emotions felt by the families for whom the 12 September 2012 was a bitter-sweet day. Sweet for it was at last a vindication of their search for truth but bitter for it was yet another re-living of their loss and grief. My own reaction expressed both the forensic and pastoral roles I had inhabited as Chair of the Panel. The conclusion of the Panel's work helped me and my wife to see it as the climax of my ministry as Bishop of Liverpool and to put in place plans for my retirement the following year on reaching my 65th birthday.

The Attorney General, Dominic Grieve MP, read the Panel's report and made an application to the High Court to re-consider the verdicts of the original inquests. The Court quashed the verdicts and ordered new inquests. To my surprise a new role began to emerge for me. The day before the Panel reported I had met with the Prime Minister in Downing Street to appraise him of the Panel's work. Then two days after the publication he rang me to enquire after the families and to seek my advice on how the Government could ensure that the Panel's work could be taken forward in the journey from truth to justice. Some months later the Prime Minister visited Liverpool on political business and expressed a wish to meet with the families face to face but away from the media glare. I was asked to host and to Chair the meeting at Bishop's Lodge. The families had various concerns about different aspects of the investigations that they shared frankly with me and robustly with the Prime Minister. What was evident was that although the families were encouraged by the fact that new inquests had been instigated they still understandably had no confidence in the authorities to deliver justice.

There were extensive discussions between the families' legal representatives and the Hillsborough team at the Home Office who liaised with the three investigative authorities – the Crown Prosecution Service (CPS) the Independent Police Complaints Commission (IPCC) and Operation Resolve, the police investigation in part supporting the Coroner's investigative team. Through an iterative process in which I myself was involved the different parties coalesced around the concept of establishing a Forum in which the families could engage with the various investigations. The Terms of Reference which were agreed by all parties including and especially the families were as follows:

- To provide clarification for the families and survivors on areas of investigation by the IPCC, Operation Resolve and (as necessary) any prosecutorial matters by the CPS.
- To facilitate an exchange between families, survivors and the investigation teams regarding the progress of investigations.
- To facilitate understanding of the processes and add to public confidence in the investigation.
- To identify and quickly address issues raised
- To ensure that the group has the opportunity to shape the agenda of these meetings as well as the IPCC, the CPS and Operation Resolve.

It was proposed by the Home Office team and concurred with by the investigative agencies and agreed by the families that I should be the Chair of the Forum. The families had confidence in me having chaired the Panel that had delivered the Report. I accepted the invitation of the Home Secretary to be her Adviser on Hillsborough and in that capacity accepted the invitation to Chair the Forum.

This summary does not do justice to the complexity of the negotiations or to the tension that frequently erupted. The purpose of this chapter is to examine the role of the Church. The significant point is that this work continued after I had vacated my See as Bishop of Liverpool, which I have done with the blessing of my successor, the Rt Revd Paul Bayes. Chairing the Forum required the trust of the families. That was a 'sine quo non' especially given the history of distrust in authority. But the Chair also needed to have the confidence of the CPS, the IPCC and Operation Resolve. Clearly my own involvement in the Panel brought its own commendation but it was I believe also built on a recognition of the way a Bishop occupies a civic role not just as a leader of the Church but as a leader in the wider community.

The meetings of the Forum have allowed the families to express emotions that they were not allowed to show in Court. They have given them the opportunity to articulate their concerns. I cannot hide my admiration for the families who for a quarter of century have fought for truth, accountability and justice. Through adversity and their own endeavours many of them have become expert in the law. Yet in spite of living for years with the issues and knowing the legal arguments inside out I was able to observe how dis-empowered they often became in the presence of authority. Chairing the Forum I often found myself articulating questions on the families' behalf and pressing the professionals to clarify or to address the real questions the families were asking. The various authorities were at pains to make themselves available and accessible to the families within the constraints of the Coroner's Court. But the truth is that those of us with power seldom fully appreciate the dis-empowering power of our own authority to those who are without it. The fact that the Church could have a role as an advocate for the powerless, a voice for those who felt strangulated by the weight of the institutions who had failed them in the past has made me re-evaluate the role of the Church in the contemporary world.

The Church can be tempted to think that its mission could be advanced by short term initiatives that are Smart – specific, measurable, achievable, realistic targets. But the Gospel is about relationship – human and Divine. Relationships do not have short cuts. They take years to build. Of course, there can be epiphanies in both human and Divine relationships when in an instant you know the other as intimately as you are known. But mostly a relationship is grown through shared experiences, reciprocal openness and mutual trust. In a human relationship it may take years before one may talk with another about God in a way that respects their history and their integrity.

I conclude with an episode from my relationship with Margaret Aspinall (Chair of the HFSG) whom I have asked permission to share this story.

Five years after I began my work with the Hillsborough Independent Panel and 16 years after I became Bishop of Liverpool I was in a small meeting with Margaret on the second anniversary of the publication of the Hillsborough Report, 12 September 2014. We were reminiscing about the day of the Report. Margaret shared with me how she would never forget the three words with which I had opened the proceedings. 'You said "I know you are all wondering if we have found anything that tells a different story." Then you said "And we have." And with those three words, Bishop, our world changed forever.'

For me the Gospel of the Christian faith is about the world changing, about a new world coming, a world of truth and justice. I then told Margaret that every day for three months I had read a passage from the New Testament. I reached for my hand-sized Bible in my brief case, laid it between us and read the Parable of the Widow and the Unjust Judge from Luke 18. Although I was reading it I heard it as I had never heard it before. It was as if it were being told for the first time to and about Margaret and her plea and that of all the families of the 96, 'grant me justice'.

Only Margaret can say what that parable means to her. For me it was the glass through which to see the Kingdom of God. In a world where justice is so often delayed or denied here's a story of hope that God is coming with a whistle to his lips ready to call out the injustices. For the families the whistle finally blew on 26 April 2016 when 27 years later the Jury returned its determination of 'Unlawful Killing'. The following day in Parliament the Home Secretary announced to the House of Commons that she was asking me continue to work with the families to collate their experiences and to bring a Report before Parliament so that we might learn from all that they have endured.

It strikes me that fairness on the playing field without which competitive sport loses all its meaning is but a microcosm of life itself which becomes meaningless if ultimately there is no justice.

Note

1 This text of this chapter was first presented as a keynote address at the Inaugural Global Congress on Sports and Christianity, 24–28 August, 2016, York St John University, UK.

References

Bowen, A. and Garnsey, P. (eds) (2003) *Lactantius Institute*, Liverpool, UK: Liverpool University Press.

Boyle, R. (1995) *Football and Cultural Identity in Glasgow and Liverpool*, PhD Thesis, University of Stirling, Scotland.

Boyle, R. (2001) Football and Religion: Merseyside and Glasgow, in J. Williams., S. Hopkins and C. Long (eds), *Passings Rhythms: Liverpool FC and the Transformation of Football*, New York: Berg: 39–52.

Brennan, M. (2008a) *Mourning and Disaster: Finding Meaning in the Mourning for Hillsborough and Diana*, Newcastle upon Tyne, UK: Cambridge Scholars Publishing.

Brennan, M. (2008b) Mourning and Loss: Finding Meaning in the Mourning for Hillsborough, *Mortality*, 13(1): 1–23.

Brennan, M. (2008c) Condolence Books: Language and Meaning in the Mourning for Hillsborough and Diana. *Death Studies*, 32(4): 326–351.

Brennan, M. (2009) Public Mourning and the Legacy of Hillsborough – 20 Years On, *Illness, Crisis & Loss*, 17(3): 261–264.

Darby, P., Johnes, M. and Mellor, G. (2005) *Soccer and Disaster: International Perspectives*, London: Routledge.

Graham, E. (2003) *Between a Rock and a Hard Place: Public Theology in a Post-Secular*, London: SCM.

Morrison, B. (1997) *As If*, London: Granta Books.

Scraton, P. (1999) *Hillsborough: The Truth*, Edinburgh, Scotland: Mainstream Publishing.

Walter, T. (1991) The Mourning after Hillsborough, *Sociological Review*, 39(3): 599–626.

Index

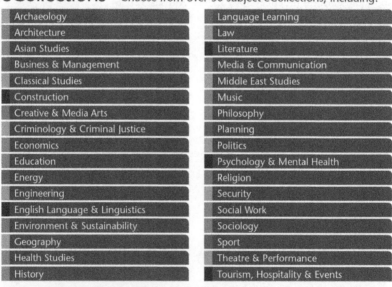